TEACH YOURSELF QUARKXPRESS FOR WINDOWS

---

by

Joseph Kasmer

**A Subsidiary of
Henry Holt and Co., Inc.**

©Copyright 1992 MIS:Press

All rights reserved. Reproduction or use of editorial or pictorial content in any manner is prohibited without express permission. No patent liability is assumed with respect to the use of the information contained herein. While every precaution has been taken in the preparation of this book, the publisher assumes no responsibility for errors or omissions. Neither is any liability assumed for damages resulting from the use of the information contained herein.

Throughout this book, trademarked names are used, in an editorial manner only, and to the benefit of the trademark owner, with no intention of infringement of the trademark. Where such designations appear in this book, they have been printed with initial caps.

First Edition—1992

ISBN 1-55828-241-6

Printed in the United States of America.

10 9 8 7 6 5 4 3 2 1

MIS:Press books are available at special discounts for bulk purchases for sales promotions, premiums, fund-raising, or educational use. Special editions or book excerpts can also be created to specification.

For details contact: Special Sales Director
MIS:Press
a subsidiary of Henry Holt and Company, Inc.
115 West 18th Street
New York, New York 10011

Dedication

For Laura

Acknowledgments

Three hundred people helped me with this book. The clients and students I have been privileged to serve and teach over the years contributed questions, problems, and deadline crises that provoked many of the solutions and approaches presented here.

Gerard Black of Black-Eye Productions, San Diego, helped with cool-headed advice, graphic assistance, equipment loans, and technical encouragement at crucial times.

Ian McLaren of San Francisco, a scientist with the mind of a detective, provided invaluable deductive assistance during early technical difficulties. And a thousand thanks to L.L. Richwood, the San Diego artist who graciously allowed paintings to be scanned and manipulated for use in Chapters 12 and 13 and elsewhere. No book can do justice to the fine detail and vibrant colors in the original works. The copyright to these images is held by L.L. Richwood, all rights reserved.

Contents

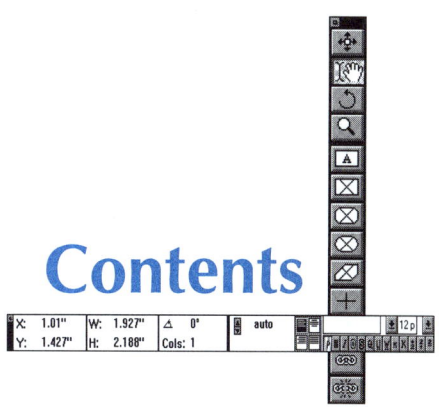

INTRODUCTION 1

Getting the Most Out of This Book 2
    Conventions 2
    A Brief Outline 3

CHAPTER 1: AN OVERVIEW 7

What You Will Learn in This Chapter 7
Is QuarkXPress a Tool? 8
Environment and Interface 8
Control Devices 10
Text 12
Pictures 12
Items 13
Where and What 14
Multiple Documents and Programs 14
Gathering Forces 14

CHAPTER 2: THE WINDOWS/QUARKXPRESS MARRIAGE 15

What You Will Learn in This Chapter 15

v

The All-Encompassing DOS? 16
    What Is DOS? 16
    Escape from DOS 17
If It's a DOS World, Why Use Windows? 18
What Windows Provides XPress 19
    Moving an Object 19
    Resizing an Object 22
    Using Dialog Boxes 24
Installing QuarkXPress into the Windows Interface 25
Windows to QuarkXpress 28
Windows Managers 30
    The Station Master 30
    The Baggage Handler 30
    The Mouse in Windows 32
Linked by Association 33
Multitasking Program Switching 35
Stepping up 37

CHAPTER 3: WORKING WITH DOCUMENTS 39

What You Will Learn In This Chapter 39
You Are Here 40
Creating a Document 41
Opening Existing Documents 43
    Adjusting Document Windows 46
Saving Documents 47
Page Views 48
    Standard Page Views on Command 48
The Pasteboard 49
    Controlling Page Views by Direct Entry 50
The QuarkXPress Workshop 51
The Tools and Measurements Palettes 52
    Using a Tool 52
    Using a Measurements Palette 54
    Page Views by Tool 57
Moving Around the Page 60
Positioning Work 61
    Selecting Items 62
    Moving Items: The Drag Method 62
    Palette Moves 63
    Moving Multiple Items 65
Manipulating Pages 65
    Adding Pages 65
    Removing Pages 66

The Document Layout Palette	67
Moving to Another Page	68
Moving Items Between Pages	69
Advanced Moves	70

CHAPTER 4: TYPE AND TEXT FORMATTING 71

Where Text Lives	72
Making a Text Box	72
Effects of Creating a Text Box	74
Text and Content Tool	75
Keying Text Directly	76
Clipboard Text	76
About File Formats: Importing and Exporting Text	77
To Import Text	78
Text Box Overruns	79
Internal Word Processing	80
Find/Change	81
Type Control	83
Selecting Text within a Box	84
Using the Text Measurements Palette	84
Type Control	85
Font and Size	85
Type Style	86
Paragraph Control	86
Paragraph Alignment	87
Adjusting Line Spacing	88
Letter Spacing	88
Kerning and Tracking	90
Columns	90
Advancing	91

CHAPTER 5: NEWSLETTERS ON THE JOB 93

What You Will Learn in This Chapter	93
The Letterhead Newsletter	94
Producing the Letterhead	94
Typesetting Body Text	99
Copyfitting	104
A Contemporary Newsletter	106
Preparing Body Text	107
Preparing the Nameplate	108
The Mailer Section	110
Text Layout on Page 2	112

Text Layout on Page 3 114
　　Text Layout on Page 1 116
　　A Table of Contents 118
　　Text Layout on Page 4 120
Advancing 122

CHAPTER 6: PICTURES, BOXES, AND INTERACTION 123

What You Will Learn in This Chapter 123
Pictures 124
Picture Forms 124
Importing into Picture Boxes 126
Picture Cropping, Picture Sizing 130
　　Shaping the Picture Box 130
The Picture Grabber 132
　　Shaping and Sizing the Image 134
Box Characteristics 135
　　Box Frames 136
　　Box Backgrounds 138
Picture Content 141
　　Content Colors 141
　　Reverse Text 143
Rotating Boxes 143
　　In-Box Picture Rotating 145
　　Picture Skewing 145
Rulers, Guides, and Grids 146
How Items Interact 147
　　Monitoring Multiple Items 147
　　Aligning and Spacing 148
　　Depths of Layering 149
　　Text Runaround 151
　　Text Box Linking 154
　　Text Box Unlinking 155
Stepping Forward 156

CHAPTER 7: GUIDES ON THE JOB 157

What You Will Learn in This Chapter 157
The Guide Brochure 158
A Museum Guidebook 167
Stepping Forward 172

CHAPTER 8: PARAGRAPHS, STORIES, AND TYPOGRAPHIC CONTROLS 173

What You Will Learn in This Chapter 173
Formatting 174
Hyphenation and Justification 179
    Gaining Access to Hyphenation and Justification Specs 180
    Changing Hyphenation Specifications 181
    Changing Justification Specifications 182
Vertical Alignment 184
The Baseline Grid 185
Widows and Orphans 187
Horizontal Scaling 188
Drop Caps 190
Tabs 190
Paragraph Rules 193
Preferred Modes of Working 193
Stepping Forward 195

CHAPTER 9: NEWSPAPERS ON THE JOB 197

What You Will Learn in this Chapter 197
The Front Page 198
    Setting Up the Newspaper Document 198
    Top Matter 200
    The Stories 202
    The Inside Box 209
Stepping Forward 212

CHAPTER 10: DOCUMENT FLOW 213

What You Will Learn in This Chapter 213
Master Pages 214
    Using Master Pages 214
    Master Page Designation 215
    Access to the Master Pages 217
    Working in Master Pages 219
    Adjustments of Master Items on Document Pages 220
    Generating Master Pages 222
    Automatic Page Numbers 224
Style Sheets 225
    Applying Style Sheets 227
    What It Means to Have No Style 228
    Creating and Adjusting Style Sheets 228
    Basing Styles Sheets on Other Style Sheets 231

Special Item Connections 234
    Grouping 234
    Anchoring Inline Items 235
Special Page Flows 239
    Multiple-Page Spreads 239
    Sectioning 241
    Automating Jump Lines 242
Stepping Forward 243

CHAPTER 11: ON THE JOB: CATSALOGS, MANUALS, AND BOOKS 245

What You Will Learn in This Chapter 245
A Catalog 246
    Starting the Catalog Page 246
    Using Style Sheets 248
    Final Work on the Page 251
A Manual 252
    Starting the Manual 253
    Working with Sections 255
    The Manual's Fine Points 260
Stepping Forward 262

CHAPTER 12: MANIPULATING IMAGES 263

What You Will Learn in This Chapter 263
Contrast and When It Matters 264
    Adjusting Contrast with Preset Controls 266
    Customized Adjustments to Contrast 269
Halftones 272
    Resolution 276
Stepping Forward 277

CHAPTER 13: ON THE JOB: MAGAZINE PAGES 279

What You Will Learn in This Chapter 279
Assembling the Elements 280
Setting the Text 284
Halftone Considerations 286
Stepping Forward 287

CHAPTER 14: MULTIPLE EDITIONS AND MULTIPLE DOCUMENTS 289

What You Will Learn in This Chapter 289
Across the Document Boundary 290
Thumbnails 292

Blind Replacements and Updating 294
Fixing Mistakes and Reverting 295
Multiple Editions and Templates 296
    Making a Template 296
    Making Templates Using Save As 297
Stepping Forward 298

CHAPTER 15: TRANSFERS WITHIN AND WITHOUT 299

What You Will Learn in This Chapter 299
The Library 300
Sending Text Out of QuarkXPress 304
Sending Layouts Out of QuarkXPress—EPS 307
Sending Layouts Out of QuarkXPress—Screen Capture 307
Stepping Forward 310

CHAPTER 16: COLOR 311

What You Will Learn in This Chapter 311
Screen Color versus Print Color 312
Other Models and Printers 315
Color Separations 316
Trapping Colors 318
The Color Palette and Blending Colors 319
Stepping Forward 320

CHAPTER 17: PRINTING 321

What You Will Learn in This Chapter 321
Checks and Connections 322
    Image Sources 322
    Updating 324
Fonts in a Document 324
    How the Program Deals with Fonts 325
    Keeping Track of Fonts 325
Readying a Print 327
To Print 328
Using the Print Manager 330
Installing Printer Drivers 332
Stepping Forward 333

CHAPTER 18: BEYOND THE USUAL METHODS 335

What You Will Learn in This Chapter 335
Keyboard Shortcuts 336

Ctrl Key Shortcuts 336
Alt Key Shortcuts 337
Momentary Item Tool 337
Text Sizing 338
Click Zooming 338
Selecting Through Layers 339
Simple, Direct Word Counting 339
Quick Page Moves 340
One-Step Hanging Indents 340
Adding Typographers' Quotes, Common Marks, and Symbols 341
Setting Defaults and Preferences 342
Where To? 342

APPENDIX A 345

APPENDIX B 361

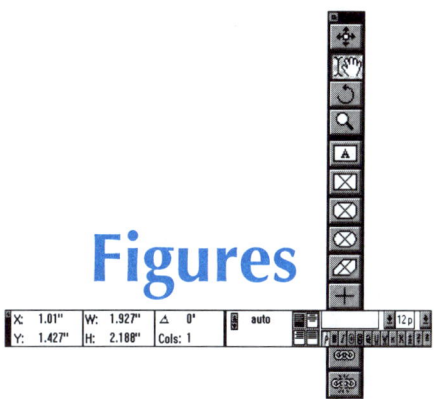

Figures

CHAPTER 1: AN OVERVIEW 7

Figure 1.1	*Text can change while format remains the same.* 9
Figure 1.2	*The interface controls of QuarkXPress.* 10
Figure 1.3	*The Measurements palette for a graphic.* 11
Figure 1.4	*Vertical justification.* 12
Figure 1.5	*The item/content duality of text.* 13

CHAPTER 2: THE WINDOWS/QUARKXPRESS MARRIAGE 15

Figure 2.2	*The Windows interface.* 18
Figure 2.2	*Selected text within a selected window.* 20
Figure 2.3	*Relocating the Program Manager window.* 20
Figure 2.4	*Open directory folder windows.* 21
Figure 2.5	*Using scroll bars in a window.* 22
Figure 2.6	*Resizing window width.* 23
Figure 2.7	*Resizing a window diagonally.* 23
Figure 2.8	*Resizing a picture item.* 24
Figure 2.9	*A dialog box.* 24
Figure 2.10	*One appearance of the Program manager window.* 26
Figure 2.11	*The Run command used for installing QuarkXPress.* 27
Figure 2.12	*The XPRESS folder created on installation.* 28
Figure 2.13	*Using the Startup folder.* 29

xiii

xiv ♦ *Teach Yourself...Quark XPress for Windows*

Figure 2.14	*The Program Manager and program group windows.*	*31*
Figure 2.15	*Two drive directories in the File Manager.*	*31*
Figure 2.16	*Using the mouse to drag a file between directories.*	*32*
Figure 2.17	*Copying a file to a floppy disk as backup.*	*33*
Figure 2.18	*Locating the program to which a file is being associated.*	*34*
Figure 2.19	*Quick ALT-TAB switching between Quark and the Program Manager.*	*36*

CHAPTER 3: WORKING WITH DOCUMENTS 39

Figure 3.1	*The first layer of the QuarkXpress interface.*	*40*
Figure 3.2	*The dialog box from the New document command.*	*41*
Figure 3.3	*Margin guides.*	*42*
Figure 3.4	*Column guides.*	*43*
Figure 3.5	*Three document windows opened in QuarkXpress.*	*44*
Figure 3.6	*Opening a document using the dialog box.*	*45*
Figure 3.7	*The cascaded view of multiple open documents.*	*46*
Figure 3.8	*The Windows menu.*	*46*
Figure 3.9	*The effect of the Tile command.*	*47*
Figure 3.10	*The View menu choices.*	*48*
Figure 3.11	*Relative sizes of preset view choices.*	*49*
Figure 3.12	*A page spread and its pasteboard in use.*	*50*
Figure 3.13	*View percent field at a Fit in Window view.*	*51*
Figure 3.14	*Lines drawn using the Rule tool.*	*53*
Figure 3.15	*A recently drawn rule with its measurements palette active.*	*54*
Figure 3.16	*Measurements palette Line Type list activated.*	*55*
Figure 3.17	*Measurements palette arrows Option list activated.*	*55*
Figure 3.18	*A rule edited through the Measurements palette.*	*56*
Figure 3.19	*Magnifying with three clicks of the Zoom tool.*	*57*
Figure 3.20	*A Fit in Window view.*	*59*
Figure 3.21	*A precise Zoom tool magnification.*	*59*
Figure 3.22	*The Grabber hand accessed using the Alt Key.*	*61*
Figure 3.23	*Caption to come.*	*61*
Figure 3.23	*Using the selecting box to select several items at once.*	*63*
Figure 3.24	*Using the Measurements palette to move an item.*	*64*
Figure 3.25	*Adding pages using the Insert Pages command.*	*66*
Figure 3.26	*The Document Layout palette mimics the order of pages.*	*67*

CHAPTER 4: TYPE AND TEXT FORMATTING 71

Figure 4.1	*Selecting the Text Box tool at the palette.*	*73*
Figure 4.2	*Creating a text box.*	*74*
Figure 4.3	*Importing text through the Get Text command.*	*79*
Figure 4.4	*Typewriter quotes versus typesetter's quotes.*	*79*
Figure 4.5	*Text over-run indicated by an "x" in the text box.*	*80*

Introduction ◆ XV

Figure 4.6	The Find/Change search and replace dialog box.	81
Figure 4.7	A document carries messages in its type.	83
Figure 4.8	A line of type and the Measurements palette monitoring its attributes.	85
Figure 4.9	Altering type font and size using the palette.	86
Figure 4.10	Effects of the palette's type style buttons.	87
Figure 4.11	The four paragraph alignments.	87
Figure 4.12	Three paragraphs with different leading.	89
Figure 4.13	Text kerned and tracked with the measurements palette.	89
Figure 4.14	Resetting text into three columns using the Measurements palette.	92
Figure 4.15	Resetting text into four columns using the Measurements palette.	92

CHAPTER 5: NEWSLETTERS ON THE JOB 93

Figure 5.1	Specifying the newsletter's document layout at the New dialog box.	95
Figure 5.2	A letterhead text box drawn over the margin guide.	97
Figure 5.3	Style adjustments applied to the title line.	98
Figure 5.4	Close view of the completed letterhead.	99
Figure 5.5	Importing the EXPL.TXT file through the Get Text command.	100
Figure 5.6	Greeked text view of original text box and Page 2 with overrun.	101
Figure 5.7	An inadvertent, odd character found in imported text.	101
Figure 5.8	The first phase of changing the odd character back to an apostrophe.	102
Figure 5.9	Inserting tabs through global replacement.	103
Figure 5.10	Setting off text lead-ins with underlining.	104
Figure 5.11	Viewing the copy-fitting challenge of Page 2.	104
Figure 5.12	Controlling the leading using the Measurements palette.	105
Figure 5.13	Adding a small Page Number text box.	106
Figure 5.14	Creating a custom sized, formatted document.	107
Figure 5.15	Moving to the new layout document.	108
Figure 5.16	Shaping the Nameplate text box.	109
Figure 5.17	Newsletter title and tag line set off.	110
Figure 5.18	Adding pages in the GR103B document.	111
Figure 5.19	The mailer return address, Page 4.	112
Figure 5.20	A Page 2 subheading.	114
Figure 5.21	Page 2 completed with heading and body text in place.	115
Figure 5.22	Partial layout of Page 3.	115
Figure 5.23	Reducing leading in the headline.	116
Figure 5.24	In-line heads adjusted.	117
Figure 5.25	Copy fitting needing head-body copy coordination.	118
Figure 5.26	Enlarging the text box vertically using the handle.	119
Figure 5.27	Contents text box drawn over the body text box	119
Figure 5.28	Page 1 completed.	120
Figure 5.29	Page 4 story pasted.	121
Figure 5.30	Text overrun on Page 4.	121
Figure 5.31	Page 4 completed.	122

xvi ♦ Teach Yourself...Quark XPress for Windows

CHAPTER 6: PICTURES, BOXES, AND INTERACTION 123

Figure 6.1   Picture box–generating tools. 125
Figure 6.2   A graphic file from outside the document. 125
Figure 6.3   Dialog box for importing graphics. 127
Figure 6.4   An imported image seated in the upper-left corner of a picture box. 128
Figure 6.5   Images imported into rounded-corner and oval picture boxes. 128
Figure 6.6   One result of using the polygon picture box tool. 130
Figure 6.7   Effect of enlarging one particular picture box. 131
Figure 6.8   An apparently empty picture box enlarged. 131
Figure 6.9   Shaping the window around a part of the image. 132
Figure 6.10 Cropping with the picture grabber hand. 133
Figure 6.11 Reshaping the image in two directions. 134
Figure 6.12 The measurements palette monitoring control of box location and size. 136
Figure 6.13 The Frame dialog box. 137
Figure 6.14 A frame of 16 points applied to a picture box. 138
Figure 6.15 The Picture Box Specifications dialog box. 139
Figure 6.16 Setting different backgrounds in adjacent boxes. 139
Figure 6.17 The three versions of the Style menu. 140
Figure 6.18 The three variations of the Specifications dialog box. 140
Figure 6.19 Three lines of different color/shade settings. 142
Figure 6.20 Effects of applying the color White, and the Negative command. 142
Figure 6.21 Reversed type. 143
Figure 6.22 A rotated text box over one not rotated. 144
Figure 6.23 Box rotation and image rotation. 145
Figure 6.24 An image and its skewed copy. 146
Figure 6.25 A set of items selected together. 148
Figure 6.26 The Space/Align dialog box. 149
Figure 6.27 Aligning to a horizontal. 150
Figure 6.28 Layering depths when a circle, square, and triangle are drawn. 151
Figure 6.29 Sending an item, the triangle, to the lowest layer. 151
Figure 6.30 The Runaround Specifications dialog box. 152
Figure 6.31 Runaround Modes: None and Item. 152
Figure 6.32 Runaround Modes: Auto Image and Manual Image. 153
Figure 6.33 Linked text boxes forming a text chain. 155

CHAPTER 7: GRIDS ON THE JOB 157

Figure 7.1   A spread format arising from the New dialog box. 158
Figure 7.2   Positioning a five-column box in a six-column grid. 159
Figure 7.3   A text box added to the grid. 160
Figure 7.4   Roughly positioned picture boxes. 161
Figure 7.5   Cropping to the useful image. 161
Figure 7.6   Cropping and enlarging proportionately using a diagonal. 162

Figure 7.7	Applying the Negative command.	163
Figure 7.8	Using Space/Align to distribute along an uppermost horizontal.	164
Figure 7.9	Using Space/Align to distribute along a leftmost vertical.	164
Figure 7.10	Using Space/Align to distribute along a bottommost horizontal.	165
Figure 7.11	A text chain established for four linked bordering boxes.	166
Figure 7.12	Linked, reversed, rotated text boxes.	166
Figure 7.13	Preliminary layout with item runaround.	168
Figure 7.14	Pushing out text by moving a runaround boundary.	168
Figure 7.15	Choosing a new picture box shape.	169
Figure 7.16	Reshaping a picture box.	169
Figure 7.17	Positioning reversed labels.	171
Figure 7.18	Positioning number keys.	171
Figure 7.19	The completed section.	172

CHAPTER 8: PARAGRAPHS, STORIES, AND TYPOGRAPHIC CONTROLS ..173

Figure 8.1	Showing nonprinting markers.	174
Figure 8.2	The Paragraph Formats dialog box.	175
Figure 8.3	A Formats dialog box for an altered paragraph.	176
Figure 8.4	Paragraph formatting variations.	178
Figure 8.5	Creating hanging indents.	178
Figure 8.6	Access to hyphenation and justification settings.	180
Figure 8.7	Specifications for hyphenation and justification.	180
Figure 8.8	A new H&J specification made available in the formats dialog box.	182
Figure 8.9	Effect of the minimum equals optimum spacing.	183
Figure 8.10	Effect of tight spacing.	183
Figure 8.11	Vertical alignments.	184
Figure 8.12	Vertically justified text.	185
Figure 8.13	The baseline grid revealed.	185
Figure 8.14	Fixed leading versus text locked to baseline.	186
Figure 8.15	Text replete with widows and orphans.	187
Figure 8.16	The widow and orphan controls.	188
Figure 8.17	A story cleared of widows and some orphans.	188
Figure 8.18	Effects of horizontal scaling to 90 percent.	189
Figure 8.19	Expanding text 400 percent.	189
Figure 8.20	A drop cap applied using the Formats dialog box.	190
Figure 8.21	Tabs revealed through Show Invisibles.	191
Figure 8.22	Tab choices.	191
Figure 8.23	Aligning the Tabs dialog with selected text box.	192
Figure 8.24	The Paragraph Rules dialog box.	193
Figure 8.25	The Rules Specification dialog box.	193
Figure 8.26	The Preferences juncture submenu.	194
Figure 8.27	General Preferences.	194

xviii ◆ *Teach Yourself...Quark XPress for Windows*

CHAPTER 9: NEWSPAPERS ON THE JOB 197

Figure 9.1   Changing measures and display features for the document. *199*
Figure 9.2   Locating the master page through submenu. *199*
Figure 9.3   Readjusting margin guides. *200*
Figure 9.4   Establishing the banner title. *201*
Figure 9.5   Inserting a center tab. *202*
Figure 9.6   Inserting a right tab. *203*
Figure 9.7   Character and rule formatting applied to a section head. *203*
Figure 9.8   Uniform spacing applied to three paragraphs. *204*
Figure 9.9   Formatting a byline. *205*
Figure 9.10   Applying a rule across the column above the byline. *205*
Figure 9.11   Body copy locked to baseline grid. *206*
Figure 9.12   Body copy with adjusted hyphenation and justification. *207*
Figure 9.13   A jump notice installed. *208*
Figure 9.14   A blank picture box as placeholder. *209*
Figure 9.15   Style formatting of the box heading. *210*
Figure 9.16   Fomatting the paragraphs. *210*
Figure 9.17   Aligning page numbers to the right with tab adjustment. *211*
Figure 9.18   Pushing down text through Runaround of the heading box. *211*

CHAPTER 10: DOCUMENT FLOW 213

Figure 10.1   The Document Layout palette of a new document. *215*
Figure 10.2   A list of applicable master pages. *215*
Figure 10.3   A Document Layout showing a variety of master pages applied. *216*
Figure 10.4   Automatic master page, M1, applied. *217*
Figure 10.5   Moving to a master page. *218*
Figure 10.6   Master page indicating automatic text box linking is inactive. *219*
Figure 10.7   The left member of a master page spread. *219*
Figure 10.8   A master page spread. *220*
Figure 10.9   Editing a master page item on the document page. *220*
Figure 10.10   A locked item changing a Tool icon. *221*
Figure 10.11   Preparing to add a new master page. *222*
Figure 10.12   Inserting a new master page. *223*
Figure 10.13   Master page number placeholder and document page number. *225*
Figure 10.14   A subheading within body text. *226*
Figure 10.15   Displaying a Style Sheets palette. *227*
Figure 10.16   Applying style sheets using the Style menu. *228*
Figure 10.17   No Style preserves formatting when the style sheet is modified. *229*
Figure 10.18   The Style Sheets dialog box. *229*
Figure 10.19   The Edit Style Sheet dialog box. *230*
Figure 10.20   Basing a style sheet, Subhead Two, on Subhead One. *232*
Figure 10.21   Two levels of subheads, one based on the other. *233*

Introduction ◆ **xix**

Figure 10.22	The result of changing just the primary subhead.	233
Figure 10.23	Three items grouped and their common bounding box.	234
Figure 10.24	The dialog box for modifying elements of a group.	235
Figure 10.25	A picture anchored to the baseline as first character.	236
Figure 10.26	A picture anchored to the baseline within a paragraph.	237
Figure 10.27	Setting picture box inline anchor.	237
Figure 10.28	A picture box anchored to the highest ascender.	238
Figure 10.29	A text box anchored to the first line of another text box.	238
Figure 10.30	Adding a third page to a spread.	240
Figure 10.31	A five-page spread.	240
Figure 10.32	Enabling section numbering.	241
Figure 10.33	Automatic jump-line page numbers in place.	243

CHAPTER 11: ON THE JOB: CATALOGS, MANUALS, AND BOOKS 245

Figure 11.1	Document setup for a catalog.	247
Figure 11.2	Layout of prototypical early page.	247
Figure 11.3	Text pushed down in columns below a heading text box.	248
Figure 11.4	Establishing a new style sheet based on selection.	249
Figure 11.5	A prototypical listing and style sheets palette.	250
Figure 11.6	Result of applying style sheets to listings.	250
Figure 11.7	Effect of 2 picas in the style sheet's Space After box.	251
Figure 11.8	Adding Rule Above to the style sheet.	252
Figure 11.9	All the styles in effect and finalized.	253
Figure 11.10	Using the Measurements palette to monitor precise text box adjustment.	254
Figure 11.11	The completed master page spread for Section A.	255
Figure 11.12	Changing one section master to another.	256
Figure 11.13	Creating a thumb-indexed book.	256
Figure 11.14	Inserting six blank pages in front of Section A.	257
Figure 11.15	A successful importing into the automatic text box in Section A.	258
Figure 11.16	Inserting the first Section B page from the M2 master.	258
Figure 11.17	Section A page numbering put into effect.	259
Figure 11.18	Inserting the back pages after the last section.	260
Figure 11.19	Graphics as separate items, and anchored within text lines.	261
Figure 11.20	Relative leading indicated in the Measurements palette.	261
Figure 11.21	Paragraph adjusted to absolute leading.	261

CHAPTER 12: MANIPULATING IMAGES 263

Figure 12.1	A grayscale image, at 50% shading, and with extreme contrast.	265
Figure 12.2	An image at Normal Contrast setting.	267
Figure 12.3	The image of 12.2 at High Contrast setting.	267
Figure 12.4	The image of 12.2 at Posterized setting	268
Figure 12.5	The Picture Contrast Specifications' plot of Normal Contrast setting.	269

Figure 12.6   The Picture Contrast Specifications' plot of the High Contrast setting. ..270
Figure 12.7   The Picture Contrast Specifications' plot of the Posterized setting. 270
Figure 12.8   Plot of High Contrast button, then inversion button specifications. 271
Figure 12.9   Effect of a drawn contrast graph. 271
Figure 12.10   Continuous tone image and halftone image. 273
Figure 12.11   Halftoning screen controls on the Style menu. 273
Figure 12.12   Picture Screening Specs dialog box from Other Screen command. 274
Figure 12.13   Halftones of Normal Screen and 20-lpi Dot Screen/45 degrees. 275
Figure 12.14   Halftones of 60-lpi/zero degrees and 30-lpi /45 degrees. 275
Figure 12.15   Effect of sizing bitmapped art on image resolution. 276

CHAPTER 13: ON THE JOB: MAGAZINE PAGES *279*

Figure 13.1   The adjusted contrast graph with Palm image. 282
Figure 13.2   The normal contrast Victorian image. 282
Figure 13.3   The effect of point-wise manipulated contrast on the Victorian image. 283
Figure 13.4   An "S" contrast graph applied to each of two images. 284
Figure 13.5   The spread of Pages 32 and 33, all text and pictures adjusted. 285
Figure 13.6   Page 34 complete. 286
Figure 13.7   Monitor display for Normal Screen halftone and the chosen halftone...287

CHAPTER 14: MULTIPLE EDITIONS AND MULTIPLE DOCUMENTS *289*

Figure 14.1   Copying by dragging items from one document to another. 291
Figure 14.2   Copying pages by dragging from a small document to a larger one. 293
Figure 14.3   A blind change of formatting made in the Find/Change dialog box.....294
Figure 14.4   The dialog box that made the changes in Figure 14.3. 295
Figure 14.5   Saving a file as a template. 297

CHAPTER 15: TRANSFERS WITHIN AND WITHOUT *299*

Figure 15.1   Three items represented as thumbnails within a library. 302
Figure 15.2   Labelling a library entry after double clicking on it. 303
Figure 15.3   Choosing a library entry by alphabetical name listing. 304
Figure 15.4   Choosing an export file type from the Save Text dialog box. 305
Figure 15.5   Document formatted text and exported with XPress Tags. 306
Figure 15.6   A portion of a screen capture in a picture box. 309

CHAPTER 16: COLOR *311*

Figure 16.1   The Colors dialog box with color wheel indicating white. 313
Figure 16.2   Red, as viewed in the CMYK color model of the Edit Color dialog box. ..315
Figure 16.3   The HSB color model presented in the Edit Color dialog box. 316
Figure 16.4   The Pantone matching system 316

Figure 16.5   The Application Preferences dialog box containing Trap specifications. 318
Figure 16.6   Applying a trapping value to the color Green. 319
Figure 16.7   The Colors palette. 319

CHAPTER 17: PRINTING 321

Figure 17.1   A document's Picture Usage dialog box indicating status of source files. 323
Figure 17.2   Using a document's Font Usage dialog box to get a list of active fonts. . 326
Figure 17.3   The Printer Setup dialog box. 327
Figure 17.4   The Print dialog box. 328
Figure 17.5   The Print Manager window. 331
Figure 17.6   The Printers window. 332

Introduction

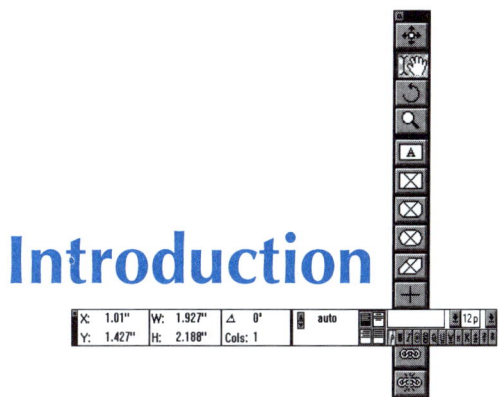

A 24-Hour Consultant

This book is for everyone seeking to understand and use QuarkXPress for Windows. It assumes that you are largely on your own in trying to achieve command of the program.

Employing a full-time consultant to tutor you on the job would be a good way to learn any software. Workshops, seminars, and classes also serve as excellent vehicles for acquiring skills. Such approaches, however, can't possibly keep pace with your requirements to learn software in a practical, cost-effective way. Being available to all clients at the precise moments they need guidance has been a professional goal of mine. Most software users, however, can't afford an immediately available, on-the-spot advisor.

Fortunately, you have just located an affordable 24-hour, on-site consultant to help you climb the learning curve. This book leads you into the working environment of QuarkXPress—its tools, its features, and the best methods for quickly achieving results. Examples provide memory-enhancers that transform what you've seen into what you know. This book is about acquiring working knowledge.

1

GETTING THE MOST OUT OF THIS BOOK

Teach Yourself...QuarkXPress for Windows guides your explorations of one of the most rewarding software packages of recent years. Wild claims about so-called "powerful" software products abound, but QuarkXPress is one of a handful of programs about which I can honestly say the claims apply. It is one of the brightest pieces of publishing technology yet available. With *Teach Yourself...QuarkXPress for Windows* as your guide, you'll discover the surest methods for creating effective publications and designs. I have taught scores of workshops, training seminars, and college classes, and one lesson has repeatedly impressed itself on me: Software skills take hold most strongly when their introduction is followed by immediate examples and practice. So, as soon as you have the opportunity, please apply the techniques revealed in the following pages to your own projects.

This book presents the tools and procedures of QuarkXPress in stages, always with an eye to putting them into practice. Each chapter leads to a set of integrated skills. And certain chapters, such as Chapter 5, comprise complete examples, start-to-finish, using the capabilities presented. You may wish to work through them in whole or in part to get a better feel for how the techniques are applied.

As your QuarkXPress abilities and skills accumulate, you'll be able to apply more of them to the publications and designs you're creating. By all means, use these skills ASAP. You'll gain mastery if you are willing to learn and experiment with work that has significance to you. If you're not currently facing project deadlines, you'll still find this cumulative approach a practical one. It will hasten your understanding of the program's functions and suggest ways to best make use of them when the time comes.

This book is developed logically. You'll find straight-ahead presentation, explanation and description of features and techniques, clear methods, and concise step-by-step procedures. Dozens of examples and nearly three hundred illustrations highlight the procedures as they unfold before you. More than one hundred easy-to-use summaries quickly refresh your memory and later provide fast referral, allowing you to quickly recall even the most complex procedures.

Conventions

Throughout the book there will be sections that require special attention. The following icons are used to mark these sections.

Indicates that you should take note of the information, which may contain a helpful hint or special condition.

Introduction ♦ 3

 Indicates that you can perform an action more quickly by using shortcut keys or by following the suggestion in the text.

 Indicates cautionary information or warnings. This symbol often provides a warning that you may lose data or crash your system if you perform an action incorrectly.

> **At-a-Glance**
>
> *You'll also find key points summarized in screened "At-a-Glance" inserts, like this one. This jogs your memory without forcing you back through the explanatory details previously presented.*

Several times throughout the book you'll notice another kind of chapter, titled "On-the-Job." These step-by-step work-through examples detail practical usage of the techniques explained in preceding chapters. They illustrate—as only a thorough, complete example can—all of the new skills presented. When you reach an On-the-Job chapter you may find you have already applied the preceding techniques successfully to your own project. If so, you may choose to skip directly to the next chapter for new techniques. If, however, you have any questions about how the methods can be applied, you should look at actual tasks being handled in the On-the-Job chapter.

Within this book you'll find skills for installing QuarkXPress, working in the Windows/QuarkXPress interface, managing QuarkXPress documents, editing text, typesetting, importing and exporting text and graphics, handling master pages, manipulating graphic images, controlling content flow through the document, customizing the QuarkXPress environment, creating multiple editions and templates, transferring files, doing print runs and color publications, as well as countless other skills.

A Brief Outline

From the Windows world to the secret shortcuts of QuarkXPress, each of the eighteen chapters in this book explores a different set of skills that combine to make for desktop publishing proficiency.

An **overview** of the program puts tools and features into perspective in Chapter 1. Scanning over the range of Quark's operation, you'll see just how far you can push the limits. We'll look at Quark-generated documents and the program's operation, and see what makes the Windows-QuarkXPress interactivity distinctive.

QuarkXPress creates an environment by virtue of other software that supports it. Thus, you will sometimes need to pass through unfamiliar stretches of an operating milieu created by **DOS and Windows**. In Chapter 2, we'll explore how QuarkXPress works within these programs, and how to approach this unique desktop publishing world. You'll also see how to manage files in Windows, and learn a few tricks that can drastically improve Quark's performance.

The best way to gain a foothold in QuarkXPress is to get a good grasp of **how documents are generated and navigated**, and how the interface controls everything on the page. In Chapter 3 we will look at working with publication and design elements on the QuarkXPress page, as well as working between pages and other documents. You'll see how to choose the right tools for creating and manipulating visual elements in your document, and how palettes provide control and feedback of these elements.

At the foundation of virtually every page or design is type. Without question, it is in this area that QuarkXPress excels. Chapter 4 reveals the **basics of type control** in QuarkXPress, from retrieving and generating text to adjusting the nuances of its appearance on the page. You'll see how to generate text, how to import it into a document, how to apply typefaces, how to style type, size it, and space it. You'll also learn how to use guides, margins, and columns to fashion text into a page proof.

Putting techniques to work makes them yours. In Chapter 5 you will construct two newsletters, using the techniques learned in the first part of the book—from setting up the document file to importing, formatting, and laying out text.

Graphics can make or break designs and publications. In QuarkXPress, graphics are imported into picture boxes, in which they can be manipulated and modified in ways explained in Chapter 6. We'll examine the graphic features of text and illustrations as they appear in a document, learning how images can be imported, cropped, sized, aligned, framed, and anchored, and how they affect other page elements.

In publications that inform, text and pictures must coordinate clearly. Chapter 7 will take you through the steps that make such coordination a success.

As the message in a publication or design becomes more crucial, the demands placed on text increase. Chapter 8 takes up the challenge of **detailed formatting** in paragraphs and stories. This chapter will show how controls work at both paragraph and story levels, how to regulate hyphenation and justification, and how to accomplish special effects with type.

Chapter 9 shows how newspaper copy must catch the reader's eye and at the same time fit in with surrounding stories.

As the complexity of a document increases, graphics can become intertwined with text. Chapter 10 explains **grouping, anchoring,** and the **movement** of text and picture combinations. In this chapter we'll look at the methods that provide unity within

Quark-generated documents, integrating text, picture, and line items.

Chapter 11 demonstrates methods used for establishing and controlling text and graphics for presentation; you'll apply your skills to the construction of both a catalog and a manual, using the unifying methods learned in previous chapters to establish and control the dynamic between text and graphics.

In QuarkXPress an imported graphic need not be a take-it-or-leave-it affair. Chapter 12 reveals the **graphics effects and modifications** possible. You will learn about halftones, contrast, and fine-tuning images.

Chapter 13 shows how the graphics in a catalog can speak for the items being sold. In this chapter we'll lay out a heavily illustrated magazine piece, preparing grayscale pictures in a document for final output with the text they accompany, and adjusting these digital images to optimum quality for output through an imagesetter.

You may wish to use certain graphical elements, layouts, and master pages more than once; building on work that went into a first effort is made practical by **publication templates**. Chapter 14 shows how to develop subsequent issues of a publication. Working with multiple documents and multiple editions of the same document, we'll look into ways to reapply whole pages, to update, to return to existing documents, and to set up and reuse whole documents in new forms.

Desktop publishing generates a torrent of file movement. Documents change computer platforms, graphics meld into new formats, text slips in and out of files. Chapter 15 unveils ways to manage the tumult, including some sophisticated methods of **file management**. You'll learn about QuarkXPress libraries, as well as ways to export text, graphics, and layouts by command and through auxiliary software.

Color can be elusive, but is manageable. Chapter 16 offers approaches for designing and printing in color.

The final incarnation for most documents is the printed page. Chapter 17 shows ways to successfully handle **printing** by proper management of fonts, printers, drivers, and odd-sized pages.

Chapter 18 presents time-saving, work-enhancing **shortcuts, tips, and suggestions** for working with QuarkXPress and Windows.

Appendix A provides a **handy reference** to the procedures outlined in the chapters; it is a compilation of all the At-a-Glance summaries, and provides outlines to the key elements of each technique. These summaries are organized by chapter so that you can locate methods quickly and easily. Appendix B offers a number of other sources that can aid you in further developing layout, typesetting, and related skills.

Every useful book is a springboard and a friend, and this book was written to be just that for you. The author welcomes your comments and reactions. Send correspondence to Studio K, Box 3562, San Diego, CA 92163.

Now, teach yourself QuarkXPress for Windows!

Chapter 1

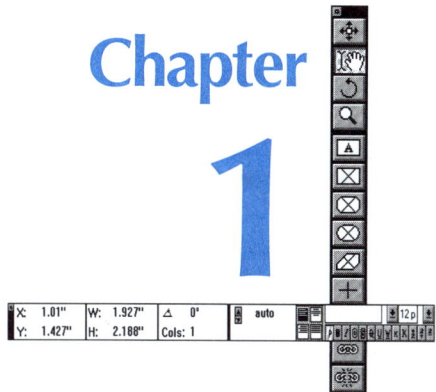

An Overview

WHAT YOU WILL LEARN IN THIS CHAPTER

- ◆ How documents are organized
- ◆ The features of the QuarkXPress interface
- ◆ Page elements
- ◆ The difference between content and items

The arrival of QuarkXPress to the Windows platform was long in coming. Many of us waited expectantly during the long gestation. Large portions of this book had to be written during the final test stages. Still, here is the program, and you may be wondering—like the proverbial kid in the candy store—just where to begin. Let's start with viewpoint.

IS QUARKXPRESS A TOOL?

Despite the oft-heard opinion that software functions just like a hammer or a power drill, no desktop publishing program is just a tool. No single tool built the Golden Gate Bridge, or the room in which you are reading this; and no single tool can make a full-color catalog or a modern consumer magazine. In describing one of the most sophisticated desktop publishing programs yet developed, the tool analogy just can't keep up with QuarkXPress.

So how best to view this software? Is it like an artist's studio? Yes. A craftsperson's workshop? OK. A builder's work crew? Sure. In fact, QuarkXPress is not so much a thing as an environment: a place providing capabilities, one from which a diversity of results can issue.

If you followed QuarkXPress in its first platform, the Macintosh, you know that it's been widely used by professionals in publishing and design to produce books, magazines, newspapers, advertising, and documentation. Others apply it to stationery, posters, forms, brochures, and corporate publications. In it, skilled designers and typesetters find features to which they are accustomed. But anyone who can operate a Windows-run computer can use QuarkXPress. (And even if you're unsteady with Windows, you'll find tips in Chapter 2 to help get you up and running with the program.)

ENVIRONMENT AND INTERFACE

Overall, the process of desktop publishing is simple: You get an idea for a publication or design. You tell the program to generate a file document on which adjustments, additions, and changes can be made. There, the idea is worked into a graphic form as completely as time and resources allow. Eventually the file document is transformed into printed pages.

At the core of every desktop publishing program is a single idea: Create a simulation of pasteup pages. Software mimics the real world by making working on digital files seem like working on actual pages. Other elements from the real world—type, lines, and other images—can be made to interact on those simulated screen pages as they might on the printed page. (Admittedly, some designs will never see the printed page, going instead into multimedia presentations, or out as FAX images between computers. In this book, however, we will use the printed page as a standard.)

Creating a convincing simulation of the graphic world leads to recreating the tools and capabilities of that world. On a simulated page generated by QuarkXPress, we enter a virtual reality where we can fashion and adjust page elements with amazing precision and speed. Type and graphics modifications take seconds instead of hours. Scaling a typeface or an image on screen is now infinitely simpler than it is in the physical world of type shops, stat cameras, and darkrooms. It has become nearly axiomatic that the more capabilities given us by the software program, the faster we will arrive at our goal.

The **document file** is where QuarkXPress simulates the graphic world. It includes much that is not obvious on screen, or on the page. Designs are made of elements that are largely type and graphics existing on the page in relation to each other. The relations among design elements can be conceptual as well as visual. Text that is indented appears as type shifted from the margin. But the document file also holds certain settings for indentation, which will be in effect even if those particular words are replaced with others, as shown in Figure 1.1.

> Text holds more than meets the eye. Text holds more than meets the eye. Text holds more than meets the eye. Text holds more than meets the eye. Text holds more than meets the eye. Text holds more than meets the eye.
>
> Consider indentation, for example. Consider indentation, for example. Consider indentation, for example. Consider indentation, for example. Consider indentation, for example. Consider indentation, for example.

Figure 1.1 *Text can change while format remains the same.*

All the relations are encoded in the document file along with what we see. These include connections between jumped text, arrangements of pages and page spreads, hyphenation standards, references to other files, and so on. Such relation-charged

10 ◆ *Teach Yourself...QuarkXPress for Windows*

QuarkXPress documents contain much more than meets the eye. When one element shifts, dozens of others can adjust to accommodate the change.

The document, then, can become quite a complex file. How are we to deal with all the relations being balanced and adjusted within it? The answer to this rather general query looks back at us from every QuarkXPress document. The answer is the **interface**—whose sole purpose is to connect us with every one of the program's capabilities. Figure 1.2 shows a page under construction. Around it appear parts of the interface: the tools, devices, controls, and command menus used to import and manage page elements in the page design. These are the most immediately accessible parts of the interface; we will look at them in Chapter 3.

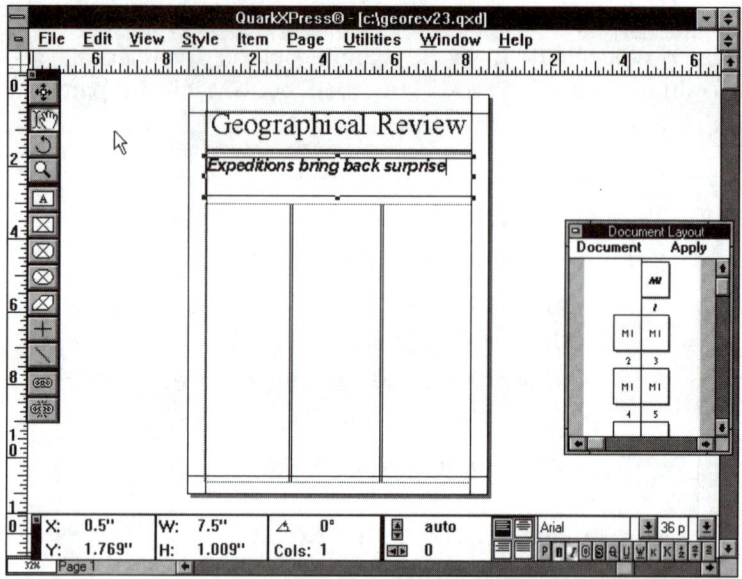

Figure 1.2 *The interface controls of QuarkXPress.*

The QuarkXPress interface also produces an environment in which to work. It is more sophisticated than it appears. The interface is not just a tool box. It leads us to the heart of the program. It may be all we ever see of the thousands of behind-the-scenes operations in which QuarkXPress responds to our directions. The interface acts as our interpreter to our work crew. To know the interface is to control the program.

CONTROL DEVICES

If you've worked with Windows, Macintosh, or one of the other graphic user interfaces that present commands through **menus**, you've probably become accustomed to the open-and-pull-down approach. It's good; it works, and it's easy to recall how to do what you want. Turn to graphics or desktop publishing software and you are sure to encounter **mouse-based tools**. Click and the mouse cursor changes function and appearance. Again, easy and functional. Maybe you've gone further and picked up power-use **keyboard strokes**, often displayed opposite the menu commands they activate, sometimes hidden as the most power-charged techniques in uncited keystroke controls. At around this point you might begin to imagine you've seen it all, in terms of interface control. Graphic user controls can start to seem like old hat.

Then, expecting more of the same, you open QuarkXPress. There are the tools: the mouse, the Menu bar, the keyboard shortcuts. But refer back to the QuarkXPress display in Figure 1.2. Look at the bottom of the window and over at the right side. The first looks like a read-out summary, the other like a miniature Layout window. These things look a little strange because they are designed to do things differently. The folks at Quark threw a new player into the game. It's called a **palette**.

When I first encountered the Quark Measurements palette (that's the long horizontal box at the bottom), I tried to get it out of the window and off the screen as quickly as I could. Ditto for the Document Layout palette (at the right). Today I use these palettes all the time. Their great virtue, especially for the Measurements palette, is that they provide instant feedback as well as control. They don't usurp the controls from tools and menus; but they continually tell you the status of an item, and let you change it at will. This feedback is a significant advance in graphic user interface design. And as anyone who's ever tried to parallel park a car by the bump method can tell you, feedback is the way to go.

A palette measuring a graphic on the page, as shown in Figure 1.3, indicates position, size, scaling, and other attributes. In addition, it will actually change that graphic when you type new numbers into it.

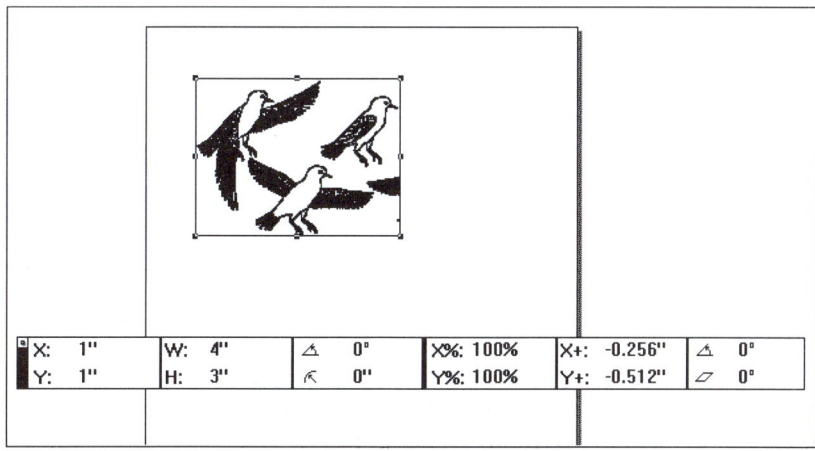

Figure 1.3 *The Measurements palette for a graphic.*

TEXT

If you're a typesetter (or if you spec type in your work), you probably have your own mental checklist of features against which to test QuarkXPress. Yes, it will align type left, right, centered, and justified. It gives fractional control of leading (line spacing) and interparagraph spacing, and it automatically jumps text. It indents, hyphenates, tracks, kerns, shifts baselines, subscripts, superscripts, spell-checks, and all the things you'd expect of it.

It also does many things you may have lusted for in your typographical heart, such as rotating type, scaling type horizontally, shading, trapping, and overprinting type. It aligns text within layouts by vertically centering lines, aligning them all to the top of the layout, to the bottom, or spreading them out in automatic vertical justification, as in Figure 1.4.

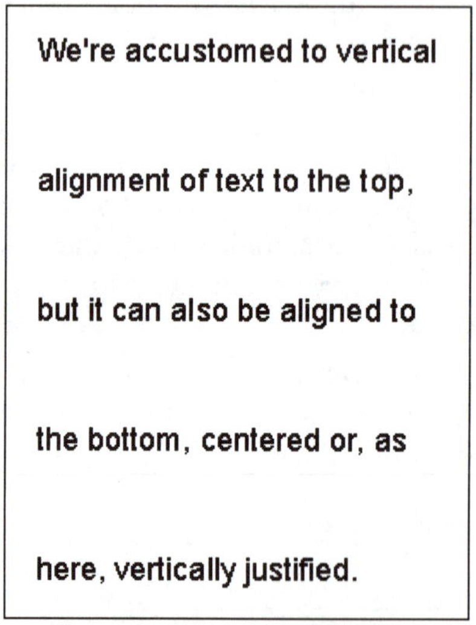

> We're accustomed to vertical
>
> alignment of text to the top,
>
> but it can also be aligned to
>
> the bottom, centered or, as
>
> here, vertically justified.

Figure 1.4 *Vertical justification.*

All of these features will be covered in detail in Chapter 4, "Type and Text Formatting," and Chapter 8, "Paragraphs, Stories, and Typographic Controls."

PICTURES

To the chagrin of graphic designers, illustration is often still treated as an afterthought in many desktop publishing programs—perhaps because of desktop publishing's origins in word processing. QuarkXPress has made strides to close the gap between type and graphics. Besides rotation, scaling, and cropping features, the image-oriented designer will encounter shading and contrast adjustments, as well as half-toning with gray levels, angle, and screen-frequency options. Don't overlook color editing and separations, based on several models, with trapping and overprinting features, of course.

ITEMS

Text, pictures, and lines are all QuarkXPress allows in a document. (All, that is, except guides, baselines, and other nonprinting particulars.) The whole basis of design is that these elements interact with one another. One way is through runaround—text flowing in columns around other text or pictures. Other ways include overlapping, abutting, aligning, and spacing.

Those design elements we deal with—text, illustrations, and rules—QuarkXPress calls **items**. Items are half of a duality that runs through QuarkXPress documents. Text appears in a text box. That's an item. Within the text box is type. That's content. Graphics appear in a picture box. That's an item. Within the picture box is the picture itself. That's content. Rules, or lines, are simpler, but they still fall into the item/content duality.

As an item, our design element is subject to being resized, moved, deleted, turned, copied, and otherwise manipulated. As content, our element might be hyphenated, spell-checked, kerned, lightened, or cropped. Figure 1.5 shows just such a dual role for one text box. Duality is easy to deal with. It's simply a matter of choosing what we want to do with the element on the page.

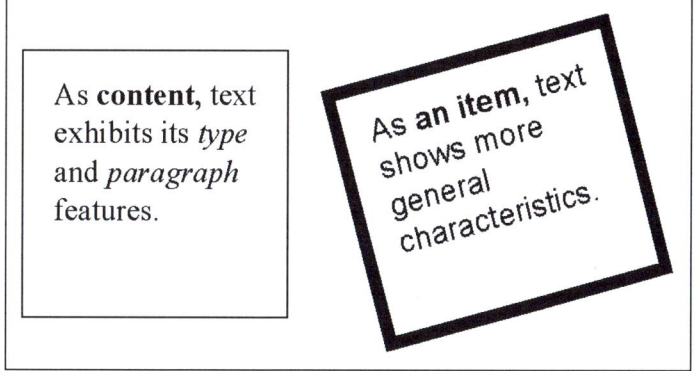

Figure 1.5 *The item/content duality of text.*

Where and What

Almost every successful feature ever devised for navigating around a page or document has been incorporated into QuarkXPress. You'll find a grabber hand, scroll bars (of course), a Miniature window, zoom tools, menu commands, keyboard strokes, typing fields, and a special technique for enlarging exactly the area of your interest. You can even locate the external files from which graphics were imported.

A sailboat's rudder and sail can both be used to direct the craft. Moving about the document is much the same—lots of options, and even more combinations. After learning what the controls are, everyone uses them in an individual fashion. In Chapter 3 we'll see how.

Multiple Documents and Programs

QuarkXPress lets you open as many as seven documents simultaneously. This is like landing on the shores of paradise if you've ever had to play the *copy element—close first document—open second document—paste element* game with an application that provided a window for only one document. But seven at once! Well, suppose you're lifting text and layouts from your last six newsletters to make a year-end review. Or what about copying design elements from work for former clients to work for a current one. If that's not enough, there's also a system of collecting elements in a library subfile that QuarkXPress can access.

With the wedding of QuarkXPress to Windows, things get even hotter. Windows running multiple programs dovetails nicely with QuarkXPress's abilities to track picture usage. This means, among other things, that you can work between your document and a graphics program concurrently. Here's the kicker: You can develop your illustrations *while you develop your layout*. QuarkXPress will update a picture already placed, even if that picture's file has been modified elsewhere. So if it's not quite right for the layout, you switch to the graphics program, revise it, return to the QuarkXPress document in a keystroke, then call up the revised picture on the page. (In Chapter 2, we'll see how to do this.)

Gathering Forces

This look at QuarkXPress is, of course, just a fly-over. Down at ground level you'll see what happens and exactly how it happens. The Windows-QuarkXPress interactivity is among the first areas we'll explore in more depth. These two software products were ready for marriage, and they have "joined hands" in a way that expands our abilities with design documents.

Chapter

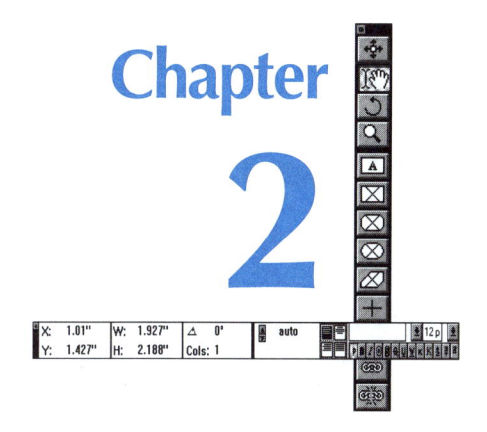

2

The Windows/QuarkXPress Marriage

WHAT YOU WILL LEARN IN THIS CHAPTER

- ◆ How to work in Windows
- ◆ How to install QuarkXPress
- ◆ How to create a start-up environment
- ◆ How to switch between QuarkXPress and other software

Before you lies your project, somewhere beyond DOS, beyond Windows, in the realm of QuarkXPress. In this chapter you'll see how to traverse the terrain that stretches between you and your document. You'll see how to install QuarkXPress on your computer. You may find that your system places you directly into Windows, or perhaps even into QuarkXPress. We'll look at how you can do it yourself. You'll also see how to manage files in Windows, and glimpse a few tricks that can drastically improve QuarkXPress's performance.

For the moment, we'll proceed under the assumption that you're starting from ground zero. We'll move step by step through the craggy foreboding mountains of DOS, across the gentler, rolling plains of Windows, and into the rich valley of QuarkXPress, where functionality on your desktop publishing projects begins.

We'll be going through the domains of the Program Manager, the File Manager, and the installation of QuarkXPress. If you've been through this before and are confident about your ability to start the program and arrive at your document, you might wish to skim over the following few sections.

THE ALL-ENCOMPASSING DOS?

Perhaps you've heard murmurs of fear about the DOS realm, without really knowing what all the bother was about. Without a doubt, DOS is challenging, a place with rules all its own, a place where the wrong letter or the loss of a colon can spell disaster for unprotected files. The general advice passed around by unfamiliar observers is: Don't go near DOS unless you know a lot about it. And the wisdom of command-weary veterans of the DOS campaign is sometimes so ridden with command jargon as to be unintelligible.

In the true spirit of the traveler, we opt for a practical approach to dealing with DOS. That means using it just enough to bring us into the Windows platform, a more intuitive atmosphere where graphic landmarks can help us to deal with QuarkXPress.

What Is DOS?

DOS is simply the world in which everything that happens in a computer running QuarkXPress for Windows takes place. DOS stands for Disk Operating System, a description true enough, but hardly any more complete than American Telephone and Telegraph is for that corporate entity. DOS was named when the major job of a system of computer instructions was to tell the disk drive when to turn, and where and when to move data on a disk. By now DOS has come to do much more than spin disks and transfer data—it can be viewed as the operating system for *all* computer functions. Right now, in the set-up you're working with, if something is going to be done in your computer, DOS will be involved in doing it. Perhaps some higher authority—like Windows, or one higher still, like QuarkXPress—will give the orders. But DOS almost always has a hand in the dirty work.

Using QuarkXPress (or any other program operating under Windows), You indirectly give commands to DOS, which acts on them after they've been translated. You key in esoteric DOS instructions, line by line, at the DOS command prompt, which is one of the first things to appear when you switch on a Windows-based computer. It looks like this:

```
C:\>
```

Our immediate concern with DOS is really very simple. All we need to do is to step gingerly across the stream of DOS commands and onto the relative safety of the Windows island. Jumping over to Windows is achieved by a single command typed at the DOS prompt.

Escape from DOS

If a computer is operating from a hard disk on which Windows is installed, DOS need not take up too much of our attention. (We'll assume you're working on such a system. If not, run the Windows-installation program, setup.exe, and follow the procedure outlined on the windows disk, Disk 1.)

NOTE A word on Windows operating modes: To work with QuarkXPress, you'll need to be in either the 386-enhanced or the standard mode.

To start windows from the DOS prompt, key *win* (for the enhanced mode) and press Enter. The screen will change more or less instantly to display a momentary Windows logo and then a screen much like the one shown in Figure 2.1, the Program Manager. You can relax. You've arrived at the Windows interface! We're only one step away from QuarkXPress now.

NOTE The Win command will send your Windows-installed computer into 386-enhanced operating mode. For reasons dependent on the hardware configuration of your system, you might wish to avoid the advantages of this enhanced mode. Advantages include the ability to operate both Windows and DOS software simultaneously from Windows—and put other demands on the speed and memory of your system, which could be annoying if your system's processor moves at the pace of a leisurely 386SX-16 MHz, for instance. On the other hand, the side effects of running in enhanced mode on a 386DX-40MHz, for example, are minor. To call up Windows in a Windows-only—no DOS access—mode, key in *win/2* at the DOS prompt and you will be in Windows standard mode.

18 ◆ *Teach Yourself...QuarkXPress for Windows*

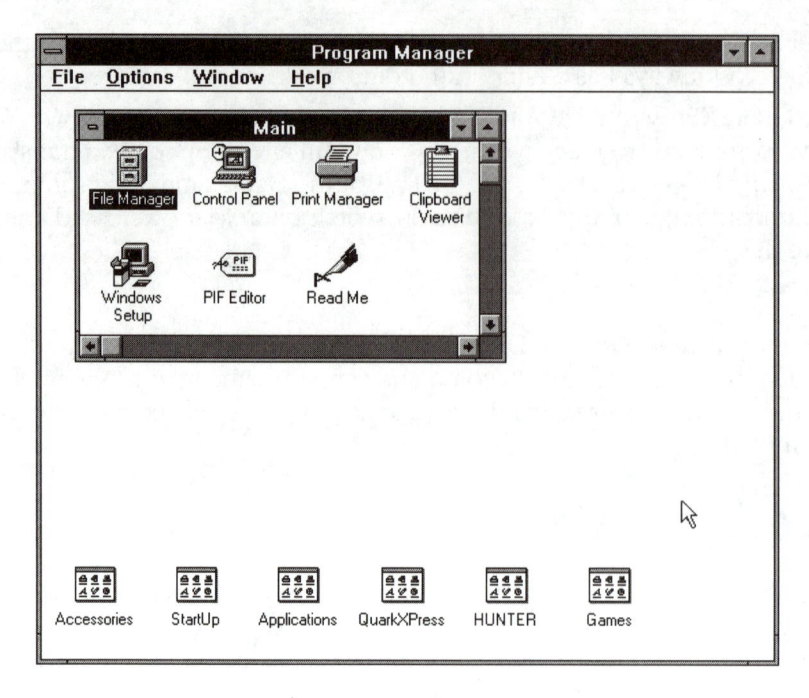

Figure 2.2 The Windows interface.

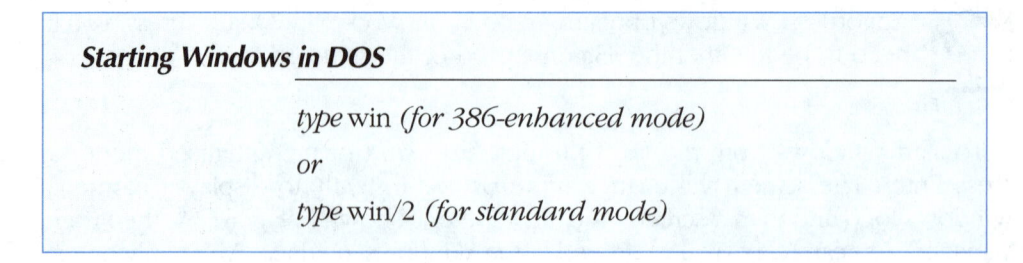

Starting Windows in DOS

    type win *(for 386-enhanced mode)*

    or

    type win/2 *(for standard mode)*

IF IT'S A DOS WORLD, WHY USE WINDOWS?

If DOS commands operate so many activities in the computer, and QuarkXPress is the program we are going to use, where does Windows fit in? Windows exists because many of us don't have the boundless patience and precision required by DOS. Imagine having to be perfectly precise in every request you ever make, every note you ever write, never making a typo or transposing letters. That is life under DOS, where simply forgetting the coded commands confounds the dutiful (but dumb) operating system.

    Windows raises the level of sophistication of what we can do, at the expense of the item-by-item precision control offered by DOS. But we will not miss that at all!

Windows responds not just to terse, linguistically forgettable phrases full of backslashes, colons, and periods, but to graphical images of commands arranged in imaginative and readily comprehended layouts.

Because of this image-oriented approach, and because Windows is now the direct interpreter of our commands to DOS, it belongs to a class of software known as **graphic user interfaces (GUI)**. An interface is just the place where two things come together—like a key that connects your hand to the door. Often an interface is a way for one thing to control the thing it meets.

We can control DOS at the Windows interface. Here we can handle graphics as well as nongraphic things like words and numbers in an I-see-you way instead of through I-hope-you-are-what-I-asked-you-to-be commands typed at the keyboard. It means desktop publishing and design. And it means QuarkXPress.

WHAT WINDOWS PROVIDES XPRESS

Windows provides an interactive overlay on top of DOS for any program written for Windows, including QuarkXPress.

Several graphic controls operate in the Windows interface and in every Windows program. In this, as in every graphic user interface, you often make choices about objects. These objects can be files, programs, circles, words—nearly anything that can be represented visually.

Often the first step in working with a graphic user interface object is to select the object in question. The universal method for selecting is to position the pointer or tool over the object and click. Sometimes dragging the cursor through or over the object will select it. The object will normally indicate its selection in some obvious way. For instance, the Header Title bar on a window may highlight or change color, small handles may appear on a graphics square, or text characters may turn light on dark background, as shown in Figure 2.2. Be sure the object you're selecting sits in a window that is itself already selected. Otherwise, your click will make the window active, and you'll need to click again to select the item.

Moving an Object

To relocate an object, first select it as above, then (holding the mouse button down) move the mouse so that the object appears to be moving onscreen. For instance, you can move any window, just as the QuarkXPress window shown in Figure 2.3 is about to be shifted downward. To move a window, grab it by the top Title bar with the **pointer** (also called a **tool**, or a **cursor**) on the screen, as shown.

20 ◆ *Teach Yourself...QuarkXPress for Windows*

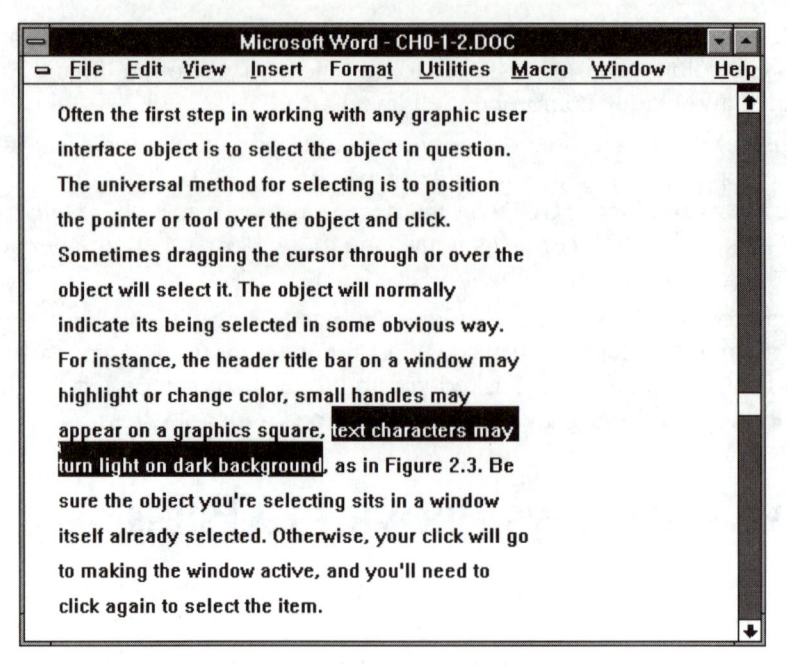

Figure 2.2   Selected text within a selected window.

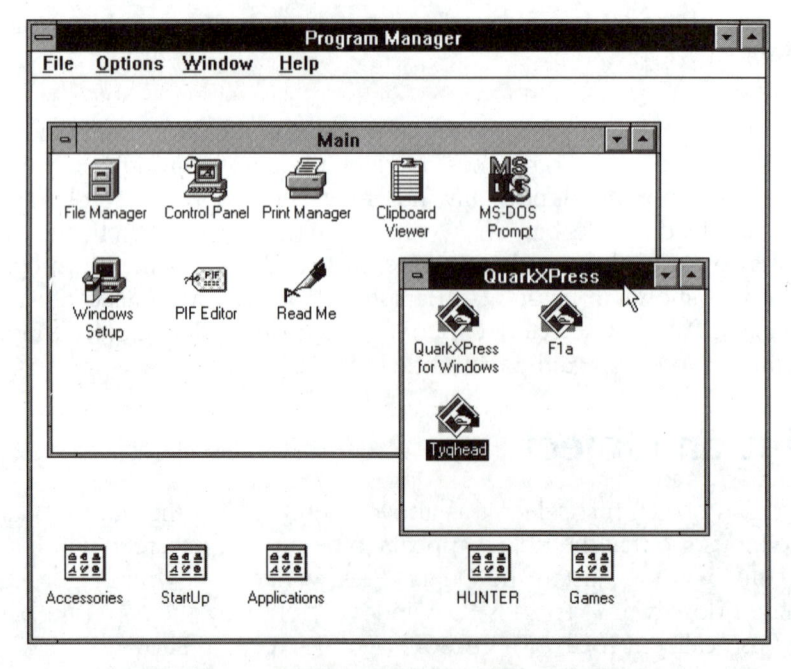

Figure 2.3   Relocating the Program Manager window.

The Windows/QuarkXpress Marriage ◆ **21**

> **Moving an object in Windows**
>
> *Select with click*
>
> *Drag to new location*
>
> *Release mouse button*

Windows gets its name from the way it displays files, objects, and command menus—always in a window display. Note all the windows open in Figure 2.4. When you open a folder or group of files by double-clicking, a window appears. If a directory or folder exists within that window, it can be opened also, and so on. The program manager of Windows is a window you will encounter often in dealing with QuarkXPress and other programs.

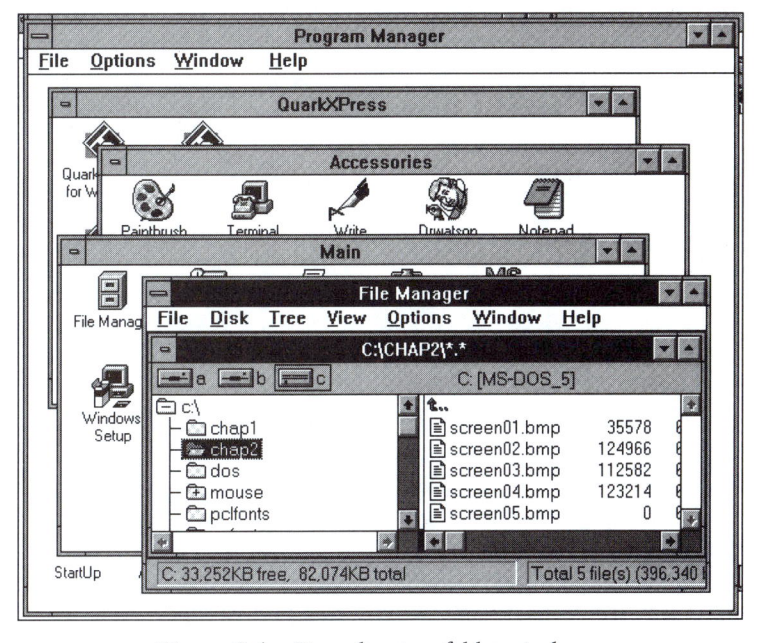

Figure 2.4   *Open directory folder windows.*

Objects can exist in the conceptual space extending beyond a visible window. To view them (or pull them into the window's purview), use the scroll bar at the bottom of the window for horizontal shifting of view, or the one on the right for vertical shifting. Clicking the mouse with the pointer over the Arrow buttons will slide the viewing window over the larger conceptual space previously out of view, as shown in Figure 2.5. The view will also slide when you click at either side of the small box in the scroll bar, or when you point the mouse arrow at the scroll box, hold down the mouse button, and drag it one way or the other. These methods come in handy when looking for a program in the Program Manager, or for a document file in File Manager.

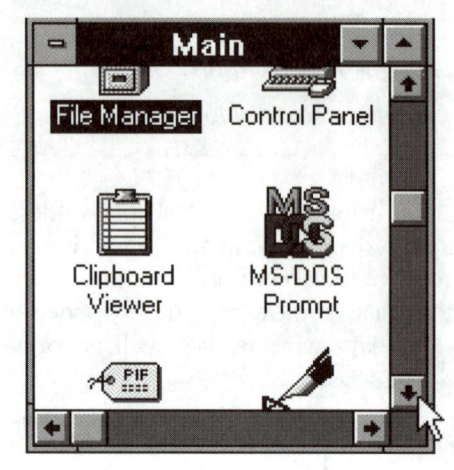

Figure 2.5   *Using scroll bars in a window.*

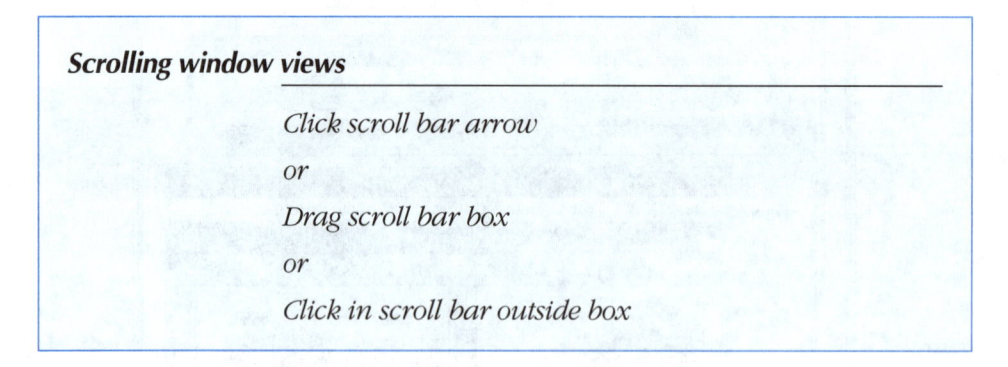

Scrolling window views

   Click scroll bar arrow

   or

   Drag scroll bar box

   or

   Click in scroll bar outside box

Resizing an Object

Objects, including windows, can be sized to be larger or smaller. To widen a window, for instance, point the arrow cursor carefully along the line of one side, as shown in Figure 2.6.

Notice that the cursor becomes a double arrow. This is a signal that you can drag the mouse in one of two directions, and make that side larger or smaller. Just drag out the side by holding down the mouse button and moving the mouse. This will work on any side. By grabbing a corner, you'll notice a diagonal double arrow appear as the mouse cursor. This is a signal that you can pull out or squeeze in the height and width concurrently, as in the diagonal stretching shown in Figure 2.7.

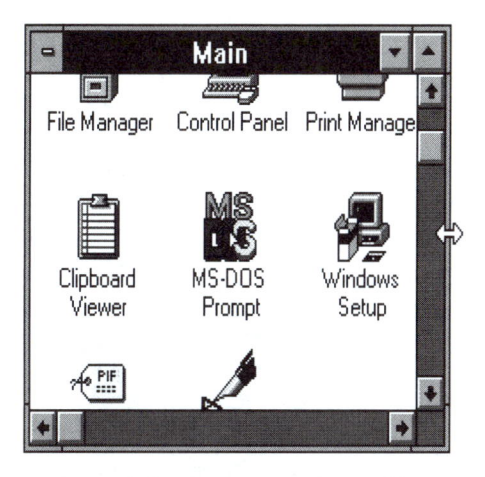

Figure 2.6   Resizing window width.

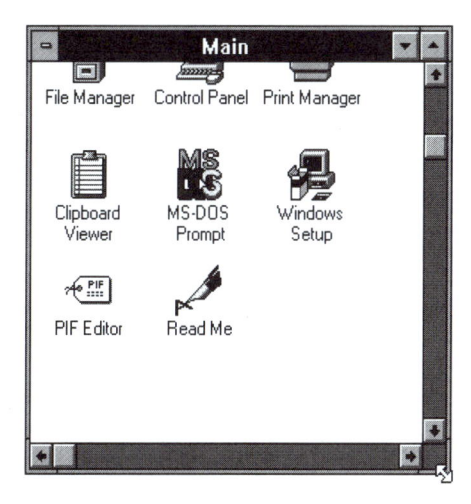

Figure 2.7   Resizing a window diagonally.

In programs like QuarkXPress, when an item is selected, small handle boxes appear at the sides and corners. These may be pulled using the mouse to resize the item, as in shown Figure 2.8. There the picture box of a scanned image is being enlarged toward the right by a pointing hand cursor to display the whole image. The tool cursor may change appearance depending on the object or the program, but the effect is essentially the same.

Figure 2.8   Resizing a picture item.

> **Sizing objects**
>
> *Position pointer (on side or corner handle) until it becomes double arrow (or other sizing tool)*
>
> *Drag to new shape and size*

Using Dialog Boxes

The graphic interface succeeds so well because the computer can talk back to you about the commands you give. It can ask for details, warn you of some impending loss, or ask for your confirmation. This feedback process is accomplished through **dialog boxes** like the one shown in Figure 2.9.

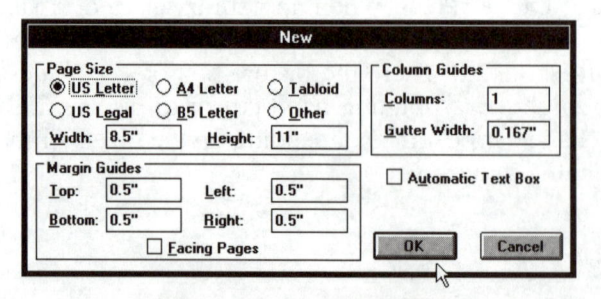

Figure 2.9   A dialog box.

Through a question-response format, you engage in a dialog with the software at work. Your response can be given using the mouse tool or the keyboard. Often it's very simple, like pressing OK or Cancel. Other times you might specify further details.

Software control buttons like those shown in the figure are a way of choosing among alternative replies. You make your choices in a dialog box from a list by using the mouse pointer to click on an item you wish to select, or by typing information into the boxes provided. When you've made all your specifications, you normally send them together by clicking an OK button. Or you can say, "Forget this whole conversation," by clicking a Cancel button.

In later sections, more uses of graphic interface techniques will be elaborated in detail. Mainly, we'll be looking at working within QuarkXPress. But there will be times when using the Program Manager or the File Manager of Windows will help greatly with documents. On some of those occasions, we will put QuarkXPress temporarily in the background and turn to another software application.

INSTALLING QUARKXPRESS INTO THE WINDOWS INTERFACE

Setting up QuarkXPress for Windows is easy. It requires a few items: the QuarkXPress Installation disks and a Windows-running computer.

Quark, Inc. currently says the program requires the following to install and run properly: a 386SX system or better (386DX is recommended), 4 megabytes of RAM (8 megabytes are recommended), version 5.0 of DOS (or later) and 3.1 of Windows, VGA color capability, and 6 megabytes of space on a hard-disk drive. In addition, users of Adobe Type Manager are advised to use version 2.0 or higher.

To install QuarkXPress onto your hard disk, make sure that Windows is operating. Next, verify that you are in the Program Manager. You should see the window shown in Figure 2.10, or one like it. If your system is operating in something other than the Program Manager, you can get to it in a couple ways.

One way is to exit whatever is operating by opening the File menu and choosing Exit.

SHORT CUT Here's a quick way to exit at the keyboard: Hold down Alt key while pressing F. Then press X.

26 ♦ *Teach Yourself...QuarkXPress for Windows*

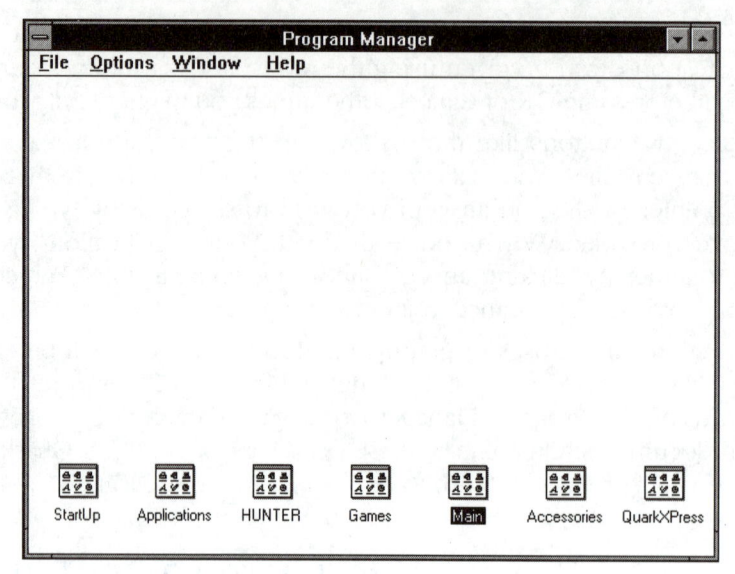

Figure 2.10 *One appearance of the Program manager window.*

Keep exiting whatever other windows are displayed this way until the Program Manager window comes into view and is active (the title, Program Manager, will be displayed as light text on a dark background).

WARNING If you reach the Program Manager then try to exit it inadvertently, a message—*This will end your Windows session*—will appear in a dialog box. Click the Cancel button to return to the Program Manager.

Another other way to reach the Program Manager is simply to turn your computer off then on again (or press the Reset button). If this sends you back to the Program Manager, perfect! If you see the DOS prompt instead, just type *win*, and press Enter. That should put you in the Program Manager.

Next comes one of the rare instances in which this book recommends that you blindly follow orders from a piece of software. Insert the QuarkXPress Installer disk (Disk 1) into your floppy drive. At the Program Manager File menu, choose Run. You can do this by clicking on the File menu. When the list of commands opens beneath it, click on Run, as shown in Figure 2.11.

Type the letter of the drive into which you've just put the Installer disk (usually A or B) then immediately type *:\INSTALL* on the same line. Thus you will have typed *A:\INSTALL* or *B:\INSTALL*. Now press the Enter (or Return) key.

If this seems a bit stark for the user-friendly Windows environment, that's because you are typing a DOS command through Windows. It is within DOS that the INSTALL program will run from the floppy disk you inserted.

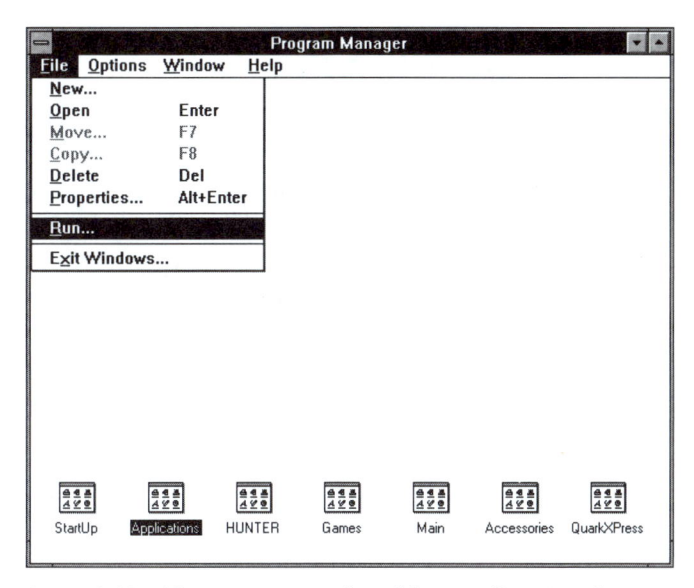

***Figure 2.11**   The Run command used for installing QuarkXPress.*

Now the installation procedure is just a matter of inserting the appropriate disk when directed by the dialog boxes that appear. First you'll be led through some dialog boxes that set up your registration file. Then the User Registration Disk will be requested. And later other disks will be asked for by number. This will involve swapping disks in the floppy drive. Note that you have some options that can customize the organization of the QuarkXPress directories and files. Unless you have a good reason to customize, it is recommended you follow the defaults by clicking OK. Customizing involves dialogs with the INSTALL program to specify paths different from the default.

The User Registration disk is a blank disk used to store information about your system, and to register the program with its publisher, Quark, Inc. After installation, you can send it back to Quark, Inc. to register. When installation is complete, you see a message indicating so. Click OK and you're out of the procedure.

> **NOTE**   Installing does not simply copy the software onto your hard drive. It creates directories, initials files, and adds lines in existing files telling Windows where and what all the associated QuarkXPress files are.

Now to you are ready to run QuarkXPress in your system. Begin at the Program Manager window.

WINDOWS TO QUARKXPRESS

When QuarkXPress has been installed according to the default set-up, you can find the following files on your hard drive. Within the Program Manager there will be a Directory window titled QuarkXPress, and within it an icon for the program. This icon is titled QuarkXPress for Windows. You can move the icon to a more convenient location, say the Applications windows of Program Manager, if you prefer. This icon is all you need to locate in order to run the program from this point on. Double-click on it and you initiate the program.

Starting a program

Locate icon in Program Manager (or File Manager directory listing)

Double-click on it

If you're interested in where the actual working files for the program are kept, you could bring up the File Manager and select the hard disk—normally C:\—directory by double-clicking on the drive icon in the File Manager window. Figure 2.12 shows the files you can find there, tucked in a directory folder called "xpress."

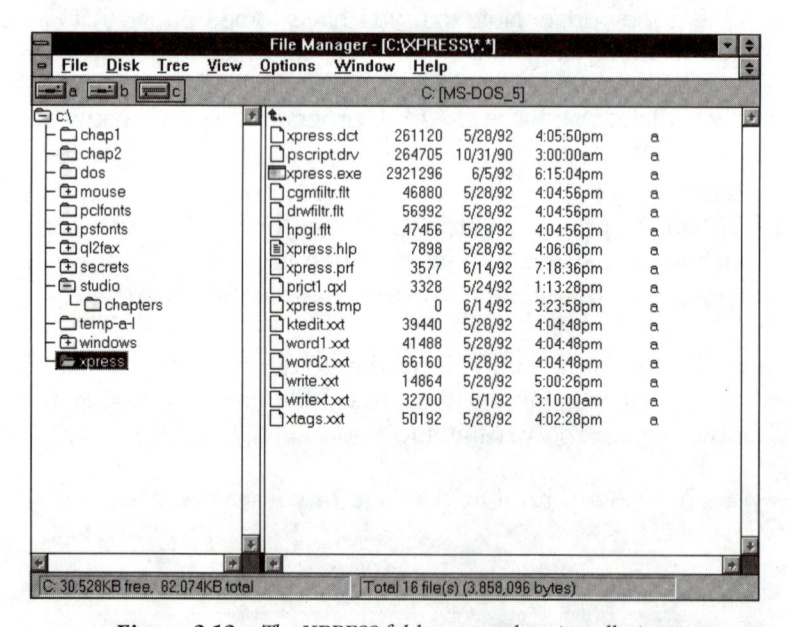

Figure 2.12 *The XPRESS folder created on installation.*

You'll learn more about the File Manager later in this chapter.

Whenever you start QuarkXPress, through the Program Manager icon or otherwise, Windows runs the program file, xpress.exe, found in the xpress folder. In fact, an alternative way to start the program is to locate and double-click on this file. Other files here store preferences and defaults that you can establish from inside the program. The QuarkXPress help files are stored here also. You really never need to open this folder. All access is available through the program icon and within QuarkXPress itself.

If Quark Xpress is the program you usually work with first when you start the computer, by all means consider making it a start-up application. If you do so, whenever the Windows environment comes up it will automatically run QuarkXPress. Here's how to set things up. Locate the Directory folder in Program Manager labeled *Startup*. It may be an open window or an icon like the one near the bottom of the screen shown in Figure 2.13. (This type of icon—you'll notice others nearby—is a called a **program group**.) Next, locate the icon for QuarkXPress—the actual program icon, not just the Directory folder. Using the mouse, click on the icon to select it. Moving the mouse with mouse button down, drag the QuarkXPress icon directly over the Startup Directory folder, or into the open Startup window, and release the mouse button. QuarkXPress's icon is now located inside this folder. Now, anytime Windows starts up, so will QuarkXPress.

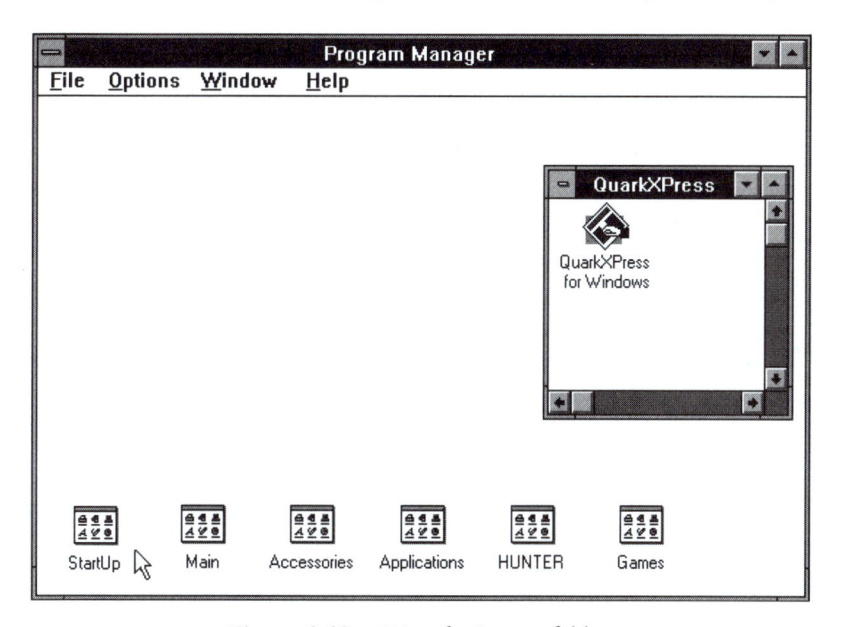

Figure 2.13   *Using the Startup folder.*

If other program icons are properly located in the Startup window, they will run automatically also. In fact, if your work sessions usually involve the same set of programs—such as QuarkXPress, a word processor, and a graphics application—you might want to locate all three programs inside the Startup folder. (When your work no longer requires one program or another, you can drag that program icon out of the Startup folder and into the program group folder it originally came from.)

We are covering Windows basics in this book as they apply to facilitating QuarkXPress operation. If you want to know more about Windows 3.1 than is covered here, refer to the bibliography in Appendix B.

WINDOWS MANAGERS

While we're touching on managing files in Windows, this is a good place to look over the ways the Program Manager and the File Manager can make your work easier—or rather, how to make the most of them. If you are new to Windows, or have worked in another environment (like the Macintosh), you might find that file-handling in Windows is somewhat friendly, but also somewhat strange.

The Station Master

In a nutshell, Windows assigns the Program Manager the status of station master, passing control to it on startup. What we might call "environmental controls" are reached through certain Directory windows of program groups in it. The Main window, the Applications window, and the Accessories window are all displayed from program group windows in the Program Manager. Icons placed in Program Manager during installation procedures (as in the INSTALL procedure for QuarkXPress) indicate and can run their respective programs. Figure 2.14 shows a typical view of the Program Manager. Notice the File Manager in the window titled Main.

The Baggage Handler

The File Manager is given the task of locating and handling the baggage by helping you copy, move, delete, and otherwise organize all files on the hard and floppy drives. Through its icon in the Main window of Program Manager, you can engage the File Manager by double-clicking. The result is a File Manager window like the one shown in Figure 2.15. In this example, two drive windows have been opened by clicking on the Drive icons at the upper-left.

Switching from Program Manager to File Manager

Open main window

Locate and double-click on File Manager

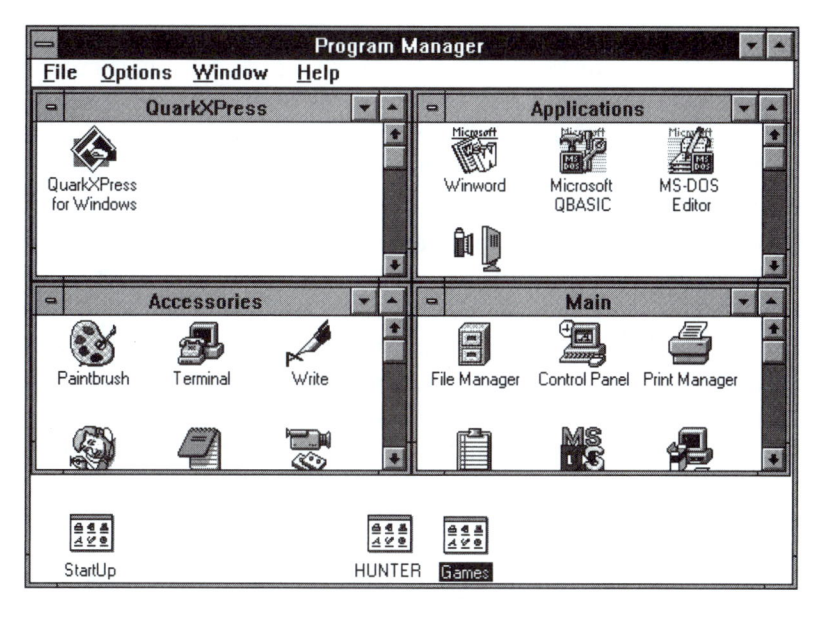

Figure 2.14 *The Program Manager and program group windows.*

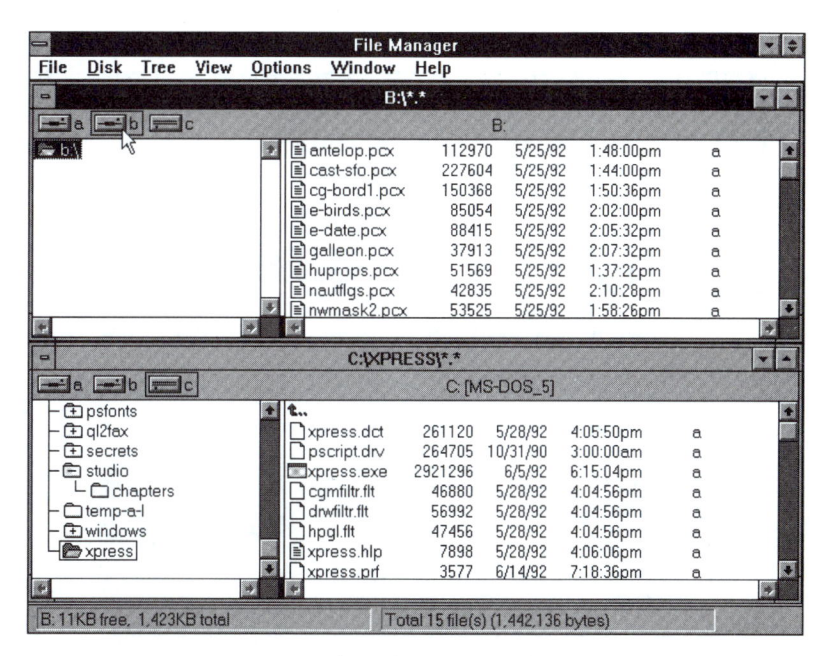

Figure 2.15 *Two drive directories in the File Manager.*

Notice the double listings in one of the drive windows. This is similar to the scheme you'll see in QuarkXPress to find, open, save, import, and otherwise deal with files. In this case the small window occupying the left half of the drive window displays directory folders. When these folders are opened to reveal other directories within them, those directories are shown branching beneath their parent. The window occupying the right half displays the contents of the directory folders selected in the left window. This list may include files and other, nested directory folders. Double-clicking on folders here includes them in the branching display on the left while displaying their content files on the right.

The File Manager's menu commands facilitate formatting blank disks, copying, deleting, and moving files (whether they be data or programs), groups of files, and whole disks. The ways you can choose to display are adjustable in the File Manager's View menu, and include alphanumeric naming order, file extension type, and by size.

When you find a program file (such as one with a name bearing the suffix ".exe"), you can run it by simply double-clicking on that name or its accompanying icon. In like fashion, under certain circumstances a file icon may be used to start the program that generated the file and to open the file within it at the same time. These circumstances are explained in the section, "Linked by Association."

The Mouse in Windows

The mouse is a major player in Windows. To start any program, you point the mouse cursor on its icon and double-click. To open a program group window, double-click on it with the mouse pointer. In fact, to open any Directory folder, just point and double-click. The mouse can be used to move things, as you've seen; for instance, it can drag a file from one directory to another in the File Manager disk window, as shown in Figure 2.16, where the pointer is placing a file into the folder temp-a-1. The procedure is to point and click-drag to a new location.

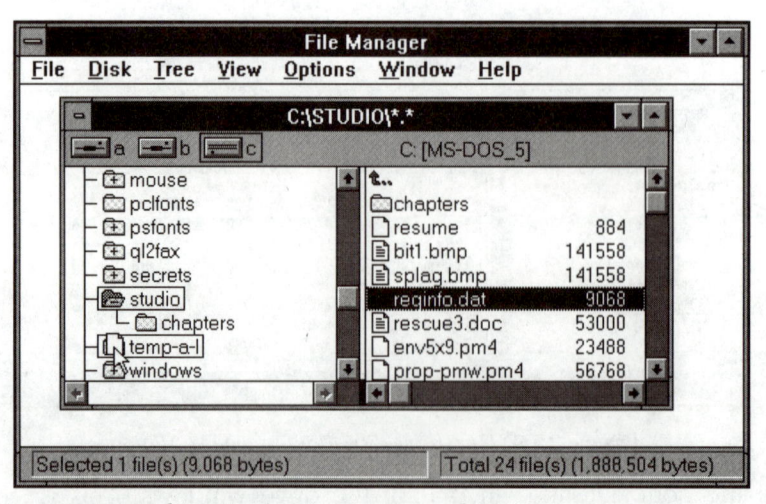

Figure 2.16 *Using the mouse to drag a file between directories.*

If you drag a file icon out of its drive directory and into another drive's, the effect in Windows is to copy it. The simple way to create additional, back-up copies of your document files is to select them on the hard-drive directory (usually C:) and drag them to the floppy disk icon (say, b:) at the upper-left corner of the window. The file icon will display a plus sign (+), as shown in Figure 2.18.

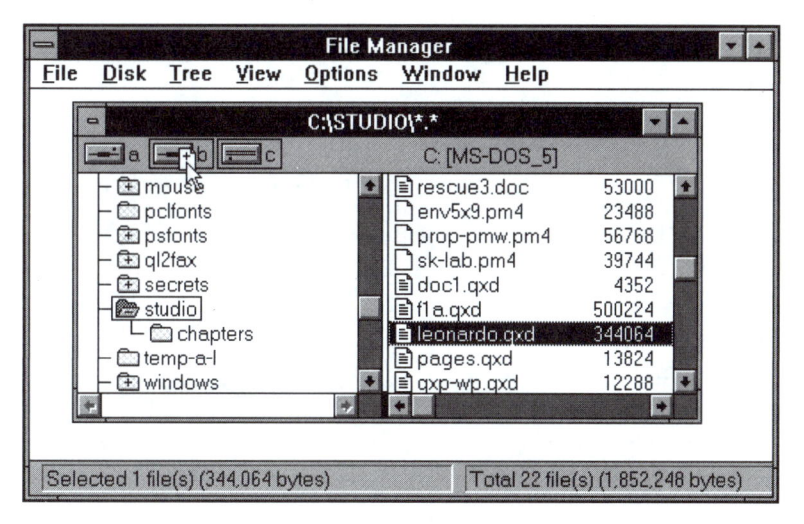

Figure 2.18 *Copying a file to a floppy disk as backup.*

Release the mouse button and the file will be copied onto the floppy in that drive. You can likewise drag a directory to another location. By clicking with the Ctrl key pressed, you can pick out a selected set of files to copy or move.

Making file backups

Drag file icon/name to another drive

LINKED BY ASSOCIATION

As we noted above, it is possible to start a program and open a file simply by double-clicking on that file. But you will find that sometimes this does not work, and you will see a *Cannot Run Program* dialog message. Why? Windows can't find a link to the program you're trying to start. You can, however, tell Windows in advance which program to run whenever the file is called up.

One way to establish this connection is to use the Associate command in the File Manager. First click on the file to select it, then open the File menu and choose the Associate command. Unless you wish to link the file to one of the Windows Accessories programs, you'll next need to use the Browse button to work your way through the Directory folders to the program, as shown in Figure 2.17. When you locate the program, select it (note that the files are in the left window and the directories are in the right) and click OK.

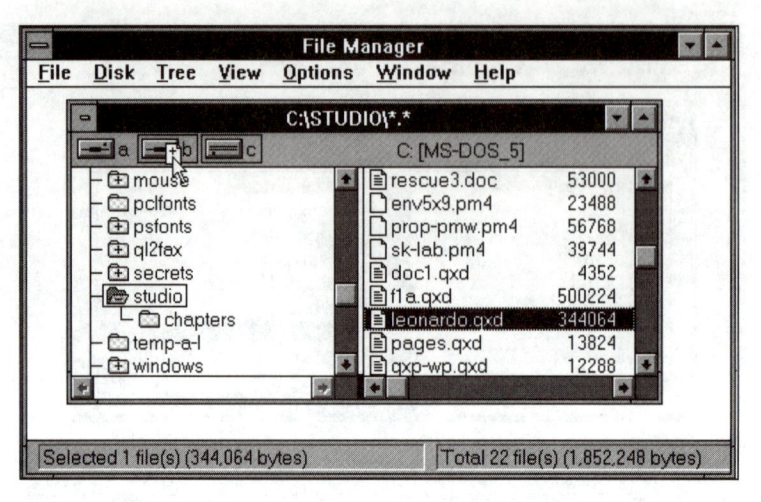

Figure 2.17 *Locating the program to which a file is being associated.*

> **Linking a file to a program**
>
> *In File Manager, select the file*
>
> *Open File menu, choose Associate*
>
> *Click Browse, locate and select program*

Another approach is to drag the file icon from File Manager to one of the Program Manager windows. Let's suppose you've found a QuarkXPress document that you want to make accessible in the QuarkXPress program group window. You can position the Program Manager and File Manager windows adjacent to each other and drag the document file to that program group window. An icon will be created for it there. Then, when you wish to start the program and open a window for that file, you only need to double-click on the file icon.

Multitasking Program Switching

On the business end of desktop publishing, we're all assembling our wish lists for the next version of whatever software we're using most. No matter how beautifully implemented programs are, it is only natural to think, "If only it did *this one other* thing." The demands of design goals frequently govern which software we choose to use. QuarkXPress can do word processing, but it's not a great word processor. It can create simple graphics and manipulate elaborate ones; but it's clearly not a graphics program. So we use a word processor and one or more graphics generators.

But even with this much of our software hunger satisfied, we really want—in our heart of hearts—one giant superprogram (fully customizable, of course) that would provide every tool and ability we've ever employed. And we'd want all of these features to be accessible at the same time. Having to quit your desktop publishing program to start up your graphics program just doesn't make the grade when you want *instant* revision on the document page. One consequence of the marriage of Windows and QuarkXPress is that you don't have to do that anymore. By taking advantage of two features, one in each environment, you can join your software into what is the functional equivalent of your own superprogram.

Remember that Windows is capable of running more than one program concurrently, and QuarkXPress is capable of keeping track of imported files and of updating them within the document. These two features can be made to dovetail perfectly, as we'll see in detail in Chapter 6. The result is that both QuarkXPress and your graphics program can be made to run at the same time—and so can your word processor, your database, and your type-manipulation software. You can switch between them with a keystroke. In the case of graphics, QuarkXPress can be instructed to seek out a graphic's source file previously imported into the document, and to update the changes into the document. So, if looking at your document page you see clearly that the background of the page 1 photo should be digitally airbrushed, you can switch to the graphics program, make the change, switch back to QuarkXPress and specify an update, and you'll see the photo on the document page now airbrushed. You could just as easily make changes to a text file in your word processor and reimport the revised text without quitting either program.

To understand how this works, you need to know that by virtue of the way Windows works, even when you are working in QuarkXPress, the Program Manager is available in the background. Many explanations of Windows describe first how you can "minimize" the current foreground application to drop into the direct Windows operation. Later, they explain how you can "maximize" your way back to the application, or to another. This works through clicking on the Minimize arrow in the upper-right corner of the Application title bar, then double-clicking on the application icon, which is usually at the bottom left below the Program Manager window.

SHORT CUT There's a more practical way: Open QuarkXPress, then (to minimize it) hold down the Alt key and press Tab once. A box like the one shown in Figure 2.19 will appear in the center of the screen. Now release the Alt key. The Program Manager window will appear over the QuarkXPress window. Open the second application—let's say you choose Paintbrush in the Accessories window. Hold down the Alt key while pressing Tab several times. You'll see a cycle in the display box: Program Manager, QuarkXPress, Paintbrush, Program Manager, QuarkXPress, Paintbrush. Windows is going backward through the most recently accessed applications. So now, in this example, you can switch instantly between Paintbrush and QuarkXPress. Of course, Paintbrush could have been any other application. In fact, you could open *several* in this fashion to set up your temporary superprogram.

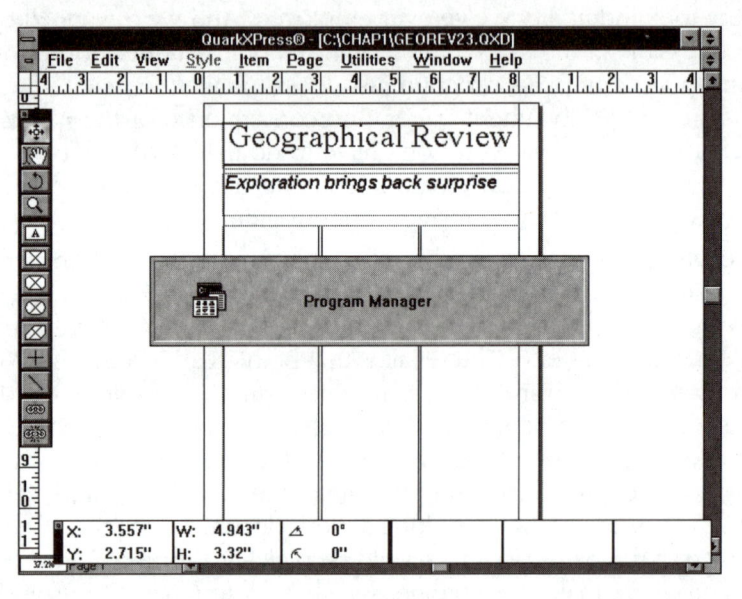

Figure 2.19   *Quick ALT-TAB switching between Quark and the Program Manager.*

Instant switching between programs

>*Hold Alt key, press Tab repeatedly until program name appears*
>
>*Release Alt*

STEPPING UP

A book devoted to QuarkXPress cannot possibly explore all the aspects of operating in the Windows environment—we can only hint at most of them here. If power Windows operation is an interest of yours, take a look at Appendix B for resources dedicated to the program. Windows offers great features, but it is peculiar and far from flawless.

By this point, you've come through DOS-land and Windows to arrive in the QuarkXPress environment. From this point on, each small effort on your part will give you more control over text, graphics, and layout. Even if you've already been working with typesetting or desktop publishing software, you'll be surprised at some of the things you can do with the features and tools we'll encounter—such as working with documents, the subject of Chapter 3.

Chapter 3

Working with Documents

WHAT YOU WILL LEARN IN THIS CHAPTER

- ◆ How to create, locate, and open documents
- ◆ How to set up guides
- ◆ How to adjust and use different page views
- ◆ How to use tools and palettes
- ◆ How to position pages and page elements

Like mighty oaks, designs and publications have humble beginnings. In QuarkXPress they all start as one-page documents, but they can grow to as many as two thousand pages. They can be as small as a one-inch square to as large as a four-foot banner. This chapter will show you how to create document files of any dimensions and page length, how to locate the exact part of any project you are working on, and how to view pages using a large range of magnifications and reductions.

This is where you will learn how to choose the right tools for creating and manipulating your document's visual elements and also how to control and monitor these elements by using palettes. Your explorations in this chapter will give you control over every region of any document you may produce.

You Are Here

The screen displayed immediately after starting QuarkXPress reveals much about the program. You can see major controls for working with documents, as shown in Figure 3.1. Virtually every manipulation, adjustment, creation, revision, activity, movement, deletion, addition, enhancement, and change can be achieved through one of the interface components displayed in the Program window. In fact, the Menu bar, the Tool box and the Measurements palette, as these parts are known, control virtually every feature of QuarkXPress.

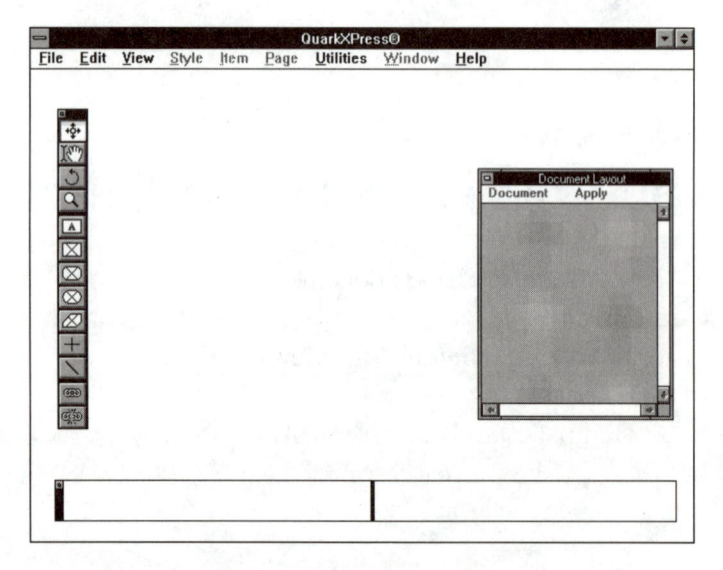

***Figure 3.1**   The first layer of the QuarkXPress interface.*

Note, for example, the small window at the right of the Program window. This Document Layout window is a key to managing pages in a document. At the left, is a vertical box called the **Tool palette**, which offers three groups of mouse-driven tools for creating, manipulating, and linking elements. Above both of them, the familiar Menu bar provides access to a multitude of functions within the program. The long horizontal blank box at the bottom of the window is a versatile layout device called the **Measurements palette**. It both controls and monitors orientations, characteristics, and dimensions of type and graphics. As you change aspects of one element or another, the values displayed there instantly reflect that change. This palette provides a speedy, precise feedback approach to page layout, as you will see.

CREATING A DOCUMENT

In QuarkXPress each new document starts as a single page. The first thing the command for a new document does is to present a dialog box like the one shown in Figure 3.2. (Dialog boxes offer such a clear way to exchange information that they are used frequently by the program.) In this case, the box shows you a preselected publication format and asks you either to accept it or to change the format parameters to something you will accept.

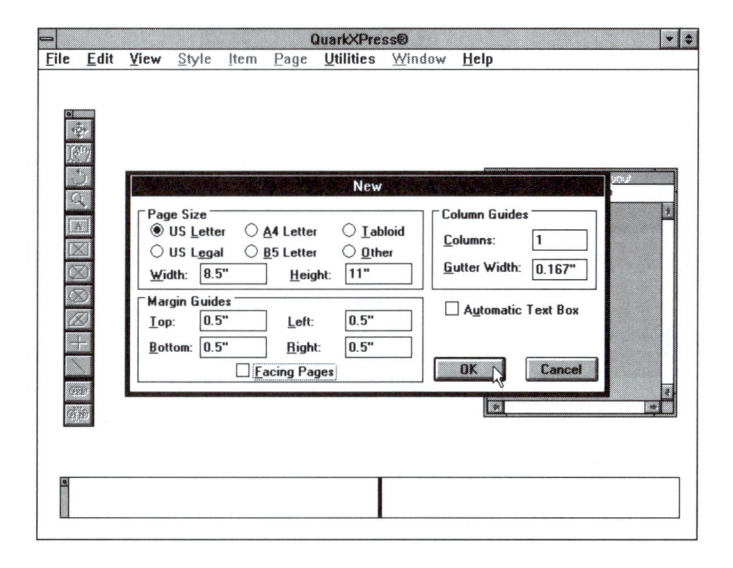

Figure 3.2 *The dialog box from the New document command.*

The steps for creating a new document are simple. First, open the File menu and choose New. The dialog box displays the default parameters. To accept them, click OK. Note that as you create new documents, QuarkXPress automatically gives them temporary names—Doc1, Doc2, Doc3, and so on.

If, on the other hand, you need to customize the publication format, consider each aspect of this dialog box with an eye to your publication page. You'll notice a number of things.

Under the Page Size section, five standard page formats are indicated by software buttons. The dimensions of each will be displayed in the Width and Height boxes as you click on them. You can key in your own custom dimensions—from one inch by one inch to 48 inches by 48 inches. (Inches are only one of several measurement units available. We'll look into others later.)

The Margin Guides section deals with the boundaries of the active page area. **Margin Guides** can be displayed on the screen, as shown in Figure 3.3, but they do not print. They help to form a visual framework during layout. In some cases they also provide for automatic text layout. You can specify any combination of the four margins that will fit on the page size selected.

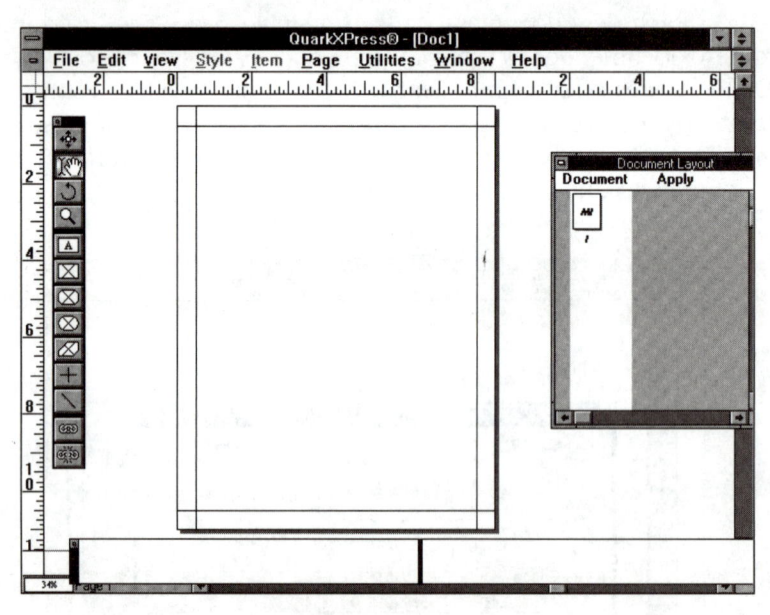

Figure 3.3 Margin guides.

The Facing Pages checkbox determines how the Left and Right margin guides will be treated, and how the pages of a multipage document can be displayed onscreen. When it is checked, Left and Right margin choices are replaced with Inside and Outside choices.

> **NOTE** Pages that are added later are then displayed in page spreads (pages 2 and 3, 4 and 5, and so on) rather than singly.

Column Guides are like Margin Guides in that they appear in the document onscreen, as shown in Figure 3.4, but do not print. They in no way constrain your layout, acting only as visual cues. Here you can choose the number of column markers to be laid out automatically as part of a grid. They will be spaced equally within the area defined by the Margin Guides selected above. You can also specify the space between columns in the field labeled Gutter Width.

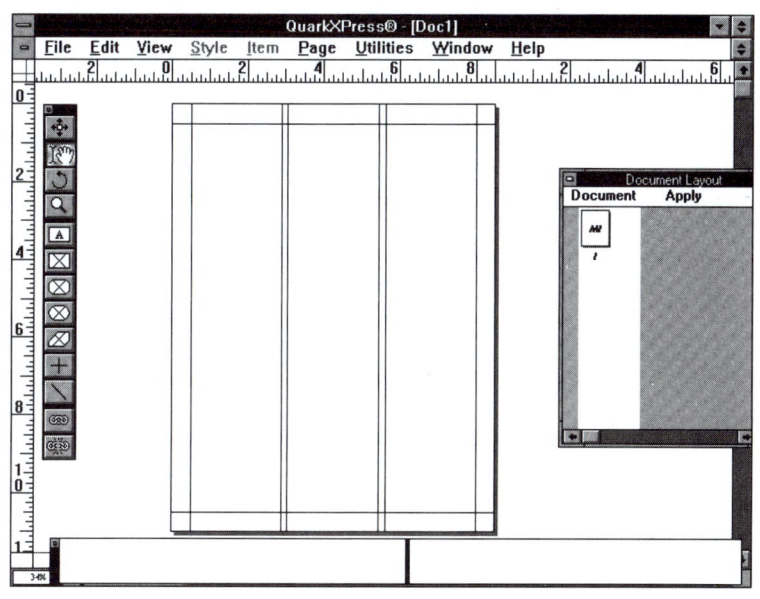

***Figure 3.4**   Column guides.*

The Automatic Text Box feature can facilitate flowing text within columns through the installation of a partitioned text box. It puts a text box (explored in depth in Chapter 4) on the hidden master page that accompanies and defines Page 1. This master page is automatically named Master A. You can derive other pages from Master A; they will have the same column characteristics as Page 1. Such a feature becomes extremely useful in typesetting book-length documents. Master pages are explained in detail in Chapter 10.

When you set up a customized document format by making revisions to the New dialog box, these specifications are saved as the default and used for the next document created through the New command.

OPENING EXISTING DOCUMENTS

More often than not, desktop publishing projects will require you to revise, update, or expand documents already in existence. Since QuarkXPress can handle seven different document windows simultaneously, you can transfer elements, groups of elements, or designs directly from one to another. Each new or existing document opens in its own window beneath the Menu bar, overlapping any windows already open. Figure 3.5 shows three such documents open in the program, each at a different view. They have been arranged side by side using the Windows Tile command (under the Window menu available in QuarkXPress).

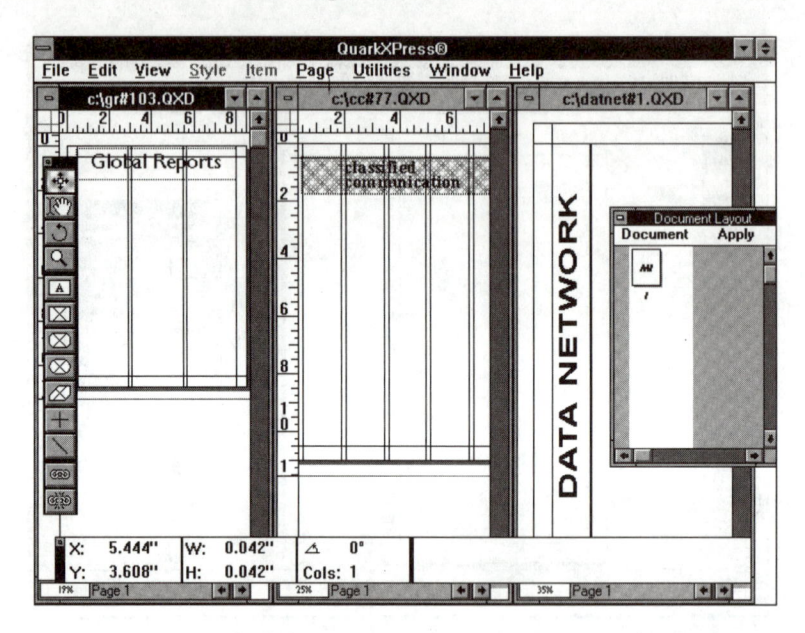

Figure 3.5   *Three document windows opened in QuarkXPress.*

Document files can be opened in any of several ways. We've already looked at opening documents from within the Program Manager and File Manager. The setup and organization of your system and directories may vary, and with it the exact steps for opening from these two Windows programs. But one method is fairly consistent: opening from within QuarkXPress itself.

The steps here vary only according to where the desired files are located. Begin by opening the File menu in QuarkXPress, and choosing Open. An Open dialog box will appear, as shown in Figure 3.6. There are two approaches to follow. You can key in the file name and path, if you know it, regardless of what appears in the File and Directory windows. To do this, give the path in DOS, and hence Windows, format. This, as you may know, follows the form:

```
(drive designation):\(directory folder name)\(directory folder
name)...\(file name.qxd).
```

For example, the document might be named *leonardo,* and reside within the Directory folder named *current*, which itself resides within the Directory folder *studio*, which is on

Working with Documents ◆ 45

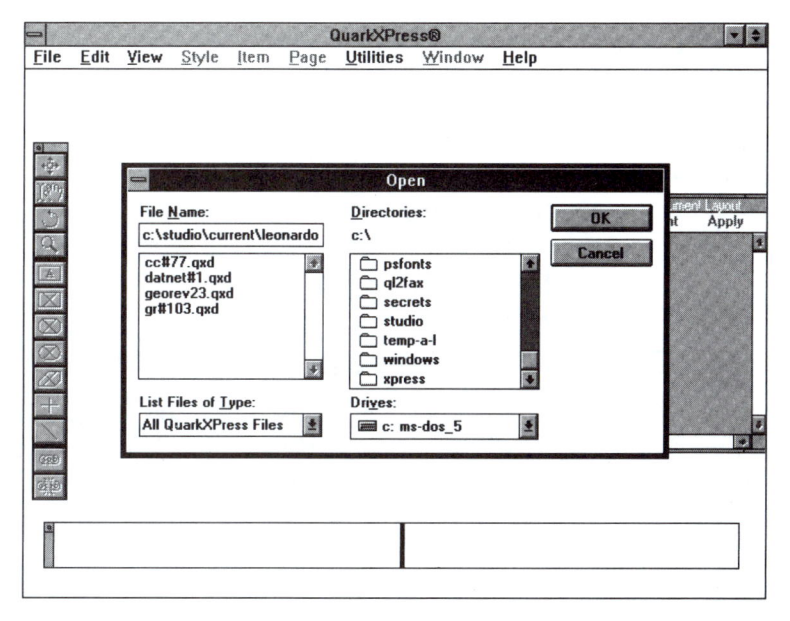

Figure 3.6 Opening a document using the dialog box.

the hard drive designated C. In that case, you would type the following into the file name field: *C:\studio\current\leonardo.qxd*. Note the backslashes (\) that separate the directories, and note also the suffix, *.qxd*, that indicates a QuarkXPress document file.

Opening a file by pathname

At the File menu choose Open

Type path to document in this form:

drive:\directory\directory...\file.qxd

The other way involves using the Open dialog box. You hunt through the directories for the file, as we did in the File Manager earlier. When you locate the document file in the File window, just double-click on it to open it. This process is quicker to describe but not always faster to do. If you remember exactly what the path to the file is, sometimes the file name approach is the way to go. Sometimes the choice is a toss-up.

NOTE Documents can be opened only one at a time. So, if you want more than one, you'll need to repeat either of the opening procedures above for each file.

Adjusting Document Windows

The documents you open, like documents you create, typically appear in the overlapping fashion shown in Figure 3.7, your most recent document being uppermost and shifted slightly down and to the right of the previous window. In Windows parlance this is known as **cascading**. Clearly there are times when you want to see parts of more than one document at the same moment. When this happens, you can adjust Document windows using the same methods for adjusting windows in the Program Manager and the File Manager.

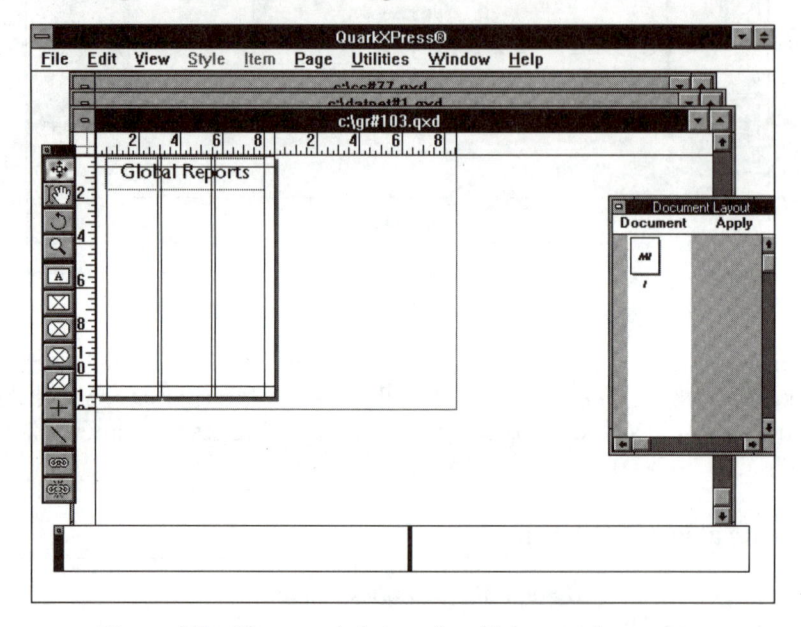

Figure 3.7   *The cascaded view of multiple open documents.*

You can also use commands under the Window menu (as shown in Figure 3.8) to rearrange open Document windows automatically. The first choice is Tile, the result of which is shown with three documents in Figure 3.9.

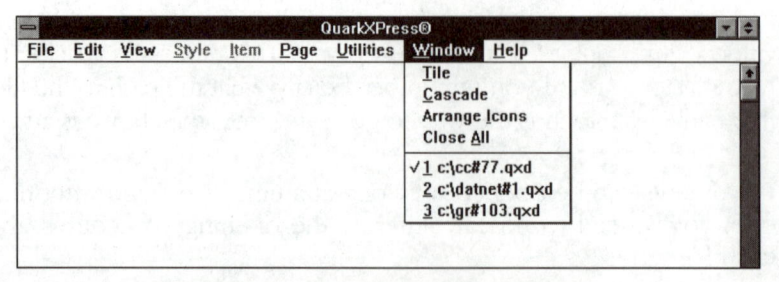

Figure 3.8   *The Windows menu.*

Working with Documents ♦ **47**

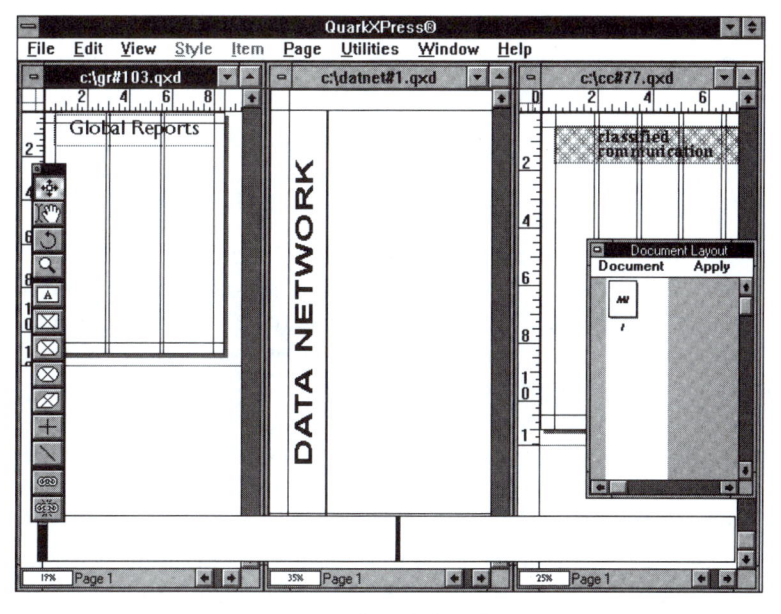

Figure 3.9 *The effect of the Tile command.*

We've already seen how the Cascade choice works. In the lower half of the menu, you'll find a listing of all the documents currently open. The one indicated by a checkmark is the active window. You can switch to another Document window by selecting another name on that list. If that document is obscured, as it is under cascaded windows, it will be lifted to the frontmost level.

Another pertinent control here is the Close All command—which does just that, asking you, when appropriate, whether changes to the document should be saved.

SAVING DOCUMENTS

You save documents in a procedure that is similar to the Opening procedure. QuarkXPress labels new documents as Doc1, Doc2, and so on, depending on how many new files are open. It automatically adds the suffix .qxd to identify the file as a QuarkXPress Document. To give your document a descriptive title, open the File Menu, choose Save, and key in an eight-character file name, following the usual DOS-Windows conventions.

You might like to save copies of your documents at different stages of completion, giving slightly differing names to each stage, such as stage1, stage2, stage3, or janmag, febmag, marmag. QuarkXPress will automatically add the .qxd suffix for you. If you are experimenting with different layouts, consider saving a file for each major change in order to have various fall-back versions to return to.

To save a document under a different name or in a different folder or disk location, open the File Menu, choose Save As, and proceed as above, either changing the name, the directory, or the disk pathname in which the document file is saved.

Page Views

When much layout work has already gone into a document, a change in page size should be undertaken only after careful consideration. Many hours of layout work can be lost by revising the page size on which elements have been laid out. You can experiment with various page dimensions and aspect (height-to-width) ratios onscreen. But altering the page size is apt to leave already positioned text and graphics in unintended places. If you try to reduce the page size so drastically that large items no longer fit in the workspace, QuarkXPress might be unable to produce the new smaller size. Moreover, take care when changing page size so as to avoid jumbling page elements. We'll discuss the use of the workspace surrounding the page in more detail later.

Changing the page setup itself is simple. Begin by opening the File menu and choosing Document Setup. Then select or key in the new format in the dialog box, much as you would choose a format in the New dialog box.

Standard Page Views on Command

Large-format documents, like newspapers, and diminutive projects, like small-display advertisements, have one thing in common: At actual size they can be difficult to work with on a typical monitor screen. One won't fit; the other needs magnification. In fact, most documents on which you work will require several views besides Actual Size.

Six ready-set views can be chosen in the View menu, as shown in Figure 3.10.

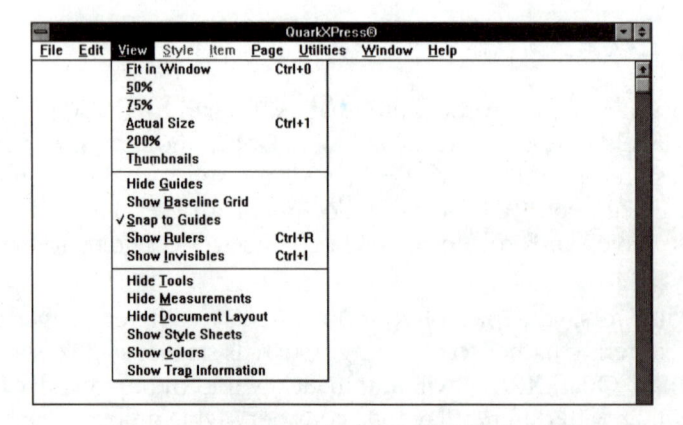

Figure 3.10   *The View menu choices.*

Four of these views are based on percentage of actual size—50%, 75%, Actual Size, and 200%. Percentages refer to measuring the proportional change along one side of the page. For example, an 11 inch–long letter-size page viewed at 50 percent would appear 5.5 inches long. In reality the page being viewed at 50 percent is one-fourth the area of actual, but we're following a different convention here, the same one used in copy machines. Figure 3.11 shows the relative size comparisons of these four views.

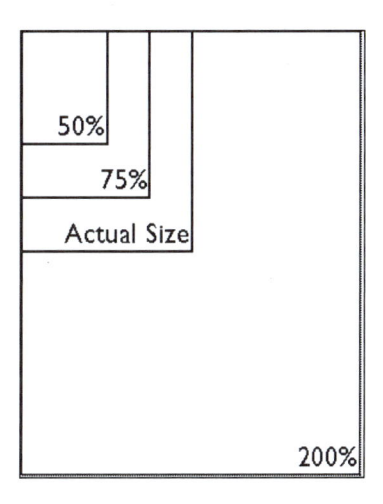

Figure 3.11   *Relative sizes of preset view choices.*

Two special views appear in the first section of the View menu. The first, Fit in Window, adjusts the display so that a page (or page spread) just fits within the active document window, whatever the size of that window. If you change the size of the window, then reapply the Fit in Window command, the page view will be scaled to fit within the new window dimensions.

The other view, Thumbnails, displays a Lilliputian view of several pages at once. This view is less than 10 percent, so QuarkXPress doesn't even try to make page elements accessible in it, even though they may be displayed. You can't select or otherwise alter items or contents in it. Its principle value is that it allows an overview of page geometry and provides a way to assemble multipage spreads, such as three- or four-page centerfolds. We'll see more about the usefulness of this later.

THE PASTEBOARD

Pages can also be displayed surrounded by a pasteboard workspace. Figure 3.12 shows this space in use during the construction of a page spread. It's a nonprinting part of the document that allows you to temporarily shuffle any design elements you want off the page while you're assembling your layout. Leave items there, and they will never print. Overlap them and only the part on the page will print.

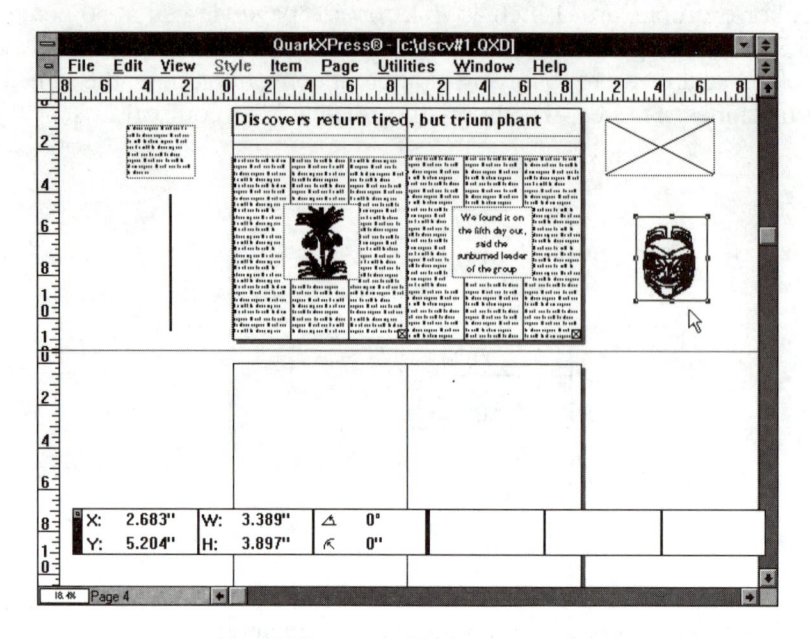

Figure 3.12 *A page spread and its pasteboard in use.*

The pasteboard serves as a handy place to leave notes on a page in progress. Separate pasteboard spaces accompany each page or spread. The relative extent of the pasteboard can be seen clearly in Thumbnail view. A thin line encloses it and its pages.

Viewing pasteboard with pages

CTRL + Fit in Window (under View Menu)

To see all of the pasteboard while being able to work with elements there, open the View menu and hold down the Ctrl key as you choose Fit in Window.

Controlling Page Views by Direct Entry

As you choose Page views, you might notice numbers changing in a small box in the lower-left corner of the Active window. This value, the Percent view, reflects precisely the percent-size currently applied. Note the View Percent field to the left of the horizontal scroll bar and page-number display in Figure 3.13. It provides

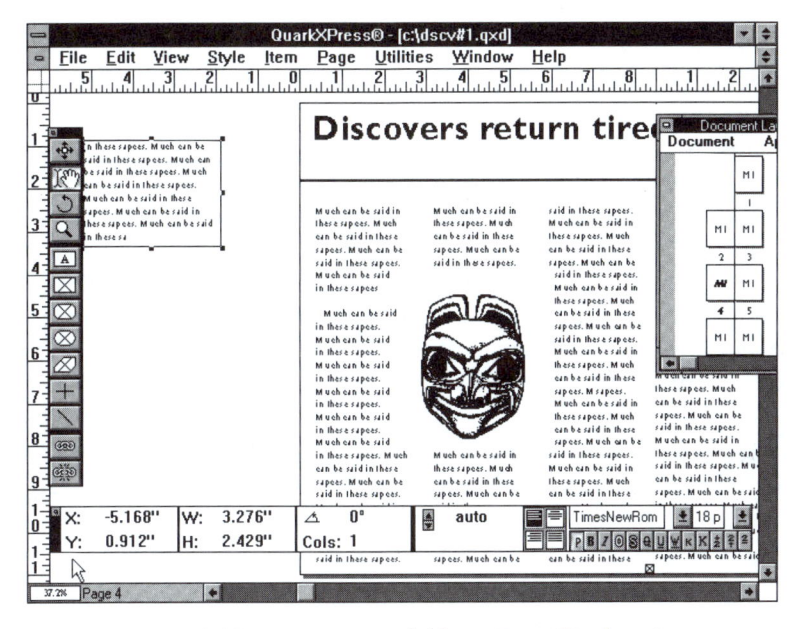

Figure 3.13   *View percent field at a Fit in Window view.*

feedback for magnifying or reducing your Page view with precision. You can use it to change the view to any percentage you prefer, from 10 percent to 400 percent. Using it, you can zoom in or out precisely as you might with a telephoto zoom lens on a camera.

To use the View Percent field, aim the cursor over it, double-click to select the value already there, then key in your preferred view, in percentage, in its place. Press Enter. The screen will redraw the window in the new magnification or reduction.

A later section will show you how to manipulate page view using your toolbox tools.

Precision percentage views

> *Double-click value in percentage view display*
>
> *Key in new percentage*
>
> *Enter*

THE QUARKXPRESS WORKSHOP

QuarkXPress can be thought of as a designer's workshop where publications and designs are created and modified. Basic materials include pages and the text and graphic elements placed onto them. The desktop publisher who gains a solid grasp of QuarkXPress tools and devices can produce excellent results.

Most of the tools and many of the features of the program are presented through various palettes, which like painters' palettes allow you to change the canvas you're working on. Since these palettes take up space on the screen, you'll find times when they are best left out of sight. Normally, the program automatically displays three of these palettes: the Tools palette, the Measurements palette, and the Document Layout palette. You can display or remove these (or any of several other palettes and guide features) from the screen through the View menu. All the Show/Hide commands under this menu allow instant display or concealment. These are toggle commands that alternate states between Show and Hide.

> **NOTE** Each palette is itself a small window, and can be moved by dragging from the Title bar—or any other bar—found at the top or left of the palette.

THE TOOLS AND MEASUREMENTS PALETTES

We can think of text and graphics as items that can be manipulated and revised. As such, they are created, imported from other files, moved about on a page, moved over or behind other items, moved between pages, stretched, shrunk, and otherwise altered. The Tool palette gives tangible devices for handling text and graphic items. Tools from this palette initiate nearly every manipulation performed on an item. Working first with one of the simplest tools demonstrates many of the ways all tools function.

Using a Tool

In laying out publication pages, one of the most indispensable graphics elements has proven to be the humble rule. As horizontal or vertical lines that typically separate text on the page, rules are perfect for helping organize a page. Quark has dubbed the tool that makes these lines the **orthogonal line tool**. But **rule tool** will describe it just as well. It draws only horizontal or vertical lines regardless of how you drag the mouse. The lines shown in Figure 3.14 were drawn with the rule tool by dragging in various nonhorizontal and nonvertical directions.

The rule tool shares the operational features of several other tools. The first step for all tool use is to select the tool. To select the rule tool, click on the fourth button from the bottom of the tool palette; it appears on the Crosshairs button indicated in Figure 3.14. By moving the mouse into the document window area, you'll see the cursor become a similar set of crosshairs.

Working with Documents ♦ 53

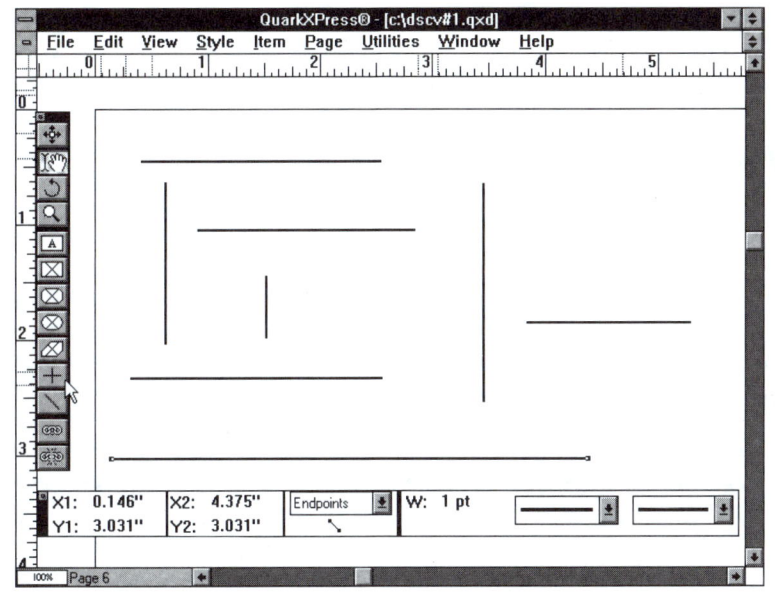

Figure 3.14   Lines drawn using the Rule tool.

SHORT CUT   Two easy ways to choose tools are available through the keyboard. To move the tool selection from one tool to the one below it, hold the Ctrl key and press Tab. Each time you press, the tool selection moves downward (you'll see the button appear depressed). Ctrl-Tab at the bottommost tool, (the unlink tool, represented by the broken chain) shifts selection back up to the first, the item tool. Ctrl-Tab cycles through all the tools like this. To cycle in the other direction, upward, hold both Ctrl and Shift keys while pressing Tab; the selection then moves upward, switching at the item tool down to the unlink tool. Note that if the Tool palette is hidden, either Ctrl-Tab or Ctrl-Shift-Tab will show it onscreen.

Selecting tools from the keyboard

Ctrl-Tab to move downward through buttons, or to show palette

Ctrl-Shift-Tab to move upward

The second step in tool use is to apply the tool. Depending on the task at hand, this may mean selecting an existing item, or making a new item. In this case we are creating a rule by drawing. To draw a rule, press the mouse button and drag from start to finish, then release the button. Even if your hand wavers, the tool will draw a line that is perfectly horizontal or vertical. You will see a long horizontal Measurements palette (seen earlier in this chapter) displayed along the bottom when you release. Also, the cursor will revert automatically to the content tool once the rule is drawn.

Using a Measurements Palette

When an item is created or moved, its Measurements palette normally appears on the screen. Each of the three kinds of items in QuarkXPress—a line, picture box, or text box—will activate its own Measurements palette when that item is selected. In fact, you can think of each individual item as having its own Measurements palette that can be displayed when the item is selected. Consider the last line drawn in Figure 3.15, under the Geographic Review nameplate. It is still selected. The Measurements palette for it appears at the bottom of the Program window.

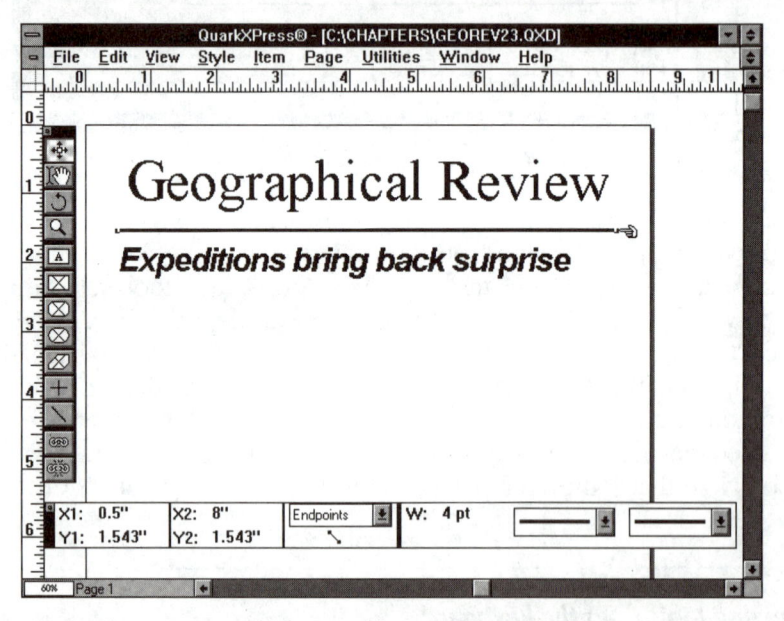

Figure 3.15   *A recently drawn rule with its measurements palette active.*

At the left side of this palette you will find the X and Y coordinates for one endpoint of the line. (These coordinates are the measurements along the horizontal ruler at the top of the window, X, and along the vertical ruler at the left of the window, Y.) Just to the right in the palette are displayed the coordinates for the other end. Then comes the method of measuring, in this case from end to end. Next comes the line weight in points. And further we see a **drop-down list** for line types—dotted, dashed, double, and so on, as shown in Figure 3.16. The final drop-down list indicates the arrows on the line; in this case none are applied (as shown in Figure 3.17).

Working with Documents ◆ 55

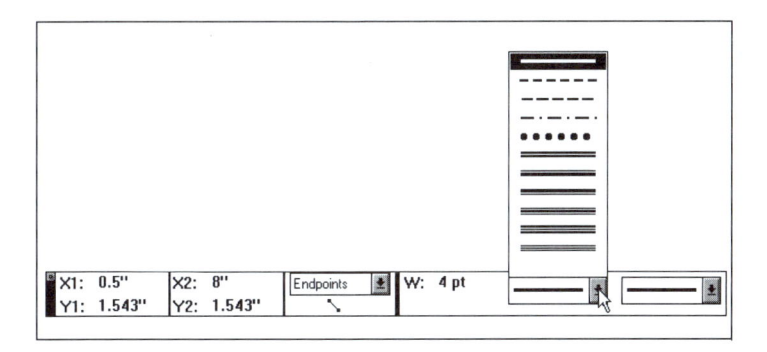

Figure 3.16   *Measurements palette Line Type list activated.*

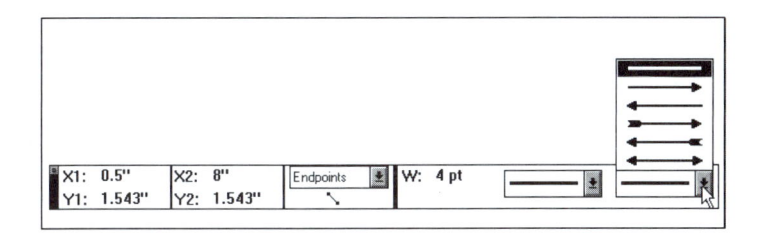

Figure 3.17   *Measurements palette arrows Option list activated.*

NOTE   These drop-down lists, as they are called, are actually dropping *up* into available window space when the list arrow is clicked.

As other kinds of items come onto the scene, we will see that their associated Measurements palettes are each somewhat different. But the most significant feature of all these palettes can be readily demonstrated in this Line palette. To understand that feature, consider the following: The values shown are really part of a **feedback loop**. They describe the item selected, and they can be changed with great precision. Changing a value in the Measurements palette changes that characteristic in the item itself. Note that we are talking about changing the item's features, not its contents.

Here's how to modify an item through a Measurements palette. First, check that the item highlighted is the one you want to change. (A large portion of the errors made in documents can be avoided simply by assuring that the selection is appropriate.) Next, move the cursor to the palette and highlight the value you wish to change, then type in the value you desire. For features with a drop-down list, make your choice by opening and highlighting a choice from the list. Do this for all the values you wish to change. Finally, press Enter to apply the new values to the item.

> **Modifying through measurements palette**
>
> *Select item and locate attribute in palette*
>
> *Highlight attribute value and type in new value*
>
> *or*
>
> *Select new value from drop-down list*
>
> *Press Enter*

By keying in a new X1 of .75 inch and a new X2 of 7.75 inches, and a new weight of 6, we have shortened and thickened the nameplate rule, as shown in Figure 3.18.

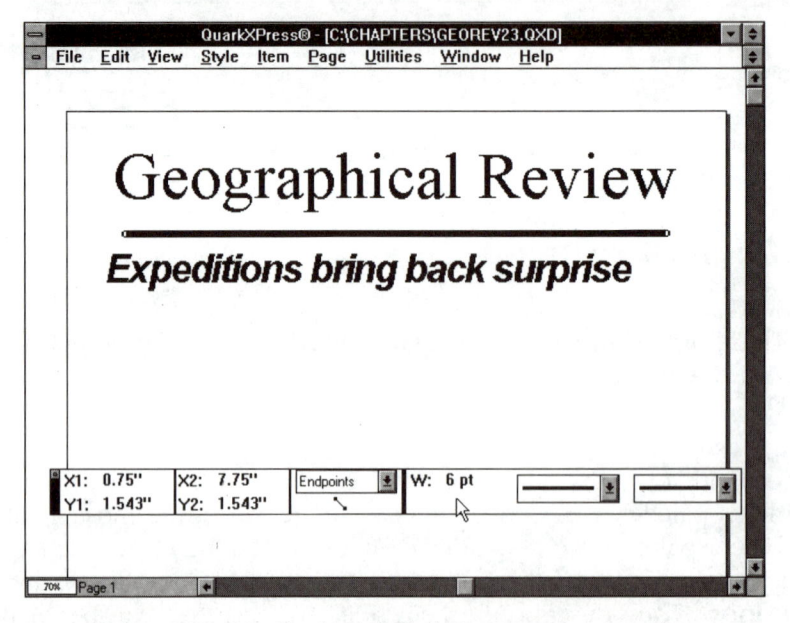

Figure 3.18 *A rule edited through the Measurements palette.*

When you try this yourself, you'll see the speed and precision inherent in using this palette for rule revision.

> **NOTE** This very special instant-feedback relationship between items and their Measurements palettes holds true for every item in every document.

Page Views by Tool

Tools provide clever alternatives to effect many modifications possible through other means, such as Menu commands. Sometimes they offer a measure of control not otherwise easily achieved, or make possible a useful try-it-out approach. For instance, consider the zoom tool. This tool (fourth down in the Tools palette) is specifically designed for changing views. Clicking with it changes the view in preset increments. (The default increment is 25 percent.) It also allows you to magnify or reduce the view around a particular point on the page. Further, with it you can indicate an area to be magnified to the full extent of the window.

Here's how it adjusts view by increments. When you select the zoom tool and move the cursor into the document window, you'll notice that the cursor changes into a magnifying-glass cursor with a dot in the center. Position it over the area of interest and click. The window will redraw in a view magnified 25 percent over the previous view. Click again and the view magnifies another 25 percent. Notice that this method seems to anchor whatever point is under the cursor—as in Figure 3.19, where we clicked three times inside the letter *e* to magnify from 100 percent to 125 percent to 150 percent to 175 percent.

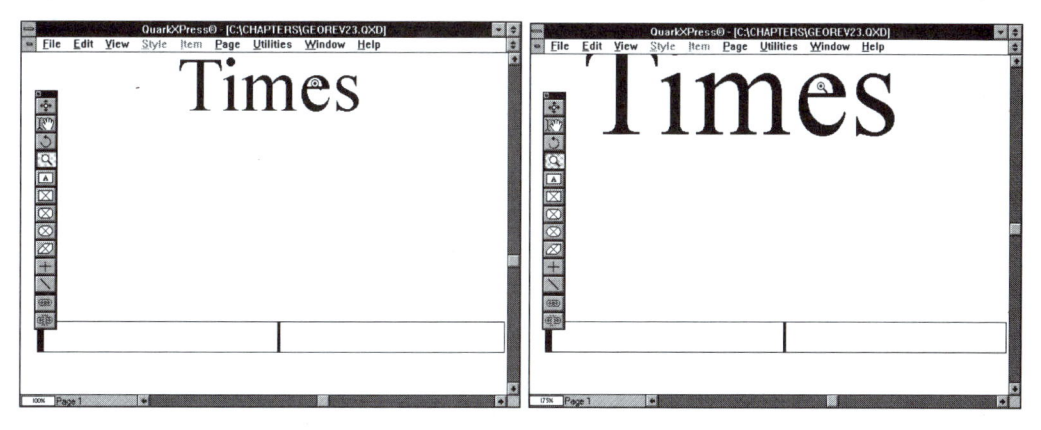

Figure 3.19 *Magnifying with three clicks of the Zoom tool.*

Magnifying view with zoom tool

Position tool over point to anchor

Click repeatedly until desired magnification is achieved

Reducing magnification works the same way, except you hold down the Ctrl key while clicking. A minus sign appears inside the lens of the tool cursor. The window will redraw to a view reduced by 25 percent. You can notice these view changes in the Percentage View box near the horizontal scroll bar.

Reducing view with zoom tool

Position tool over point to anchor

Hold Ctrl key and click repeatedly until desired reduction is achieved

---

NOTE: The limits of view magnification/reduction are 10 percent to 400 percent.

The zoom tool permits one additional method of view change, that of **magnifying by area**. Here's how it works. Let's say we are looking at the mask in the Document window of Figure 3.20. Notice the view in the Fit in Window; in this case, 37.2 percent. Now suppose you want to look closely at one of the eyes; that is, you want to enlarge the view to fit the eye into the window. You can do this in one precise step with the zoom tool. The procedure is as follows: Hold down the Alt key, press the mouse button, and drag until the dotted box covers just the area of interest. As you're doing this, notice the Percentage value indicator in the corner box changing. It's keeping pace with the percentage view your box-into-window drag calls for. When you've enclosed the area to be magnified, let go of the button. The subject will fill the screen as in Figure 3.21.

Precision magnification with zoom tool

Choose rectangular area to magnify

Position zoom tool at one corner

Hold Alt key and drag diagonally to create enclosing box

Release

Working with Documents ◆ 59

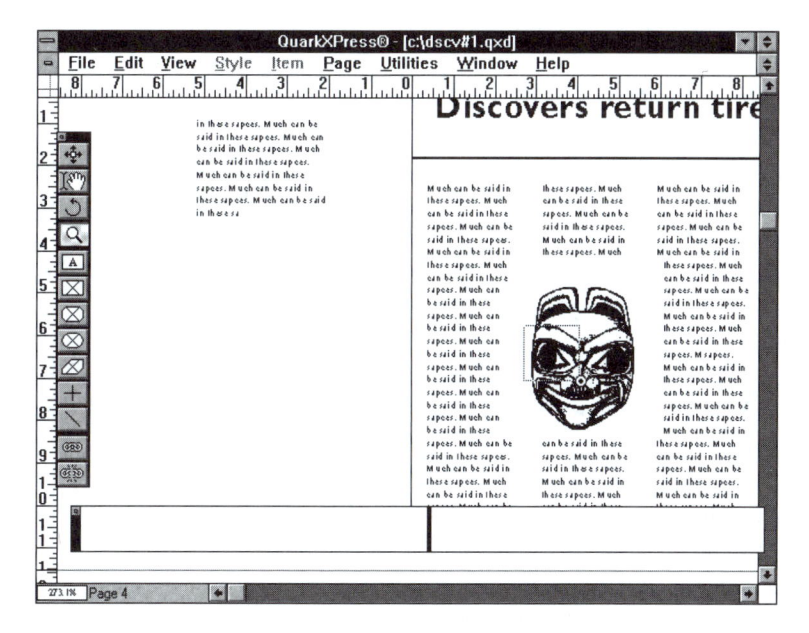

Figure 3.20   *A Fit in Window view.*

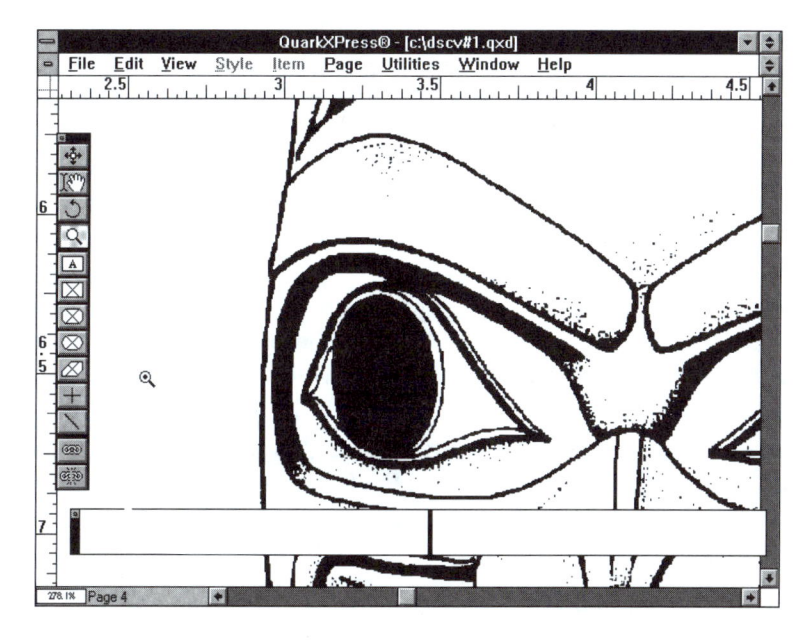

Figure 3.21   *A precise Zoom tool magnification.*

Moving Around the Page

As you may be starting to suspect, you often can do something in more than one way in QuarkXPress. Moreover, some functions interact with other functions. This is part of the richness of the program. The overlap and interaction though, can sometimes be confusing at first. But the more you see of the program in operation, the more each implementation makes sense.

In desktop publishing, we're always changing what we're looking at. Quite simply, as visual communicators we're seldom satisfied with just one look at a design or layout. We insist on seeing close up, at arm's length, or across the room. We sometimes want to focus on one area, other times on another. We examine and re-examine until we're convinced that the design, the page, or the ad works as it should. Page view and page movement are things we do over and over. So we want them to become second nature.

Going from one part of a page to another really means encompassing different areas within the purview of the window. If magnification remains unchanged, this is a simple move. You can think of moving the new area to inside the frame of the window, or of moving yourself (as a viewer behind the window frame) over a stationary page.

There are two basic ways to accomplish a simple move. One is to use the scroll bars, in the way common to Windows and most Windows applications. This approach can become tedious if the distance of the move or the magnification is large. After all, it requires separate adjustments to move in horizontal and vertical directions. Added complications arise in multipage documents, where large moves on the vertical scroll bar can send you off to other pages in the document.

Another, more versatile method involves bringing out the **grabber hand**. This is one of the hidden tools. From any cursor tool already selected, with the exception of the zoom tool, we can make the grabber hand momentarily appear. The grabber, which can be seen in Figure 3.22, has the effect of reaching down through the document window, grasping onto the page and sliding it by as you move the mouse.

To use the grabber tool, start with any but the zoom tool selected. Hold down the Alt key. You'll see the hand cursor appear. Press the mouse button, and drag the page in the direction you wish it to move.

Using the grabber hand

With any tool but the Zoom selected, hold the Alt key

Press mouse button and drag page through window view

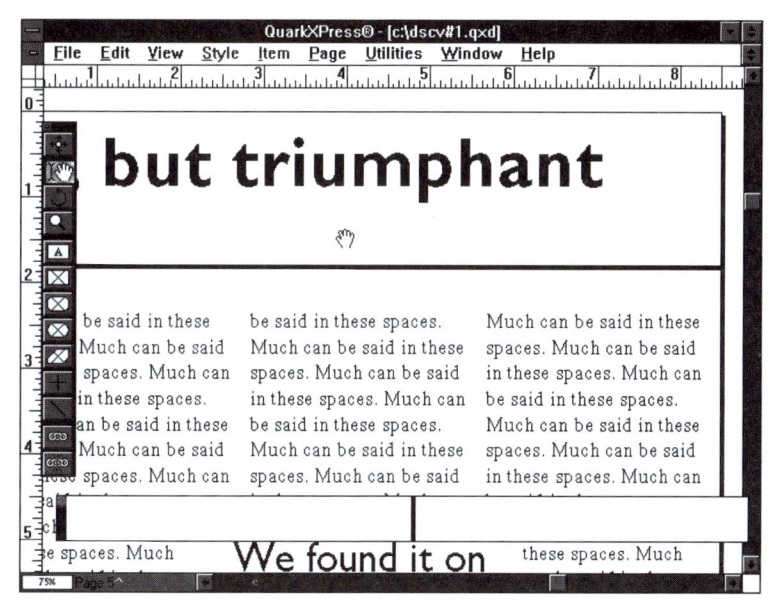

Figure 3.22 *The Grabber hand accessed using the Alt Key.*

The grabber tool works at any magnification, and it can even be used for moving the window from page to page.

Positioning Work

As you develop the layout of a publication, you come to rely increasingly on your ability to position page elements at just the right locations. Positioning work requires three capabilities: one, changing the view or magnification; two, bringing an area of interest within the window; and three, shifting an item from one location to another.

Moving an item can be as simple as dragging it from one place to another. Certainly you need this skill. But what if you would like to position the item more precisely than you can easily manage by dragging with the mouse? What if you wish to move several items at once? What if the item's destination is hundreds of pages away from its starting point?

We've already started to answer these questions by acquiring the abilities to examine a page at any practical view, and to examine any location on the page. We can extend these skills to help us with the task of relocating items from one place to another.

Selecting Items

Not surprisingly, the first step in moving an item is selecting the element to be moved. This can be anything from a box of text, to an elaborate color illustration, to a simple rule. The selection tool for any element is the same. That tool is the item tool, uppermost in the Tool palette. Recall that elements in a document are treated according to two aspects: the content within them, and their status as an item.

To activate the item tool, point the tool cursor over the uppermost button in the Tool palette and click.

Select with the item tool by pointing over the item in question, then clicking once. The item will be selected and small handles will appear around its periphery or ends. (Click just once. Double-clicking will engage a QuarkXPress dialog box.) You'll also see the Four Arrows tool cursor appear.

In some cases, at some reduced views or with some small items, you may find it difficult to select the item you want using this approach. In these hard-to-grasp cases, a sight variation is more effective. If you find a rule just too thin to be selected at a reduced view, or if you want to grasp several items together, this alternate method will serve well. Both cases can be handled by enclosing part of the item, or items, in a selecting box.

To define a Selecting box with the item tool, hold down the mouse button anywhere in open space, drag the resulting dashed box so that it encloses a piece of the item (or items) to be selected, as shown in Figure 3.23, then release. Item handles should appear on all those elements inside the box, signifying selection.

> **Using the selecting box**
>
> With item tool drag a box to enclose any part of item(s)

Moving Items: The Drag Method

The direct method for moving a selected item is to drag it to a new location. It's simple: Select the item, and keep the mouse button pressed. Then drag the cursor and the item to its new position. Release the mouse button to deposit the item.

Dragging is the method common to nearly all graphics applications. Its advantage is that you can see clearly where the item is moving. A disadvantage is that at larger magnifications the drag can take a long time. Depending on the speed of your computer, the screen may redraw each advance of the mouse in a plodding fashion, further slowing the move.

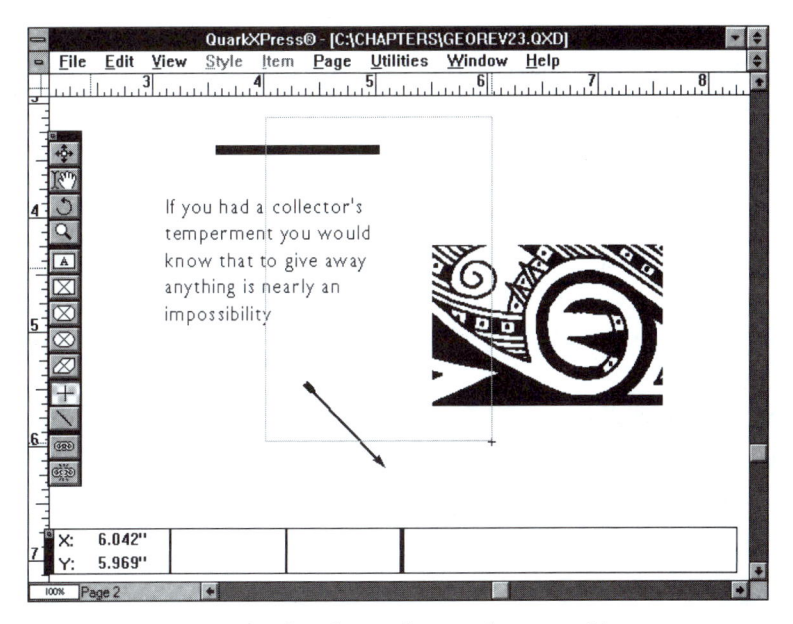

Figure 3.23 *Using the selecting box to select several items at once.*

But more important, this is only as accurate as your hand movements with the mouse. And don't even think about the time it would take to move a graphic from page 356 up to page 4.

Palette Moves

Have you ever had the frustrating experience of trying unsuccessfully to use a mouse to position a design element? You know exactly where you want it to go. You know your motor coordination is up to the task. But for some reason—it's 3 A.M. before a project meeting at eight, you're trying to center a half-point line in a one-point space, and you just can't seem to get your 16 MHz wonder to cooperate—the element won't go right where you need it. These things happen.

When precision becomes important, select the item, and don't try to force your hand-to-eye coordination. Sure, it's challenging. But is it worth a half hour or more of trial and error? You'll get better results by turning to the Measurements palette. Recall how we moved the rule in that earlier example. Now consider that the Measurements palette is a feedback device. So, keying in new coordinates will relocate an item.

The coordinates of any item on the page, other than lines, refer to the upper-left corner of the box that bounds that item. The same is true for a text box and a picture box. (All text in QuarkXPress exists in a text box; you'll see how in Chapter 4.) Even nonrectilinear items like ovals can be located by the coordinates of the box that would fit around them.

> **Positioning with the Measurements palette**
>
> *Select item*
>
> *Key in new location as X and Y values*

You've seen how to change the location of a rule. Suppose you wanted to move the Text Box sidebar that's sitting at the lower-left corner of the page in Figure 3.24 to the upper-left corner, within the margins.

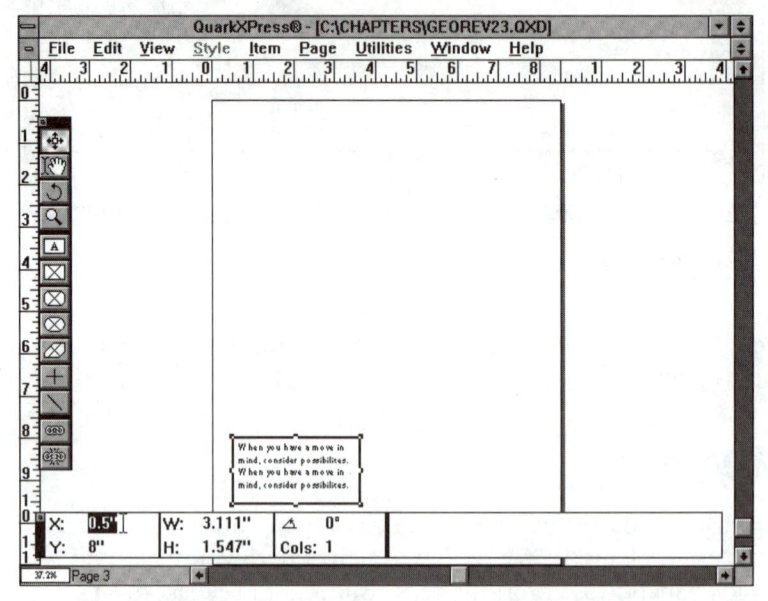

***Figure 3.24** Using the Measurements palette to move an item.*

To do this, select the box, and release the mouse button. At the Measurements palette, double-click on the X coordinate. Key in the value for the new location, in this case 1.5. Make a similar adjustment to the Y coordinate, in this case 1. Then press Enter. The item, in this case the text box, will reappear at the new location, even if part of it is out of the Window view. In this case the sidebar settles in at X=1.5 inches, Y=1 inch.

The Measurements palette approach to moving items on the page has the advantage of precision and, often, speed. It requires you to have a sense of where coordinates are on the page. With the help of the rulers displayed at the top and at the left side of the window, you can pick up this coordinate sense easily as you develop your layout.

Moving Multiple Items

Both of the methods described for moving a single item also apply to moving more than one item. Indeed, you can select as many items as you wish to move.

To select more than one item, use the item tool to drag a Selection box that intersects the items in question. Dragging a selected set is straightforward enough. Just grab any selected item with the mouse button, and drag the whole set to the new location. Click to release them all.

Alternatively, you can select multiple items individually. To do this, hold down the Shift key as you click on each item in turn. They will become selected and stay selected. If you decide to remove any of the items from the Selection set, just point and click again with the Shift key down. This will de-select the indicated item.

Selecting scattered items

Hold Shift key and click on each item

(De-select with second click)

What about using the Measurements palette with a set of items? Having selected items, you'll notice that the X and Y coordinates in the Measurements palette have changed. Now they reflect the upper-left corner position of the aggregate of items selected. Keeping this in mind, decide where you want the upper-left corner of the set to go, and key in the values in the palette as before.

MANIPULATING PAGES

Adding Pages

Every QuarkXPress document starts as one page. But life is seldom simple, so assume you will be adding pages. Whether assembling books, newspapers, magazines, company reports, or just augmenting a proposal with a second and third version of a display ad, you'll need additional pages. QuarkXPress will let you add as many as a hundred pages at a time. The program tops out at a total document length of 2,000 pages.

The procedure to add pages is this: Open the Page menu and choose Insert Pages. In the first Field box, key in the number of pages to add. Then click the button indicating relative location (Before, After, At end) and key in the page that the new page or pages should precede or follow. Before you click OK, check your choices by reading through them. If the command reads the way you want your new pages to appear, click OK.

For instance, to expand a new document to thirty-two pages you would set up the dialog to read: *Insert 31 page(s) after page: 1* (as shown in Figure 3.25).

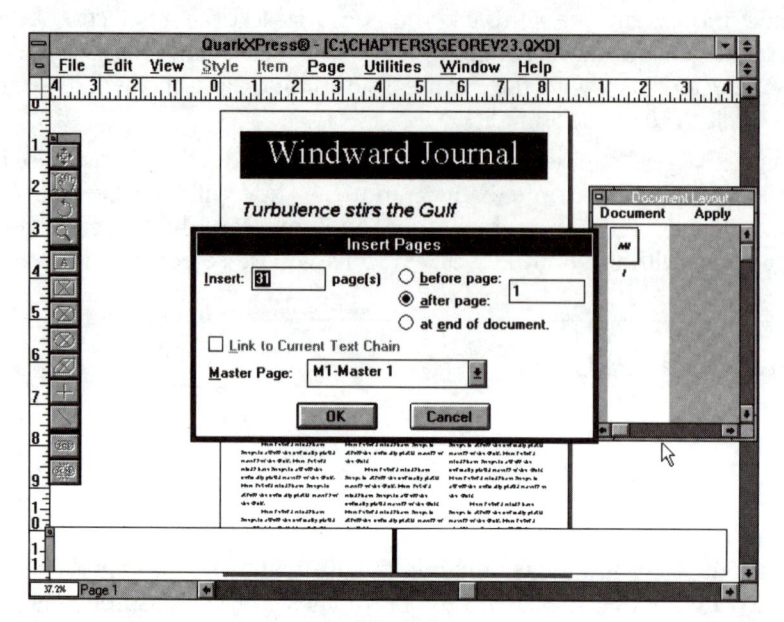

Figure 3.25 *Adding pages using the Insert Pages command.*

You can use the Insert Pages command at any point, and repeatedly as necessary, to lengthen the document. When you add pages between existing pages, automatic page numbering will be activated.

WARNING In facing-pages documents you should consider carefully the effect that adding or removing an odd number of pages may have on page spreads downstream. For instance, by bumping them forward unevenly, the new batch of inserted pages can turn your well-designed spreads into so much visual confusion. By doing so, you could inadvertently split elements planned for a two-page design into two separated pages.

Removing Pages

Pages can be dropped from a document at any time. But any items laid out on those pages will be lost from the document as well. In fact, even if an item merely overlaps slightly onto the page from the pasteboard (and this is an easy oversight to make), it will be lost. (If a text box has text linked from an earlier page, however, the text will *not* be lost.)

To remove one or more pages, open the Pages menu and choose Delete. Key in the page number, or the numbers for a range of pages, and click OK. These pages will drop out, and the subsequent pages that remain will be renumbered. (Note that the warning issued under "Adding Pages" about consequences to downstream page-spreads applies here too.)

The Document Layout Palette

It's time that we consider the Document Layout palette. It mimics the ordering of pages you see through the document window, as shown in Figure 3.26. You can use it to insert and delete pages, as well as to deal with master pages (as we shall explore in Chapter 10). Every page in the document is represented here.

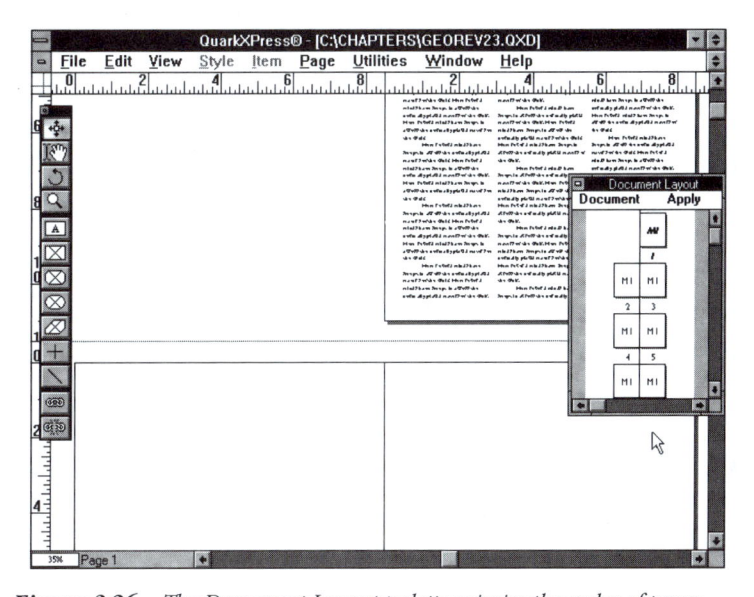

Figure 3.26   *The Document Layout palette mimics the order of pages.*

To remove a page, locate the page icon in the Document Layout Palette window, select it by clicking on it, then open the palette's Document menu and choose the Delete command as appropriate. You can select a range of pages in this palette by clicking on the icon for one end of the range, then, with the Shift key down, clicking on the icon for the other end. The pages at either end and all those in between will become selected.

> **Selecting a range of pages in Document Layout**
>
> *Click on page at one end of range*
> *Scroll to other end in Document Layout*
> *Hold Shift key and click on page at other end*

You can also select an assorted set of pages that may not be consecutive. Simply Ctrl-click on each one in turn. To remove individual pages from the selection, Ctrl-click again.

> **Selecting scattered pages in Document Layout**
>
> *Hold Ctrl key and click on each page*
> *(De-select with second click)*

To add one or more pages, you open the Document menu in the palette, and choose Insert. This command leads to a submenu with options regarding master pages. (This will be explained in Chapter 10). The short story on this approach is this: Following your choice of page type, you can move the cursor into the Document Layout window and click next to a page before or after it, or between pages of a spread to insert between them. Later we'll see how to use this to build multipage spreads.

Moving to Another Page

Facing a document from two to 2,000 pages, you're confronted with the simple expediency of how to shift your view to the page you want at the moment. There are four quick ways to move to pages or page-spreads out of view of the document window. Whichever you use, keep in mind the following: The document pages, or page-spreads, are arranged from first to last, one below the other. That is, Page 1 is *above* Pages 2 and 3, and so on. So, to move through the document in this arrangement, move the window *down*.

First, you can always call up the grabber hand. If you can drag parts of a page or pasteboard into view, you can drag pages of the document window into view. To do this, use the grabber hand to drag sideways to adjacent page-spreads, and upward for higher-numbered, downstream pages (downward for lower-numbered pages). This method works well for nearby pages, but proves too slow for skimming through magazines or books, or even that 16-page newsletter.

> **Moving to adjacent pages using the grabber hand**
>
> *Hold Alt key and drag pages through window view:*
> - *up to higher numbers*
> - *down to lower*
> - *sideways on spreads*

Alternately, you can use the vertical scroll bar as you have on the single page. This works if you can estimate the relative location of the new page on the scroll bar.

Or you can use the Document Layout palette. To do this, bring the page icon in the Palette window by the palette scroll bar (which works like every other vertical scroll bar). Double-click on the page you want. It will appear in the document window.

> **Moving to a page using Document Layout**
>
> *In the palette, scroll to locate page icon*
>
> *Double-click to bring page into window*

And you can use a Menu command. To do this, open the Page menu and choose Go, then key in the page number you seek. The page will appear in the Document window.

Moving Items Between Pages

Many elements found in a publication-in-progress seldom remain on one page for long. Here are two methods for moving items. They both start after you select the item or items in question.

First is the drag method. To do this, simply drag the items to their destination page. Clearly this direct approach works best for neighboring pages.

An alternative is the **cut-and-paste** method. To do this, use the Edit menu choice or the keyboard to give the Cut command with the intended items selected. They will disappear off the page into the Clipboard. Then use any of the methods discussed for moving to another page. Finally, open the Edit menu and choose the Paste command at the destination page. Your item or items will appear on the page.

> **Moving items to distant pages in the document**
>
> *Select item(s) and at Edit menu choose Cut*
>
> *Locate destination page*
>
> *At Edit menu choose Paste*

Advanced Moves

Sure control over items and parts of the page will speed the rest of your work. By adding these skills in some of the more powerful document maneuvers, you have simplified the labor that will go into every document you ever call up in QuarkXPress.

These are major activities affecting large areas of work in any document. Remember that you can use the At-a-Glance boxes and procedure highlights for quick recall, while applying techniques to your documents-in-progress. With skills from this chapter you are ready to make good use of text in your documents. Text has the greatest range of variability, and usually the greatest effect on the reader. The type and text capabilities you will find in QuarkXPress can accentuate, strengthen, and emphasize any message to make your design achieve maximum effectiveness. Let's see how.

Chapter 4

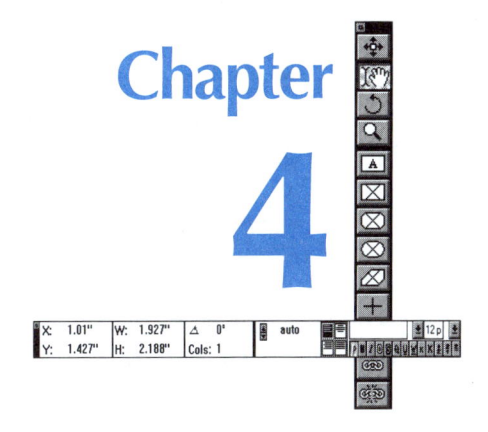

Type and Text Formatting

WHAT YOU WILL LEARN IN THIS CHAPTER

- ◆ How to create and adjust text boxes
- ◆ How to import and export text
- ◆ Word processing in QuarkXPress
- ◆ How to find and replace text
- ◆ How to use type and paragraph controls

Type carries visual messages. It is always saying something like, "This is important! Look further. Take your time. Look how easy. Urgent, read immediately! This is trifling detail. How dignified. Don't miss this!" and a million other things.

Enticement, priority, pacing, emphasis, mood—these are what type lives for. No text takes the form of type on the page without these messages accompanying it, whether intentional or accidental. Text attempts to convey information and conceptual meaning, while the type in which it is set supports or betrays these efforts.

QuarkXPress has gained something of a reputation for its extraordinary abilities with type. This chapter shows you the fundamentals of controlling type and text in QuarkXPress. You will see how to generate and how to bring text into a document, how to apply typefaces, how to style type, to size it, to space it, and generally to distinguish it. Here also will be found the ways to do word processing within QuarkXPress. You'll learn how to use guides, margins, and columns to fashion raw text into the beauty and strength found in a well-set page.

Where Text Lives

As you recall, the item/content duality permeates every design element in QuarkXPress. Both text and graphics demonstrate this directly. Simply put, you won't find text or graphics without finding a box containing them. The first step to creating or importing text, then, involves generating a text box.

The importation of any text into a document must be preceded by the creation of a text box, similar to the way people are not let onto an airplane until a seat has been designated for them. You can create text boxes, or (as we shall see later) you can have QuarkXPress create them.

Once text boxes are created, they can be resized, relocated, cut, and otherwise modified (except in special circumstances, which we will cover later). That is, they can be treated like an item, with or without text inside them. And the text they contain, or will contain, can be treated like typographic contents, capable of being formatted and typeset in its own right. Keeping a clear mind on this distinction between the item-nature of text, and its content-nature, will enable you to exert maximum control over text boxes with relative ease.

Making a Text Box

Let's assume you know where in your layout you want some text to appear. It's not crucial that you be exact and final in your idea. Everything we do here can be easily modified after the fact. For text box creation to work smoothly, you can follow three simple steps: Bring the space into view, bring the tool to the space, and drag the text box into existence.

The tool in this case is the text box tool; it's displayed on the palette button as a letter *A* enclosed by a box. Fifth from the top of the tool palette, as shown in Figure 4.1, it's grouped with similar tools that produce picture boxes and lines. More about these in Chapter 6.

Figure 4.1 *Selecting the Text Box tool at the palette.*

The idea behind making a text box is one borrowed from every graphics program you've ever seen. It's the following venerable procedure: Hold down the mouse button and drag a box onto the page. As happens with other creation tools, the mouse tool takes the form of crosshairs as you pull it into the document window.

NOTE
The moment you bring the tool to the document, the faithful Measurements palette begins tracking the X and Y coordinates of the crosshairs.

The first step in forming the box is to position these crosshairs on what you imagine would be one corner of the text box. Press the mouse button and drag diagonally to where you plan to put the opposite corner. A box will grow in size proportionally as you do this. Before you release the mouse button, you can pull the box smaller again, or drag it narrower, wider, taller, or shorter, according to your whim or plan.

> **Making a text box**
>
> *Choose text box tool*
>
> *Choose rectangular area in which to place box*
>
> *Position text box tool at one corner of chosen area*
>
> *Drag diagonally until box fits area chosen*

Note that as you're dragging out the box, the Measurements palette displays changing W and H values. These are, as you have no doubt concluded, width and height measurements of the box. If you are going for precision control from the start, you can use these values to fashion the exact box you want. When you release the mouse button, the text box will be in place and selected.

Effects of Creating a Text Box

What an avalanche of changes creating a text box generates! Four significant alterations can occur immediately, as shown in Figure 4.2. A pointing hand replaces the crosshairs tool at the last-drawn corner of the text box. The new Measurements palette, which you saw tracking the creation, replaces any previous one. One of the two uppermost tools, the item tool or the content tool, will become active. If the content tool activates, a flashing cursor will appear in the upper-left corner of the box.

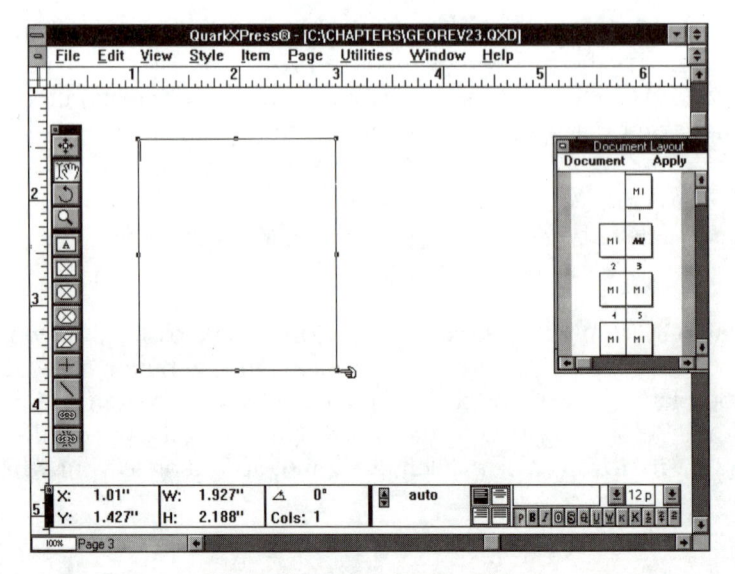

Figure 4.2 *Creating a text box.*

The pointing hand is a sort of automatic tic in tool–text box interaction. Since you've dragged diagonal-to-diagonal, the cursor has fallen over a corner point, one of eight that become active when any item box is selected. This box is now selected, ready for content (that's why the cursor's flashing), but still treatable as an item (as indicated by the pointing hand). That hand is displayed when any tool touches an active box handle. Since the content tool is selected, and it touches a corner handle, the hand is ready. Its function is to resize the box. If you wish to now or later, just press the mouse button and drag the text box to a new size and shape.

The Measurements palette you noticed tracking your moves earlier is now monitoring several characteristics of the box, including the coordinate point of origin (X and Y), the height and width (H and W), the angle of rotation of the box (0), and the number of columns to divide the text into.

These are some of the features of the text box as an item. The values given in the right half of the palette all indicate features of the text content within the box, including typographic characteristics, as you are about to see.

> **NOTE** Text boxes possess many other features besides the ones shown in the Measurements palette. Some are of an item nature; some are of content nature. They include box background color, text runaround, box framing, and text inset. We'll be looking at them in later chapters.

The tool change comes about when the program automatically switches to a previously selected mode, item, or content. If the content tool comes up, the presumption is that since you've just created a text box, you will wish to enter something in it immediately. The flashing cursor is an entry point for text. You're free to ignore the box you've just created and return to it later should you desire. You can, on the other hand, type in from the keyboard and have text appear directly in the box.

TEXT AND THE CONTENT TOOL

Basically, a text box can accept text from two sources: the keyboard and files existing outside the document. In both cases, the box must be in a ready condition before the insertion of text can proceed. Remember the dictum of tool use we happened on earlier: *Always select first.*

Text inside a box is content. In order to insert text into the box, the text box should be selected and the content tool should be active. When this is so, you'll see the selection handles of the box in all four corners and on all four sides, and inside the text box a text cursor will be flashing (or, if previously selected, the text may be highlighted within the box).

> **NOTE** The content tool shows up as an arrow until you click on a text box. Then, the I-beam is displayed as a text insertion point is designated and the flashing cursor shows up.

When the text box is empty—as it is when it's newly created—the flashing text cursor will normally be found at the top-left corner of the box, as shown in Figure 4.2. This reflects the default setting for text (left aligned, top justified). All inserted text will flow from that point onward into the box.

When text is already present, the cursor may, of course, be positioned anywhere within the text. Its location will determine where incoming text is inserted, whether from an imported file or by keyboard typing.

Keying Text Directly

Let's assume you've just created a text box like the one in shown Figure 4.2. The box is in a ready condition; its cursor is blinking. Let's say you're composing a headline at the keyboard as you're working on layout. In this case, you can type immediately, and text will appear starting at the location of the cursor.

When you'd like to enter text into an existing text box, you'll need first to put the box in the ready condition. Do this by choosing the content tool, then clicking on the box in question with it. If the box is empty, the cursor will normally appear at the upper-left corner. Then, when you type, the words will appear within the box.

If there is text already in the box, the flashing cursor will be found where it was last placed before the box was de-selected. If a section of text was highlighted then, it will become highlighted again. Very simply, QuarkXPress remembers. This is engineered into most of the functions in the program. It's a seemingly small feature that, over the course of developing a publication, will save you appreciable time and effort.

Clipboard Text

A variation of the direct keyboard method involves the clipboard. As you may know, the clipboard is a Windows-supplied file that works with most applications to temporarily store whatever is Cut or Copied. That's Cut or Copied with a capital *C*, as in the command you can give under the Edit menu or through the keyboard shortcuts Ctrl-X and Ctrl-C, respectively. (When you select text and then dispose of it by the Delete or Backspace keys, it does *not* go to the clipboard.) The clipboard can be a way of moving text from place to place inside a document or between files of different programs. It can be a quick way to paste text or graphics from a word processor or other desktop publishing software into QuarkXPress, and vice versa. Of course, you can also use it to do internal document housecleaning, like moving text fragments from one text box to another.

When you've loaded the clipboard with the Cut or Copy command, just select the text box in which you'd like to deposit the material as above. Make sure that the text insertion cursor or selection is where you'd like the text to go. Then open the Edit menu and choose Paste (or just give the Ctrl-V keystroke). A copy of the clipboard contents floods into the text box.

To move text from one box to another, select it in the first box, open the Edit menu, and choose Cut. Then select the second box, locate the cursor, open the Edit menu, and choose Paste.

Clipboard text transfers

Select the text with content tool and at the Edit menu choose Cut or Copy

Select the recipient text box with content tool

(Set insertion cursor or selection if necessary)

At the Edit menu choose Paste

ABOUT FILE FORMATS: IMPORTING AND EXPORTING TEXT

Most long texts that find their way into a QuarkXPress document will have originated in word processing software. There they will have been saved as word processing files. During the make-up of the publication, you will insert this text into your document. Bringing in file contents from one software into another is known as **importing**.

Just like importing from one country to another, this procedure involves issues of **compatibility**. If you've made a train journey from France to Spain, you may appreciate the idea of compatibility. If you were on the French train heading south, at the border you would have to disembark and haul yourself and your luggage to board the waiting Spanish train on the other side to continue onward. The reason is lack of compatibility. The Spanish rails are narrower than the French rails; they cannot accommodate French trains. You can still move the contents of the trains between countries, but not in the carriages they started in, and it is a lot more work.

QuarkXPress deals with text-file compatibility by using individual files known as **filters** that in essence make the trains from one set of rails fit on the other set. These filters decode formatting and type style information about the text being imported. They can preserve much or all of the formatting work already performed in the word processor. These filters also work in reverse to **export** text files from QuarkXPress for use by word processors. To import text from, or export it to, a particular word processing program, the filter for that word processor must reside in the QuarkXPress directory prior to launching QuarkXPress. You need not designate a filter to import a file; it's done automatically.

Two nonspecific file formats that can be used to import or export text files avoid this necessity. One is called Text Format, also known as ASCII Format, often bearing the suffix .TXT. Text saved by a word processor in this format contains only raw, unformatted text characters. The other file type is called Rich Text Format, or RTF. It is a standard PC file type that contains basic character style and formatting.

It is unlikely that you will find yourself without a filter available for a word processor file you need. But if that happens, you can probably take the following measure. In the word processor, save your material in one of the two nonspecific standard formats (ASCII or RTF), as provided for in the Save As command in that program. It's the rare word processor that does not have capacity to save in RTF, or rarer still that can't save ASCII Format. (In this latter eventuality, you can still try the clipboard method to transfer the whole file.)

To Import Text

Assuming filter-file compatibility, importing text is usually a smooth process. To import a text file into a text box, activate the content tool and select the text box. If the flashing text cursor is visible, or if text is highlighted with the text box, you're ready to import. Next, open the File menu and choose Get Text. You should see a Get Text dialog box like that shown in Figure 4.3. Key in the file name and path, or locate the file using the appropriate window (as in the File Manager) and select the file. Then click OK. The text will flow into the text box.

> **Importing text**
>
> *Assure that text box is selected with content tool active*
>
> *At File menu choose Get Text*
>
> *Select file in dialog listings or by pathname*

There are ways you can actually improve on the text just by importing it. Standard straight typewriter quotes can be converted to curving typesetter's quotes. The convert quotes checkbox in the dialog box, when active, will cause typewriter-style quotes to become matched typesetter's quotes, as shown in Figure 4.4.

Type and Text Formatting ♦ **79**

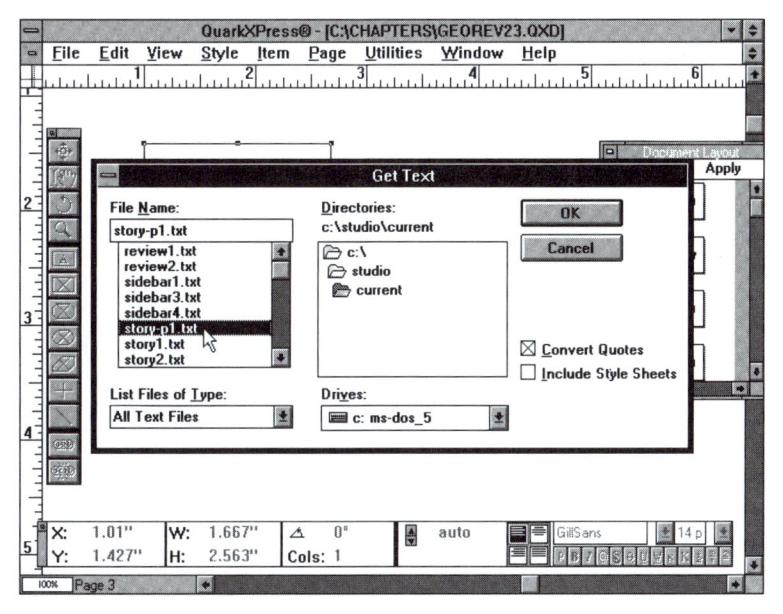

Figure 4.3   *Importing text through the Get Text command.*

Figure 4.4   *Typewriter quotes versus typesetter's quotes.*

Text Box Overruns

What if there is more text than your text box can hold? If that's the case, QuarkXPress will keep the rest recorded in the document file, even though it will be unseen. If the text is formatted wider than the box, you may not be able to see it at all. In cases like these, the box will be tagged with a small x in the lower-right corner to indicate that text assigned to the box does not end in the box. Figure 4.5 shows such a instance.

SHORT CUT   If you are working with relatively little text—a headline, for example—and have plenty of space around the text box, you can simply enlarge the box, stretching it by dragging one of its handles until the continuation x disappears and all the text shows. This is just one approach to bringing out all the text. You will see others as we continue.

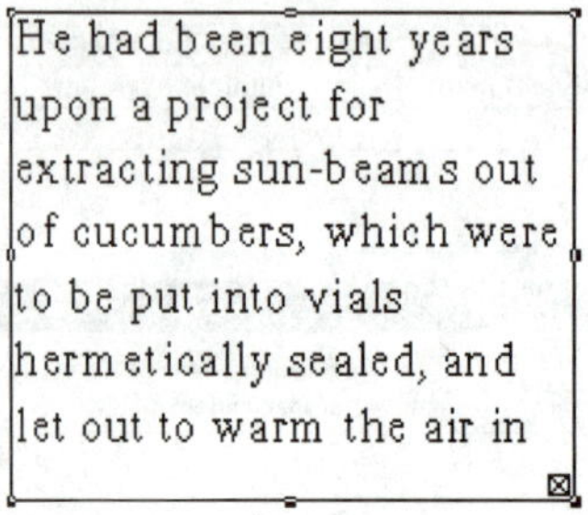

> He had been eight years
> upon a project for
> extracting sun-beams out
> of cucumbers, which were
> to be put into vials
> hermetically sealed, and
> let out to warm the air in

Figure 4.5 *Text over-run indicated by an "x" in the text box.*

INTERNAL WORD PROCESSING

By now you might be wondering, "How does QuarkXPress handle word processing?" Look at the features you've already encountered regarding text, keeping in mind that word processing (also known as text editing) relies on keying in text in a form that can be readily revised. We have available the text box, column control, facing-pages adjustment, and automatic text box generation.

You could, of course, prepare your text layout with boxes in place and key in the text directly to its destination. This method works best on a single-page layout. If there are multiple columns in the box, the text cursor will jump between columns as you type or revise. If there is more than one page, the cursor will jump between pages as it follows the text flow.

If, however, you wish QuarkXPress to emulate a straightforward word processor, without the distractions of layout while editing text, you'll find the following method useful. It involves setting up a separate QuarkXPress document as your word processing file. This approach offers you the flexibility of text editing at any size of type available on your system, and the ease of scrolling by using the Up and Down arrow keys. When your text is ready, you can either export it through the File menu's Save Text command—one of the QuarkXPress word processing filters—then import it through the Get Text command. Or you can simply copy it, move to the layout document, and paste it into the appropriate text box.

To set up a word processing document, open the File menu and choose New. At the dialog box, set up a page size and margins that will fit easily on your screen. Then make sure that the number of columns is set at 1, that the facing pages box is unchecked, and that the automatic text box is checked. Click OK. The result will be, as usual, a one-page document. Adjust the view so that the text box is centered and contained within the window.

NOTE You can achieve this on a 14-inch monitor in VGA mode on a letter-sized page by opening the View menu and choosing 75 percent, and by opening the Control Menu box, the menu left of File under the small shadow icon, and choosing Maximize.)

At this point you can select a typeface font and size, as outlined in the "Type Control" section below. You can remove the palettes and rulers from the window through the Hide Tools, Hide Measurements, Hide Document Layout, and Hide Rulers commands under the View menu. (When you return to the layout document, you can choose the View menu's Show command for each to display them again.)

What you have is a document that is stripped for text entry. As you key in more material than a single page can hold, QuarkXPress will generate additional pages and move the cursor into them as you type.

NOTE There are many worthy word processors offering specialized features—thesauri, numbering, indexing, footnoting, and table-of-contents generators. But it's good to know that you can generate text easily from within your desktop publisher.

FIND/CHANGE

One feature pumps real strength into the text editing capabilities of any word processor: The capability to locate a word or phrase, and to replace it with another. QuarkXPress implements these controls in a way outclassing many dedicated word processors. You engage this command from the Edit menu by choosing Find/Change. Figure 4.6 shows the dialog window that appears.

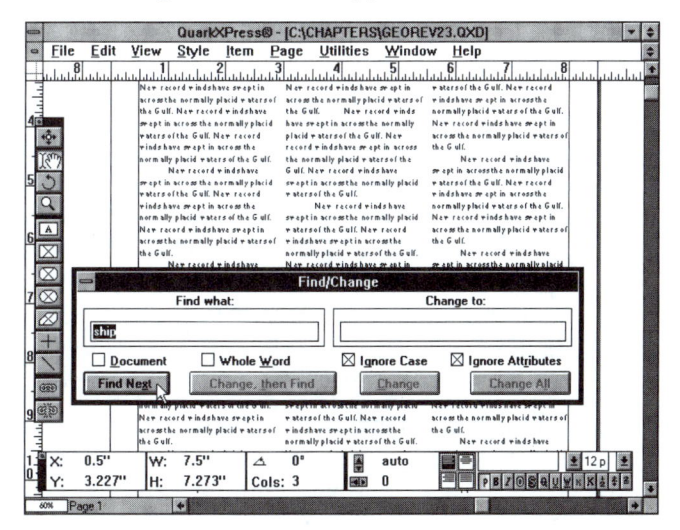

Figure 4.6 *The Find/Change search and replace dialog box.*

To locate a word or phrase, key it into the Find what: field and click the Find Next button. The field will handle up to 80 characters. QuarkXPress conducts all its searches downstream, from beginning to end. So be sure the text cursor is positioned upstream of the area you will search—at the beginning of a story, for example, if you wish to search the whole story. (If you select a segment of text, the program will commence the search at the upstream end of the selection and continue until the end, or until you stop the search by closing the Find/Change dialog window.)

Checkboxes switch on various Search options. The Document box chooses to search the whole document rather than just the story. The Whole Word box chooses to search for a word, such as "ship" rather than the sequence "...ship..." which also would find "ships," "shipmate," and "relationship." The Ignore Case box lets the search locate all occurrences of the character string in the Find what: field rather than just the characters as given. It would locate "read on," "READ ON," as well as "Read On." The Ignore Attributes checkbox adds a new depth of control by allowing us to search and change type features. We'll look into it more later on.

QuarkXPress shows the first instance of "found text" by highlighting it in its text box. You can order further instances found by clicking again on the Find Next button. Even though the text is highlighted, you can't key in changes directly until you switch control from the Find/Change box back to the document window. Click on the Document Title bar to do so; this will keep the selection active. That way you can make your revision directly.

You might want to use the Find feature to locate the occurrence of a phrase in your document—"the Caribbean," for example—for citation elsewhere in your text or for inclusion in an index. If you've marked the heads and subheads, you might use a marker (an asterisk or other notation) as a key for finding each one in turn. You might want to check for clarity by looking over personal pronouns. For instance, you can search for the word "she" to revise some occurrences in order to distinguish between a ship's captain and the vessel she commands.

To replace text, key the substitution into the Change to: field. Notice that even without an entry typed in here, the Change then Find, Change, and Change All buttons can become active. This means, of course, that under this circumstance you can change the found text to nothing; that is, you can eliminate it. In any case, until the first occurrence of Find What text is located, only the Find button is active. But thereafter the other buttons become accessible. The Change then Find button makes only a single substitution, but it does go on to locate the next occurrence. The Change button makes the substitution of found text, then turns control back to the Find Next button. The Change All button automatically makes all substitutions without pausing, and presents a dialog box noting how many substitutions were made.

A good way to use the global replacement features of the Find/Change dialog window is first to try one, two, or three instances with the Change then Find button. If all goes according to your wishes, click the Change All button.

Type Control

The universally recognized strength of the QuarkXPress system is type control. While text is what's been written, type is the form in which it's finally displayed. The virtues of various type treatments have been discussed at length by a variety of authors, some of them listed in Appendix B. At some point, it may be worth your time to examine some of these sources to get a firm grasp of the many uses that the procedures revealed in this book can be put to.

Before we go any further, however, take a moment to look at a daily newspaper. Like the document shown in Figure 4.7, it delivers all sorts of unrecognized messages. Immediately, the type sends messages to your brain before you have read a word. A nameplate spread in a sturdy but dignified type across the top says "solid, established." A large and bold headline says, "this story is of special importance." Smaller headlines say, "read me, too." The teasers under the headlines say "come closer, take a look." And the body type of the stories themselves—functional and quick-to-read—says, "here are the facts."

Figure 4.7 *A document carries messages in its type.*

Type is more than typeface. Size, line spacing, letter spacing, emphasis and weight, boldface and italic can create a multitude of effects. Type can be formatted into columns, and aligned straight or flexible. Most importantly, in QuarkXPress nearly everything that type is can be controlled, so you can precisely adjust the medium that carries the message.

Selecting Text within a Box

By now you can guess the first step for most of the type control procedures in QuarkXPress. It is the simplest and the one most easily overlooked during a deadline rush. First, select the text to be modified. If you've worked with word processors, you have some notion of the basic methods of text selection.

To select any section of text that's visible to you, begin with the text cursor at one end of the segment, press the mouse button, and drag the mouse to the other end of the segment. Release the mouse button and proceed to make your text adjustments. Alternatively, click the cursor in place at one end of the segment. Move to the other end. Holding down the Shift key, click there. Either way, you will highlight the text in between.

The following powerstrokes will prove useful in working with text:

- To select exactly one word of text, begin with the text cursor blinking anywhere in that word. Double click the mouse button. The word will be selected.
- To select exactly one line of text, begin with the text cursor blinking anywhere in that line. Triple click the mouse button. The line will be selected.
- To select exactly one paragraph, begin with the text cursor blinking anywhere in that paragraph. Quadruple click the mouse button. The paragraph will be selected.

Selecting text by powerstrokes

Use the content tool to do the following:

- *One word—double-click*
- *One line—triple-click*
- *One paragraph—quadruple-click*

USING THE TEXT MEASUREMENTS PALETTE

We will now look at the way the Measurements palette controls type and paragraphs. These are accessible when the content tool is active in text. For convenience we'll refer to the Measurements palette for text as the Text palette.

Here you'll find adjustments in basic type style and other features that are most often immediately useful in layout and copyfitting. Almost all the functions found here are additionally accessible through the Style menu and the commands Font, Size, Type Style, Track, Baseline Shift, Alignment, Leading, and Formats.

Type Control

What can happen to type? Consider the text box shown in Figure 4.8. In it sit several lines of plain type. For all its simple appearance, this type already has many attributes. The Text palette below it indicates what they are.

Font and Size

What does it look like? And how big is it? These basic standards hold for all sorts of things, from tomatoes to tattoos. Consider type in this light, and look again at the selected text and the text palette in Figure 4.8. Starting at the right side of the palette you'll notice the size indicted as *12pt,* meaning 12 points. A **point** is a measurement that equals 1/72 of an inch, or 1/12 of a **pica**. You encountered them before in adjusting the rule line. In this case 12pt indicates the height of the uppercase letters of the font. It's the standard method of measurement used by typesetters, and it should come as no surprise to anyone to find QuarkXPress using it.

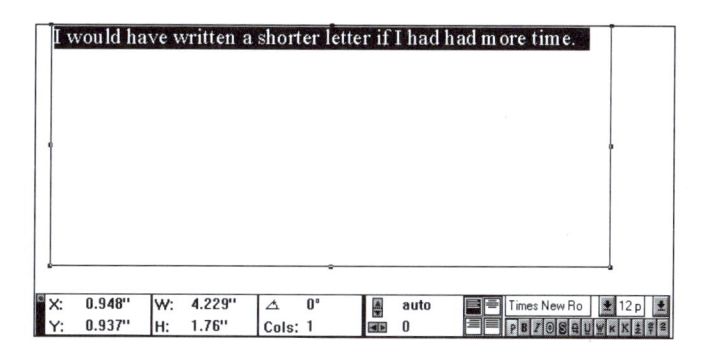

Figure 4.8 *A line of type and the Measurements palette monitoring its attributes.*

Immediately to the left you will see the name of the font or typeface. In this case it is Times New Roman (truncated in the small display box to Times New Ro).

To adjust either font or size in the palette, select the text you wish to change with the content tool. Click on the drop down list arrow next to font or size. After the list opens, click on the choice you prefer.

Select the value in the palette by double-clicking on the font or size field box. Then key in the replacement name or size. Figure 4.9 shows modified text and its Text palette. The Times New Roman body type has been replaced with Arial and enlarged. Its appearance has changed from that of body text to one more suited to a heading.

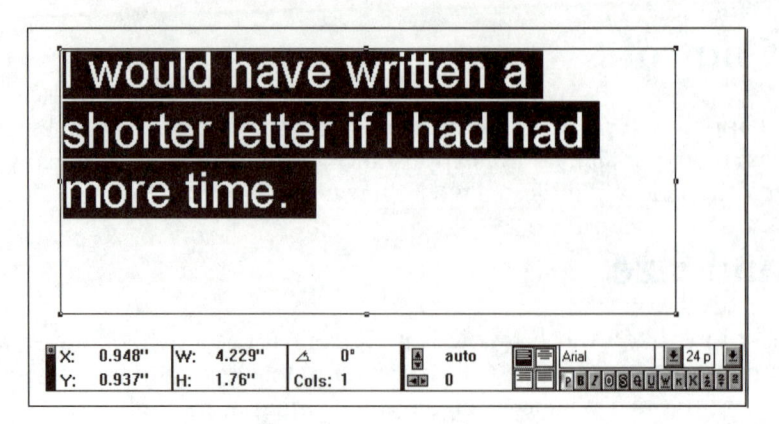

Figure 4.9 *Altering type font and size using the palette.*

NOTE: The Text palette will actively monitor whatever text is currently selected. If you change your selection, the palette will reflect values for the current selection. And you can have countless variations within a text box (though for design's sake you usually shouldn't).

Type Style

Below the font and the size are a series of buttons that control type style. These buttons activate in the following way, starting at the left: plain type, bold, italic, outline, doublestrike, strikethrough, underline continuously, underline word by word, small capitals, all capitals, superscript, subscript, and superior (a reduced size superscript). Figure 4.10 shows the effects of these style controls on two words of each line, top to bottom from plain to superior.

To adjust type style, you first select the text in question, then click on the button to apply or remove the style feature. None of these buttons mutually exclude others, except the P for plain button, which wipes off any of the other styles from selected text. All the other buttons toggle the features on or off, like a light switch.

PARAGRAPH CONTROL

While type choices control the appearance of individual characters, paragraph formatting controls the look of the lines of type that greet the eye. They create a mood before a single word is absorbed. How many times have you turned away from tightly spaced lines, or got lost trying to read right-aligned body copy?

Lines and paragraphs can flow loose, cram tight, stretch wide, or tuck in narrow. They can project an impression of openness or dense seriousness. Whatever they may be, formatting and alignment choices always affect readability.

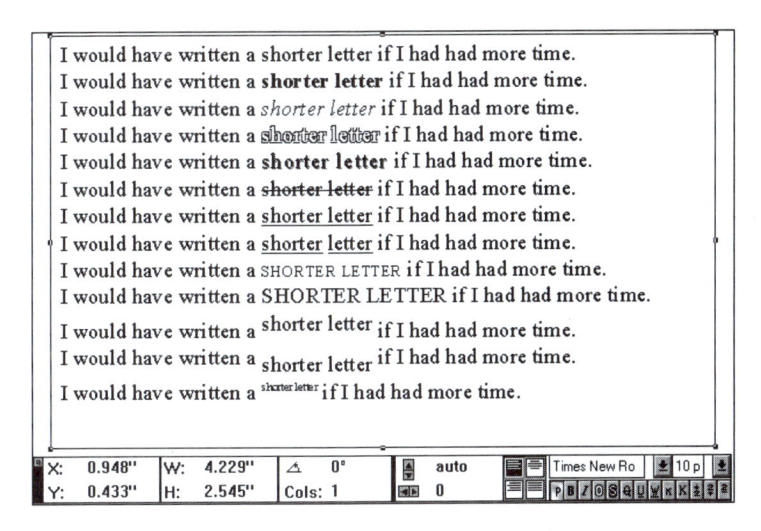

Figure 4.10 Effects of the palette's type style buttons.

Paragraph Alignment

In the Text palette, four lined boxes adjacent to the font name represent paragraph formatting. As you know, aligned-left forms a paragraph with lines of text aligned at the left, allowed to end randomly ragged on the right according to line length, as in typical typewritten correspondence. The Aligned-left control is the little Box button in the upper-left of the group. The Aligned-right button sits just below it. The centered button stands upper-right in the group. Lower right is the Justified button. Justified text achieves paragraphs aligned to both the right and left by adding or removing fractional bits of space between words and letters of each line. The alignment of the four passages shown in Figure 4.11 corresponds to the arrangement of the four alignment buttons of the Measurements palette.

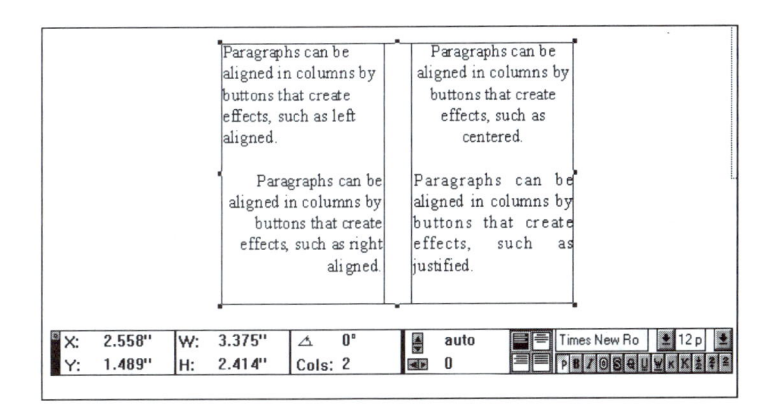

Figure 4.11 The four paragraph alignments.

These buttons apply to whichever paragraph you've placed the cursor in, whether all the text is selected or not. The method to adjust paragraph formatting follows the select-click pattern. First, position the text cursor within the paragraph in question, or select text in that paragraph. Then click on the appropriate Alignment button. The entire paragraph will be aligned. If the selection extends over several paragraphs, they will all be aligned.

Adjusting Line Spacing

Type and space are in constant balance in any document. The more of one there is, the less of the other. Spaces between lines interact with spaces between words in such a way to speed up or slow down reading. The eye will tend to stay with type and to leap only the narrowest white space. If space between lines is narrower than between words, look out! The eye will keep jumping down to the next line instead of finishing the line. Of course, we are thinking creatures, so we'll struggle to keep the eye on course. But the effort will take its toll, and reader fatigue can often defeat any desire to finish the text.

Line spacing has a profound effect on readability. This space, known as **leading** (rhymes with "wedding"), from the lead strips typesetters once used to insert space into lines, is generally measured between the baselines on which the lowercase letters sit. On the Text palette you'll see the leading measured in points. The value of the currently selected paragraph is indicated in a box to the left of the paragraph Alignment buttons. You may find the term "auto," which indicates automatic leading. (In this approach, a percentage is added over the font size, usually 20 percent. So 10 point type would be set at 12 points in the default autoleading of QuarkXPress.) Leading affects all the lines in the paragraph in which the cursor or selection appears.

The first step in adjusting leading is to position the text cursor or to select text.

To adjust leading in small steps on the Text palette, click on the Up or Down arrow next to the value. This will separate or push together all the lines of the paragraph(s) in increments of one point for each click.

To adjust leading precisely, select the value in the leading field box and key in a value you prefer. Press Enter and line spacing will change to the new value. In Figure 4.12 the autoleading of the first paragraph has been "tightened" (reduced) in the second paragraph, and "opened up" (increased) in the third.

LETTER SPACING

Tracking and **kerning** may be terms familiar to you. Anyone who works with type will at some time be engaged in conversation about the merits or desirability of these two features. That such small changes as the space between words could engender so much discussion suggests that their application is still an esoteric art. But they merely signify changing the space between adjacent type characters, as shown in Figure 4.13.

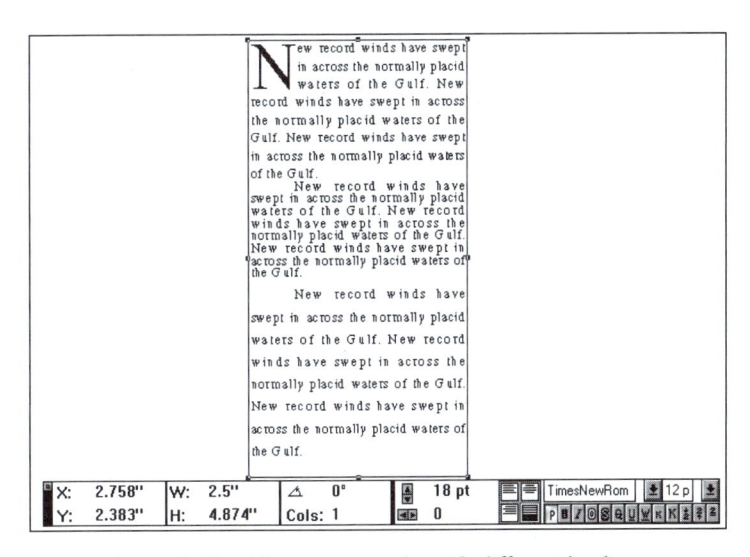

Figure 4.12 *Three paragraphs with different leading.*

Here, the first line has had only the letters W and A moved closer to each other, by eliminating some of the space normally put between them. This is **kerning**, changing the space between individual letters. Kerning certain pairs of letters often creates a more unified, pleasing appearance. When you kern with QuarkXPress, you are removing some of the space ahead of—that is, to the right of—a character. Notice that the last line has had all the letters moved further apart. This is **tracking**, changing the spacing between *all* of a group of letters. Tracking can often subtly open or close text so that it fits more neatly into the area intended for it.

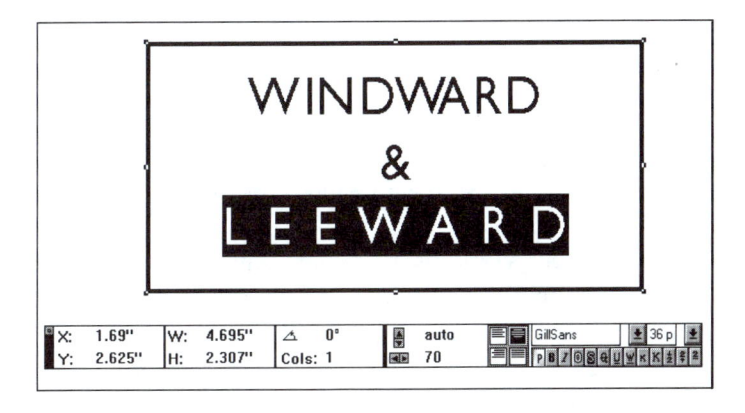

Figure 4.13 *Text kerned and tracked with the measurements palette.*

Kerning and Tracking

Kerning is a spacing relationship between two adjacent letters. Some groups of letters can be automatically kerned from tables of values kept by QuarkXPress. Here we will deal with kerning of individual pairs of letters.

To kern in increments, position the blinking text cursor between the two letters in question. At the Text palette below the leading value, find the two arrowheads. (If the cursor is not between two letters, or if text has not been selected, the kerning/tracking value is not displayed.) Click on the left arrow to close, or the right arrow to open up the space between the letters. The kern value will change normally in units of 10.

To kern by direct entry, position the text cursor and select the Kern field showing in the Text palette. Key in your preferred value. Press Enter to apply.

Kerning at the text palette

Position I-beam text cursor between letters

Use palette arrows for incremental changes (10 units each)

or

Key in kern value and press ENTER

Since kerning and tracking are similar processes applied to individual pairs and to groups of letters, respectively, you'll find tracking adjustments similar to those for kerning.

To adjust tracking, first select the range of text to be tracked. Then proceed, as with kerning, using the Text palette arrowheads for incremental changes, or utilize the direct entry method for precision tracking.

COLUMNS

One of the most obvious strengths of QuarkXPress is instant column control. You can adjust a text box from a single column to several in one step. You can experiment easily and quickly with page layouts and copyfitting. The burning eleventh-hour question—"Do three or four columns fit better here?"—can now be answered in about two seconds. Columns are incredibly easy to control from the Text palette.

As you look to the left of the heavy dark line dividing the Text palette in half, you'll encounter a section labeled Cols. This palette setting governs the number of columns into which the text in a text box is to be divided. As you may recall, crossing to the left half of the palette technically puts us in the section designed for item control. However, the setting of text in columns has such profound consequences for the effects of many type features that we'll look into it here.

If you have a text box of body copy spanning most of a letter-size page, you have a problem. Clearly, visually scanning long lines of 70 or 80 characters across an eight-inch expanse is much too taxing for most readers. Shorter lines of text are obviously preferred. Shorter lines in the same space lead to more columns, and setting type in columns provides a more graceful and practical result.

Because QuarkXPress treats text boxes as if they possessed the characteristics of adjustable columns, creating and changing columns on the page is a process you'll find instantly endearing if you have ever worked with galleys or other approaches that call for you to roll down window shades of text.

Adjusting columns at the palette

Select text box with either item or content tool

Select value in Cols field at palette

Key in new value and press ENTER

NOTE Remember that the text box always has some column setting in effect, even if that setting is only 1.

To change the number of columns in a text box, first select the box with either the item or the content tool. Then select the Cols value in the Text palette and key in the number you desire. Press Enter. The same text can be reset in three or four columns, as shown in Figures 4.14 and 4.15, in a matter of seconds.

WARNING Resetting text to fewer columns can create text box overruns. This may necessitate changing type specifications, as we have done, or engaging new text boxes to take up the surplus, as we shall see later.

ADVANCING

The typesetting functions you've learned in this chapter will do much to help you get your messages across. By fitting and fashioning the basic material of your documents through the Text palette, these controls provide some of the highest levels of productivity of all the features of the program.

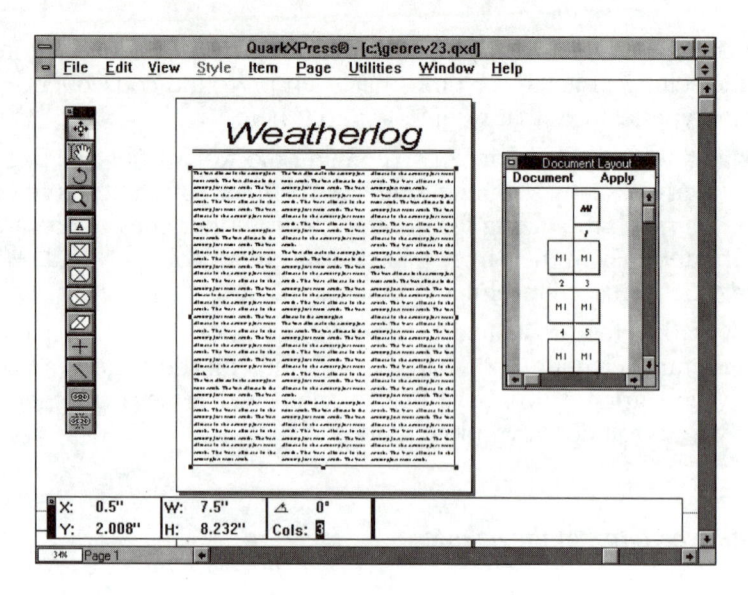

Figure 4.14 *Resetting text into three columns using the Measurements palette.*

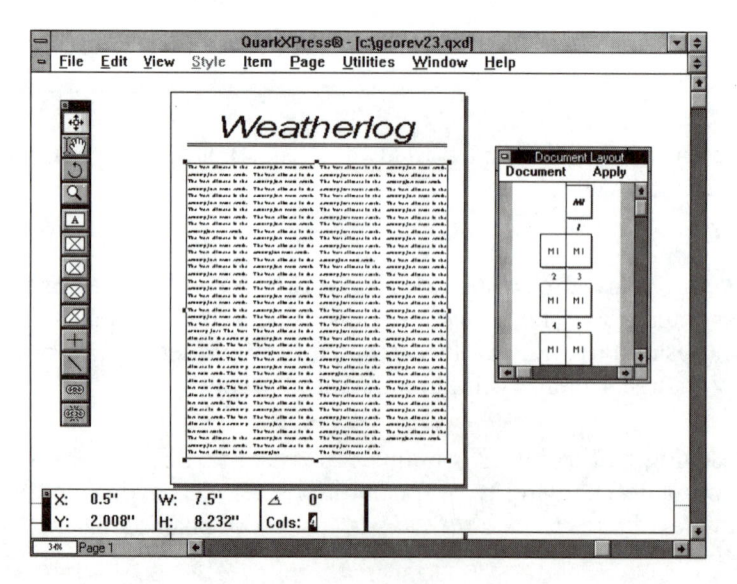

Figure 4.15 *Resetting text into four columns using the Measurements palette.*

Now you can apply your skills to a production project. In the next chapter we will go on the job at two newsletters to see how every one of the features seen here is used.

Chapter 5

Newsletters on the Job

WHAT YOU WILL LEARN IN THIS CHAPTER

- How to construct a document
- How to apply type features and layout techniques
- Copyfitting
- How to work with multiple documents

What could be simpler than a letter?

Classic newsletter layout simply requires typing information and opinions onto a letterhead. Although the letter style continues to enjoy success, the field it spawned has broadened tremendously. The term "newsletter" has come to include anything from a single page of text typed onto a letterhead to a four-color, graphic-intensive, magazinelike publication. While the number of other periodicals fluctuate, newsletters have enjoyed an era of wide proliferation. They function in every way imaginable. Some promote products and services. Others report international news or carry specialized information. Some serve as the social glue for various groups. Any design and every function can be found in newsletters, which now surge in mighty currents through the world's postal systems.

In this chapter we will use techniques you've already encountered in this book to construct two newsletters as QuarkXPress documents. From start to finish we'll move through all the steps, from setting up the document file to importing, formatting, and laying out the text. These two newsletters will in fact be two versions of the same material. To assemble the first, the classic letterhead newsletter, we'll start by setting up the letterhead, then adding and formatting text files to produce a traditional single-column piece. The second version, a contemporary design, will draw on the whole range of skills encountered so far.

As you proceed through these examples the At-a-Glance sections you encountered before will reappear to remind you of certain procedures.

NOTE You may wish to work along on your computer with text of your own, building parallel newsletters for the experience. You can also benefit by tracking the development of each newsletter in the pages that follow. In either case, you will discover how QuarkXPress works under the demands of an actual project.

THE LETTERHEAD NEWSLETTER

We have five text files (drink.txt, japan.txt, expl.txt, inside.txt, and sf-maps.txt) to work with and the following information: The Global Review, A snapshot of the world, No. 103, The Studio K Editors, Box 3562, San Diego, California 92103. We're told that the final newsletter is to be on a letter-size sheet, front and back, in traditional letterhead style, to be mailed in a standard #10 envelope.

Producing the Letterhead

Our first task is to produce the letterhead itself. We have a title, a tag line, a credit, and an address. We'll create a QuarkXPress document, then proceed to develop this information into a letterhead.

We'll assume that the computer has booted up properly, QuarkXPress has been installed, and we are at Window's Program Manager. The first step, then, is to run QuarkXPress. We do this by opening the QuarkXPress program group, and starting the program within it.

Starting a program

Locate icon in Program Manager (or File Manager directory listing)

Double click on it

After the Quark ID-logo window appears momentarily, we reach the program window where we can create our document file. We open the File menu and choose New. The New dialog box is displayed where we select the button that makes this document letter-size. Key in values of 1.25-inch margins all around, uncheck the facing pages checkbox, accept a one-column layout, and make sure the Automatic Text box function is engaged, as shown in Figure 5.1.

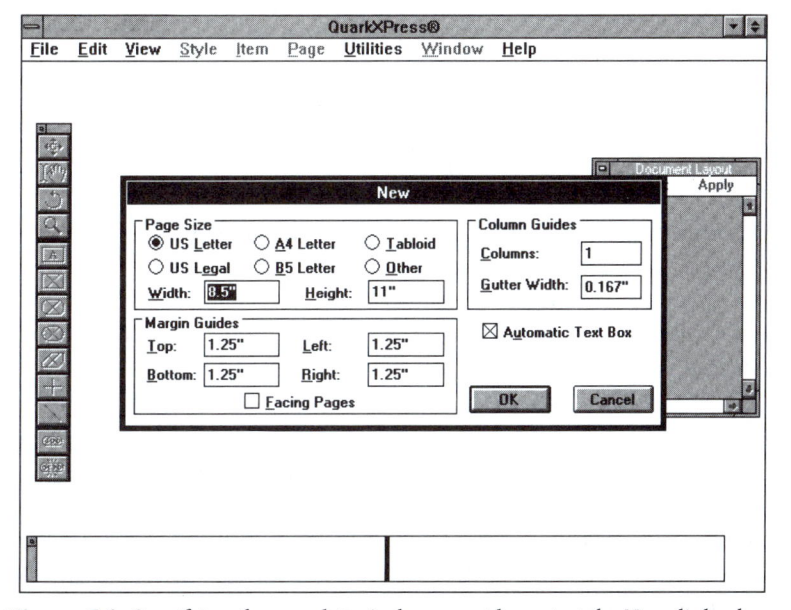

Figure 5.1 *Specifying the newsletter's document layout at the New dialog box.*

Next appears the view, Actual size, of the corner where top and left margins meet. We'll back off a bit and have a look at the whole page while we decide just where to arrange the letterhead information. Opening the View menu, we choose Fit in Window, and can then see all the margin guides clearly. On our color monitor these appear as blue lines. An automatic text box is already contained within these margins. We'll use it later for the body copy.

For the letterhead we need another, smaller text box. For the moment we've decided we want to center the letterhead information at the top, using the traditional Times typeface. We select the text box tool, position it at the left margin guide, above the top margin guide. Since we're using these guides just for convenience, we're free to ignore them when we wish. A one-inch-high text box running down about three-quarters of an inch from the top should be about right. The Tool palette happens to be obscuring the vertical ruler, so we point at the bar at the top of that palette and drag it to the right, away from the ruler. Next, we drag a text box across from the upper left over to the right and down past the top margin guide.

NOTE At this early stage, we'll usually choose to save the file to the hard disk, which makes the document window clearly identified in the event other documents are opened. Also, though we've just begun the document and not yet put much work into it, saving the file now initiates a good habit: frequent saving. As survivors of countless software crashes will testify, the habit of saving frequently eventually pays back the small effort it requires. From now on, we'll take it as given that this document and all other documents are being saved whenever some significant bit of work goes into them.

Opening the File menu and choosing Save, we use the Save As... dialog box to title the document GR103A.QXD. We're locating it in the directory folder 1-KASMER (previously created in File Manager). We find it and double-click to open it before clicking OK.

We need to type in the letterhead data through the keyboard. Since we're planning to center the text and to use a Times typeface, we'll first choose these at the Measurements palette. Making sure that the text box is selected and that the content tool is active at the Tool palette, we click on the Centering button, open the fonts list, then click on TimesNewRoman (a Times-style TrueType font installed in our Windows program).

Before keying in the Global Review data we return to Actual size through the Ctrl-1 keyboard shortcut. Because the Document Layout palette obscures the text box at this view, we'll hide it by double-clicking on the tiny box in the upper-left corner of that palette. (We could also have opened the View menu and chosen Hide Document Layout.) We use the grabber hand to slide the page so that the text box is clearly visible. Then we type the data.

Using the grabber hand

With any tool but the zoom selected, hold the Alt key

Press mouse button and drag page through window view

Pausing a moment, we consider the appearance of this text box, shown in Figure 5.2. In between the left and right guides, this text box sits over the top margin guide, which we can see running through the third line. We ignore the top margin for the moment, because these guides don't print. To take a closer look at the text itself, we open the View menu and choose 200 percent, and then use the grabber hand again to position the Window view so we can see all the text.

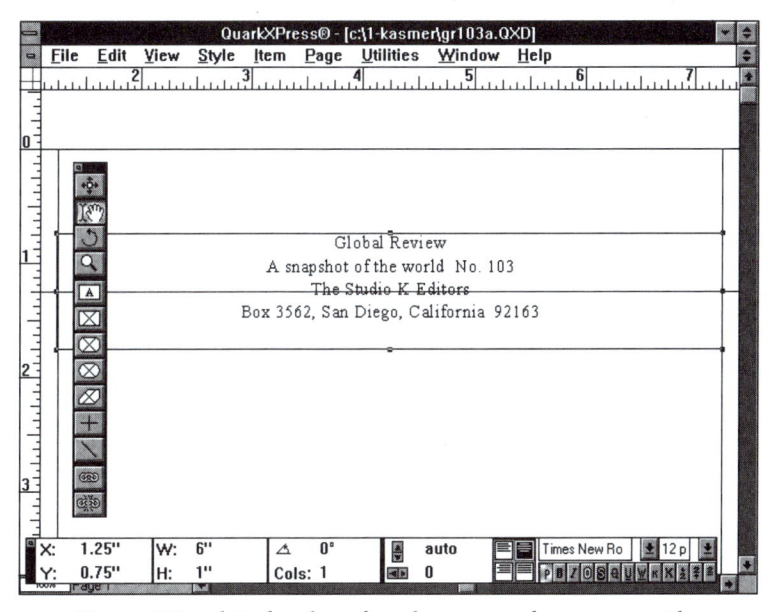

Figure 5.2 *A letterhead text box drawn over the margin guide.*

We want our letterhead to appear traditional, so we will emphasize the first line, our title, by making it larger, bolding it, and using all capital letters. Our first step is to select the text line; triple-click on it. Next, at the Measurements palette we open the Font Size list and click on 18pt. Then we click on the Bold (B) button and the All Caps (K) button. And to pull the title into a tighter group, we click once on the Reduce Tracking arrow, setting that value at -10. These type revisions yield the line shown in Figure 5.3.

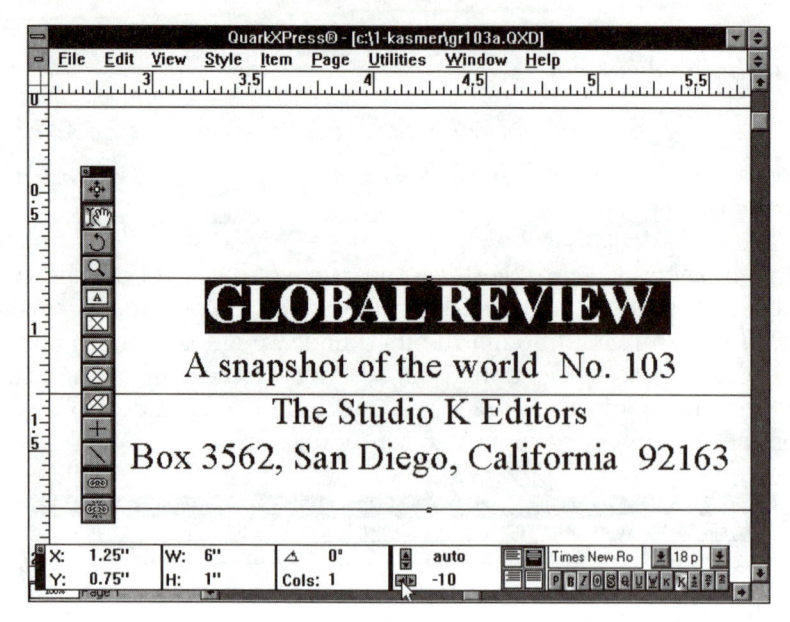

Figure 5.3 *Style adjustments applied to the title line.*

Note that a selected line is displayed in inverse or highlighted text—white on black in this case. We're setting our type to be black on white (like ink on paper). QuarkXPress remembers its selections, so selected text will appear unselected when the text box is deactivated, but it will appear highlighted and selected when the box is activated again. While examining our changes, we can click in a area outside the box. This deactivates the box, and the text inside shows up in normal display, black on white. When we click on the text box again, the contents are reactivated and the selected line appears highlighted as before.

> **NOTE** A note to typographic purists. Yes, it is true that there are specific typefaces for bold, italic, and so on, and a strong case can be made for preferring them in particular circumstances. But throughout this book, we choose to use the automatic type style capabilities of the program, in order to demonstrate their use. The decision of using a bold typeface or a plain face with bolding applied will be left to the user-designer.

Turning next to the tag line under the title, we select that line with a triple-click and return again to the Measurements palette. We apply a smaller size by selecting the Font Size field and typing *8*, italicize by clicking the I button, and decrease leading to 9pt by clicking on the Leading down arrow to bring the tag line up closer to the title.

Moving to the third line, The Studio K Editors, we triple-click to select it, and at the palette apply bolding and small capitals through the buttons. To drop this line away from the tag line we increase the leading to 17pt by clicking the Leading Up arrow. To tighten the line's letter spacing, we decrease tracking -10 by clicking the Tracking down arrow.

Finally, selecting the address line, we reduce its size by clicking in the Font Size field and typing *8pt*. And here again we decrease letter spacing -10 by clicking the Tracking down arrow.

At this point it becomes apparent that the title line should be larger, so we triple-click that first line again and increase the font size to 24pt by opening the Palette Font Size list, then clicking. At the 200 percent view shown in Figure 5.4, the letterhead portion now appears completed.

Figure 5.4 *Close view of the completed letterhead.*

Typesetting Body Text

Next our attention turns to the text that will make up the body of the newsletter. Since this text was generated elsewhere, our task is to bring it in, order it, then format it. At this point we're using the text box that was placed automatically within the margins when we created the GR103A.QXD document. It is into this box that we'll import those text files.

NOTE Note that the automatic text box and the letterhead text box overlap. Generally, text runaround is engaged—it is a default setting—and one text box may force text in another box to reposition. However, this works in our favor here, because the features of text runaround are pushing the body text downward from the letterhead text box. Text runaround controls will be explored in detail later.

To import the first part of the text, we first choose the content tool, then click on the large, automatically generated text box. A flashing text cursor is displayed beneath the letterhead text box (because of the runaround feature pushing it there), indicating where text will be inserted. At this point we decide to establish the font and size by selecting TimesNewRoman and 12pt at the Measurements palette. Opening the File menu, we choose Get Text. Locating the file EXPL.TXT within the directory (as shown in Figure 5.5), double-click to import it. The text comes into the box in the selected size and font, and the cursor flashes at the end of the text.

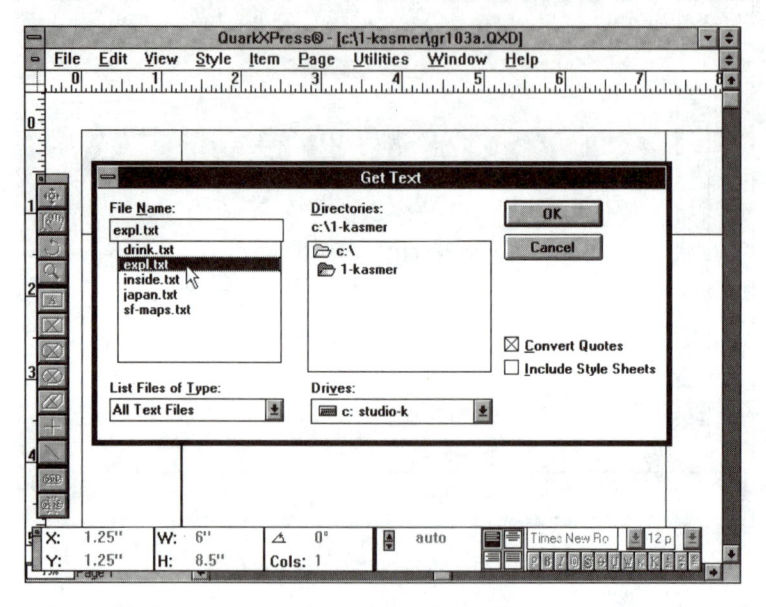

Figure 5.5 *Importing the EXPL.TXT file through the Get Text command.*

Deciding to import all the text at this time, we again choose Get Text to bring in the JAPAN.TXT file, then the INSIDE.TXT file. At this point the program flows the text to the bottom of the text box on Page 1, and automatically inserts Page 2 into the document with a similar text box. The program continues to flow in the balance of the INSIDE.TXT file, as shown in the greeked text of Figure 5.6.

Now we continue, importing next the DRINK.TXT file, and finally SF-MAPS.TXT. With all the text now in place, we decide to have a look, returning to Actual Size view. There will almost always be some cleanup or "massaging" necessary before final formatting. Often word processors (the people, not the software) put in two spaces between sentences. Sometimes extra carriage returns are entered between paragraphs.

In Figure 5.7, something else is awry. A character, ô, has been inserted wherever apostrophes were originally typed by the (human) word processor.

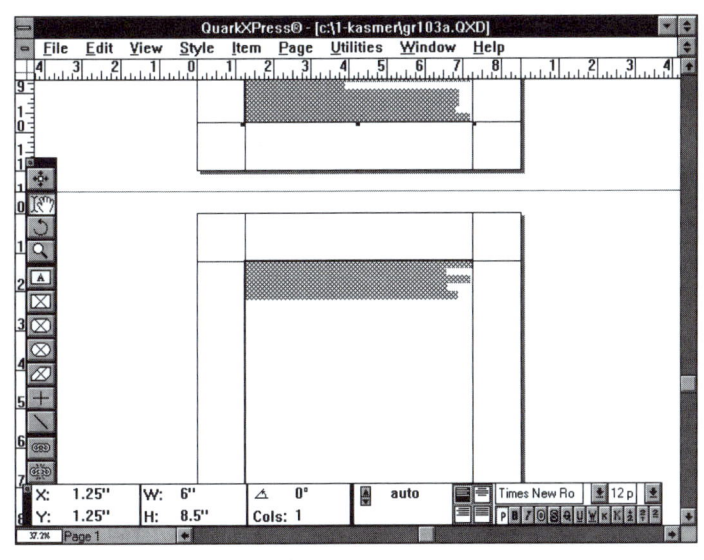

Figure 5.6 *Greeked text view of original text box and Page 2 generated to handle overrun.*

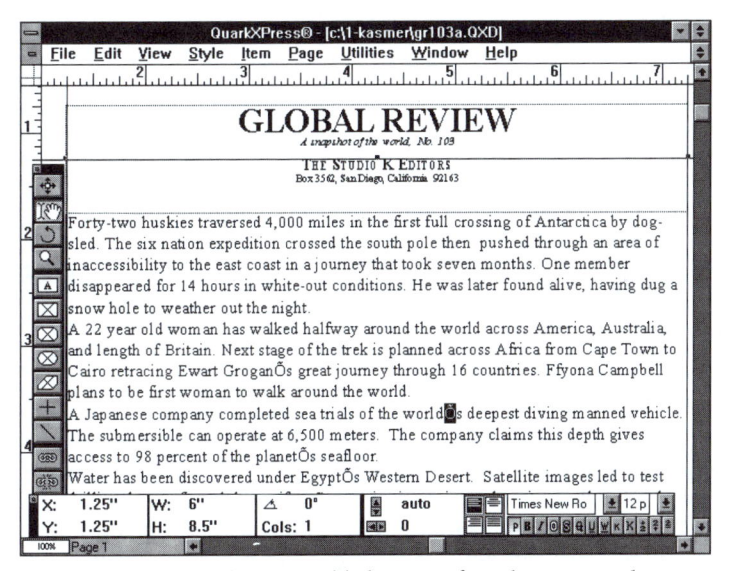

Figure 5.7 *An inadvertent, odd character found in imported text.*

These odd translations can happen unexpectedly. In this instance, the files have passed through five separate software programs, and from the Macintosh to the Windows platform. Undoubtedly, those apostrophes were lost somewhere in the several translations, and the õs were blindly substituted for them.

Also, we've been informed that the Fyona Campbell story of paragraph 2 is dated and should be removed. We attend to this first by quadruple-clicking in that paragraph to select it, and pressing the Backspace key to delete it.

Next we take on the õs. The obvious thing to do here is make a **global replacement**. Since we don't know off the top of our head what character code produced the õs, we first select one from the text with a drag of the mouse and copy it to the clipboard, using the Edit menu shortcut Ctrl-C. Next we click the cursor to the beginning of the text. Then, at the Edit menu, we choose Find/Change.

At the Find/Change dialog box, with the text cursor flashing in the Find What field box, we use the shortcut Ctrl-V to paste in the õ. Then we tab to the Change To field and key in an apostrophe. We click the only button accessible now, Find Next, and the process begins. The first õ is located and selected by the Change function. We click the Change button and examine the result, shown in Figure 5.8, to be sure it's what we want—with no unintended spaces or other surprises. Satisfied, we then click the Change All button. The Change dialog substitutes apostrophes for all õs throughout the story.

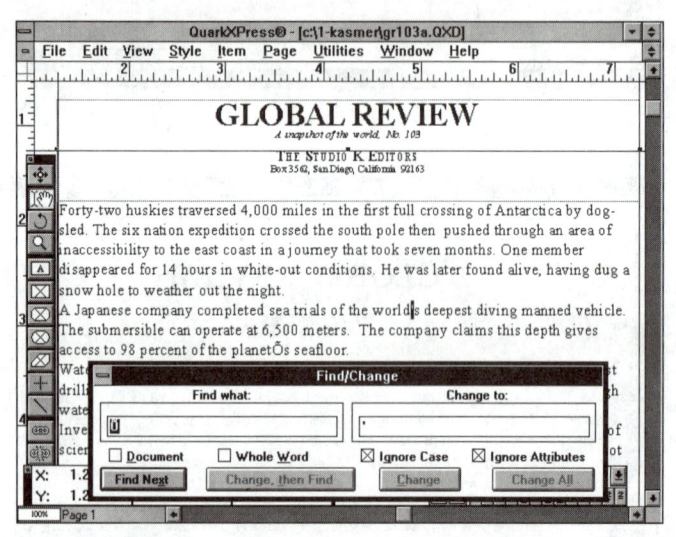

Figure 5.8 The first phase of changing the odd character back to an apostrophe.

Now we position the text cursor back at the beginning of the story, and prepare to use the Find/Change dialog box to remove double spaces. We do this by typing in two spaces in the Find What field, and then typing a single space in the Change To field. Proceeding as before, we direct global replacement through the dialog Change all button.

Next we move into the area of paragraph formatting. Although there are other ways of handling paragraph spacing, we plan to use the Change feature. To make our text self-consistent, we'll eliminate any double carriage returns. With the text cursor at the story's beginning and with the Find/Change dialog box active, we key in two new paragraph codes in the Find What field, \p\p, and a single new-paragraph code in the Change To field, \p. These new-paragraph codes are generated each time the Enter key is pressed.

Basic QuarkXPress character codes

New line	\n
New paragraph	\p
Tab	\t

NOTE: In case there might be unnoticed *triple* carriage returns, we also run the same global change from the beginning of the text a second time.

Next we want to put a tab at the beginning of every paragraph. We use the Find/Change dialog box to replace every paragraph with a paragraph and a tab, using the codes \p and \t, as in shown Figure 5.9. These codes indent every paragraph except the first (since it has no carriage return preceding it). To take care of the first paragraph, we set the text cursor at the beginning of the text box and type in a tab by hand.

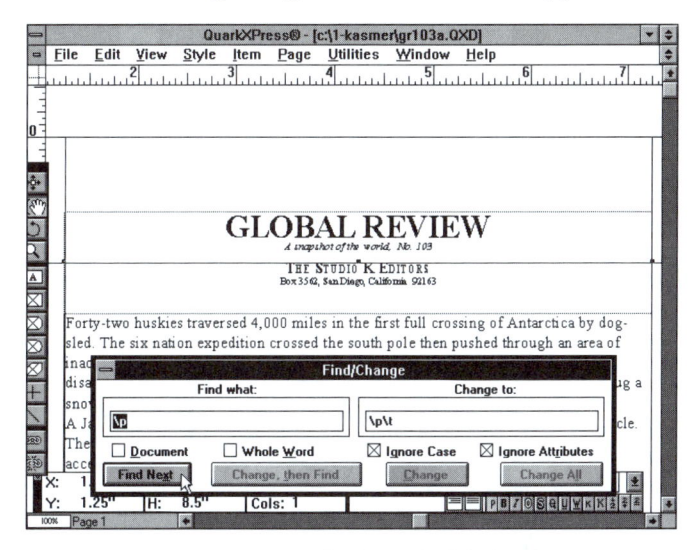

Figure 5.9 Inserting tabs through global replacement.

We are dealing with simple formatting here. In order to separate articles, we go through visually, insert the text cursor and add a carriage return to create additional space between them.

In keeping with the traditional look of this piece, we'll put a simple typewriterlike emphasis on each new article by dragging to select lead-in text and then underlining using the Text palette's Continuous Underline button, as shown in Figure 5.10.

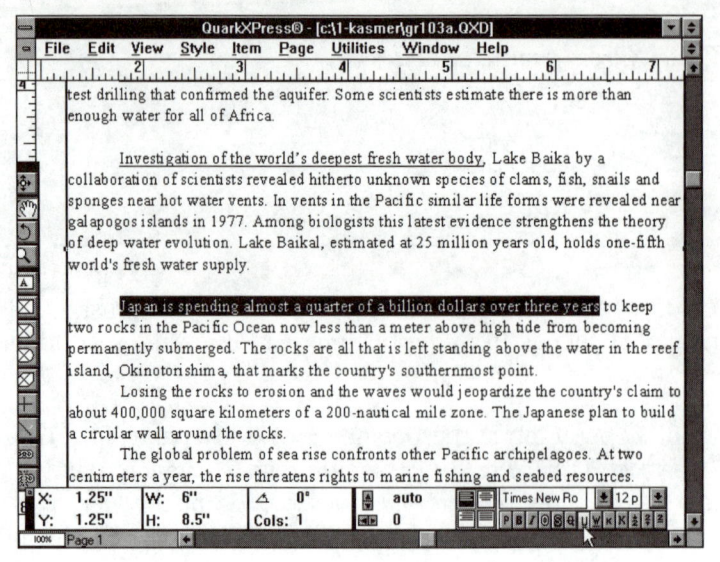

Figure 5.10 Setting off text lead-ins with underlining.

Copyfitting

Now we can pull our view back and take an overall look at this newsletter. A glance at Page 2 reveals that we have yet to fill out the publication. (See Figure 5.11.) And in this case there is no more text coming in, so it's up to design alone to balance the page without impeding readability—always a fundamental consideration in a newsletter.

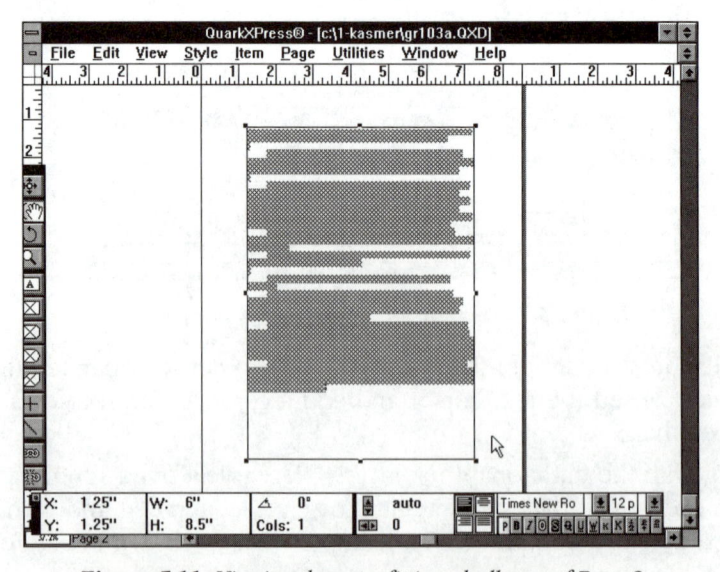

Figure 5.11 Viewing the copy-fitting challenge of Page 2.

Here our choice is to try increasing the leading. Making sure that the content tool is selected, we click to insert the text cursor in the story, and then select it all.

SHORT CUT An alternative way to select all the story's text is to quintuple-click with the cursor in the story. Depending on the coordination of the operator and the double-click speed setting for the mouse in the Control Panel of Windows, this *might* be easier than the Edit menu or Ctrl-A keyboard techniques.

With all the text selected, we move to the Measurements palette and click on the Leading Up arrow while monitoring the change at Page 2. At 16pt we are rewarded. Our text has just filled the text box without running over, as shown in Figure 5.12. And the separation between the lines is not in the least distracting.

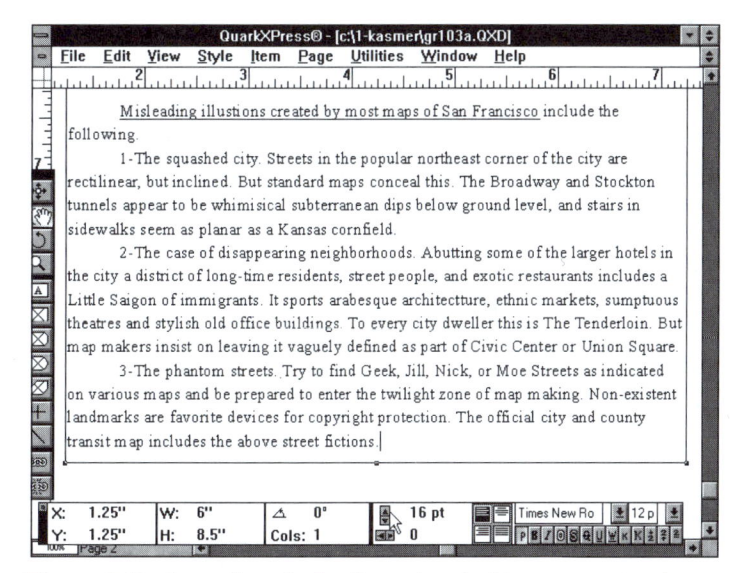

Figure 5.12 *Controlling the leading using the Measurements palette.*

Our final addition to this document is a page number added at the top of Page 2. We select the text box tool and drag a small box into the position shown in Figure 5.13, centering the box at four-and-a-quarter inches, the horizontal center of the page. We use the Measurements palette to choose TimesNewRoman again and to center the text. We type in - *2* -, and with one final Save command put document GR103A.QXD to bed.

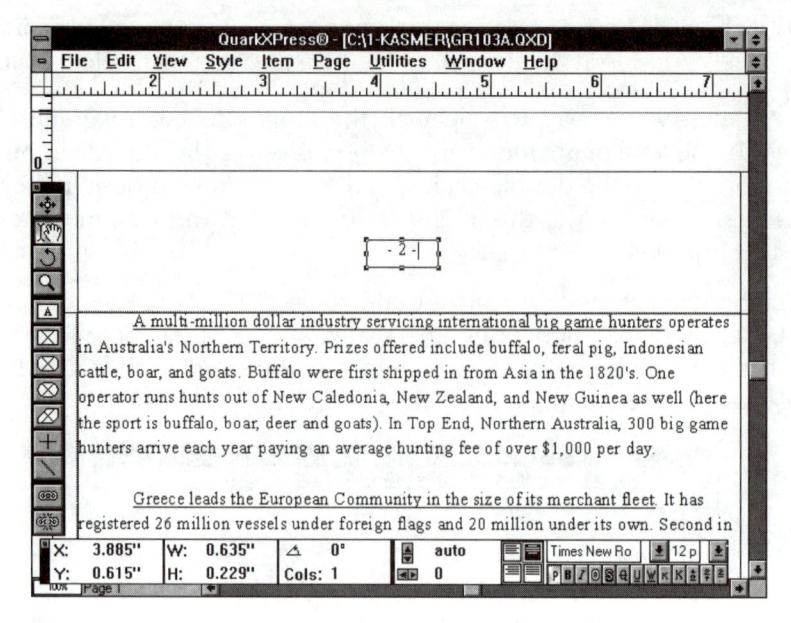

Figure 5.13 *Adding a small Page Number text box.*

A Contemporary Newsletter

Using other skills from preceding chapters, we can make a very different newsletter using the same sources that went into the classic newsletter above.

We'll be working with the same text (from the files EXPL.TXT, JAPAN.TXT, DRNK.TXT, INSIDE.TXT, and SF-MAPS.TXT), and the same title, tag line, credit, and address as before. In this case, though, we've taken on the task of redesigning the previous format. We want a special-size, four-page self-mailer that will fold into a 5.5-inch-by-8.5-inch format.

The new page format will call for narrower columns and a different layout altogether. The articles will be broken into separate stories and given more individual play within the layout. We'll add headlines and rule elements to set the stories apart from each other. We'll set the type in multiple columns to make for an easier read. And we'll create a space for adding an address label for mailing.

Our first step is generating the document. As shown in Figure 5.14, at the File menu's New dialog box, we've set the page size to match, chosen .3-inch margins, facing pages, and a two-column format with a .167-inch separation. Here, because we want more flexibility in layout, the automatic text box feature was turned off by clicking to remove the x in that field box. Clicking OK at the dialog box gives us a single page of the new smaller document. We'll add the others as needed.

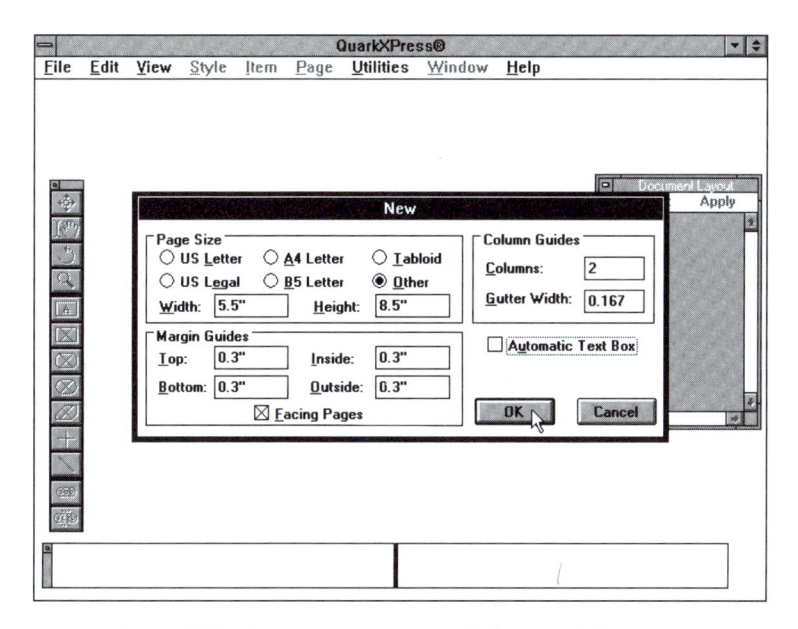

Figure 5.14 *Creating a custom sized, formatted document.*

As we proceed, we start with the body text as it appears in the letterhead document. Often, we import text first into a simple, single column document with the automatic text box feature engaged. This has already been done in the first design of the newsletter, so we'll make use of it. We call up GR103.QXD using the Open command or the Windows menu and rename this first version 103TEXT.QXD by opening the File menu and choosing Save As. Here we can easily prepare our text for the more elaborate design document, GR103B.QXD.

Preparing Body Text

Our first step in 103TEXT is to remove all the special type-formatting in the text document's body copy—in this case, the underlining. We engage the content tool, put the cursor into the body text, and select All (Edit menu and Select All, or quintuple-click). Then at the Measurements palette we press the P button (for plain text). The underlining disappears. This is the same method that will also clear out any bolding, italics, and other type styles that may have been applied by the word processor. Granted, many times preserving type styles is important. But here, as we transform the Global Review material from a traditional letter form to typeset-pages form, underlines are out.

Also, we prefer to start layout work with autoleading (normally set at 120 percent). This will prove useful at whatever size we may work with. So, with all the text selected, at the Measurements palette we select the Leading field and key in *auto*.

Preparing the Nameplate

Let's prepare the new document's nameplate. We're going to cut items and text from the 103TEXT document as we move them to the GR103B document. This will help us keep track of what remains to be included in the new layout. So, we use the item tool, select the Global Review letterhead text box in 103TEXT by clicking on it, then open the Edit menu and choose Cut. Then we open the Window menu and choose the GR103B document from the list of open documents, as shown in Figure 5.15. There, we open the Edit menu and choose Paste. The letterhead text box appears.

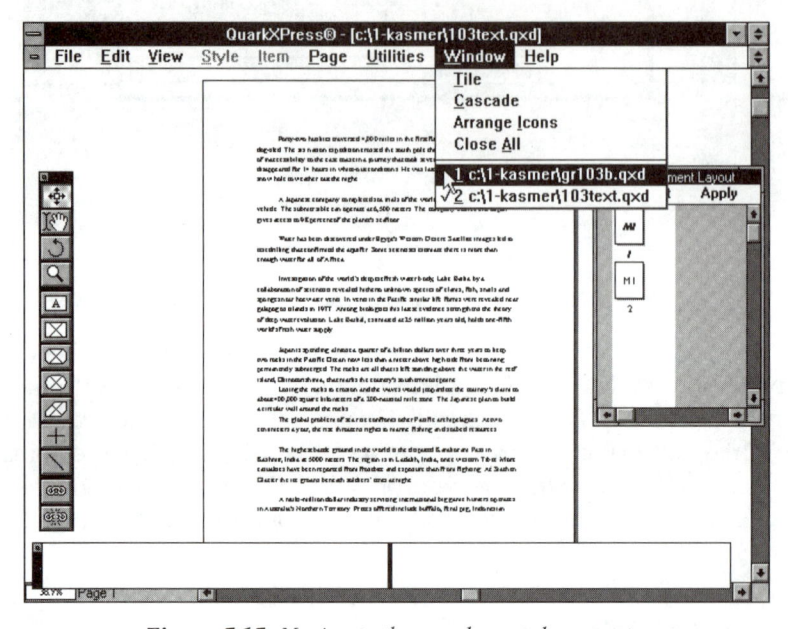

Figure 5.15 *Moving to the new layout document.*

By pointing onto the upper-left selection handle, we drag the text box, adjusting its shape so that it is seated into the upper-left corner of the margin guides. Grasping the box's lower-right corner similarly, we drag the shape into that shown in Figure 5.16, establishing the newsletter's nameplate text box. While making these adjustments, we change views and use the grabber hand to position the page, and hide or show palettes to accommodate our efforts.

NOTE There is an alternative to cutting items from the source window and pasting them into the destination window. We could display both windows concurrently by choosing the Windows menu's Tile command. This will fit all open windows adjacent to each other, automatically resizing them as it does so. It's a Windows feature that helps when we want to see parts of two documents simultaneously. Additionally, this concurrent window display allows us to copy easily. The method is simply to drag the items from one window to the other. As the mouse cursor appears in the second window, so does an outline of the item. Releasing the mouse button causes the paste function to engage. However, as useful as this feature can be, we've chosen the cut–switch Windows–Paste method because we're deliberately paring away the available source document.

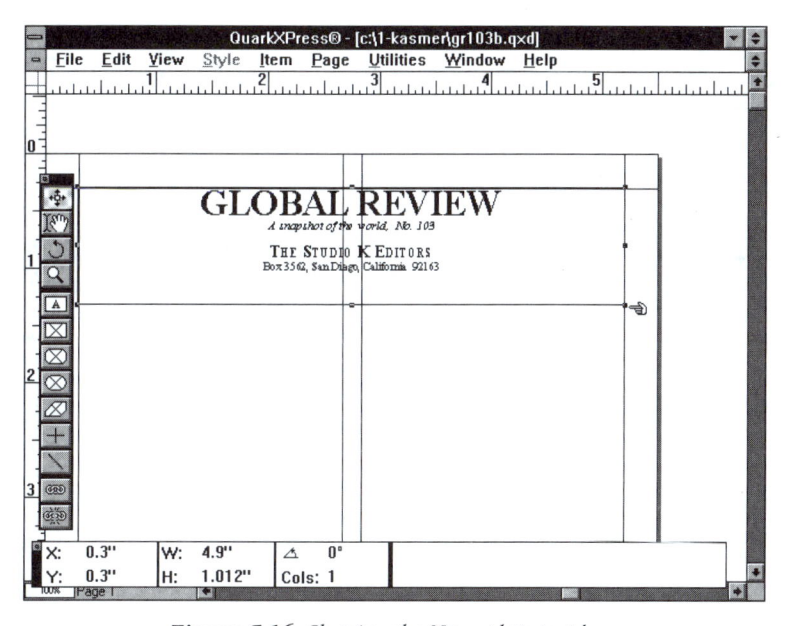

Figure 5.16 *Shaping the Nameplate text box.*

Quick copying between documents

Display both documents concurrently (Windows menu, Tile)

Select item in source document window

Drag to destination document window and release

Now we work on the newsletter's nameplate. Here's what we plan. The title will be larger, and accompanied by the tag line and issue number, but the credit and address will be excluded from Page 1. Most of the publication information will be included on the back page.

One of the first things we're doing to the nameplate is making the title larger. We drop the cursor in Global Review and triple-click to select the line. Experimenting with its appearance through the Measurements palette, we remove the bold style, enlarge the font to 48pt, then set the tracking to -15.

We stretch out the tag line and issue number with tracking of 120 at a size of 8pt. For use later on the back page, we copy the text box with the item tool and move it temporarily to the pasteboard at the right. Then we remove the credit and address lines from the nameplate text box by drag-selecting with the content tool text cursor, and shorten the box by grasping the bottom-center handle of the selected box and pulling upward.

Next we select the rule (the orthogonal line) tool to add a rule to set off the nameplate, dragging the rule into place beneath it. At the Measurements palette, we select the Thickness field by clicking, then key in a point size of 6pt for the line. Using the Hide Guides command from the View menu, we remove the blue guides, and survey what we've done so far in Figure 5.17.

Figure 5.17 Newsletter title and tag line set off.

The Mailer Section

Before we retypeset and layout the body text, we're going to prepare the back page mailer space. This way we'll have a clearer idea of how much space is available for the body copy. To proceed, we'll need to create three more pages. We can do this either through the Document palette or through the Page menu. The Document palette method is piecemeal, one page at a time. In this case, we'll use the Menu command. We open the Page menu and choose Insert. In the Insert Pages dialog box of Figure 5.18 we type *3* into the Pages field, leave pressed the round button that indicates After Page 1, and leave the Master page selection at the default (M1-Master 1) we set up when we created the document at the New dialog box.

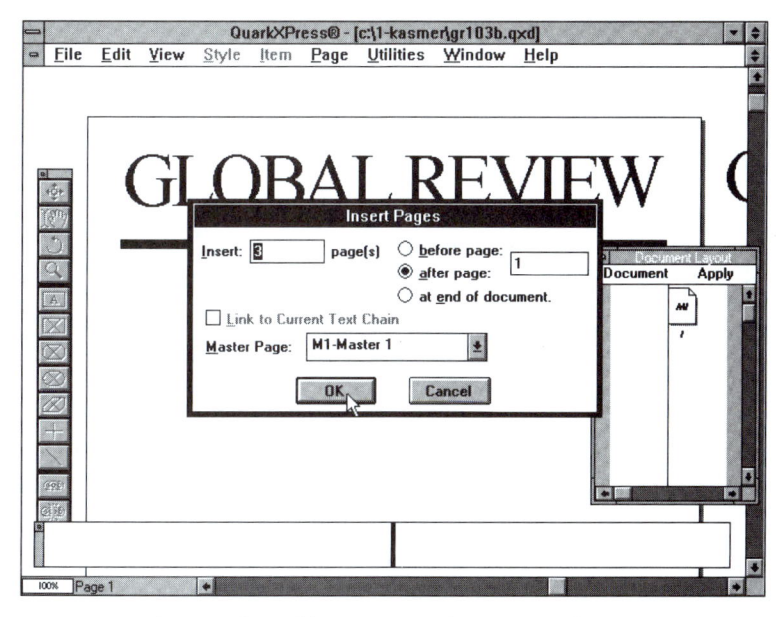

Figure 5.18 *Adding pages in the GR103B document.*

Turning to the Document Layout palette (we've brought it up through the View menu Show command) we now see the icons for all four pages, with Pages 2 and 3 shown as facing pages. The designation M1 sits in each page as an indication of the master page format applied to it. Our object is to move that text box which sits on the pasteboard of Page 1 to Page 4. We could drag through the pages, but we prefer another way. Engaging the item tool, we select the text box and give the Cut command. Then at the Document Layout palette we double-click on the Page 4 icon. Page 4 appears in the window, then we select the Fit in Window view. Now we give the Paste command, and the text box appears on Page 4.

To develop the mailer section of the newsletter, we decide to use the lower half of the page. From the View menu the guides are switched to Show guides. The rule tool is chosen and a rule is drawn across the middle of the page at 4.25 inches, left to right margin. We select the Thickness field and type the desired thickness, 4pt, into the Measurements palette.

Next, we make some adjustments to the text box just brought from Page 1. The text would sit well as a return address in the upper-left corner of the lower half of the page. So, using the content tool, we select the first-line title with a triple-click, and after some experimentation reduce it to *22pt*, typed in at the Measurements palette. Next, after triple-click-selecting the tag line—*A snapshot of the world*—we reduce tracking on it (in the palette) to 20. Then, manipulating the box handles, we size it down to fit in the left column under the rule. Using a zoom-tool click to view in at 100 percent, we turn to the content tool again to select the issue number and, pressing the Backspace key, delete it, leaving the return address of the mailer as shown in Figure 5.19.

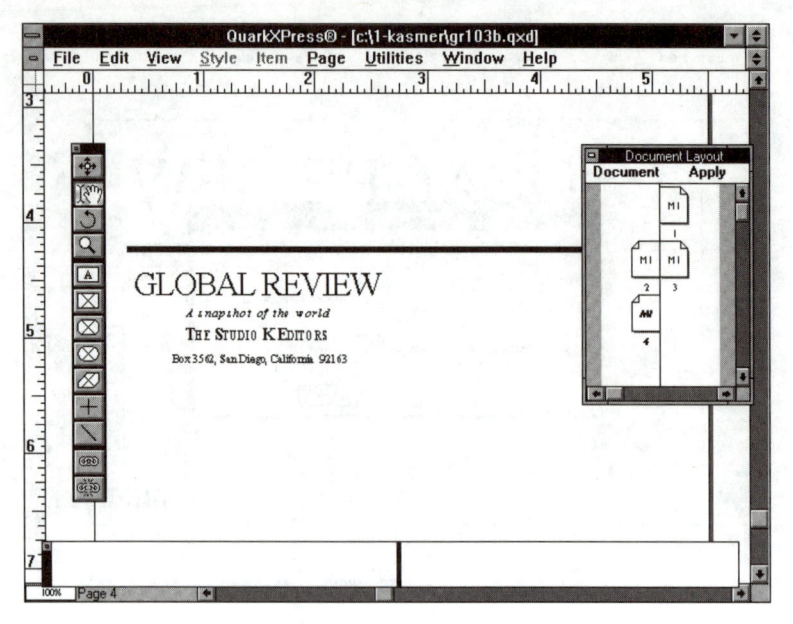

Figure 5.19 *The mailer return address, Page 4.*

Text Layout on Page 2

Now our attention turns to the text in the 103TEXT document. Our layout area for text has been reduced slightly. The format before us in GR103B suggests headlines and groupings of articles. A theme the articles share is that of water. We'll turn to the text document to see about gathering them together for a unified page spread on Pages 2 and 3. Using the Windows menu document list we select 103TEXT and locate the consecutive articles on the Japanese submersible, the Egyptian desert, Lake Baikal, and the disappearing islands—then select by dragging the text cursor. Estimating these will fit on one of the inside pages, we cut them into the Clipboard (using the keyboard Ctrl-X command). At the Windows menu we then select the GR103B document again.

Using the Document Layout palette to double-click on the Page 2 icon, we bring that page into the window, choosing Fit in Window from the View menu. Next, we select the text box tool from the Tool palette, and draw a box within an area of Page 2 where we imagine the body copy will fit.

NOTE If your preference for fitting copy runs to using accurate word counts and calculating numbers of lines, here's a method in QuarkXPress that overcomes the program's lack of a specific word-count function. This method relies on this fact: When the program does automatic replacement, it notifies you of the number of changes made. Indeed, this method will work with any word processor that offers similar notification.

Go to the Find/Change dialog box under the Edit menu. In the Find What field, type one space. Likewise, in the Change To field, key in one space. Make sure that the text cursor is at the beginning of the text. Click the Find Next button, and then the Change All button when it becomes accessible. The Find/Change function will then run through the text, changing every space to…a space. The net result is no change. But in the process of doing each substitution, the Change function will tally the number of changes and display that number in a dialog box at the end of the search. Since nearly every word in a typeset-ready text file is followed by a space, the number of space changes will virtually equal the number of words.

Word counting

In Find/Change dialog Find What field type in one space, and in the Change To field type in one space.

Select Change all

The number of changes cited equals virtually the number of words

---

To bring in the water articles, we make sure that a text cursor is flashing in the text box on Page 2. We then issue the Paste command (at the keyboard, Ctrl-V). The text of the articles selected previously flows into the text box. At the Measurements palette we select the Cols field and type in *2*.

Next, we hunt through each piece in the text box for subheadings, at Actual size. Selecting a suitable phrase with a drag of the text cursor, we copy the phrase (at the keyboard, Ctrl-C). We then insert the cursor at the beginning of the article and paste in the subheading phrase (at the keyboard, Ctrl-V). Two carriage returns with the Enter key are added for separation. We edit our prospective subheading to a paraphrase where appropriate, and remove the tab of the lead paragraph of each article.

Selecting the subheading, we add style features of bold and all capitals. Figure 5.20 shows how the Japanese submersible piece looks. From each article of the water group an extracted subheading is in turn formatted. With the cursor still in the text, we then select All (quintuple-click) and click the Justify button on the Measurements palette.

Finally, to achieve the right fit for this text box we drag down the center handle of the top side until all the copy fills the resized box (without generating an overflow x in the lower-right corner).

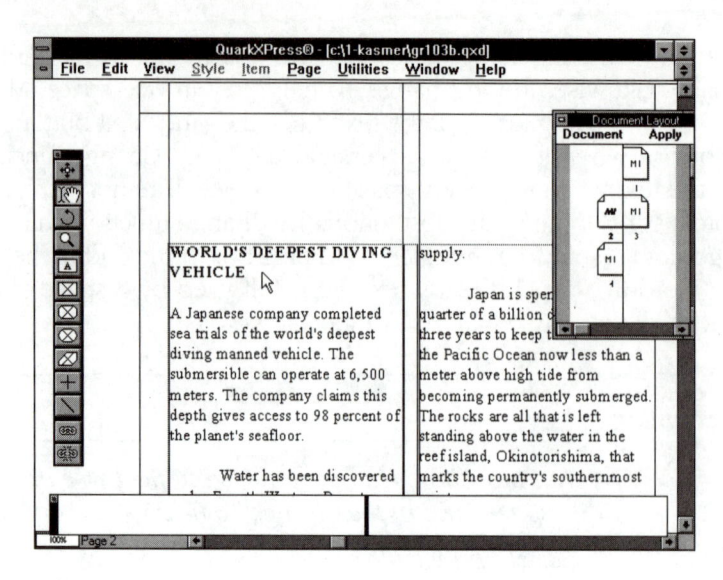

Figure 5.20 *A Page 2 subheading.*

To headline the piece, we choose the text box tool and drag a box into the space above the body text box. Into it we type the heading *Waterlogs* on the first line, then a return, and then *from the Pacific, Egypt, Japan, Siberia* on the next line. To format the headline, we select all the text (quintuple-click). At the Measurements palette we open the Font list by a click on the arrow and choose Arial. For style, the choice is italic. Next, to size the Waterlogs line we set the cursor in the word and triple-click to select the line. Experimenting with the choices in the list, we finally click in the Size field and type *44,* for 44 points. At the second line of the heading box we insert the cursor and triple-click to select the line. Here we choose 14pt from the Size list, and click the Right Align button in the palette. The result is seen in the partial view of Page 2 in Figure 5.21.

Text Layout on Page 3

We complete the Pages 2 and 3 spread by returning through the Windows menu to the 103TEXT document and selecting, then cutting the "drinking hazards" story in the same way we cut the "water group" pieces. Through the Windows menu choice we return again to GR103B. Here we set the View to Fit in Window (at the keyboard, Ctrl-0) and ensure that the guides are showing. After the text box tool is selected, a text box is drawn across into the lower four-fifths of Page 3, within the margins. With the text cursor flashing within it, we paste the clipboard-held text (at the keyboard, Ctrl-V), and the text flows in.

Experimenting with view sizes and the grabber hand (Alt-drag) we arrive at a 50 percent view that gives a clear perspective of the text box's cautionary story. Working at the Measurements palette, we type *2* in the Cols box for a consistent layout. Once all the text is selected, we set it at a larger font size (16pt) and increase the leading, using the Up arrow, until an appropriate display is achieved. A top text box handle is then dragged up, enlarging the box and pulling in all the text until we reach the partial layout of Figure 5.22.

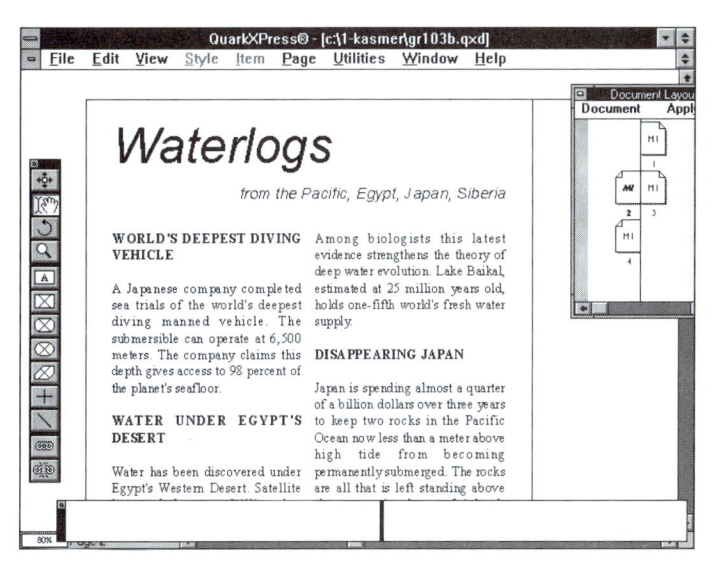

Figure 5.21 *Page 2 completed with heading and body text in place.*

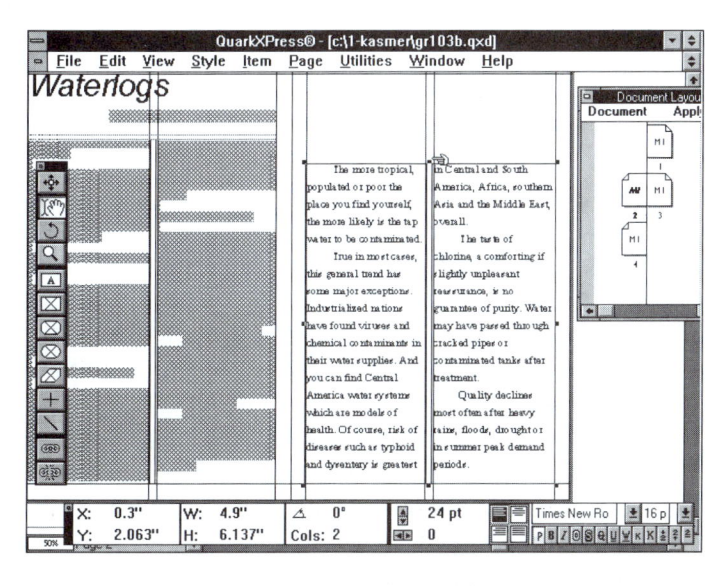

Figure 5.22 *Partial layout of Page 3.*

Next, we'll create a Page 3 heading. With the text box tool we drag a box into place above the body text. The heading, *Drinking the water, or not,* is typed. We deliberately key a return before the phrase "or not" to drop it to a second line. Then Select All is invoked. Experimenting, we settle on Arial in a font size of 36pt through the drop-down lists of the Measurements palette. For an italic headline, we click the I button. To bring the heading lines closer together, the down arrow for leading is clicked until an agreeable 29pts is reached, as shown in Figure 5.23.

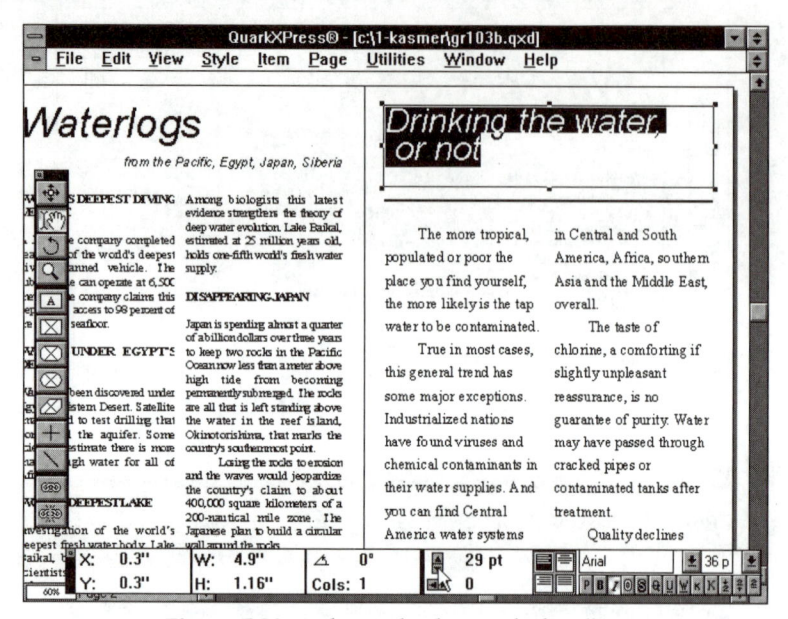

Figure 5.23 *Reducing leading in the headline.*

Text Layout on Page 1

Double-clicking on its icon in the Document Layout palette, we move to complete Page 1. We're going to insert short articles here from the 103TEXT document. We'll also add a small table of contents for articles on the other pages. In 103TEXT we drag-select and cut the articles on crossing Antarctica, the highest battleground, big-game hunting, and the Greek merchant fleet, leaving only the piece on San Francisco maps behind in the text document. We'll fit this on Page 4 later.

We proceed in much the same manner as we did with Page 2, dragging out the text box, pasting in the text, setting 2 columns at the Measurements palette, eliminating first paragraph tabs and creating small headlines for each piece.

Here, however, we want these in-line headings to stand out more, since the articles are unrelated. Selecting the first head, "Antarctica Crossed by Dog-sled," we choose Arial, 18 point, at the Measurements palette, where we also click the buttons for bold

Newsletters on the Job ♦ **117**

and italics. After brief experimentation, we close up the headlines by selecting the entire headline text and applying a tracking of -10. To close up the vertical spacing, which looks awkward when the headline is this large, the selection is clicked off and the text cursor is clicked into place in the first line of the head. At the Measurements palette, the Leading down arrow is used to reduce the leading to 21, as in Figure 5.24. At this point we apply a shortcut to each of the other heads on Page 1, using an approach that works in almost any program that deals with text.

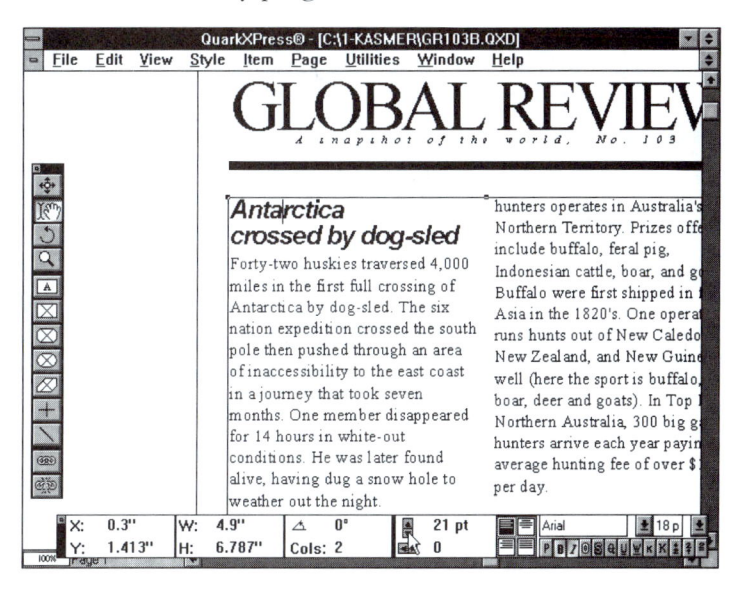

Figure 5.24 *In-line heads adjusted.*

SHORT CUT

You don't have to apply type styles and other text formatting repeatedly. Nor do you always need to set up style sheets. For instance, headings might all require the same style and format. First set up the headline, exactly as it and its sibling heads should appear. Select and copy it, then move to the next head location and paste in that first headline. Select this pasted text and type the wording of the new headline in its place. Using this method for each of the remaining three heads on Page 1, we copy all of the formatting except the leading reduction at each heading location. For leading, we place the text cursor in the first line of text for each head and again click the Leading down arrow. In this way, all the heads are adjusted within a minute or so.

NOTE

The other way to apply recurring styles to a series of paragraphs involves the creation and use of style sheets, a subject explored in detail in Chapter 10. These are the tried-and-true way to preserve style and format selections for later reapplication. For our present purposes, however, this technique would be no faster than the above shortcut.

In adjusting the Page 1 heads, all goes well—except for one small thing. As shown in Figure 5.25, the text fits within the box, leaving room in the lower-right corner for that table of contents we'll be adding. In the left column, however, we find that the "Australia big game hunts" head is followed by just a single line of body text. We'd prefer at least two lines of body copy under a head.

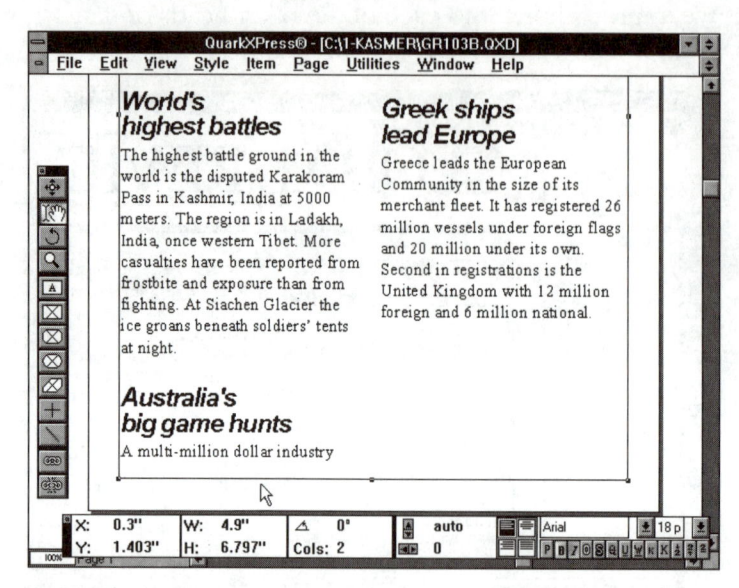

Figure 5.25 *Copy fitting needing head-body copy coordination.*

In this case, we apply a simple solution. We enlarge the text box slightly to lengthen columns just enough so that another line of body text flows to the bottom of the left column from the top of the right one. This is accomplished easily. Pulling upward, ever so slightly, on the middle box handle into the ample space below the title rule (as shown in Figure 5.26).

A Table of Contents

Now we set up a table of contents. A small listing in the lower-right corner should entice readers on to the other articles. We first choose the rule tool and draw a line across the right column to help separate copy above it from the contents below it. After clicking the text box Tool button, a small text box is drawn within the available space of the corner, as shown in Figure 5.27. (Note that text runaround function, which will be described in detail later, is not a factor here, since the new text box is clear of any text.)

Figure 5.26 *Enlarging the text box vertically using the handle.*

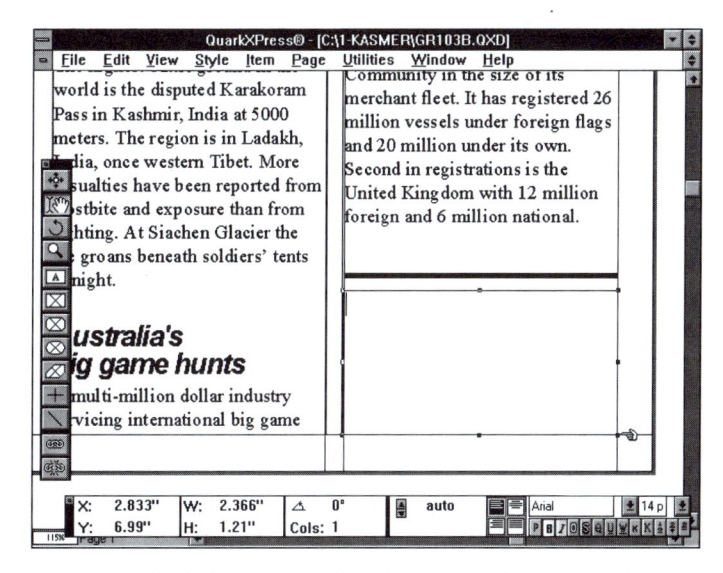

Figure 5.27 *Contents text box drawn over the body text box*

All the stories are now in place, except the one destined for Page 4, so we can set up a list, headed "Also in This Issue," describing the contents of Pages 2, 3, and 4. Using the Measurements palette we apply Arial, italics, and 16 points to the contents heading, 14 to the list. And we adjust tracking in each, positive tracking to spread out the heading, and negative tracking to tighten the listed lines. As these final adjustments are completed, so is Page 1, shown in figure 5.28.

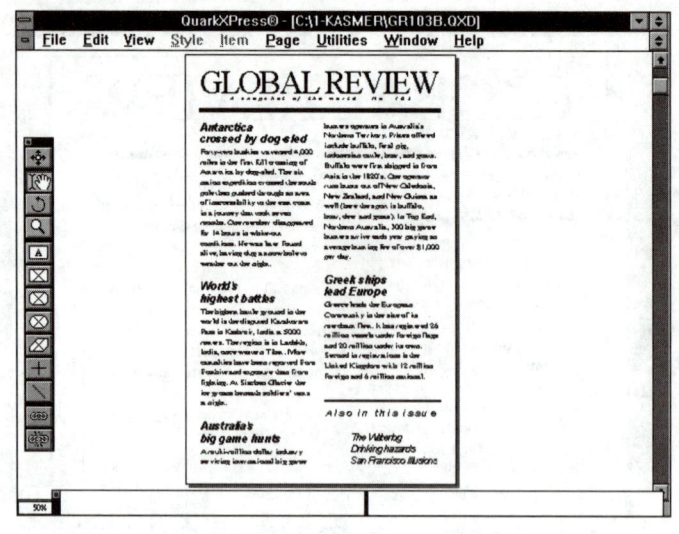

Figure 5.28 Page 1 completed.

Text Layout on Page 4

Now our attention shifts to Page 4 and to placing the last story of the newsletter. We bring the Document Layout palette onto the screen through the View menu, double-click on the icon for Page 4, and use the grabber hand (from Alt-drag) to slide the page to the center of the window. At the Tool palette, click on the text box Tool button, then draw-drag a box within the margins of the half of the page above the rule. After making sure that the text cursor is flashing there, we use the Paste command and see the text of the San Francisco piece flow into place, as shown in Figure 5.29.

We specify *2* in the Cols field. Next we'll have a look at the text. We select it all (Ctrl-A) for adjusting style and format. Now, what is immediately clear is that at 12 points, the text will not all fit into the box we've drawn. Also clear is that we have three points we want to call special attention to. We choose to cut out the first paragraph and make it into a heading, we quadruple-click to select it, and cut (Ctrl-X). We pull down the top of the text box by the middle handle to shorten it and make room for the Heading box. (Of course, this generates more text overrun, but we'll come back to that problem soon.)

Now, we click on the text box button at the Tool palette and draw another text box the width of both columns above the copy already in place. The cursor appears in it and we transfer the first paragraph text by pasting (Ctrl-V). Once we key in changes that edit it into headline form, we select all (Ctrl-A) and change font and size to Arial, 24 point. We then use the down arrow to reduce the leading to 22 points. *Voila!*—we have a proper headline for the piece.

Newsletters on the Job ♦ **121**

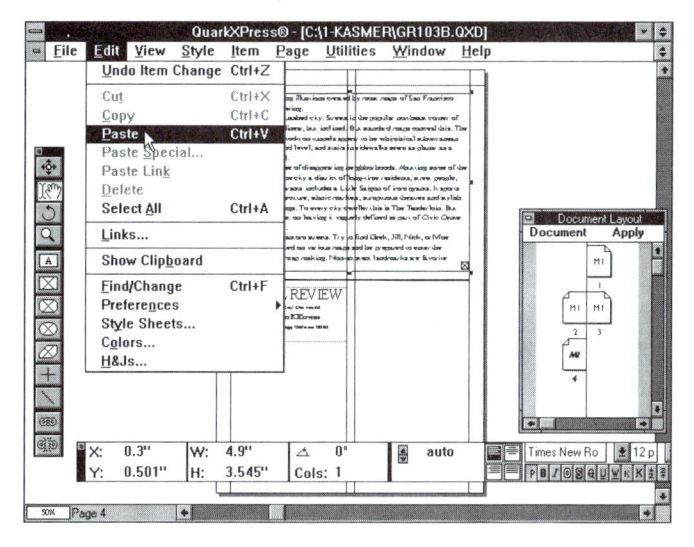

Figure 5.29 *Page 4 story pasted.*

In order to highlight each of the three points in the text, we drag-select the phrase leading into each paragraph and apply bold style through the Measurements palette button (B). As we look at our layout in Figure 5.30, the x in the lower-right corner of the text box indicates that the overrun problem is still with us. To fit in all the body text, we choose to reduce the font size. (Since we're leaving the leading at Auto, this will reduce the line spacing concurrently.) Experimenting with values typed into the selected size field in the palette, we arrive at the size, 11.2 points, that allows the text of the San Francisco piece to fit without being noticeably different in size from the basic body copy in the newsletter. Figure 5.31 shows the final version of Page 4.

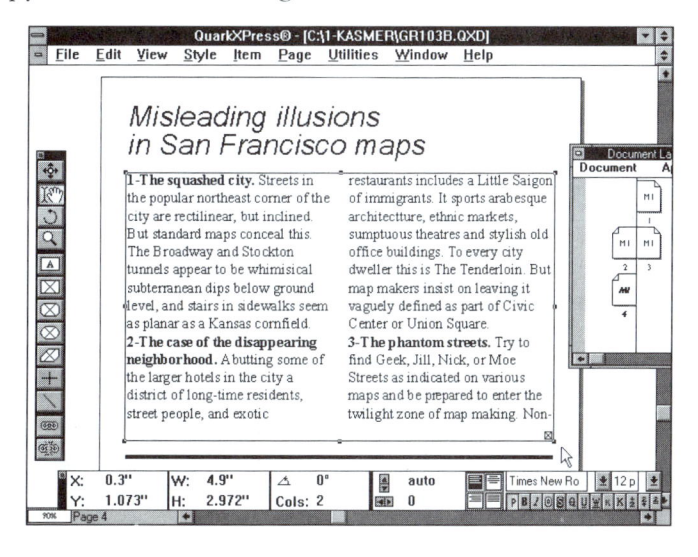

Figure 5.30 *Text overrun on Page 4.*

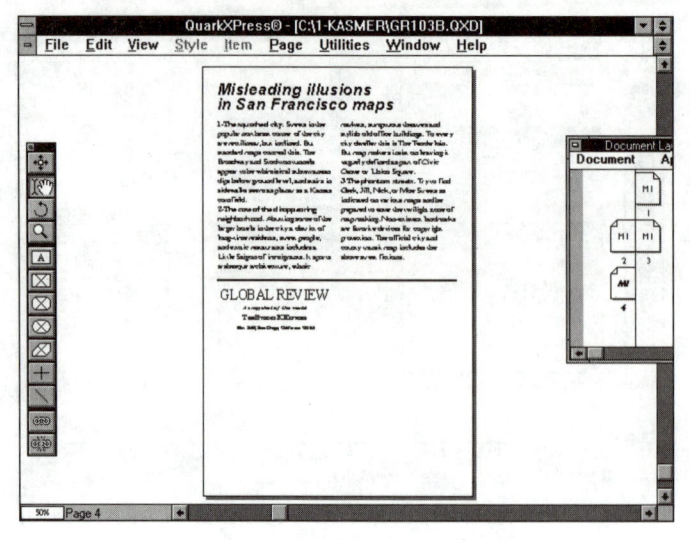

Figure 5.31 Page 4 completed.

ADVANCING

In developing these newsletter layouts, we've seen how basic text features can be managed in QuarkXPress. We have by no means explored all the typographical features of the program. Chapter 8 will reveal much more about global-document features, formatting, style sheets, linking text and precision controls. At this point, however, we've established a solid basis for using the program's text features.

The next logical step is to see what QuarkXPress can do with graphics and the graphical features of both text and pictures. From there, we can apply these features to handle graphics, and to accomplish more with text in all our documents.

Chapter 6

Pictures, Boxes, and Interaction

What You Will Learn in this Chapter

- How to use picture boxes
- How to import graphics
- How to crop, size, and shape boxed images
- How to skew and rotate pictures
- How to reverse text
- How to align items
- How to set text runaround
- How to chain text boxes

Every element on the page can be considered a graphic, even text. Drawings, photographs, rules, even black type flowing in columns on white paper create imagery. QuarkXPress recognizes the graphics nature of every item in a page layout, whether it is formed by text or pictures.

In this chapter we examine the graphic features of both text and illustrations as they appear in the document. We'll see which images can be brought into the program and how, the ways to size and crop them, and the effects that their presence can have on other page elements. We will begin to learn how to use guides and rulers, and uncover the text runaround properties inherent in all items. We'll look into aligning, layering, and framing, as well as locking and rotating items and their contents.

To put all these qualities and controls in perspective, let's start with an investigation of the images that can be brought into a document.

Pictures

QuarkXPress sees any imported content as either text, which we've already begun to explore, or pictures, more generally referred to as **graphics** or illustrations. Text and pictures, though mutually exclusive as content types, share many traits—and exhibit some marked differences.

Unlike text, picture content cannot be generated directly inside QuarkXPress. While you can set up QuarkXPress documents that function adequately for word processing, you would be hard-pressed to do the same for generating images. On the other hand, you'll find a broad range of manipulation and enhancement features that apply to pictures imported into the document.

Picture Forms

Let's look at how QuarkXPress provides Item boxes for picture content. The Tool palette is the starting point. Notice the four Tool buttons indicated in Figure 6.1. These are item-creating tools for pictures. They parallel in function the text box tool above them. The one you will probably use the most is the simplest: The basic **rectangle picture box tool** produces square-cornered boxes like those of the text box tool. The other picture box tools all produce boxes that function as alternatively shaped mattes through which canvases of imported graphics can be displayed. To create a rectangle picture box, you select the tool and drag out a box, as you do for a text box.

Your imported graphics files will almost certainly define a rectangular format. This will be true even if the image within a file appears circular or otherwise nonrectilinear. However, the display mattes through which graphics are seen in a document can be infinitely varied.

Pictures, Boxes, and Interaction ♦ **125**

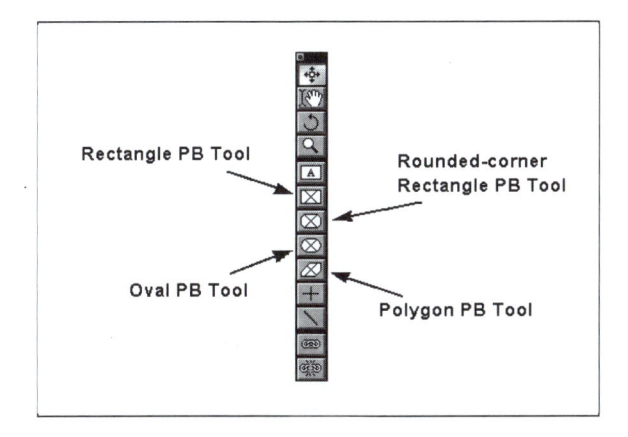

Figure 6.1 *Picture box–generating tools.*

The palette buttons for both the rounded-corner rectangle and the oval picture box tools show general likenesses of the boxes they make. The rounded-corner rectangle boxes are simply variations on the rectangle box. The oval boxes are actually ellipses—that is, regular circles and circles elongated either horizontally or vertically.

Polygon picture boxes, as created with the final box tool, turn out to be much more variable. They are the odd uncles of the picture box family, being the only irregular—that is asymmetrical—shapes. This tool, in fact, creates no particular shape at all, but facilitates the line-by-line drawing of "boxes" composed of multiple sides in variable orientations—triangles, octagons, trapezoids, stars, and a multitude of irregular, flat-sided polygons.

The best way to see what these boxes can do is to see how they contain imported illustrations. A graphic illustration can begin as a file outside of QuarkXPress, like that shown in Figure 6.2.

Figure 6.2 *A graphic file from outside the document.*

Such an illustration may have been produced in a Windows-based graphics program like Paintbrush or CorelDraw. It could have come from a Macintosh platform program such as DeskDraw or ImageStudio. It might have originated from software such as Adobe Illustrator, found in both software platforms. The illustration might have been generated through a screen-capture program such as Collage. It may have come through a scanner system, a digital camera, or a video-frame-capture system.

NOTE The type of file being imported can be Bitmap, TIFF, Encapsulated Postscript, Windows Metafiles, Computer Graphics Metafiles, Scitext, and others. Importable files can be recognized by these filename extensions: BMP, DIB, RLE, GIF, CGM, EPS, PLT, PCT, DRW, PCX, DRW, CT, TIF, and WMF. Most will import directly, but certain of these types require the presence of an import filter in the QuarkXPress directory folder, in the same way text file import filters are required. These special cases are file formats designated by CGM, DRW, and PLT extensions.

IMPORTING INTO PICTURE BOXES

Whatever the file type, whatever the picture, the content is imported into a document in essentially the same way. The illustration in Figure 6.2 has been scanned, adjusted in a graphics program, and captured off the screen as a bitmapped image. Figure 6.2 is a drawing in white on a black background with a narrow white border. Imported into a QuarkXPress document to various boxes, it can be masked in different forms to produce different pictures.

The method for bringing a picture into a QuarkXPress document is as follows. First, draw the box with one of the four picture box tools. Make sure that the box is selected and the content tool is active, open the File menu and choose Get Picture. The displayed dialog box (shown in Figure 6.3) is similar to the Get Text dialog box, and a graphics file can be selected and opened the same way—locate it and double-click. The graphic then appears within the picture box in the document.

> **Importing a graphic**
>
> *Activate a picture box tool and draw a box*
> *Assure the content tool is selected*
> *At the File menu choose Get Picture*
> *Locate the graphic file in the dialog box and double-click*

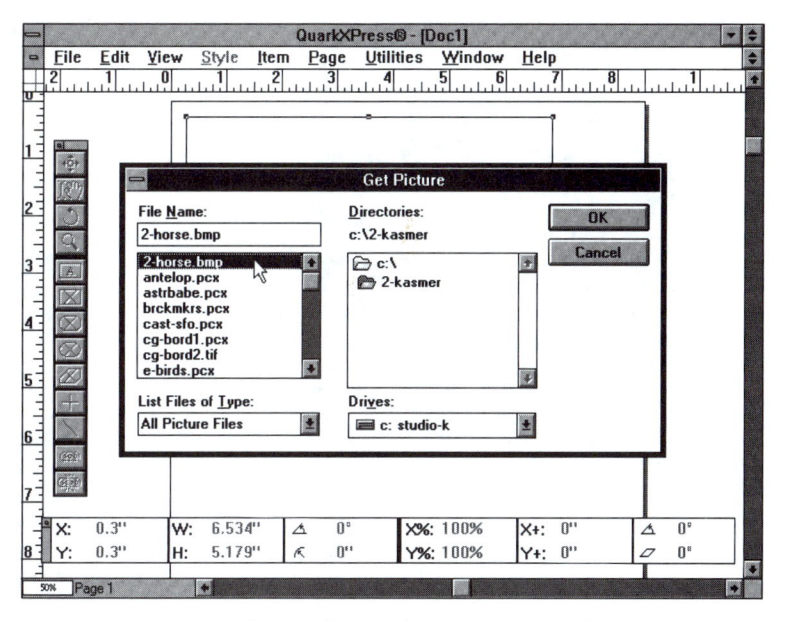

Figure 6.3 Dialog box for importing graphics.

NOTE Notice in the Get Picture dialog box that the drop-down list field labeled List Files of Type: includes all the file formats we discussed, as well as two other settings, All Picture Files and All Files. You can use the format categories to restrict the files displayed in the list above the field. Generally, you might find the All Picture Files a reasonable display for locating the file you're after. When the files collected within a directory become unwieldy in number and type, you can easily restrict your search by limiting the listing to the specific file type that interests you.

When a file is imported to a picture box, as shown in Figure 6.4, it is automatically seated in the upper-left corner of the rectangle that describes that box. In other words, the upper-left corner of the graphic is positioned in the upper-left corner of the box. In the case of Figure 6.4, the original image had a narrow white border around it. In the picture box this border can be seen between the box corner and the image. Note that large white spaces extend to the right and bottom of the picture box (where you see what looks like a grabber hand). This picture box was larger than the picture being imported.

When a picture box is smaller than the incoming graphic, some of the graphic can be obscured at the right and at the bottom. It seems to be cropped off, but it's still accessible, as we shall soon see.

128 ♦ *Teach Yourself...QuarkXPress for Windows*

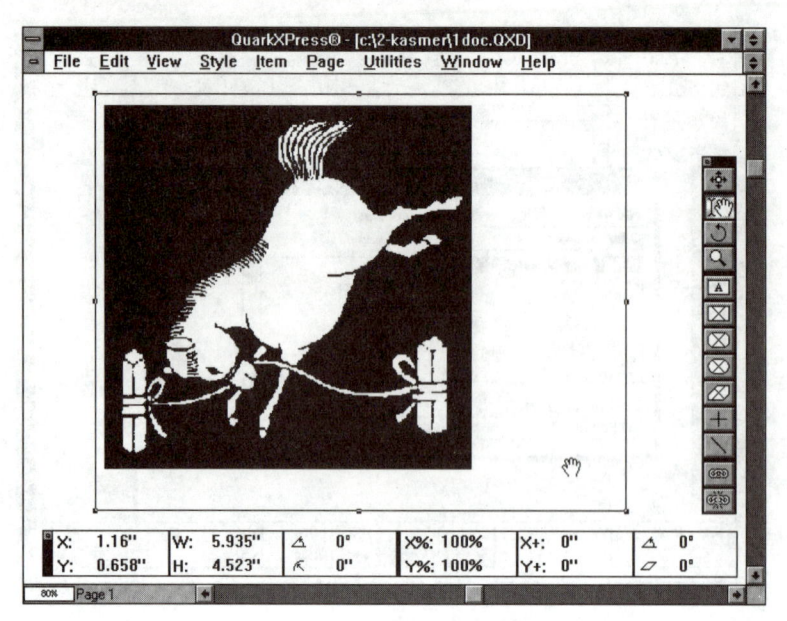

Figure 6.4 An imported image seated in the upper-left corner of a picture box.

As a file is being imported, the page-number indicator in the horizontal scroll bar becomes an indicator of the percentage of the file received, growing as the file is taken in. Often with 100K-or-smaller files, the importation process is so quick that it seems instantaneous (it would seem so on a 386DX 40 MHz computer, for instance). A large file—a scanned photograph of several megabytes, for example—is another matter (especially so on an SX computer running at 16 MHz). This can signal an opportunity to examine your other page proofs, call the printer, or make that postponed trip to the water cooler.

Imported graphics are seated in the upper-left corner in the other types of picture boxes, but in a way that may render them obscured. In Figure 6.5 we see the results of importing the same graphic, 2-HORSE.BMP, into a rounded rectangle and an oval picture box.

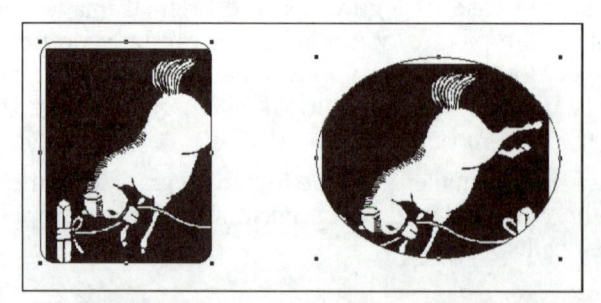

Figure 6.5 Images imported into rounded-corner and oval picture boxes.

Noticeable in both, especially in the oval, is that the upper-left corner of the image is obscured. In fact, QuarkXPress, in using the same graphic-seating scheme, has put the upper-left portion of the graphic against the upper-left corner of the item box that would enclose the picture box. You can visually define this area by noting the set of eight manipulation handles that surround each in a bounding rectangle. The oval, for instance, masks off the horse in an elliptical shape, but it still contains all the graphic underneath the mask.

To create a picture box with either of these two tools, follow the same approach you used with the rectangle picture box, noting that when you drag out a diagonal you are defining the item-area bounding box, which is not quite the same as the oval or rounded rectangle box.

NOTE How rectangular is a rectangle? The rounded-corner box is really just a square-cornered box with an adjustment. That adjustment can be found in the Measurements palette for the picture box. The value is on the item half (left side) of the palette and is indicated by a small quarter-circle with a radial arrow pointing toward it. Look at the value for a rectangle picture box; you'll see it's zero. By keying in a new value you can adjust the corners of either of these box types. This adjustment is also found in the Picture Box Specifications dialog box as Corner Radius.

The final picture box tool to consider creates not one form, but countless forms. The polygon picture box tool might take a little getting accustomed to. Its operation is simple, though. Imagine a shape you wish to form out of straight sides (a star, a lopsided triangle, and so forth). Select the tool and click at one of the corners of the shape. Drag the mouse to an adjacent angle point (noticing that a side stretches into place as you do so) and click there. Continue until you've come full circuit back to the first point, and double-click. This creates a polygon—that is, a many-sided figure. The simplest polygon picture box you can make is a triangle.

Making a polygon picture box

Using the polygon tool, click at each angle in turn

Return to the first click point and double-click

Figure 6.6 shows a polygon picture box made this way in the form of a jagged-topped box. The 2-HORSE.BMP file was imported into it also. Notice that, once selected, the box's manipulation handles are displayed in a rectangular boundary around the polygon shape, and that the horse image as we know it would fit into the upper-left of that boundary.

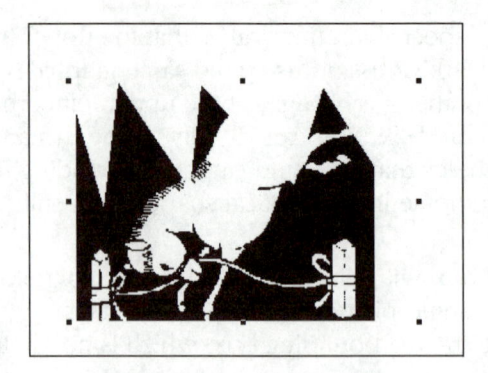

Figure 6.6 *One result of using the polygon picture box tool.*

SHORT CUT   A shortcut for closing the polygon is to double-click at the last angle point. The final side will automatically be drawn back to the first point, completing the picture box .

The contents of a picture box bear the same relation to the box as text to a text box. Similarly, a new image can be imported into a picture box that is selected and filled, replacing existing contents. Contents can likewise be cut, copied, and pasted from one box to another, replacing the images already there.

Picture Cropping, Picture Sizing

Few images are accepted "as is" for page design. Choosing the form of the box enclosing the image is one of your first layout decisions. The ability to precisely select which portion of the image should appear in the layout is another. Like a photographer in the darkroom, we can mask away all that is extraneous, and enlarge or reduce where necessary. (Modifications of the image in contrast, color, and so forth, are also possible. The methods for achieving these modifications will be explained later.)

The elements of graphic treatment include sizing and shaping the picture box, positioning the content image within the picture box, and sizing and shaping the image.

Shaping the Picture Box

A picture box is like a document window, and also like a text box. For instance, you can size the picture box by dragging any of the eight manipulation handles that bound it, just as you can with text boxes. With pictures, enlarging the picture "window" sometimes reveals images or portions of them that are completely hidden after they have been imported—as shown in Figure 6.7, where a single arch visible in a small picture box on the left is seen to be part of a much larger structure when the box is enlarged on the right. If the area visible in a small picture box is just white space, you might be tricked into thinking the image wasn't successfully imported. Figure 6.8 shows just such a situation. None of the twenty-six nautical flags visible in the enlarged box on the right side was apparent when the file was first imported into the box on the left.

Figure 6.7 Effect of enlarging one particular picture box.

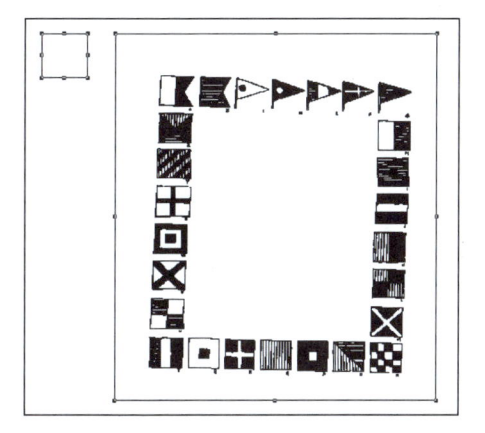

Figure 6.8 An apparently empty picture box enlarged.

If a page design calls for the checkerboard flag seen at the lower right, you could use the box handles to resize the picture box to display only that flag. In this case you could drag the upper-left corner handle diagonally toward the lower right until it bounded the checkerboard flag only, excluding the other twenty-five behind the mask of the shrunken window, as shown in Figure 6.9.

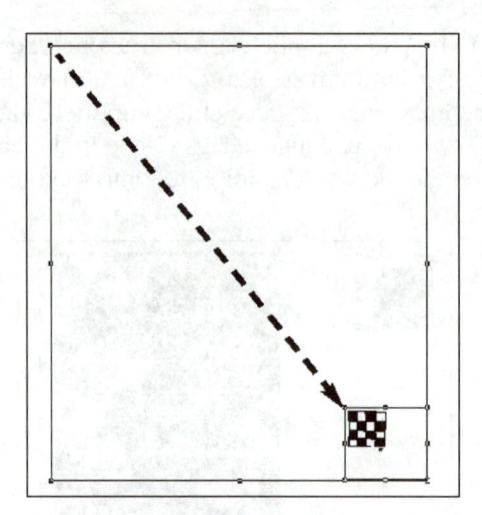

Figure 6.9 *Shaping the window around a part of the image.*

> **NOTE** Be advised that the above method can sometimes lead to enormous document files. Keep in mind that we have imported a representation of the entire image file in order to use a small portion of it. Note that the document will grow by a size determined by the entire image representation, not just the part displayed. Individually displaying—in different text boxes—each of the twenty-six flags would result in a document file with twenty-six times the kilobytes devoted to graphics in it. If the original image file is large—a scanned gray-scale photograph of two or three megabytes, for example—the resulting document file could threaten to overwhelm some already burdened hard-disk drives. It would also drastically increase processing time during printing.

When document size must be kept within certain limits, you can cut the sections out of the original image file in a graphics-manipulation program and save each section as a separate image file. These sectioned files can then be imported to the QuarkXPress document where specifically called for. This takes more time, of course, so it is appropriate only when limiting document size is more important than saving time.

THE PICTURE GRABBER

In the preceding section we changed a small picture box at one corner of the image to a large, all-encompassing box, and then back to a small picture box over a different part of the image. Basically, we moved the view through the picture box. The content grabber hand tool does the same thing. It works within the picture box as the grabber hand works in a document window. When the content tool is put over a selected box, the hand cursor appears.

To use the picture grabber, position the content tool over a selected picture box and press the mouse button, then drag the picture within the box, sliding into view the portion to be displayed. For example, the image of birds in the rectangular graphic shown in Figure 6.10 was imported into the small oval picture box—shown below it on the left. Using the picture grabber, the image was moved within the oval until the seated bird came into view, as seen in the oval on the right.

Figure 6.10 Cropping with the picture grabber hand.

Using the picture grabber

Position the content tool over the picture box

Drag the image through the window

The picture grabber is especially useful in conjunction with your ability to adjust the extent of the picture box around an image. In fitting a scanned photograph of a person, for instance, you can perform cropping by pulling down the top side of the picture box to exclude some sky in the background, and use the grabber to position the image of the person so it appears to be balanced in the box.

The picture grabber hand is useful for precise positioning within a box, but it is by no means the only way to move an image. The Measurements palette often provides a handy alternative, monitoring and controlling the shift of an image from its original seating at the upper-left of the picture box's bounding box. These values are labeled there as X+ and Y+. Keying in new values will shift the image within the box.

Shaping and Sizing the Image

The third important manual control for pictures is sizing the image within the picture box. As you know, dragging a box handle simply allows you to extend or reduce the box's window without affecting the image. Changing the image's size and shape, however, is an ability we'll need if we're to make use of graphics within a document file.

Fortunately, this is as easy as reshaping the picture box. To resize an image residing inside a picture box, hold down the Ctrl key while dragging one of the box handles. The image will grow as the picture box grows. Note that if you pull disproportionately in one direction, the image will be distorted, appearing squashed or stretched. The North American tribal mask in Figure 6.11 is shown (left to right) first as it was imported, next as it was after a Ctrl-drag in the downward direction only, then as it was after a Ctrl-drag in the rightward direction only.

Figure 6.11 *Reshaping the image in two directions.*

Reshaping, resizing the picture image

Ctrl-drag the picture box handles

A more numerical approach is to use the right side of the Measurements palette, which affects content. There you'll find two values, labeled X% and Y%, that monitor and control the amount of stretch and compression in the horizontal and vertical directions, respectively. Note that this will expand or reduce the image within an unchanging picture box, and will almost certainly require repositioning the image within the box.

It's easy to see how after a series of adjustments by dragging the image, and positioning with the picture grabber, the picture on the page can get away from an experimenting designer. Two picture features, useful in their own right, are available to impose instant order on an image that has grown unruly within a picture box.

These are both keyboard commands. The first resizes and reshapes the image to fit within the picture box, distorting it if necessary. It is activated by selecting the picture box with the content tool, then holding down the Ctrl and Shift keys while pressing F.

> **Instant fitting of image within picture box**
>
> *Ctrl-Shift-F*

The second command resizes the image to its original proportions to fit the picture box. It is engaged by selecting as above, then holding down the Ctrl, Shift, and Alt keys while pressing F.

> **Instant fitting of image proportionally within picture box**
>
> *Ctrl-Shift-Alt-F*

Clearly, each of these functions can expedite image arrangement when certain picture box dimensions are to be adhered to. Additionally, they help to pull a picture's image onto center stage, where it can be further manipulated.

BOX CHARACTERISTICS

All boxes in QuarkXPress, whether text or picture boxes, possess certain characteristics that greatly affect their contents. Many of these characteristics are not noticed until they're changed. Others are obvious. Now that you've gained some understanding of text boxes and picture boxes, let's investigate those QuarkXPress features that can most enhance their contents.

Two of these characteristics you've already explored; the Measurements palette will help identify them. Recall how the X and Y values located the horizontal and vertical coordinates of a text box's upper-left corner on the page? These coordinate values have the same significance for boxes of text or graphic content.

Likewise, the width and height values can apply to both text and picture boxes. The left half of the Measurements palette monitors item features, as shown in Figure 6.12. We've already seen how you can use the palette as a control device by keying in or selecting values to replace those displayed. This approach can be followed with all the box features.

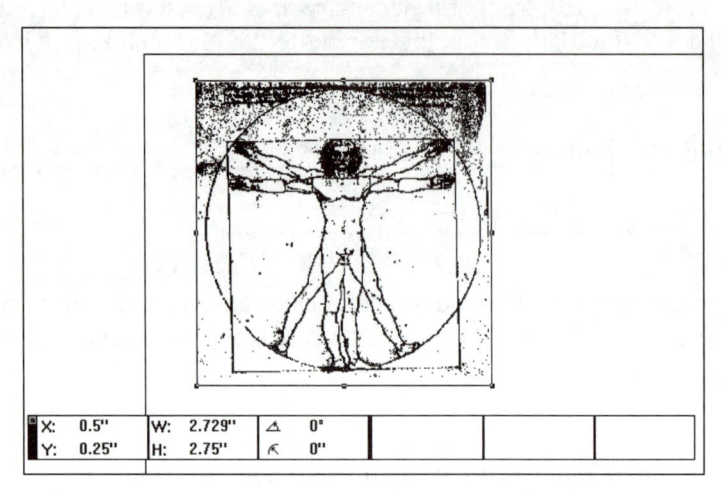

Figure 6.12 The measurements palette monitoring control of box location and size.

Box Frames

Let's look at an altogether different item feature, one common to both text and picture boxes. So far we have let the content of items in our document form their own frames. The alignment characteristics in justified text does this. The white space surrounding picture images does so as well. But the simplest way to make text or pictures stand apart is by drawing a frame around it. QuarkXPress has such a feature. To control the frame around any item box, select the box with an item or content tool, then open the Item menu and choose Frame.

When this is done for the picture shown in Figure 6.12, we arrive at the dialog box shown in Figure 6.13. The apparent absence of a frame here is brought about by the settings in the dialog box. A frame was chosen in the default setting, but the width was set at zero points, and it was automatically applied to the box when it was created. A look around the dialog reveals that four sorts of options are offered: frame type, frame thickness (or width), frame color, and frame shade (or color density).

At the left is a scrolling window of frame types. Seven come with the Windows version of QuarkXPress: a single-line type, three types of double-line frames, and three of the triple-line variety. Clicking on a frame type produces a small replica frame at the top of the dialog box.

Pictures, Boxes, and Interaction ◆ **137**

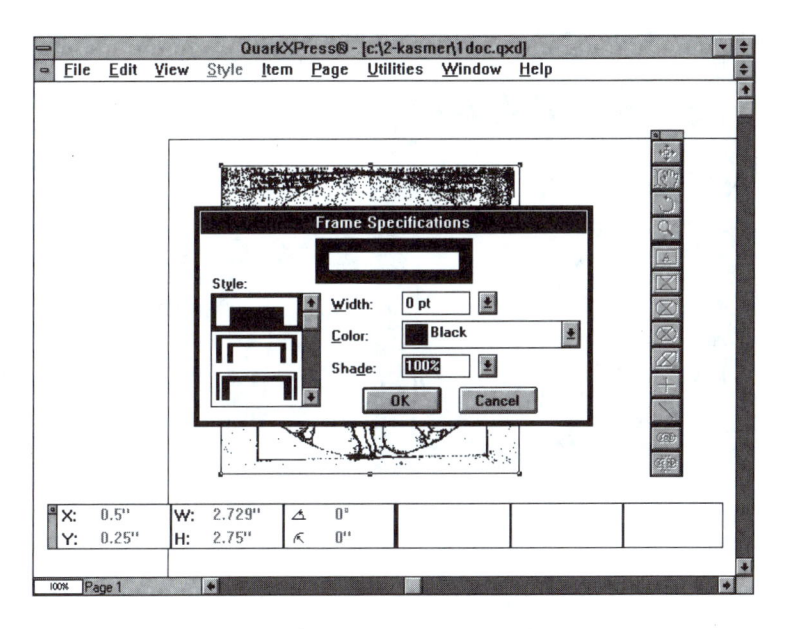

Figure 6.13 The Frame dialog box.

At the right is a drop-down List field for width, with choices to 12 points. You can also type in values not given in this listing, such as 4.5 points or 24 points.

Below is a drop-down list for color, set by default to zero. If you plan to separate colors later, other choices could come in handy.

> **NOTE** Certain colors are made available automatically within the document. These include the RGB colors on which color monitors rely and those of the color model called CMYK. Together they provide the color choices seen on the drop-down list: blue, cyan, green, magenta, red, yellow, as well as black and white, of course. Others can be added, as you will see. (There will be more to say about color in Chapter 16.)

At the bottom is the drop-down list for shade. The percentage chosen (or typed in) for shade is applied to the color chosen in the field above, lightening or intensifying the effect of that color.

Figure 6.14 shows the result of keying in a frame width of 16 points. You'll notice that the frame was applied from the limit of the picture box inward, so that in this case it actually obscures part of the picture image. This method, inside the box, is a default setting that can be adjusted through the Edit menu's Preferences choice, by choosing General. We'll look into preferences as we move along.

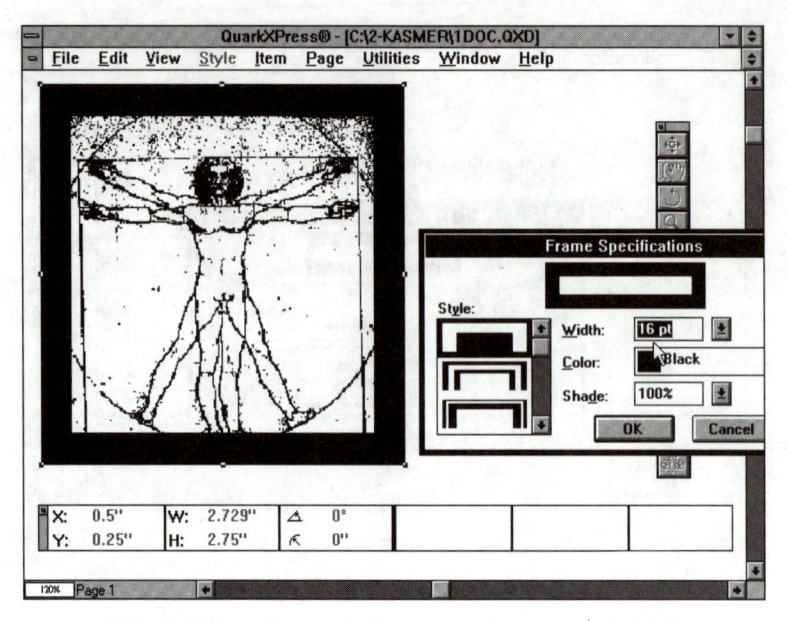

Figure 6.14 *A frame of 16 points applied to a picture box.*

Box Backgrounds

QuarkXPress boxes have another feature that is easily overlooked. It's accessible through the content or item tool, and it's set for each text and bitmapped picture box in a document. This is the background. Box backgrounds may vary according to color and shade.

This feature is often overlooked because the default is normally set to white, and text and images coming into boxes are most often black. However, a background need not be white. To change it, select the box by item or content tool, open the Item menu and choose Modify. A dialog box titled Text Box Specifications or Picture Box Specifications will appear, depending on the item. The Modify command automatically presents a different dialog according to the type of item that has been selected.

Figure 6.15 shows one such example. Although a host of apparently unfamiliar values seem to occupy this box, you'll find at least half of them have already come under your control using the manual and Measurements palette methods described earlier. We shall return to all these values later. For now, look directly to the lower-right corner of the dialog box, where the background controls are. The adjustments are simple. Color can be set to any of those available in the drop-down list. The shading of any selected color can be fixed at values between 0 percent and 100 percent, chosen from the drop-down list or keyed into the field. The same Background section is available in the Specifications dialog box for both text and picture boxes.

Pictures, Boxes, and Interaction ◆ **139**

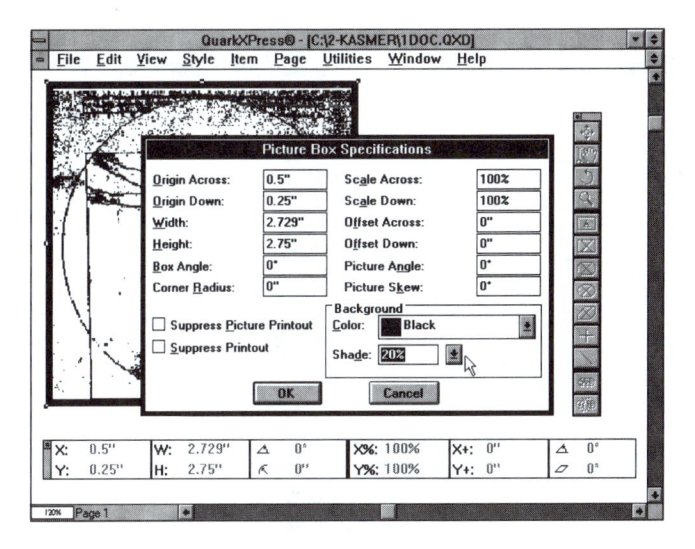

Figure 6.15 The Picture Box Specifications dialog box.

In Figure 6.16, the picture box background has been set to Black, 20 percent while the background of the text box next to it has been adjusted to Black, 10 percent, each by using the Item menu's Modify command.

Figure 6.16 Setting different backgrounds in adjacent boxes.

NOTE Working with pictures, text, and lines, you will notice that the dialog boxes and even the menu listings change according to what type of item is selected. This can be disorienting if you think you've chosen a picture item and are presented with typographical choices. Most notable is the change in the Style menu, which is really a switchable control, altering its menu listing behind the scenes as either line, text, or picture is selected. Figure 6.17 shows the three variations of the Style menu. Also significant are the sibling Specifications dialog boxes arising from the Modify command of the Item menu. These different dialogs are shown in Figure 6.18.

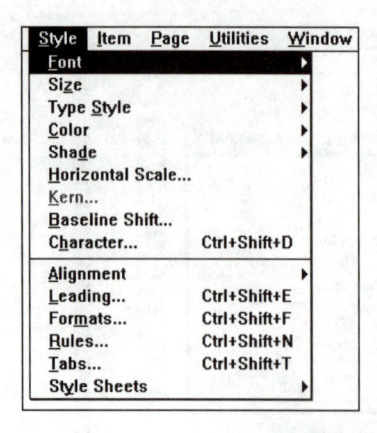

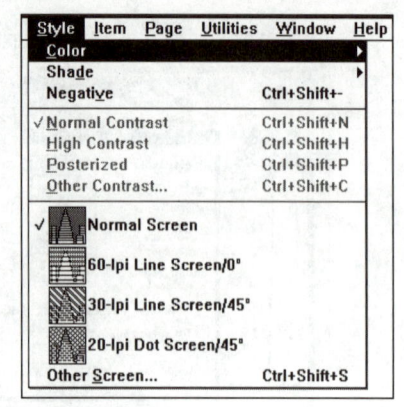

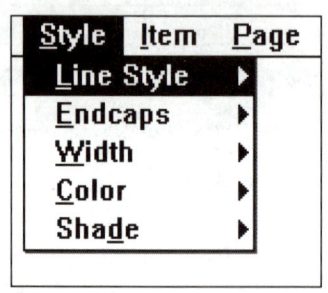

Figure 6.17 *The three versions of the Style menu.*

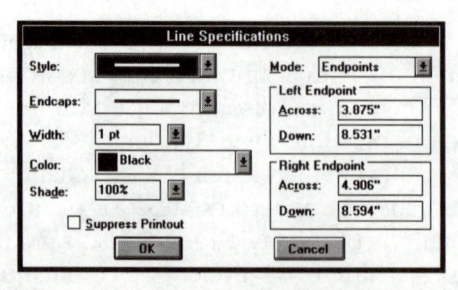

Figure 6.18 *The three variations of the Specifications dialog box.*

SHORT CUT — A quick way to bring up an item's Specifications dialog box is to double-click on that item with the item tool.

Of course, backgrounds can be useful all by themselves. By creating boxes that contain nothing but gray or black backgrounds, for instance, you can include QuarkXPress-generated shadows behind text or picture boxes to make them appear to float on the page.

Picture Content

You can modify picture boxes the same way you would any type of picture. But adjustments to the image within the box can be made only to bitmapped images. As you may know, bitmapped images are composed of pixel dots arranged in a very fine mosaic, in which each square pixel is either black, white, gray, or a color. When QuarkXPress encounters bitmapped images, it is able to perform changes in color, contrast, and so forth. Bitmapped images include files with the extensions, BMP, DIB, RLE, and TIF. Let's look at what we can do with any imported image file.

Content Colors

There are several adjustments that affect the nature of any image, text, or line. One of them is color. QuarkXPress assigns a color to every text, image, and line as it is created or imported. That color, which we take for granted, is black.

But you can assign a color of your choosing to any of the items in a document. Of course, elements in documents destined for color separations definitely require this kind of adjustment. But, as you'll notice, color is useful for indicating nonprinting features on the screen as well. Margin, rule, and grid lines are displayed in distinct colors. Even if you're not planning on printing in color, you can use it to make certain pieces stand out for easy recognition during layout, as you might with a story that is being jumped between several pages. You can color each of several stories differently to see how they play throughout your document.

For the moment, we'll consider color variations of the black-and-white variety. The same principles will apply for all the colors available in QuarkXPress. (Chapter 16 details color use.) We'll begin with the simplest of items, the line. To demonstrate variability, three lines have been dragged across the classic drawing shown in Figure 6.19. The line above the head has been changed to white through the Style menu, Color list; the line at the midsection has been changed to Black on the Color list, 40 percent on the Shades list; the line through the knees to Black, 65 percent.

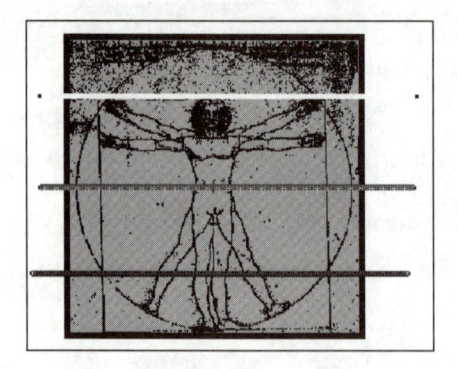

Figure 6.19 Three lines of different color/shade settings.

To change a color, select the item (if picture or text, use the content tool), open the Style menu, open the Color list, and click on the color. To change a shading, do likewise, opening the Shade list and clicking, or choosing Other and keying in a value.

NOTE: Shading choices are *not* available with White, simply because in the "print world" white is the absence of any color.

With picture elements, changes in color and shading can have dramatic effects. Notice how changing the color of the sketch picture to white has given an etched appearance to the image on the left side of the illustration shown in Figure 6.20.

With picture elements, there is another option on the Style menu that changes the image features to the background color and shading, and vice versa. This choice is labeled Negative. It's effects on the image shown in Figure 6.16 are seen on the right side of the illustration shown in Figure 6.20.

Figure 6.20 Effects of applying the color White, and the Negative command.

Reverse Text

It is with text that color and shading adjustments are perhaps most frequently used. Used in coordination with the background controls, text coloring can produce the attention-getting reverse-type effect.

Achieving this sort of typographic "shout" is a two-step process. Begin by selecting the text box with the content tool, then select the text to be reversed. Use the Item menu's Modify command to go to the Text Box Specifications dialog box. There, set the background to Black, 100 percent. Using the Style menu's Color list, choose White for the selected text. The result is white text in a black box, as shown in Figure 6.21.

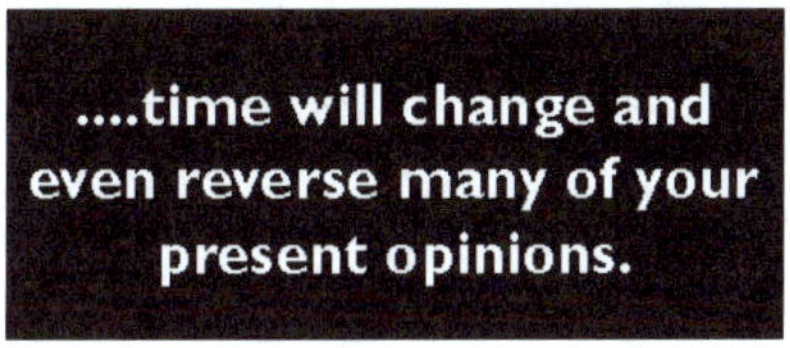

> ....time will change and even reverse many of your present opinions.

Figure 6.21 *Reversed type.*

Reversing type

Select text

Open Specifications dialog box, set background to Black, 100 percent

Open Style menu, choosing Color as White

Instead of choosing white, you could choose a faint shade of a text color, as in Black, 20 percent, though this tends to diminish the reversed text's impact. Note that shading text on a white background can produce interesting headlines and subheads.

ROTATING BOXES

Another feature shared by text and picture boxes is their **orientation**. Typically, we see boxes created in the upright position. For instance, all text begins in lines running horizontally across the page. And imported pictures normally are brought in upright. But the box that encloses type or image need not remain horizontally fixed.

Any picture, any text box can be rotated. You can rotate items from the Measurements palette. You might have noticed a value in the Text palette not yet explained. This is the rotation value for the box, or the **box angle**. In Figure 6.22, two text boxes have been created, one to serve as a simulated note, the other as a caption. The Note box was rotated 15 degrees by selecting that field above the column value in the Measurements palette and keying in the amount. Any box can be similarly rotated, simply by adjusting the box angle in its Measurements palette. Positive values indicate counterclockwise rotation; negative values indicate clockwise rotation.

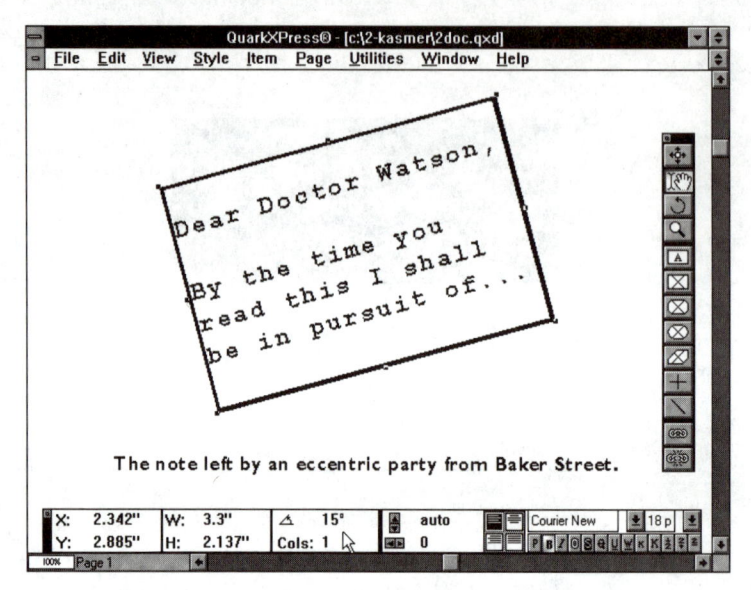

Figure 6.22 *A rotated text box over one not rotated.*

Two other means of rotation exist in QuarkXPress. One is through adjusting the Box Angle value in the Specifications dialog boxes seen earlier. The other is through the **rotation tool**, found below the content tool in the Tools palette. This method is especially suited for those who like the live action of seeing the box and contents roll around on the screen. It's also chosen as the method most likely to leave "detritus images" on the screen, and to bewilder anyone who uses it from time to time. However, as it provides active real-time control, it might be best used when trying to achieve some sort of precise, visual angular fit.

Here's how to use the tool: First, imagine that you're using a lever to turn the box. The lever can be anywhere, inside or outside the box. Select the box. Then using the rotation tool, press the mouse button down at a point that will serve as the fulcrum; a small registration-style image will be displayed. Then, still holding the button down, drag out the lever arm, and lift or pull down around the fulcrum point (with the arrowhead cursor that appears). The box will move as you do. Release the button when you've finished the rotation.

Using the rotation tool

> Select the box
>
> Click a fulcrum point
>
> Drag out a rotation lever
>
> Pull the lever around the point

It's usually wisest to select a fulcrum rotation point *outside* the box, and to drag out a long lever arm to gain the best torque control. Otherwise, you might notice the box moving rather wildly.

In-Box Picture Rotating

In the case of picture boxes, two forms of rotation can be achieved. The second form moves the image within the box *independently* of the box. In Figure 6.23, the picture in the box on the left has been rotated 45 degrees. The picture in the box on the right has also been rotated 45 degrees and the box itself has been rotated -45 degrees. This feature is labeled Picture Angle in the Picture Box Specifications dialog box, and is also located at the extreme right of the Measurements palette.

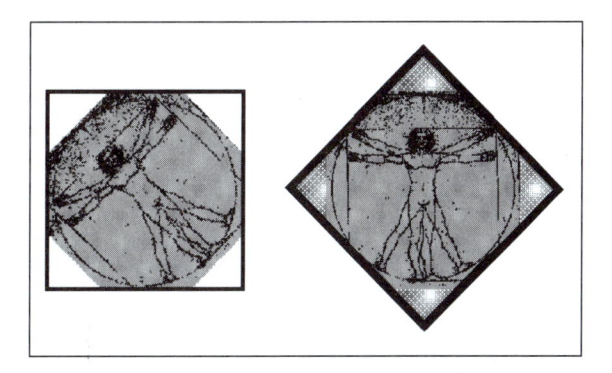

Figure 6.23 *Box rotation and image rotation.*

Picture Skewing

Another feature peculiar to pictures is **skewing**, which is somewhat like dealing with a rubber canvas. The bottom side of the canvas can be imagined to be anchored in place while the top and the two vertical sides are unjoined at their corners, left free to move sideways. If the rest of the canvas were then flexible and the free sides were pulled left or right horizontally, you would see a distortion in one dimension only, or a skew. Figure 6.24 shows an image of the now-familiar Tool palette next to the same image skewed to 45 degrees. Notice how the buttons are at precisely the same heights they were on the original unskewed image, though they have been drastically shifted horizontally.

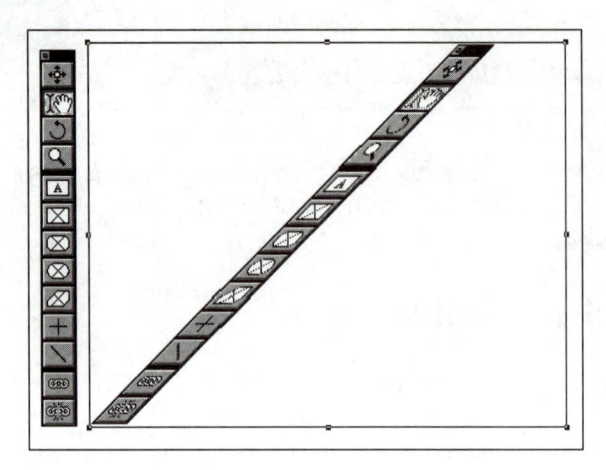

Figure 6.24 *An image and its skewed copy.*

To skew the image in a picture box, select the box with the content tool and key in an angle value in the Measurements palette at the lower-right corner, or in the Picture Box Specifications dialog box. Skewing can be used more subtly to create surprising effects, or to simulate shadows, especially when the color black and shading are applied to the skewed image.

RULERS, GUIDES, AND GRIDS

It's hard to imagine laying out complex pages without the help of rulers and guides. QuarkXPress provides every document window with a pair of rulers that can be displayed or hidden through the View menu Show Rulers/Hide Rulers toggle command. These are active monitors, indicating by faint dotted markers when the item tool is dragging out a selection box, or when an item box is being created or moved. They help when you want a little feedback about your hand-eye coordination on the page. You can adjust the units in which they are marked just as you can adjust the units in which measurements are displayed—by the Preferences commands (which are explained later).

The hidden usefulness of the rulers is their ability to release guidelines that show onscreen (in contrasting color) but don't print. To pull out a guide, point the cursor on the ruler and drag onto the page. A guide will come out of the ruler when you do so. You can pull out as many guidelines as you desire or move guides already in place as you create a design grid.

> **Creating a guideline**
>
> *Assure that the rulers are displayed*
>
> *Point on the rule, oriented as the guideline will be, and drag out a line*

Note that the display of these guides is controlled through the View menu's Show Guides/Hide Guides toggle command. The Snap to Guides feature can be set through the View menu as well.

NOTE The Snap to Guides feature exerts a pull on any item being dragged near a guide. When one approaches within a minimum distance set in Preferences, it is forced toward that guide, its nearest side stopping against the guide. This is a handy, automatic method for quick, precise alignment. You will find, though, many times you'll want to deactivate the feature and turn off its "helpfulness."

How Items Interact

On the page we find that text, pictures, and lines are neighbors to each other. They overlap. Sometimes one box pushes the contents out of another box altogether. When layout juxtaposes elements in close proximity in a design, no item remains unaffected by its fellows.

In what follows, you'll see what effects text, pictures, and lines have on each other, and how these effects can be exploited in fulfilling your design plans.

Monitoring Multiple Items

What happens when more than one item is selected? And what can we do if we've chosen a set of disparate elements like the line, text box, and picture box, shown in Figure 6.25? QuarkXPress treats every set of selected items as though a great bounding box had been established around them all. This imaginary bounding box extends as far as each of the bounding boxes within it. When multiple items are selected, the program monitors and allows control of the origin point (X and Y coordinates), the box angle, and the background of the set of items. In such a case, the origin (the upper-left corner) indicates the position of the great bounding box that would contain all the items.

Look at the Measurements palette or at the Specifications dialog box (from the Modify command) shown in Figure 6.25, and you'll see that the options there have been limited to those few qualities that can be handled collectively.

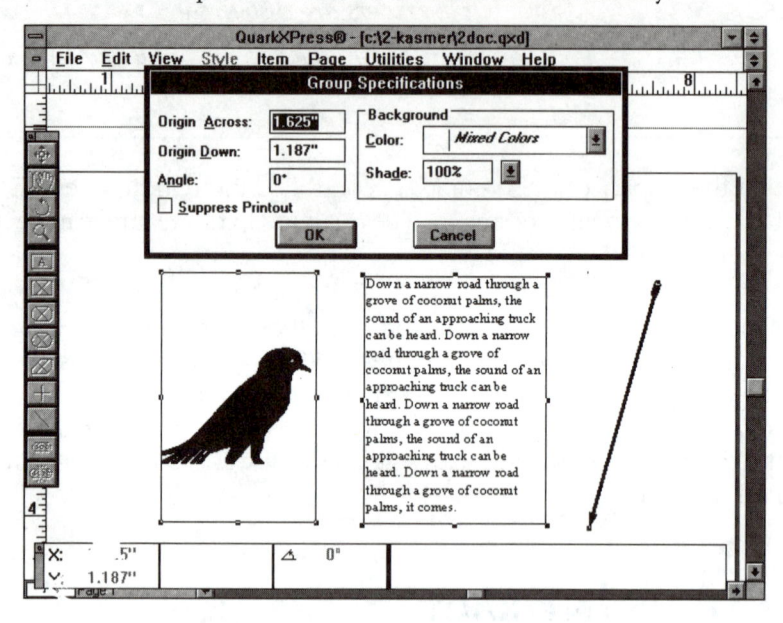

Figure 6.25 *A set of items selected together.*

Aligning and Spacing

Let's consider items on a page. True, they can be positioned and ordered by manual methods. More precise, however, are the automatic methods. QuarkXPress provides a dialog command that allows you to position items in relation to one another. You can specify a vertical or horizontal alignment. You can call for a particular spacing of items on the page. This spacing can be accomplished by measurement, as in setting items so many inches apart, in the range from 0 inches to 10 inches. It can be achieved by percentage (as in moving items to, say, 50 percent of their previous separation, or 200 percent) in range from 0 percent to 1,000 percent. You space items by setting a distance between them, one of their sides, or their centers. You can also direct the program to space the items evenly within the limits set by their farthest members.

The Space/Align command is found under the Item menu. To use it, first select the items, then choose the command. At the dialog box (shown in Figure 6.26) click on the checkbox for the orientation you wish to space: Horizontal, Vertical, or both. If you have a specific separation, make sure that the Space button is engaged before you key in your value. Next, in the Between drop-down list choose one of the four options. (Note that the Space/Align command considers each item as the bounding box that surrounds it.) Click Apply to preview the change, and OK when it's to your liking.

Alternatively, you might have the program arrange for uniform separation of the items selected. Do this by clicking the Distribute Evenly button. (Note that in this case at least three items must be selected.)

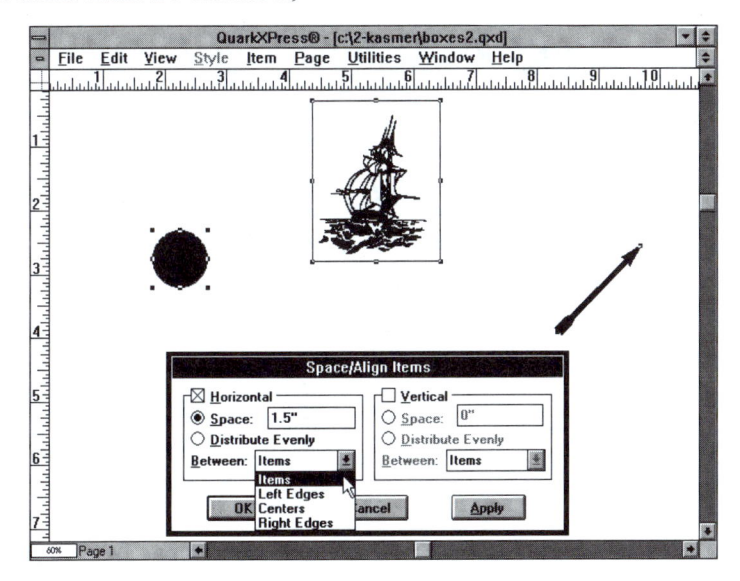

Figure 6.26 The Space/Align dialog box.

When aligning or spacing horizontally, the program will keep the leftmost item fixed and move the others to accomplish the spacing. In aligning or spacing vertically, the uppermost item is kept fixed as the others are moved.

To align items along a horizontal or vertical axis, activate the checkbox that represents the other direction, and key in *0*. In Figure 6.27 for instance, the ball, ship, and arrow were all aligned flush to the top by checking Vertical, keying in *0*, then choosing Between Top edges.

Depths of Layering

Items are added to a document in layers. Layering provides a way to manage images, text runaround, and visually interactive overlays. If you limit yourself to arranging items side-by-side, you'll never deal with layering, and you'll also miss the many functions it provides.

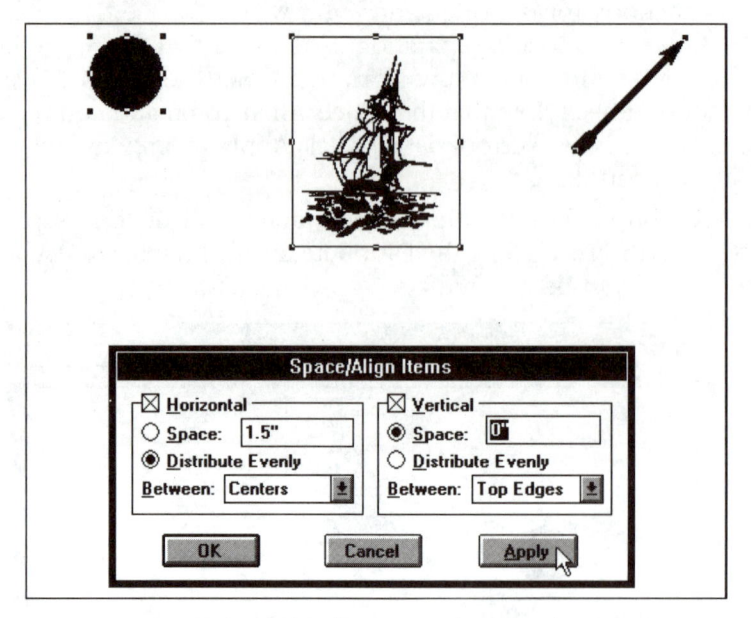

Figure 6.27 Aligning to a horizontal.

As soon as two items overlap, the effects of relative depth become significant. As an item is created, one specific layer is established that belongs to that item alone. Until it is specifically assigned to another layer, it will remain at a certain depth on your document, no matter where it may be shifted horizontally or vertically. The first item created on a page resides in the layer closest to the page. As other items are created, they are put on layers of their own, each above the earlier items. This is demonstrated in Figure 6.28, where first a circle was drawn, then a square, then a triangle.

Item-depth order is established as items are created. But an item may be reshuffled within the layers. Four controls exist for this in the Item menu: sending an item backward one layer at a time, sending it back to the layer closest to the page, bringing it forward in steps, and bringing it to the topmost layer.

Note that moving an item to the top layer, for instance, does not put it at the same depth as the item already there. Rather, this action reshuffles the layers so that the item previously on top becomes second to the top.

To move an item to a different layer, select it and choose the appropriate command from the Item menu.

Pictures, Boxes, and Interaction ♦ **151**

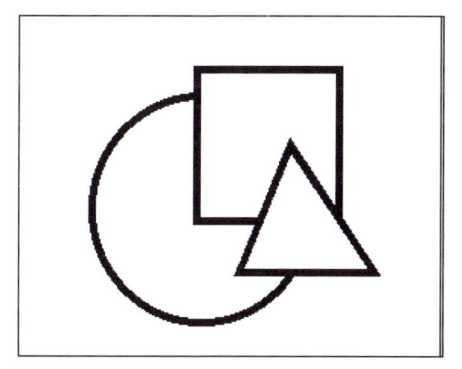

Figure 6.28 *Layering depths created when a circle, then square, then triangle are drawn.*

In Figure 6.29, the triangle is shown being sent to the backmost layer using the Send to Back command. In layering, background becomes especially significant. Although the backgrounds, White and None, often look identical, the former *obscures* items behind it, the latter *reveals* them.

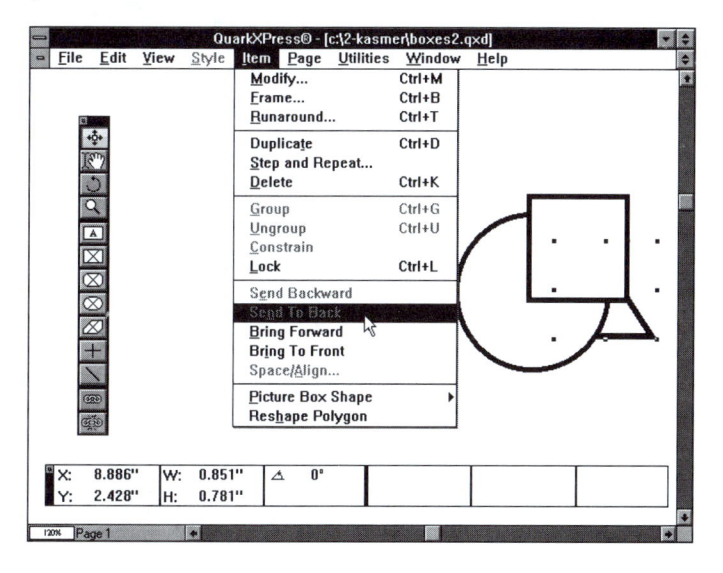

Figure 6.29 *Sending an item, the triangle, to the lowest layer.*

Text Runaround

Every item in a document bears a special relationship to text with which it comes into contact. Text reacts when it flows into space occupied by some other item. It may write over the item, flow around the item, flow around the bounding box of the item, or be otherwise redirected in its layout. This effect is known as **text runaround**.

There are two conditions that determine when text flow will be affected by another item: when the text box sits on a layer behind the item, and when the item has a runaround applied to it. Using the layer control discussed above, you can easily satisfy the first of these conditions. The second is adjustable through a dialog box when the item is selected. Although there are countless variations of effects, they all come from one of four settings in QuarkXPress. Figure 6.30 shows the Runaround Specifications dialog box, which is reached through the Item menu by choosing Runaround.

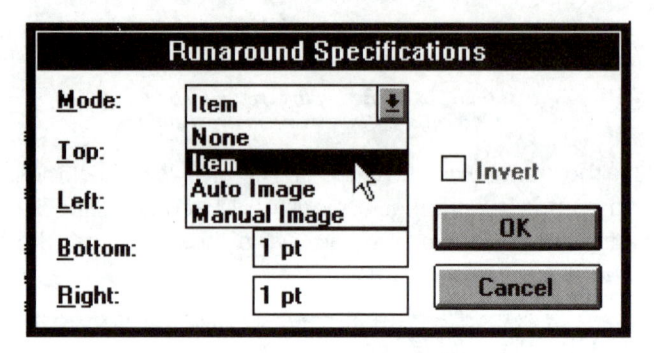

Figure 6.30 *The Runaround Specifications dialog box.*

Figure 6.31 shows two modes of text runaround. The text on the left has simply run over the picture image. In this case there was no runaround in effect; the runaround mode was specified as None. The text on the right has flowed around the rectangular bounding box of the image. Here the runaround mode was specified as Item.

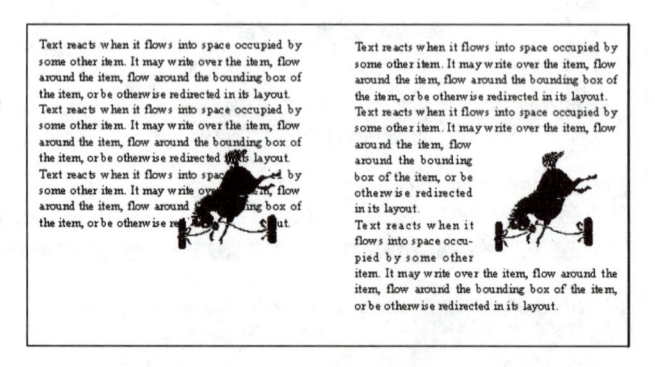

Figure 6.31 *Runaround Modes: None and Item.*

In the Runaround Specifications dialog box, four fields—labeled Top, Left, Bottom, and Right—sit below the Mode field. Each designates the offset of text from the object in question—that is, how close text can be to the object before it breaks to the next line. Be aware that QuarkXPress will flow text lines only to one side of the runaround object. The program is designed to make a line-by-line determination of which side provides the most horizontal space, and to place the text on that side.

Establishing text runaround

Assure the runaround item is selected and above the text

At the Item menu choose Runaround, select the Mode and set the offset spacing

---

Two other modes of runaround are shown in Figure 6.32. The left side gives an example of Auto Image mode. Here QuarkXPress detects the extent of the image and wraps it in a kind of unseen fence to which the text is allowed to approach each line according to the offset value entered in the dialog box.

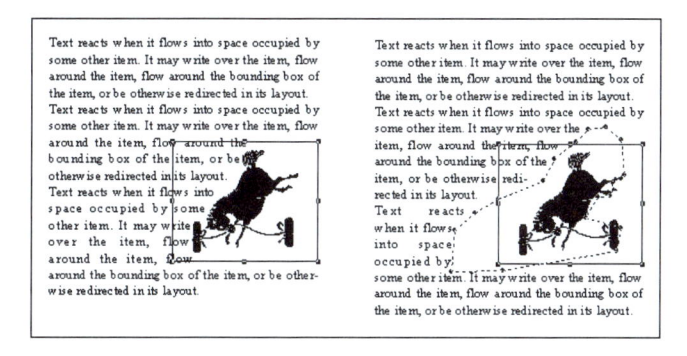

Figure 6.32 *Runaround Modes: Auto Image and Manual Image.*

The right side shows what happens with Manual Image mode—and a bit of tinkering. In Manual Image, the "fence" is displayed in the form of a runaround polygon, complete with handles connecting line segments. You can move a handle or a line by clicking on it and dragging. That's just what was done in the figure. By holding down the Ctrl key and clicking you can insert new handles, or remove existing ones. You can drag the runaround polygon sides and handles anywhere, inside or outside the item bounding box.

Adjusting a manual image

Drag the side or handle into place

Add or remove handles by Ctrl-click

Text Box Linking

Since we're dealing with relations among items, one special area deserves attention: the connection between one text box and another. We've seen picture boxes, lines, and text boxes interacting on the page, most often as a result of proximity. A different sort of association arises between some text boxes, one that is independent of nearness or visual connection: **text chaining**.

We've already seen that QuarkXPress's automatic text box feature generates a flow of text through boxes on different pages. In fact, you can direct the flow of text through *any* set of boxes in a document. Should the boxes be moved, resized, made to runaround, or otherwise modified, the linkage you've established will stay intact unless you break it. And you can break the linkage at any point of a chain and establish it through some new text chain.

Here then is the means for jumping stories from Page 1 to Page 23—or for fragmenting text to create an ad that jogs the reader's eyes through a design, or for trying page-layout possibilities when your text exceeds the limits of a text box. In the last chapter we let QuarkXPress establish this link automatically in the letterhead version of Global Review. Now we're doing it manually. You can link boxes that contain text or ones that don't. (Text can be added after linking.) We'll use the Linking tool. Second from the bottom on the Tools palette, this tool resembles three joined chain-links.

To link text boxes, choose the Linking tool at the palette, and click on the text box in which the text flow originates, or will originate. A dashed-line bounding box will appear around it. Then click on the box that is second in the text link. A gray arrow will appear, tailfeather in the first box, arrowhead in the second. If there are more boxes to be added to the chain, simply click on them in succession. An arrow will appear between each pair of linked boxes. The text will be chained to flow through the boxes successively in the order that the links were established.

> **Establishing a text chain**
>
> *Using the Linking tool click on the first box in the chain*
> *Click on every other box in order*

Any time the linking tool is chosen after a box is selected by content or item tool, the arrows indicating links between all the boxes will appear, and the chain of text flow will become visible, as shown in Figure 6.33. If the boxes are empty of text and you click content in any box in the chain, all the boxes in the chain will display as though active, but the cursor will appear in the first box.

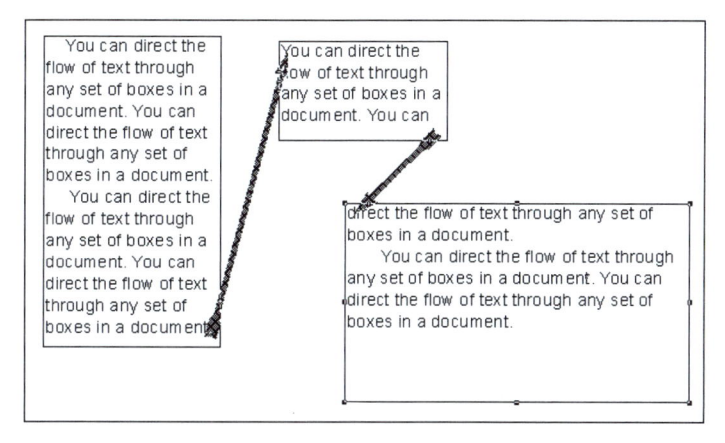

Figure 6.33 Linked text boxes forming a text chain.

Once you've established a text chain, you can include another text box within that chain, even in the middle of it. You do this by using the link tool. First click on the box already linked (box A, let's say), then click on the box you wish to include in the chain (box B, let's call it). The result will be a linkage through the new box (showing arrows from box A to box B to the box that previously followed box A in the chain).

Linking a text box in an existing text chain

Using the Linking tool click on the box before the insertion point

Click on the new text box

Text Box Unlinking

Breaking up a text chain can be done surprisingly quickly. Choose the unlink tool from the palette, and click on the arrowhead or tailfeathers pointing to the box at which you'd like to sever the link. Be sure to aim carefully. That box and all that follow will then be disconnected from the chain. All text that may have run through them in a story will be consigned to the boxes upstream that remain in the chain.

Breaking a text chain

Select the Unlinking tool

Click on an arrowhead or tailfeather

You might want to remove only one box from the chain, while keeping boxes downstream still in the text flow. Holding the Shift key, use the Unlinking tool and click on the unwanted box. It will go empty and the arrows will bypass it as they point onward through the downstream part of the text chain.

> **Removing one box from a text chain**
>
> *Select the Unlinking tool*
>
> *Shift-click on the unwanted box*

STEPPING FORWARD

You've covered text, pictures, and boxes. You're ready to apply the preceding methods to some layout challenges. In Chapter 7 you'll prepare two documents, putting to work the skills with items, pictures, and interactions that you've learned so far.

Chapter 7

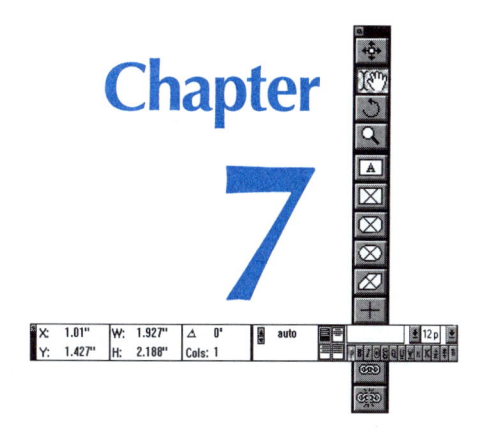

Guides on the Job

WHAT YOU WILL LEARN IN THIS CHAPTER

- How to lay out pictures with text
- How to apply picture adjustments in a spread
- How to align borders
- How to key text to a picture

In QuarkXPress documents, text and graphics can be made to play off one another to great effect.

In this chapter we follow the development of two guides. The first is a piece designed as part of a brochure to generate interest in the newly opened wing of a museum by summarizing the exhibits there. The second uses similar files to different effect; it's a section of a walking guide to be used by exhibit-goers. As these pieces are assembled, the techniques of previous chapters will be used to juxtapose picture and text elements. The underlying intent of each piece is to lead readers by coordinated visual and verbal cues. Our task is to use QuarkXPress to supply the coordination.

THE GUIDE BROCHURE

Imagine someone saying to you, "Here are several bitmapped images and a text file. Now make a two-page spread that will be the interior of a brochure to promote our new exhibition." That's the task put to us in this first document.

We decide to make a largely graphic display, since the pieces are what interest these museum-goers most. We're going to include a border that bleeds to the edge of the page, but we want the main elements in the design to be contained at least .75 inch from the edges.

We start by opening the File menu and choosing New, then clicking on the Facing Pages checkbox and setting the margin guides at 0.75 inch for the Top, Bottom, and Outside fields, and at zero for the Inside field. With Page 1 in front of us, we open the Pages menu, choosing Insert, and type *2* (leaving the master page selection created for Page 1). Next we move to the Pages 2 and 3 spread with the scroll bars. Figure 7.1 shows the spread with the New dialog box that established its format.

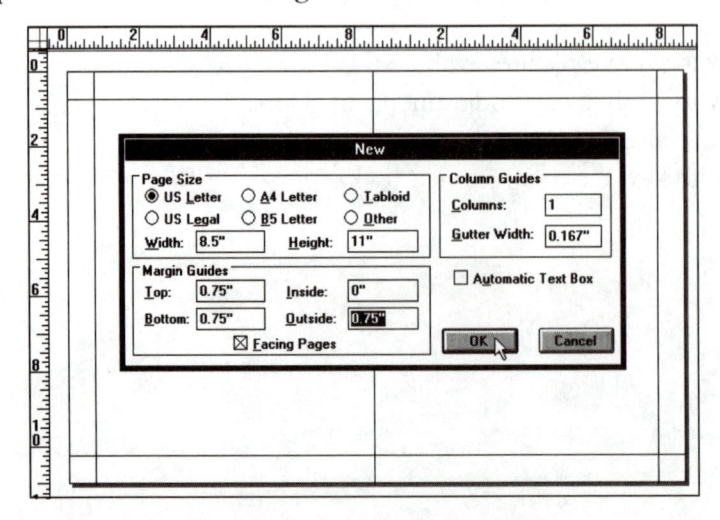

Figure 7.1 *A spread format arising from the New dialog box.*

Now we'll concentrate on setting up our spread design. It is a simple one that sets the text in columns along the lower fifth of the page, distributes pictures in the upper area, and allows for a border to run within the margins. We'll want that border to be offset from the rest of the design by .75 inch. To allocate our spaces and provide for alignment, we pull out guides from the rulers to all these limits. From the vertical ruler we pull two guides, one to the .5-inch and another to the 8-inch mark on the horizontal ruler.

Normally, pulling from the ruler produces a guide that extends across just one page. From the horizontal ruler we'll use a trick that pulls out guides across the whole spread and into the pasteboard. The technique is to pull the guide into a space off the page, into the pasteboard. In this case a guide extends across our spread as we pull it into an area of pasteboard showing at the right of the spread.

> **Pulling a guide that extends across a spread**
>
> *Point the cursor in the horizontal ruler above the pasteboard*
>
> *Pull directly down*

The first item added to the spread will be the text box at the bottom. We want it at the bottom, but not all across the bottom, because we're planning on putting a title at the lower right. We want to put a text box that would fit into a six column grid across the spread. Since we want to use some of the space for the title, we'll fit in five columns, leaving what amounts to the sixth column empty. The text box will then occupy three columns on Page 2 and two columns on Page 3. By dragging out a text box within the bottom space, but limiting its extent on the right side of Page 3, we create such a text box. The centerfold will be our guide as we adjust the box. We pull out to the right so that the column gutter falls centered over the break, as indicated by the arrow shown in Figure 7.2.

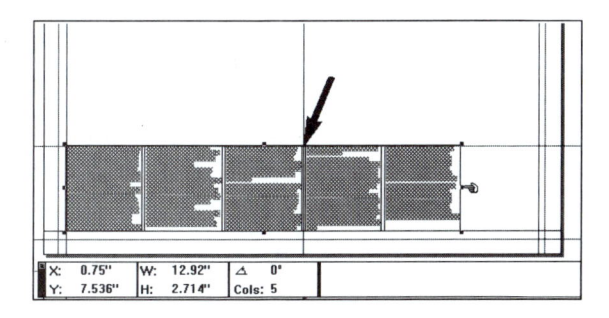

Figure 7.2 *Positioning a five-column box in a six-column grid.*

Text is next imported through the Get Text dialog box. (This text is partly dummied and will serve as a place-holder for the final file.)

Next, we put the title in place by drawing out a text box and typing *The Egyptian Hall*. After some experimenting, we use the Measurements palette to adjust the text to Arial, 26 point. We use the Frame dialog box choice under Item to apply a 1 point simple frame. Then we call up the Text Box Specifications dialog box. To do so quickly we hold down the Ctrl key, which gives us temporary partial item tool functionality. Then we use the double-click method to open the Specifications dialog box.

> **Momentarily switching to the item tool**
>
> *With any but the zoom tool engaged, hold down the Ctrl key*

At the Specifications dialog we key in a value of *8 pt*. in the Text Inset: field to bring our text away from the frame. This inset pushes our title text, *The Egyptian Hall*, down and to the right slightly, as shown in Figure 7.3. We leave the text area for the moment to bring the graphics files onto the spread.

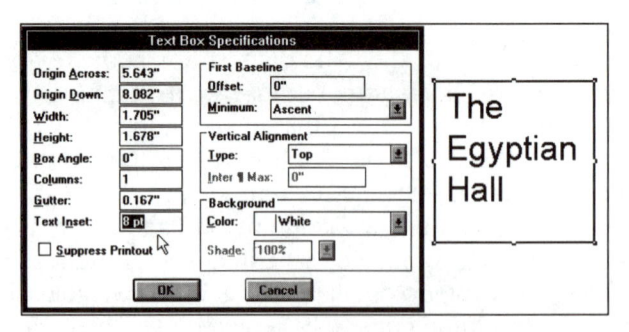

Figure 7.3 *A text box added to the grid.*

After following the draw picture boxes then Get Picture approach for the first three files, we can see that the images coming in are so large that our spread could never accommodate the whole lot at that scale. We thus drag the boxes smaller, using the Ctrl-Shift-Alt-F keyboard command to force-fit each image proportionately into each box in turn.

Now we have all the picture boxes (with images centered within them) positioned roughly around the spread, as shown in Figure 7.4.

NOTE: What QuarkXPress interprets as an image might not coincide exactly with our idea. The useful image could be surrounded by stray pixels or a large white space. Individual adjustments will be required at each box.

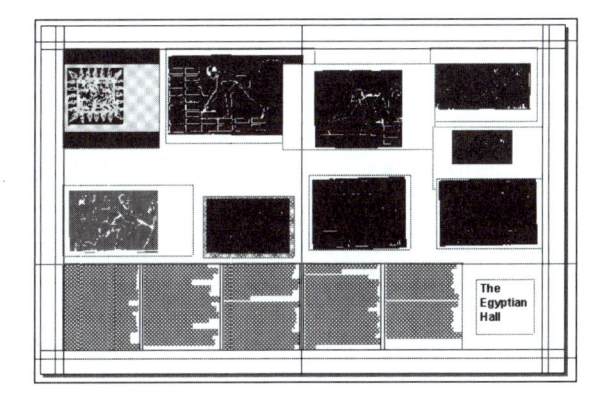

Figure 7.4   Roughly positioned picture boxes.

We turn first to the picture box in the upper-left corner. To enlarge the image proportionately, we select the picture box with the content tool, then change the X% and Y% values to 60 percent each. Then we drag on the box handles until the box encloses the image tightly, and use the grabber hand for finely positioning the image within the box. The result is shown in Figure 7.5. The importance of pulling the box in to a tight fit will become apparent when we apply the Space/Align command. (Recall that alignment and spacing are relative to the picture box, not necessarily to the image inside it.)

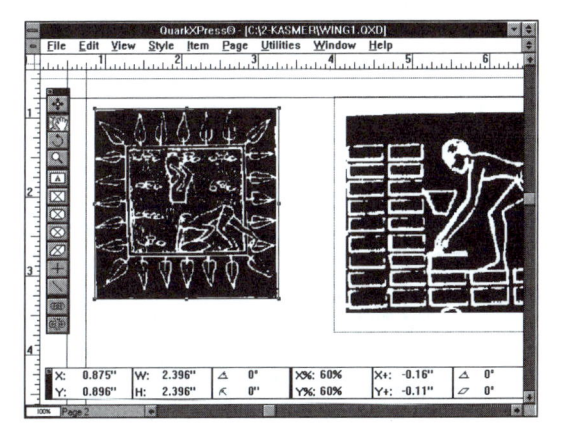

Figure 7.5   Cropping to the useful image.

Following the same approach, we resize and prepare all the remaining picture boxes. Our object is to achieve a pleasing fit and proportion within the space remaining on the spread.

As we turn to the second box (a brickworker facing left), we find, as we size it, that the box next to it obscures our view, so we apply the Item Menu command, Bring to Front, which raises the picture box to the uppermost layer and reveals *all* of the brickworker scene. But now we notice that in trying to size the box, it is being forced toward the centerfold line. This problem is the result of the Snap to Guides feature. We open the View menu and highlight this toggle feature to switch it off. Now we proceed to adjust the bounding box of this second image into a tight image fit of appropriate size.

In making up the page spread, we see that there is a preponderance of landscape-oriented (long-side horizontal) images. To break up this uniformity, we exclude part of an image from view and enlarge the remaining part, as shown in Figure 7.6. The worker on the left is cropped using the box handles to pull the box narrower. Then, to enlarge proportionately, we use the old trick of drawing a diagonal line through opposite corners with the line tool. We next hold down the Ctrl key (to pull the image as we pulled the box) while dragging the lower-right corner of the box along that line to the size we want. Then we delete the diagonal line.

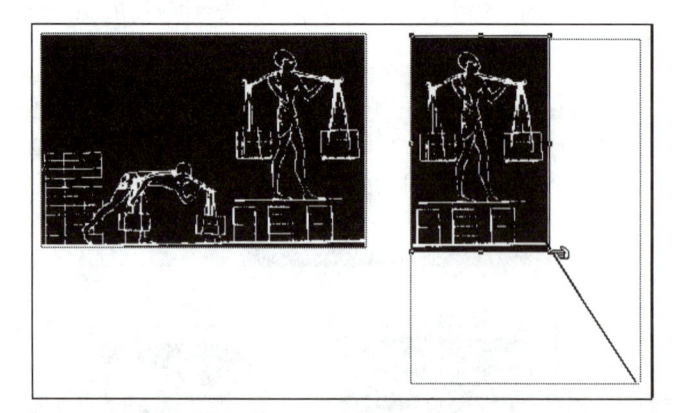

Figure 7.6 *Cropping and enlarging proportionately using a diagonal.*

Scaling a box proportionately by sight

> *Draw a line through and beyond the opposite corners of the box*
>
> *Resize the box by dragging one corner along the line*

Notice that the original images were all white on black, which tends to make the page seem heavy and uniform. To counteract for this effect, we do two things. First we select each box and individually apply color to some of the images through the Style menu. (This, of course, does not show in the Figures here. You can imagine the use of the Color list to set one to Blue, another to Red, and so on.) Remember that the image is the aggregate of black pixels on the screen, not the figures that are represented in white here. So, we change the images to White on Blue, White on Red, and so on. We also change some of the images to shades of gray, using the Style menu's Shade listing.

Second, we take a bit of liberty with the two montage images. As shown in Figure 7.7, by applying the Negative command from the Style menu one at a time we are able to reverse their White on Black to Black on White, reducing some of the black that is weighing heavily on the page.

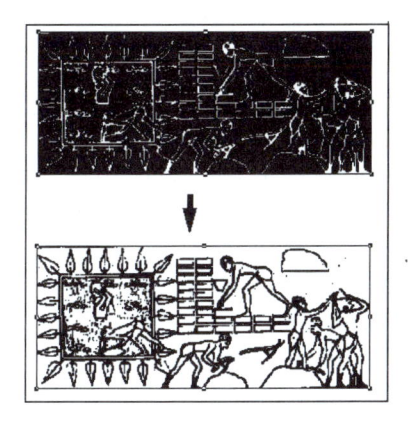

Figure 7.7 *Applying the Negative command.*

Our final task in laying out the pictorial part of the spread involves positioning the picture boxes. For this we will use the top and outside margin guides, in conjunction with the Space/Align dialog box. Recalling that this command anchors the item in the upper-left area of a set of items, we first move that item into the upper-left margin corner. To help with this, the Snap to Guides feature is reactivated in the View menu. Then, at a Fit in Window view we drag the item enough to let it snap into place. Now, since we want even spacing of picture items across the top from the left-to-right margin, the rightmost item is dragged until it too snaps into place against the right guide line. (Its vertical positioning is unimportant for the moment.)

By dragging an enclosing box with the item tool, we select all the picture boxes at the top of the spread and, opening the Item menu, choose Space/Align. Figure 7.8 shows the dialog box with this arrangement. We've used the Apply button to make sure that the spacing is just what we want. Since we seek to have all the boxes flush with the top margin, the Vertical checkbox is clicked and a Space value of zero is left in the field. From the Between: list, Top Edges is selected. Because we want the pictures evenly spaced across the spread, the Horizontal checkbox is clicked and the Distribute Evenly button is engaged with the Between setting at Items.

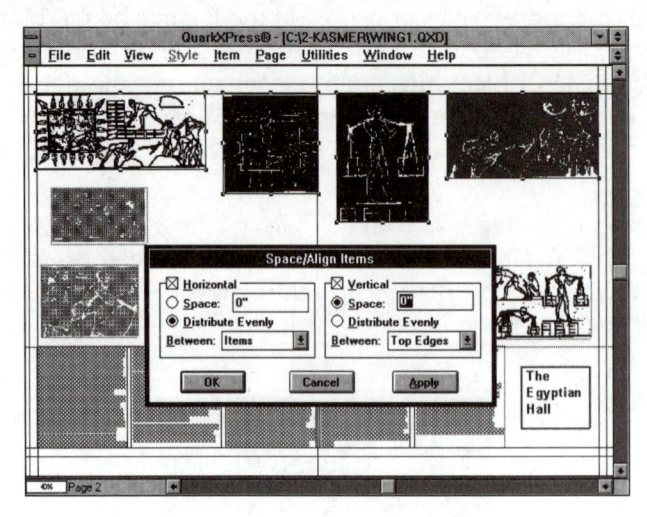

Figure 7.8 *Using Space/Align to distribute along an uppermost horizontal.*

We select the three picture boxes along the left margin next. Using the same command, we similarly arrange the picture boxes along the left margin with the same top-left picture box acting as an anchor, with the Vertical Distribute Evenly feature chosen this time. The dialog box and its result are shown in Figure 7.9. Notice that horizontal spacing was set for zero along the left edges.

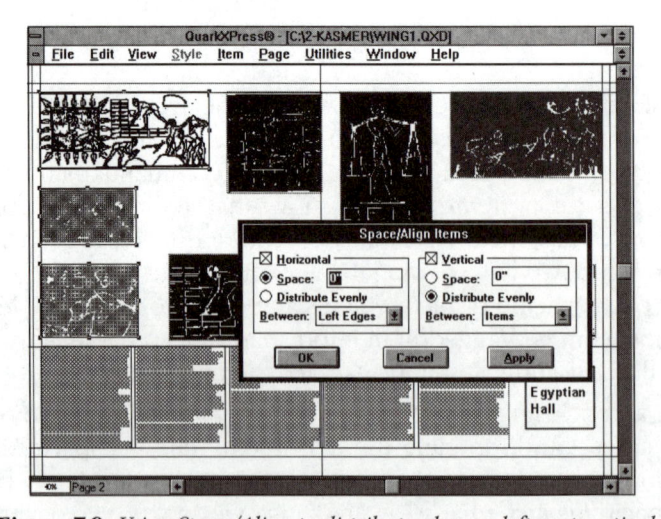

Figure 7.9 *Using Space/Align to distribute along a leftmost vertical.*

The last phase of positioning requires working with those remaining picture boxes along the bottom. Dragging the rightmost picture box to the right margin guide, we prepare for another spacing change. We drag a selection box around those bottom items, then use the Space/Align command to set up the dialog box shown in Figure 7.10. Here the Apply button has aligned the items. This time we've designated a vertical zero space along the bottom edges, and an even distribution between items in the horizontal. Now all the picture boxes are in place.

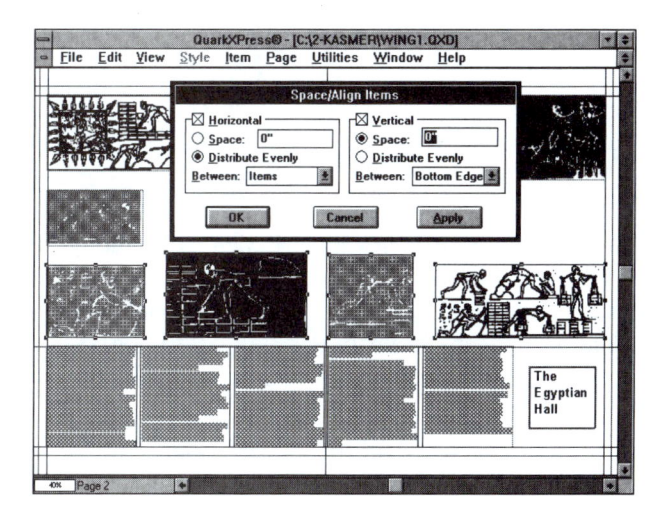

Figure 7.10 Using Space/Align to distribute along a bottommost horizontal.

The border is all that remains. For this project we've chosen to use text in the form of all the artifact names in the exhibit. This border will be a band of reverse type running around the spread.

Using the Text Box tool, we create a text box, type in the names (with spaces between them), then select all the text (keystroke Ctrl-A), copy it to the clipboard (keystroke Ctrl-C), and paste it (Ctrl-V) several times to provide plenty of text for our border. Next we draw out three more text boxes. Using the Linking tool we click on the first (the one with all the text), then click on the second. An arrow forms to show the text chain. Next we click on the second, then the third, and repeat this process until the fourth box is clicked on. This establishes the text chain shown in Figure 7.11.

Coming very close to completion now, we have to rotate, size, and position the text-chain boxes. But first, we reverse the text. (Recall that this is done by setting the color of the text to white and the background of the text box to black.) We select all the boxes as a set of items, then, opening the Item menu, we choose Modify. In this dialog box we set the background to Black, 100 percent. Next we use the content tool to select all the text. Opening the Style menu, we choose White from the Color list.

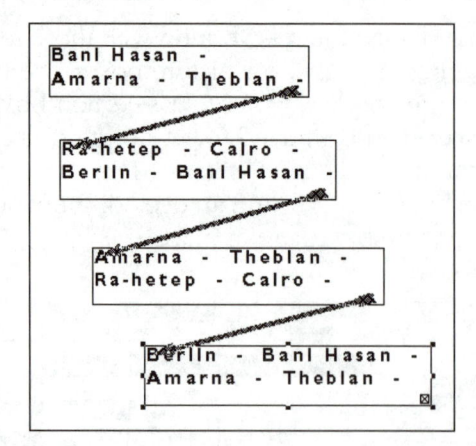

Figure 7.11 A text chain established for four linked bordering boxes.

Now we rotate the text boxes through the Measurements palette with an eye to where we will put them in the margin spaces, keeping the order clear. The first box at the top is horizontal, so there's no change; the second box, at the right, will be rotated -90 degrees; the third box, at the bottom, will be rotated -180 degrees; the fourth box, at the left, will be rotated 90 degrees (-270 degrees would do as well).

This leaves us with the text boxes shown in Figure 7.12. Putting each in its own margin around both the main text and the picture boxes, and stretching each border text box to fit as we do so, we complete the document.

Figure 7.12 Linked, reversed, rotated text boxes.

A Museum Guidebook

Now let's turn to a somewhat different document, one meant to lead visitors through a new exhibit. We're going to create one section of a museum guidebook. In this two-page spread our task is to provide clear visual links between the floor plan of the hall through which visitors will be passing and the exhibits they will encounter.

We begin by using the New command to set up a document 5.25 inches wide by 7.25 inches high. And because we want to work with a spread, we add two pages through the Pages menu and move directly to those facing pages.

There will be text on each page in three columns separated by .25 inch. We use the Text Box tool, draw out a box to fit within the margin guides of Page 2, then select Modify at the Item menu. In the Text Box Specifications, we key in *3* after Columns, and *.25* after Gutter.

Now we turn to the graphics that will grace this spread. One of them is crucial, a floor plan of the exhibit hall. We draw a box with the picture box tool and use the Get Picture dialog box. In comes the floor plan. We move this picture box to the upper-right corner, where it will be prominent enough to be noticed. Soon we will overlay numbered boxes on it, corresponding to similar boxes cited in the text.

It's time to bring in the other graphics now. For each one we draw out a box for the next image with the picture box tool, then use Get Picture. Following the procedures we've used before, we size the images to their approximate final proportions. This includes using the Ctrl-Shift-Alt-F keystroke to scale the image to the box, dragging on the handles to crop the box, using the grabber hand to position the significant image within the box, and so on.

We're almost ready to set up text runaround for the pictures. In order to proceed, though, we want to see how the runaround is interacting with our text. So we click the content tool in the text box on Page 2, and use the Get Text command to import the copy. We select all the text (Ctrl-A) and use the Measurements palette to set the text to Times 10 point. In a short time the layout shown in Figure 7.13 is before us.

NOTE All the pictures are in the runaround default mode, which is Item. This "boxy" runaround works fine for the three smaller images within the columns. But we decide that custom text runaround is called for in the picture in the lower left and in the floor plan. We select the floor plan picture first and, opening the Item menu, choose Runaround. At the dialog box we select the manual mode, and set an 8 point offset. The manual choice actually creates an automatic runaround with the option to adjust. We use that one because, if the program does an adequate job, we can leave the runaround as it turns out. On the other hand, we can easily adjust it if we have to.

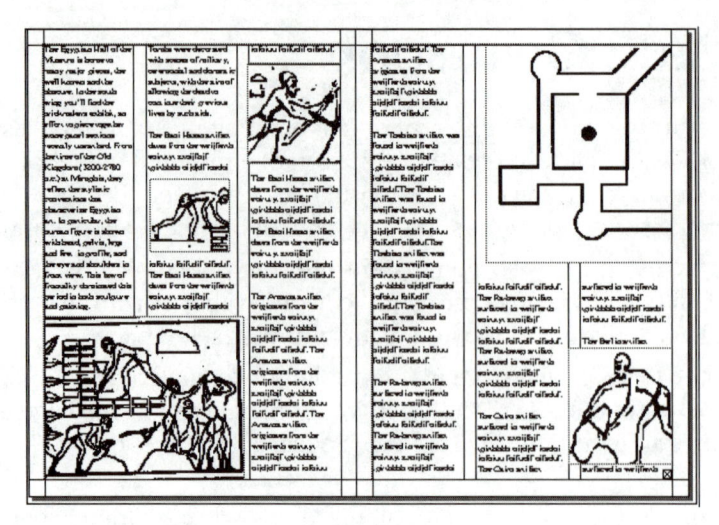

Figure 7.13 *Preliminary layout with item runaround.*

In the case of the image of the floor plan, the automatic runaround is fine except for the bit of text that's slipped into the third column. We adjust this by pulling a side of the runaround fence to the right, as shown by the arrow in Figure 7.14.

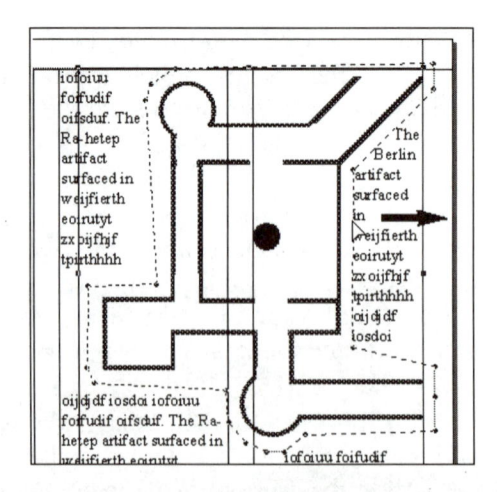

Figure 7.14 *Pushing out text by moving a runaround boundary.*

At the large image on the lower left, however, we have some custom box reshaping and cropping to do. In order to create a tapered image, we are going to convert the rectangular picture box to an adjustable polygon one. To do so, we select the picture box, then at the Item menu choose Picture Box Shape. A pictorial list of boxes appears (as shown in Figure 7.15). These are alternative box shapes. Choosing one redefines the apparent matte around the picture, but within the same bounding box. (Sometimes reaching this box list by mouse requires a deft slide from the Menu list.

Persistence pays here.) We choose the bottom figure, the polygon shape, because we wish to customize the picture box around this image.

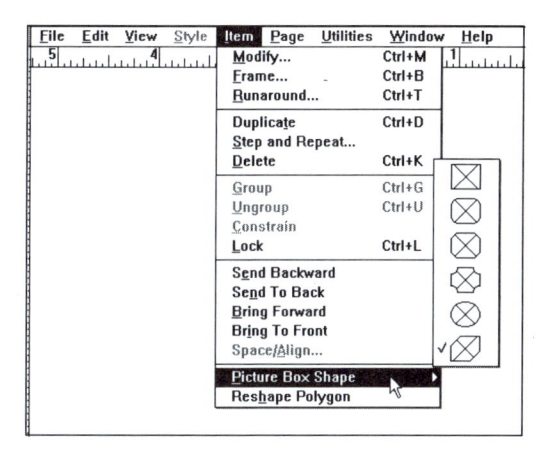

Figure 7.15 Choosing a new picture box shape.

Next we choose the last command on the Item list, Reshape Polygon. This gives our cursor tool the abilities to add and remove handle points, and to pull sides into new positions, the same abilities available when the polygon picture box tool is active. The difference here is that we can now work on revising an existing box form.

Positioning the mouse on a box side, we see the tool change to a small arrow head. By holding down the Ctrl key, we call up a tool shaped like a little rounded box. Clicking, we add a handle where we want the box to angle. We add similar handles around the corner of the box we want to adjust, and remove other handles until the box appears as shown in Figure 7.16. (Over an existing handle, the cursor changes to an "X-ed" circle.) The arrowhead allows us to move entire sides, and the familiar pointing hand allows us to move handle points.

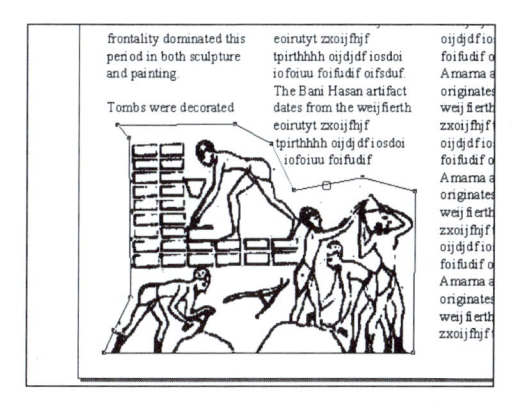

Figure 7.16 Reshaping a picture box.

An advantage to using the Reshape Polygon feature is that we adjust the text runaround at the same time we precisely crop the image. This occurs when the runaround is set to Item.

Our next task involves reversing text, the approach we've chosen to connect the floor plan map visually with the rest of the layout elements. First, to set the section apart, we'll manually insert a large reversed "out-drop" cap at the start of the page. We do this by creating a text box with the text box tool, setting the box background to Black, 100 percent, in the Specifications dialog box (from the Item menu's Modify command) and choosing White from the Color list in the Style menu. The typeface chosen is Arial, set at 48 points in the Measurements palette. Keying in the first letter of the body copy, we then delete that letter from the copy itself. In the Measurements palette the formatting is set to center, and in the Specifications dialog box the text offset to 6 points (to position the letter more centrally within the box). We assure that the Runaround is set to Item, and move this text box to the extreme upper-left of the spread. It pushes down and over on the body text, which reflows around it. (This is the manual method. We'll soon see how to generate standard drop caps automatically through paragraph formatting.)

Now we set about making label captions for the pictures. The choice is a reversed out text box with bolded Arial typeface of text taken from the copy. We set this up for one of the illustrations first. Then, to save effort, we'll copy this text box and modify the duplication. After formatting the first, we use the keyboard copy command (Ctrl-C), then a few paste commands (Ctrl-V) that produce a stack of identical text boxes. For each of the other illustrations we select the text in each (Ctrl-A) and key in the text appropriate to it.

To point body copy to the floor plan, we use the same text box clone from above, drag it to be narrower, and key in *1*. At the pasteboard, we use the item tool to select it. Then we copy (Ctrl-C) and paste (Ctrl-V) several boxes, and using the content tool we select the text in each (Ctrl-A) and key in subsequent numbers. The appropriate number will then visually point each artifact paragraph to a location on the map. Figure 7.17 shows labels—captions and number boxes—in the process of being positioned.

Each of those numbers will be needed to label locations on the floor plan. So we also select and copy the whole set of numbered boxes to use as markers there. Moving to the pasteboard adjacent to the map, we paste them near it. To complete the visual linking of the map to the text and pictures, we drag each of the duplicate numbers to its appropriate location on the map, as shown in Figure 7.18.

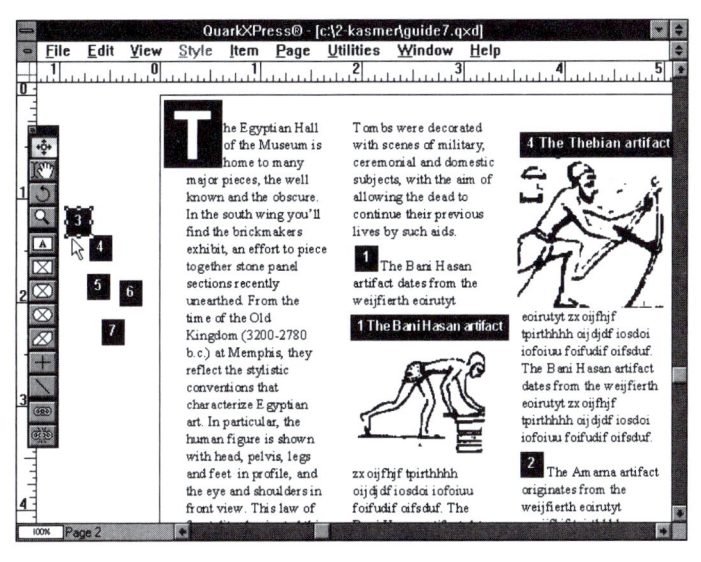

Figure 7.17 *Positioning reversed labels.*

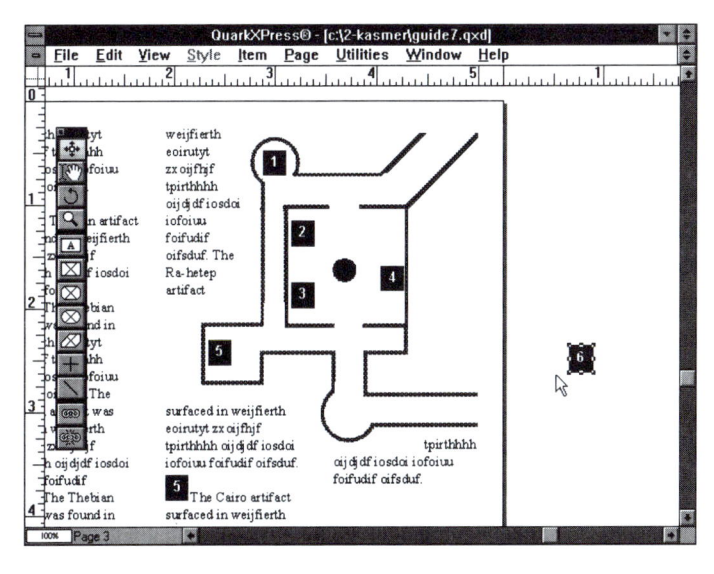

Figure 7.18 *Positioning number keys.*

To guide visitors to the hall, we select the line tool and draw lines leading in through the entrance at the top of the map and out through the exit below. Through the Measurements palette we select the arrow endcaps and a width of 6 points.

After one final minor adjustment to the map runaround boundary, the section completes the spread (as shown in Figure 7.19).

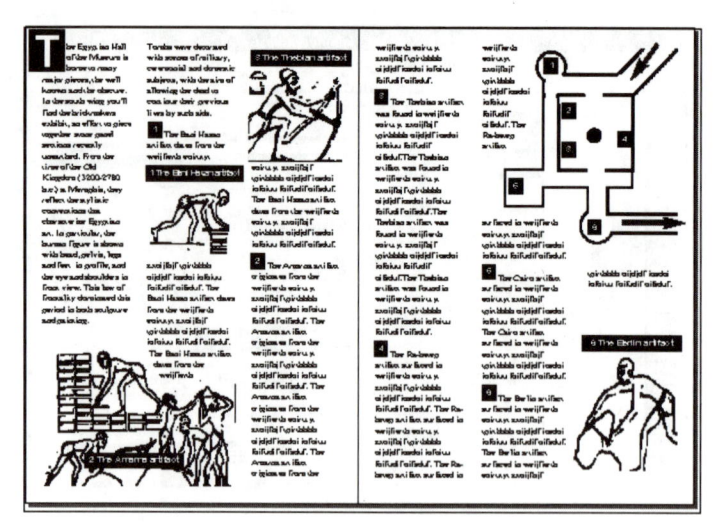

Figure 7.19 *The completed section.*

STEPPING FORWARD

Controlling the interactions of text and text, text and graphics, and items in general is possible by gaining a grasp of the graphic and content natures of items. Armed with an understanding of these qualities, and practiced in the ways of exploiting them on the page, you can now make use of even finer control over page design. Formatting stories and paragraphs to the finest degree is one of the major strengths of QuarkXPress. In Chapter 8 we'll see why and how.

Chapter 8

Paragraphs, Stories, and Typographic Controls

WHAT YOU WILL LEARN IN THIS CHAPTER

- How to format paragraphs
- How to set tabs and create hanging indents
- How to set hyphenation and justification
- Widow and orphan control
- How to control horizontal scaling and vertical justification
- How to create drop caps

Enter the realm of the typesetter.

Few desktop publishing applications come close to the broad strokes and skillful subtleties managed by the controls of QuarkXPress. This chapter will show you how these strokes and subtleties work at the paragraph and story levels, how to regulate hyphenation and justification, and how to accomplish special effects with type.

These are controls to which every serious publication producer and page designer pays close attention. Regardless of whether you have extensive experience with typography, you'll find techniques described in this chapter that can give your documents an appearance of the highest caliber.

FORMATTING

At the crossroads of text control is the Paragraph Formats dialog box, which manages paragraphs and groups of paragraphs. QuarkXPress treats any text separated by a tap of the Enter key (on the main section of the keyboard), as a paragraph. Such paragraph markers, however, can be difficult to find in relatively unformatted text.

One way to identify them is through a toggle command in the View menu called Show Invisibles and Hide Invisibles, shown in Figure 8.1 (with text in which the paragraphs might be otherwise overlooked). The invisibles referred to here include tabs, spaces, new line codes, special indent codes, and paragraph markers. These are all treated as nonprinting characters by QuarkXPress, which identifies the paragraph by the standard ¶. While these symbols might be distracting during layout, it's good to know how to bring them forward when you need them.

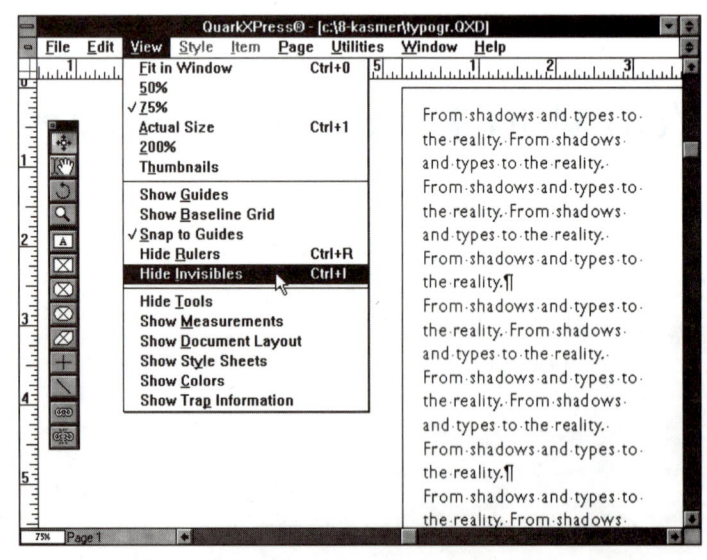

Figure 8.1   *Showing nonprinting markers.*

> **Locating nonprinting character codes in text**
>
> Open the View menu and choose Show Invisibles

Once you start to format a paragraph—for instance, by adding an indent at the first line, or an extra space after the paragraph—you will be able to discern paragraphs *without* the Show Invisibles function.

Adding and otherwise modifying formatting is what the Paragraph Formats dialog box is all about. This feature is accessible when the content tool has selected a text box. To reach it, open the Style menu and choose Formats. A dialog box such as the one shown in Figure 8.2 will be displayed. Figure 8.2 depicts a default dialog box detailing an unformatted text box.

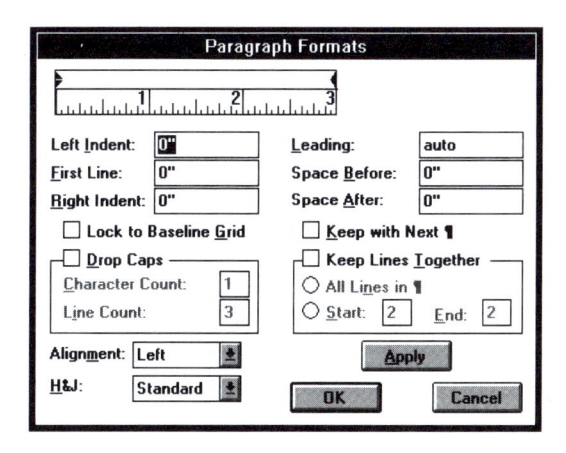

Figure 8.2 The Paragraph Formats dialog box.

Here is a good place to apply some of the formatting that makes typeset paragraphs look like, well, typeset paragraphs. Note that the Paragraph Formats dialog box makes changes to whichever paragraph the text cursor is in, or to wherever the text selection exists. If a group of paragraphs has been selected and is highlighted, each paragraph in that group will be reformatted according to the dialog box entries. If a selection extends into two paragraphs, for instance, *both* paragraphs will be formatted by your dialog box entries.

In the example shown in Figure 8.3, the cursor sits in the first paragraph of the text box at the right. Changes have been made in the Formats dialog box next to it. It is not strictly accurate to say that the paragraph began with *no* formatting. Even the zero values shown in Figure 8.2 indicate a state to which the paragraph could be returned by using the Formats dialog box to key in and select those undistinguishing attributes.

The text, for example, was initially set in 18 point Gill Sans typeface with automatic leading (here 120 percent, or about 21.6 point leading); it's left-aligned, with no indentations and no extra space before or after the paragraphs.

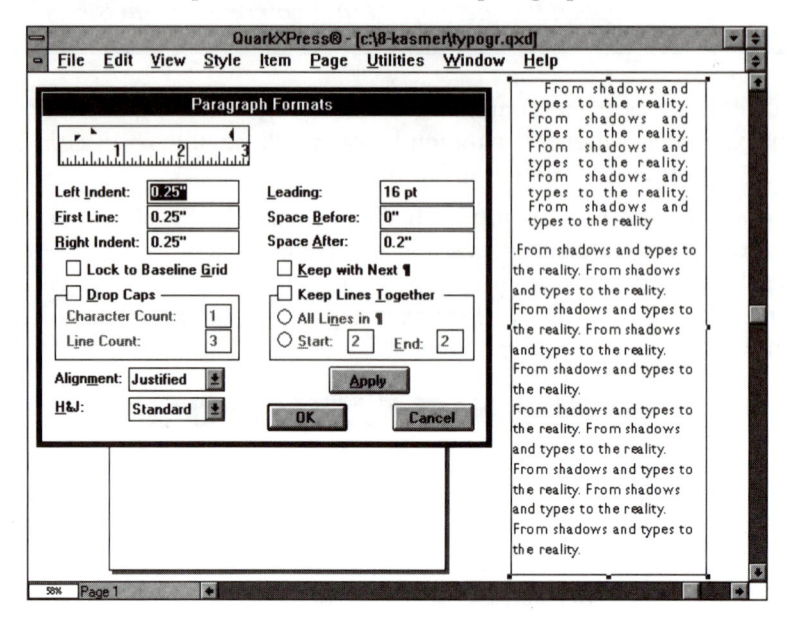

Figure 8.3   *A Formats dialog box for an altered paragraph.*

Now let's examine the dialog box to see how the changes were made to that first paragraph shown in Figure 8.3. In the upper-left corner you'll see a ruler. You might note that the two small black triangular marks on the left have been slid over, and that the large triangle on the right has been similarly moved. The functions of these three triangles are repeated through the first three fields, labeled Left Indent, First Line, and Right Indent. The indentation of the entire paragraph from the left edge can be controlled by the lower of the two small triangles as well as by the First Numerical field. In this case, a value was entered as .25 inch. The same effect would have been achieved by pointing the cursor on the triangle and dragging it rightward to the .25-inch mark on the dialog box ruler. Incidentally, as any of these marks is dragged, the location on the ruler is tracked and indicated actively within the fields.

The First Line field controls the indentation of the paragraph's first line, where a typist normally presses the typewriter's tab key. This same feature is also controlled by the small triangle in the upper portion of the dialog box ruler. We've chosen the same value, .25 inches. This first-line indentation is added to the indentation applied to all the lines of the paragraph.

The Right Indent field controls the extent to which text lines can move across the text column. This control can also be accomplished by dragging the large triangle from the right.

> **Adjusting indents**
>
> Select the paragraph(s)
>
> In the Paragraph Formats dialog box, locate the ruler
>
> Slide the triangular markers into place as follows: first-line indent, small top marker; left-indent, small bottom marker; right-indent, large marker
>
> Or, key values into corresponding fields

NOTE As you fashion a paragraph selection through Paragraph Formats, QuarkXPress provides for step-by-step changes. That is, you need not decide on *all* your changes at once. Rather, you can try changing some particular attribute, click the Apply button, observe the change, and then decide whether you wish to make your change definite. If you decide yes, you can click OK. Or you can continue adding formatting instructions to the dialog box, and trying them with the Apply button. When you reach a satisfying format, you click OK to fix your changes to the selection.

Another obvious change is the reduced spacing between the lines of the first paragraph. The rest of the text carries an automatic leading, which for 18 point type is 21.6 point spacing. However, here in the dialog box we keyed in a value of 16 point, to bring the lines closer to each other. This is the same leading control available through the Measurements palette, as well as through the Style menu.

The paragraph has been separated from its successor by added spacing. Note the Space After field, and its entry of .2 inch. In similar fashion, the Space Before field can be altered for all paragraphs—except the first.

One final change that distinguishes this paragraph from its neighbors is the alignment. We've seen that flush-left, flush-right, centered, and justified features can be set from both the Measurements palette and the Style menu. Here we've used the drop-down list near the bottom of the dialog box to justify the text of the first paragraph.

There are countless variations that can be achieved with just these few controls in the Formats dialog box. Figure 8.4 shows examples of paragraph formats brought about by adjustments in indents, leading, alignment, and spacing.

One special format that you'll find causes paragraphs to stand out is **hanging indents**. In this case, the bulk of the text appears to be indented from the left, while the first line is not. The effect is that text appears to be "hanging" from the first line. Figure 8.5 shows a series of paragraphs to which the hanging indent feature has been applied.

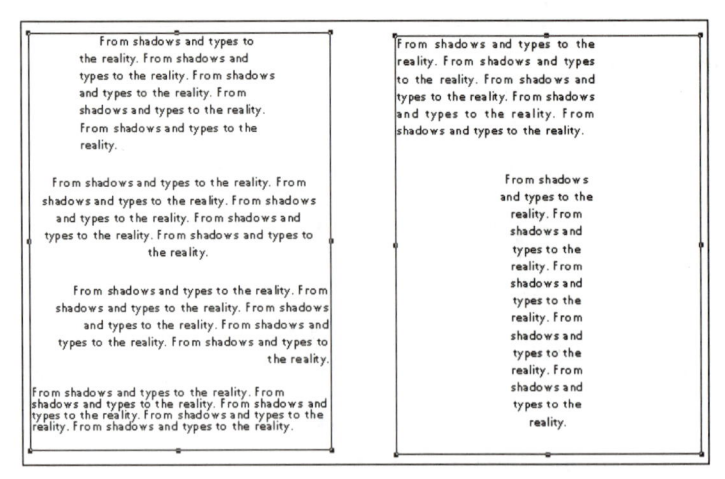

Figure 8.4 Paragraph formatting variations.

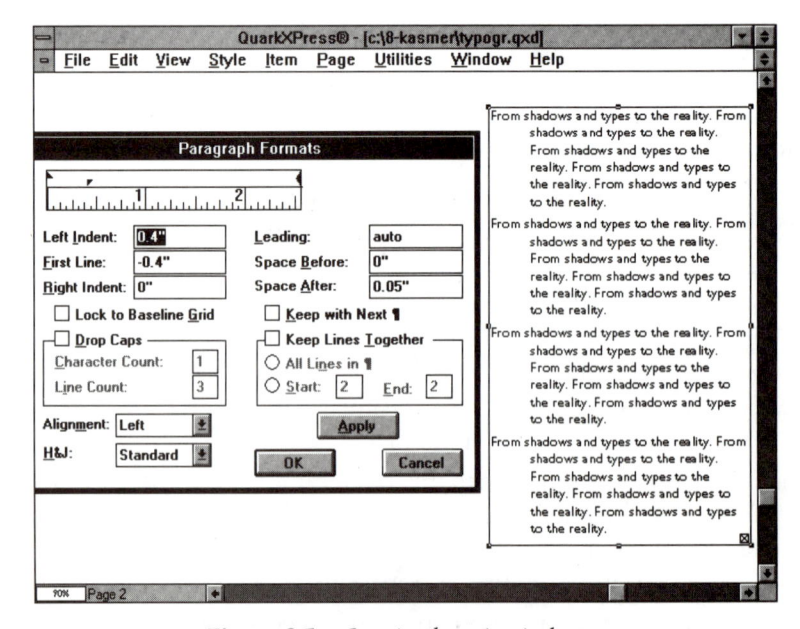

Figure 8.5 Creating hanging indents.

The technique for achieving hanging indents relies on the ability of QuarkXPress to set the first line to a negative value. Note that the first line's indent value is relative to the left indent. So a zero-first-line indent results in the first line being flush left with the rest of the lines of the paragraph. A first-line indent with a positive value results in an apparent tab over. A negative first-line indent pulls the line to the left. So, in Figure 8.5 the First Line -0.4" signifies .4 inch to the left of the Left Indent of +0.4". In other words, the first line is set at zero. The left triangular markers in the Formats ruler make this more apparent.

> **Creating hanging indents**
>
> In the Paragraph Formats dialog box, drag the left indent over
>
> Drag the first line indent back leftward of the left indent

NOTE As you work with paragraph formatting, you'll need to see what happens with each new formatting change. Admittedly, the Paragraph Formats dialog box takes up a large amount of space, especially on a typical fourteen-inch monitor operating in standard VGA mode. And even with the benefit of the Apply button to try out formatting changes, you might feel it's necessary to quit the dialog box just to see what you've done. A better way is to recall that, like every window and dialog box, this one can be moved. So, in order to see your paragraph changes, you would do better to move the Formats dialog box by clicking on its title bar to grab and drag it temporarily to another location. As long as you can see part of the title bar, you can always drag the whole dialog box on screen.

NOTE When you choose the Formats dialog, the cursor or the selection in the text seems to disappear. This is only a temporary display lapse. QuarkXPress keeps track of those paragraphs you want formatted. When you leave the dialog box, the paragraph selection will be returned just as you left it, and the formatting changes will have been made.

HYPHENATION AND JUSTIFICATION

There are other adjustments that can be made from the Formats dialog box, including hyphenation and justification control, labeled here as H&J. While the Formats dialog box facilitates choosing from among the available methods, the methods themselves are set up from within an H&J dialog box. We now turn to that dialog box to see about controlling those features.

Within the QuarkXPress document there is a standard set of specifications that controls how each line is fit within a column, given the various indents in effect. These specifications determine when to break words with hyphens—**hyphenation**. Specifications also determine how to increase or diminish space between words and characters in order to align paragraphs in justified mode—**justification**.

Gaining Access to Hyphenation and Justification Specs

When you start work on a QuarkXPress document, no lines end with hyphenated words. The reason can be found in the Formats dialog box under the heading H&J Standard. In this specification, automatic hyphenation is normally switched off for a new document. You can modify the specifications, create new ones, delete them, copy them, or transfer them from other QuarkXPress documents.

To gain access to the H&J specifications, open the Edit menu and choose H&J. You'll see the dialog box shown in Figure 8.6. To get to the specifications, click on the Edit button, and the dialog box shown in Figure 8.7 will be displayed. In it you'll see all the preset values and choices made for every new document.

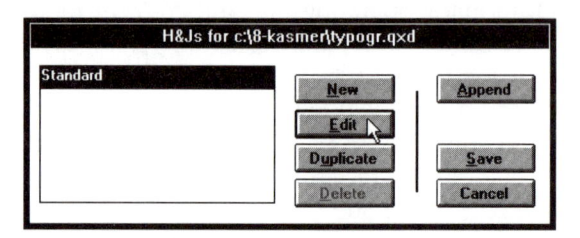

Figure 8.6 *Access to hyphenation and justification settings.*

Figure 8.7 *Specifications for hyphenation and justification.*

One way to switch hyphenation on is simply to click the Auto Hyphenation checkbox. All the paragraphs in the document will then be automatically hyphenated according to the specifications in this dialog box. This is an all-or-nothing approach.

Changing Hyphenation Specifications

Another way to apply hyphenation is to create another set of H&J specifications. Click the Cancel button, and you'll be at the H&Js dialog box shown in Figure 8.6.

Now click the New button and you'll return to an Edit Hyphenation and Justification dialog box that resembles the one shown in Figure 8.7, except that the name will be blank. If all you want to do is switch on hyphenation, click the checkbox to put an *x* in Auto Hyphenation. Key in a name, such as Hyphen On. Then Click the OK button, and you return to the H&Js dialog box. Here, click the Save button. When you call up the Formats dialog box, now you'll be able to choose Hyphen On from the drop-down list under H&Js, as shown in Figure 8.8, and apply hyphenation selectively to paragraphs.

This is the simplest H&J specifications change. You can detail the ways that both hyphenation and justification will be applied to your text. Let's suppose we wanted to elaborate the methods to be applied in the Hyphen On specifications. To do so, we again open the Edit menu, choose H&Js, then select from the H&Js Hyphen On list. Click the Edit button. You'll see a dialog box like the one shown in Figure 8.7 again.

Let's consider features under Auto Hyphenation first. In the box, the three fields indicate how and where words may be broken. Smallest Word indicates the minimum number of characters a word must have before Auto Hyphenation affects it. The default is for six characters. The possible range is three to twenty characters. Minimum Before sets the lower limit on the number of characters that must be present before an automatic hyphen is inserted. The default is three characters; the range is two to eight. Minimum After sets a lower limit on the number of characters that are made to follow an automatic hyphen. The default is two characters; the range is two to eight.

The defaults indicate that five-letter words will not be hyphenated. They cause even the word *before* to be passed over for hyphenation, because the *be-* syllable is to short to qualify, while a word like *yesterday* could be hyphenated at the first syllable, *yes-*.

In the field labeled Hyphens in a Row, you can restrict the number of consecutive lines that will end in a hyphenated word. The default, Unlimited, means "anything goes." For work that is more artistic than practical—where you don't want hyphens stabbing the right indent willy-nilly—you might want to limit this value to 1.

Hyphenation Zone sounds a bit imposing. Here's what QuarkXPress does with it. Applied to nonjustified text, the Zone is measured from the right indent of the text. It sets up conditions for hyphenating. If a word that does not require hyphenation falls into the Zone, the word after it will not be hyphenated. On the other hand, if the hyphenation fragment of a potentially hyphenatable word falls inside the Zone, the word will be hyphenated there.

These are the hyphenation specifications. With them, you can limit word splits to very large words, to occasional words, to words of large syllables, and so on.

Changing Justification Specifications

Adjacent to the hyphenation specifications in the dialog box are the justification specifications. The first six fields in the Justification Method box can have profound effects on how tight or loose the lines in your justified text appear. In particular, the tighter the text, the less chance that dread rivers of white space can flow through your paragraphs, leading the reader's eye astray.

Each typeface has implicit in its design a predetermined optimum spacing value. QuarkXPress interprets an optimum value for word and letter spacing, which it designates as 100 percent. We can see this designation is applied to the default values for specifications. The first row of the Justification Method box, Space, manipulates the spacing of words. In order for justification to work, an optimum value is specified for maximum and minimum spacing variations. Similarly, the second row, Char. (for character), manipulates spacing variations among adjacent letters and other characters, from the optimum spacing (0%). The values shown in Figure 8.7 represent the default method chosen for justification.

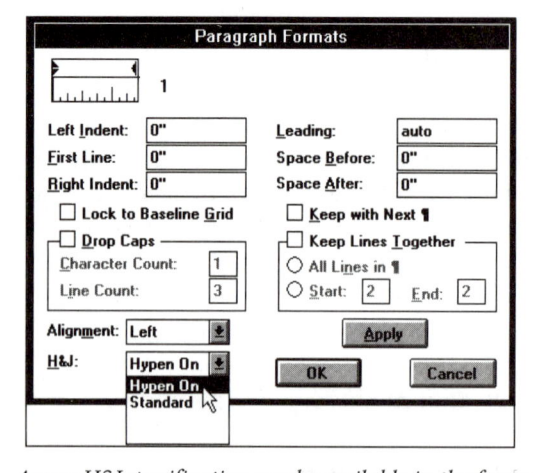

Figure 8.8 *A new H&J specification made available in the formats dialog box.*

There are two distinct schools of thought regarding justification methods. One holds that the minimum letter and word spacing must not drop below the optimum value. In this approach, the minimums are set to the optimum and the maximum values are given a wide range. The second school believes that it is best to *reduce* the range of variation but make the minimum lower than the optimum level. In this second scheme, the values might run Minimum at 85 percent and Maximum at 110 percent. Figures 8.9 and 8.10 illustrate the two preferences respectively, on one section of text.

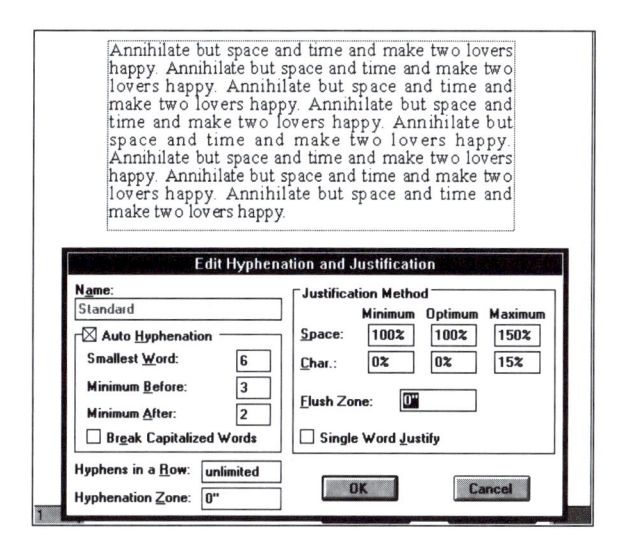

Figure 8.9   Effect of the minimum equals optimum spacing.

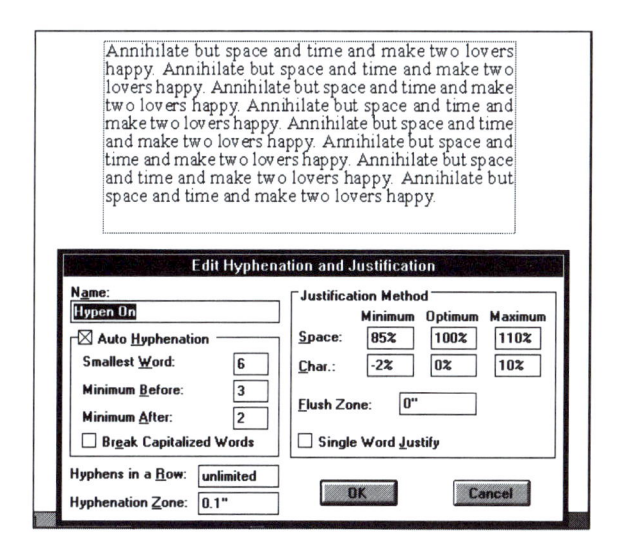

Figure 8.10   Effect of tight spacing.

As shown in Figure 8.10, you can adjust the justification spacing values to alter the setting of your justified type. You can also adjust other factors in justification. You can determine, for instance, the circumstances under which a paragraph's last line of justified text will be extended across the indents. QuarkXPress handles this control through a feature known as the **Flush Zone**. When the last line enters the Flush Zone (measured from the right indent), space is added between words and characters to make the line fill the entire space from left margin to right margin. At the default of zero inches, of course, this will never happen.

The Single Word Justify checkbox might prove useful for a special type effect, such as stretching an unusual headline across a wide space.

Remember that the H&Js edit function can only create or modify these options. It's through the Style menu's Formats dialog box that you actually apply them to text. But if you apply an H&J model to text and then edit that H&J, the text will reflect the change without being reformatted once the Save button on the Edit H&J dialog box is clicked.

VERTICAL ALIGNMENT

Another feature that can determine the formatting of text is a powerful control tucked away in the Text Box Specifications dialog box. As paragraph alignment works on text in the horizontal, this function works in the vertical. With it you can accomplish broad-brush vertical position and spacing within a text box. The Vertical Alignment drop-down list provides four choices. The first three—Top, Centered, and Bottom—are shown in Figure 8.11 and correspond roughly to the positioning within the text box. More specifically, they work between the first baseline and the text inset at the bottom of the box.

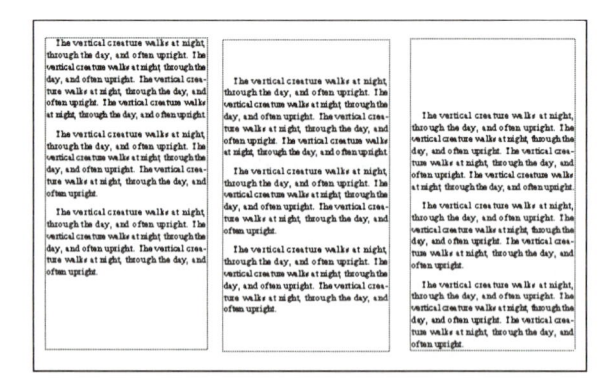

Figure 8.11 Vertical alignments.

Another option, even more drastic, is the Justified choice in this same drop-down list. With Justified, you can automatically spread out lines of text to fit the text box you're working with. Leaving the Interparagraph Spacing field at zero, choosing the Vertical Alignment of Justified, and clicking OK produces the text box at the left in Figure 8.12. By entering a value into that Spacing field and clicking OK, you'll force the paragraphs to spread apart by that value—at the expense of line spacing, as is shown in the text box on the right.

All these vertical justifications can be applied throughout a single-column text box. In a multicolumn text box, however, the effects will be exerted only on the final (rightmost) column.

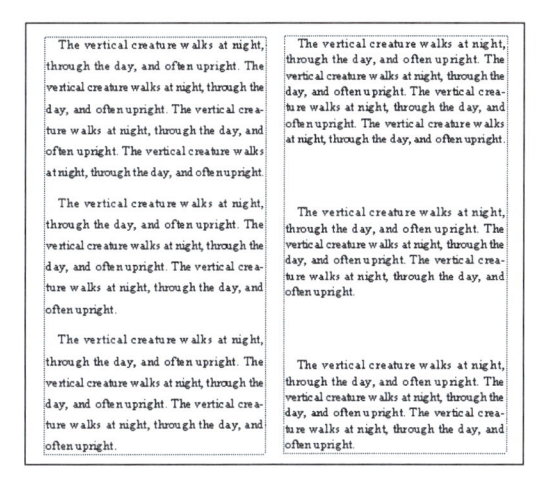

Figure 8.12 *Vertically justified text.*

THE BASELINE GRID

Leading and vertical justification would seem to be the extent of line-spacing controls. There is, however, another means by which the lines of type in a paragraph can be set. It's available throughout your document, but it's invisible unless you switch it on. This is the **baseline grid**, a set of guidelines that provides the ability to align every line of text in the document to the same spacing. To gain full control over this ability requires adjustments in three different commands. We'll start simply.

The first step in using the baseline grid is to make it visible through the View menu's Show Baseline Grid command. What you see is a set of horizontal lines running through the page and across into the pasteboard, as shown in Figure 8.13.

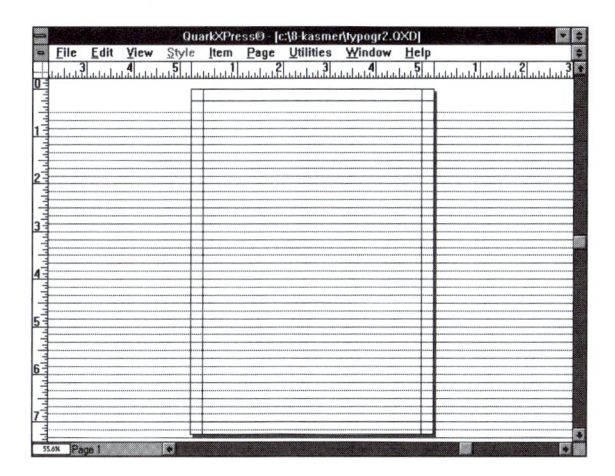

Figure 8.13 *The baseline grid revealed.*

In this case, the lines appear at the .5-inch mark on the vertical ruler and repeat every 12 points, the default set in the Typographic Preferences dialog box.

The value of baseline grids is that every paragraph in every page of an entire document can be locked to the same line spacing. This is accomplished in a per-paragraph control determined by the Paragraph Formats dialog box. You can display the baselines or not, but the control still engages either way.

To lock lines of text to a baseline grid, first select the paragraphs involved (as you would for any formatting change), then, in the Paragraph Formats dialog box, click the Lock to Baseline checkbox to *x* it.

Notice the difference in leading between the left text box and the right text box shown in Figure 8.14. Both have corresponding paragraphs set to the same point sizes, and to autoleading. However, in the right-hand box all the text has been selected and the Formats dialog box's Lock to Baseline checkbox has been applied. This command is a powerful one, overriding all local leading and providing a quick method to achieve leading consistency, so that text in adjacent columns lines up, for instance.

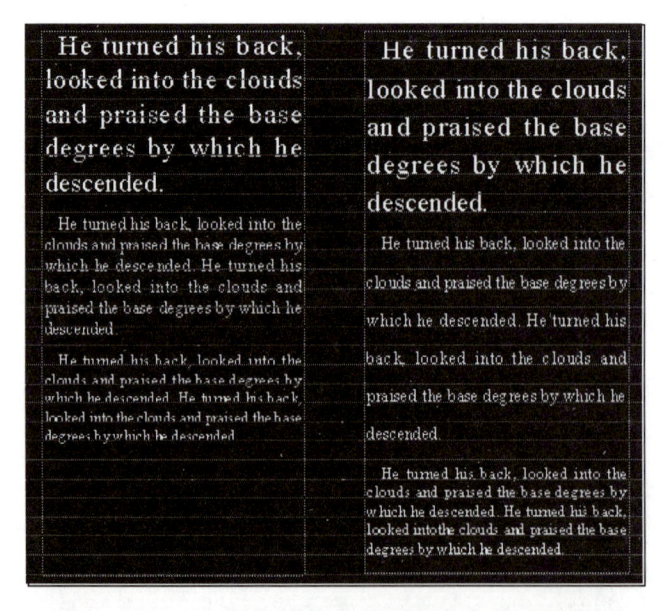

Figure 8.14 *Fixed leading versus text locked to baseline.*

Notice that the smaller text in the right-hand box has lined up exactly with each of the baselines, while the other paragraphs have lined up with every other baseline. The Lock feature works out the nearest match in baseline multiples. Notice also that the first line of text is placed on the first baseline at the top of the box that will accommodate it fully within the box (allowing for text inset, if any).

You can specify how far down in the text box your text will begin. To do so, in the Text Box Specifications dialog box, type a distance into the First Baseline box in the field marked Offset. QuarkXPress will then locate the first line of text on the first baseline it encounters from that distance down.

WIDOWS AND ORPHANS

Now we come to some typographical surprises that are the scourge of typesetters everywhere. Widows and orphans are no welcome visitors when they deflate a precisely set story or book layout. **Widows** are single lines of paragraphs that find themselves alone at the top of a column or page. And **orphans** are small words that often fall on the last line of a paragraph, as well as those first lines of paragraphs to be stranded alone at the bottom of a column or page. In Figure 8.15 you can see an invasion of widows and orphans in one box of hapless text.

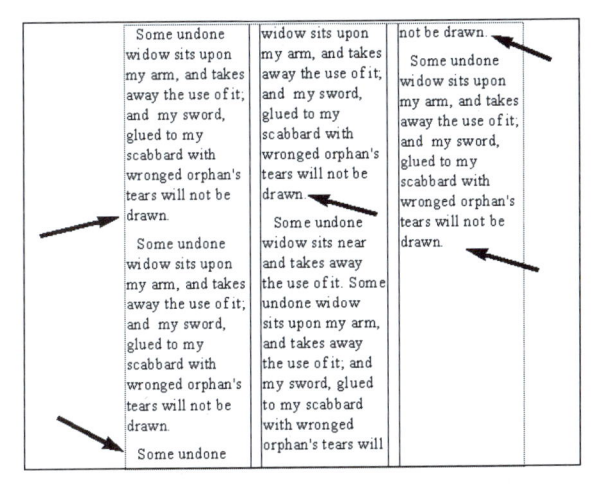

Figure 8.15 *Text replete with widows and orphans.*

QuarkXPress deals with widows and orphans through the Paragraph Formats dialog box. The program's approach is to hold the paragraphs together entirely, or in pieces. It will do this when directed through the Paragraph Line controls shown in Figure 8.16. The primary widow and orphan eliminator is the Keep Lines Together box. To engage it, click an *x* into the checkbox you see there. If you are absolutely adamant that a paragraph not be broken up in any way, then click the All Lines in Paragraph button. To keep single lines from appearing in isolated locations, click the button below it. The default requires that at least two lines are needed to start a paragraph at a given location. This is the widow-killer. The other part of the default allows a paragraph to break only if at least two lines will appear in the next column. This is the orphan-killer. You can apply this feature to a single paragraph, or to all the paragraphs in a story. Figure 8.17 shows the results of applying it to all the text in the previous text box.

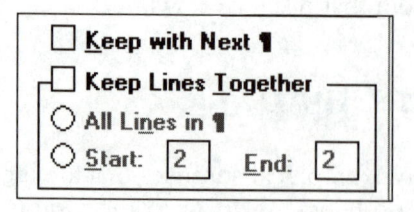

Figure 8.16   The widow and orphan controls.

Figure 8.17   A story cleared of widows and some orphans.

All the single lines, top and bottom, are gone. But notice that some single-word lines still linger. The way to fix these is by adjusting tracking, or by horizontal scaling.

Horizontal Scaling

Let's face it, some typesetting controls are more fun than others. Horizontal scaling must be nominated as one of typesetting's most pleasing controls. This feature, after all, is easy to use and powerful. It affects individual type characters. And it's highly visual. Horizontal scaling is a way of stretching or compressing characters. Purists might be inclined to scorn its use. After all, it distorts the design of the typeface. But it can be so useful in subtle ways, and can produce heavy-handed effects with such ease (when you want them, of course), that you can't afford to overlook it if you face any sort of typesetting challenge.

To compress or expand any selected text characters, open the Style menu and key in the value. The range is from 25 percent to 400 percent, in tenth-of-a-percent increments. As shown in Figure 8.18, the text of the upper box was selected and scaled to 90 percent of the original character width to produce the fit in the lower text box, by using the dialog box shown. Some would argue that the compressed appearance is an improvement. Clearly, this feature is of great value in subtly reducing the space required for a given body of text. A 95 percent scaling, for instance, would go unnoticed by almost all readers.

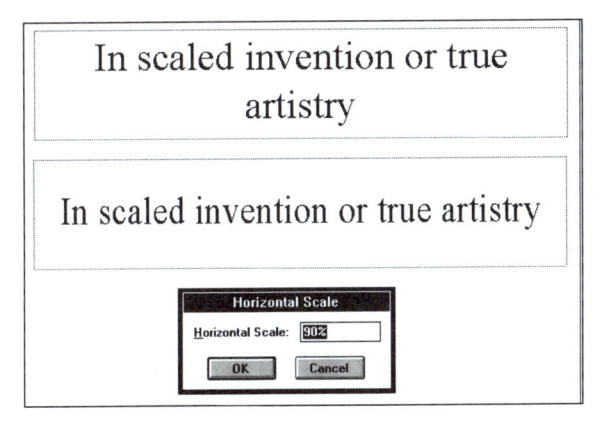

Figure 8.18 *Effects of horizontal scaling to 90 percent.*

You can, of course, go to an extreme with this feature. Figure 8.19 shows the upper box text expanded into the lower box text.

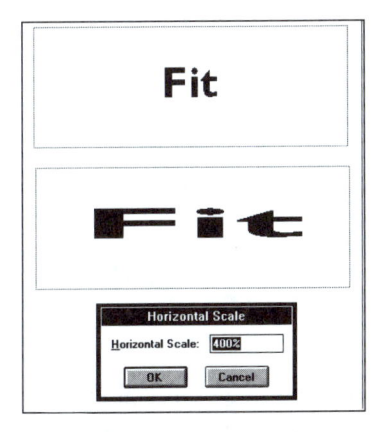

Figure 8.19 *Expanding text 400 percent.*

Drop Caps

It's safe to predict that **drop caps** will become one of your favorite features. Drop caps are the large initial capital letters that often lead off in stories and sections of newspapers, magazines, and books. They're popular because they can signal the beginning of a segment of text in ways that add visual spice to a text-heavy document. QuarkXPress has a highly effective method for producing drop caps.

If you've used desktop publishing programs before, you might have had to create a large capital, send it out to the clipboard or another program, then import it back as a graphic to use with text runaround features.

The method here is quite direct. To make an initial drop cap, first insert the cursor in the paragraph to receive the capital, then open the Paragraph Formats dialog box and click an *x* in the Drop Caps checkbox. Figure 8.20 shows the drop cap applied to the first line of the text box. The default for the number of characters rendered as drop caps is 1, and the number of lines in which to fit the drop cap is 3. These defaults are quite serviceable, but changing them and experimenting is quite a simple matter.

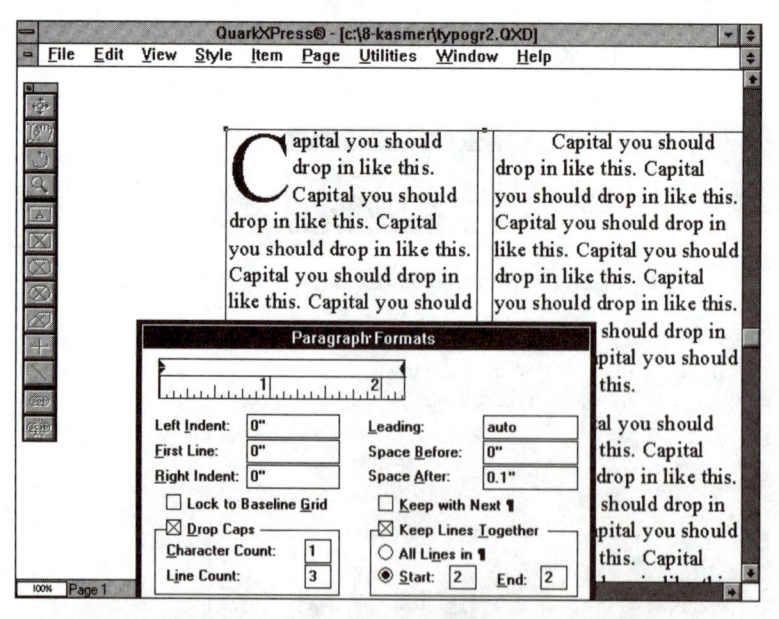

Figure 8.20 *A drop cap applied using the Formats dialog box.*

Tabs

Tabs, those markers that send text over to a certain position within a line, were simple things in the days when typewriters ruled. Now the choices have grown. The typewriter was suited for tabs measured over from the left. If you wanted to center your tabs, or align on a decimal as for a column of prices, you had to count spaces or rely on an unwavering eye.

We've already made use of the preset tabs provided in Documents (left tabs at half-inch intervals). With QuarkXPress you can precisely align tabs to the left, center, and right, to a decimal, to a comma, or to any other character you designate. You gain access to tab adjustments through a dialog box in which you can position new tabs or adjust or remove existing tabs. This dialog box is opened through the Style menu when the content tool is active and one or more paragraphs are selected. Tabs apply to paragraphs. There is also limited left tab adjustment through the Paragraph Formats box.

When you are working in the text, each time you press the Tab key in a line the program will move the cursor over as though a wide invisible character had been keyed in. The width of this character is determined by the positioning of the tab markers. You can see the tab characters represented in the text by switching on Show Invisibles. In Figure 8.21 this has been done for a text box in which the tab key was pressed several times to engage the preset default half-inch tabs.

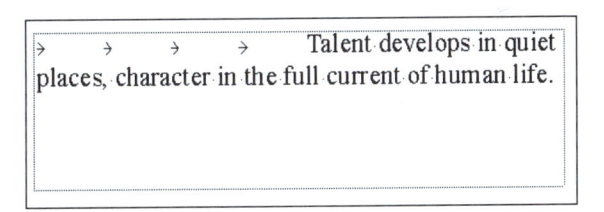

Figure 8.21 Tabs revealed through Show Invisibles.

To work on tabs, open the Style menu and choose Tabs. A dialog box will be displayed. Initially there will be a drop-down list and three fields for entering specifications. Figure 8.22 shows the dialog box with the drop-down list opened to reveal the types of tabs available.

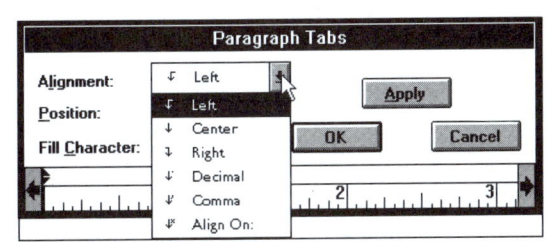

Figure 8.22 Tab choices.

There are two methods for inserting tabs. In each you first select one of the types in the drop-down list. In one method you then simply click in the ruler. A marker corresponding to the tab chosen in the list will appear.

For a more precise approach, do the following: Key in the position measured from the left origin of the text area in the Position box. A tab marker will likewise appear.

> **NOTE** Each time you click in a tab, its location will be indicated in the Position field. If you change the position value here, rather than move the tab, the dialog box will create a new tab marker when you press the Apply or OK button. You can insert two, three, even up to twenty tab markers per paragraph.

To remove a tab, drag it out of the ruler space. To reposition a tab, drag it along the ruler to the new location. To modify tab features, drag out the old tab and insert a new one according to the procedure given above.

Normally, each tab will be preceded by blank space. You can, however, modify this so that the space will be filled with a character typed at the keyboard. To do so, click on the tab in question, key in the character you wish to precede that position—that is, the character to fill that tab space—then click the Apply or OK button. You can modify tabs already present in the text, or set up tab markers to be applied to text tabs yet to be keyed.

One very useful way to use the Paragraph Tabs dialog box is to position it in line with the text to which tabs are being applied. In Figure 8.23 the dialog has been moved above the text box. This way you can visually correlate tab markers with the actual tabs that will be displayed. Note in the figure how the periods have filled the tab space in the paragraph.

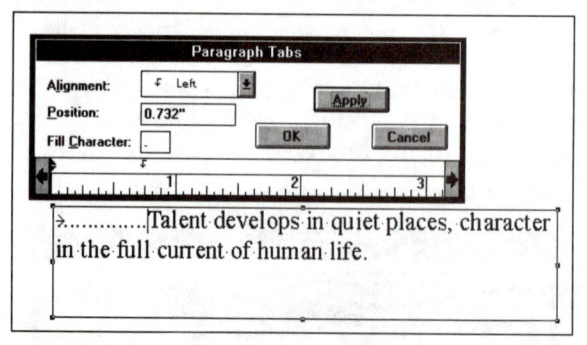

Figure 8.23 *Aligning the Tabs dialog with selected text box.*

Choosing Right Tabs gives a justified appearance to tabular text; choosing Center Tabs produces very orderly columns. Choosing Decimal Tabs will cause items in each line to align on the decimal point. Similarly, you can choose some other character, such as an apostrophe, to align a list of possessive names. When you choose Align On from the Alignment list, a field will be displayed next to it—that's where you key in the alignment character you wish.

Paragraph Rules

Rules, those nifty delineators, can be drawn out with the line tools, as we have seen. But you can also specify them through a command that will apply them automatically to text. Like formatting features, they will be applied to the paragraphs selected.

To initiate the command that does this, first select the text with the content tool. Then open the Style menu and choose Rules. You'll see the dialog box shown in Figure 8.24. Click an *x* into one or both of the checkboxes, Rule Above and Rule Below, and the dialog box will expand into one like that shown in Figure 8.25. The controls here are consistent with others we have encountered thus far, and you can install rules that will follow the paragraph, wherever it may appear in the text box.

Figure 8.24 *The Paragraph Rules dialog box.*

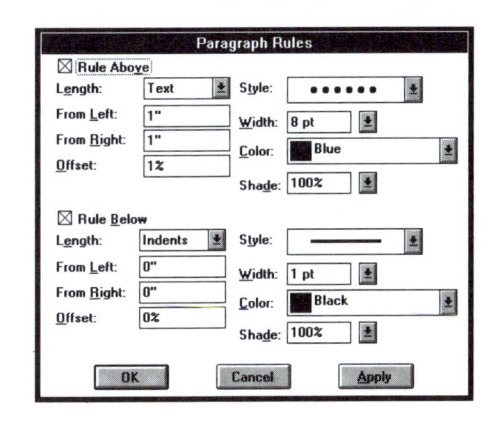

Figure 8.25 *The Rules Specification dialog box.*

Preferred modes of working

Let's turn to the subject of measurement. Surely no typesetter would feel at home if only the English system of inches were available. For the specialized world of type and page layout, measurement by pica is better. Picas provide flexibility and compatibility that correlates directly to type, rules, measuring, and positioning. A pica is defined by QuarkXPress as one-sixth of an inch, the equivalent of twelve points.

You can easily switch between measuring systems within the document, using whichever one is appropriate to the circumstance. The default, as we've seen, is inches. To switch to picas open the Edit menu and choose Preferences. Another menu will be displayed, as shown in Figure 8.26. From this menu, choose General to open the dialog box shown in Figure 8.27. Notice the Horizontal Measure and Vertical Measure fields. By opening their drop-down lists, you can select picas and convert the rulers, all the dialog boxes, and the Measurements palette to that system. You can just as easily convert back to inches, or to one of the other systems offered.

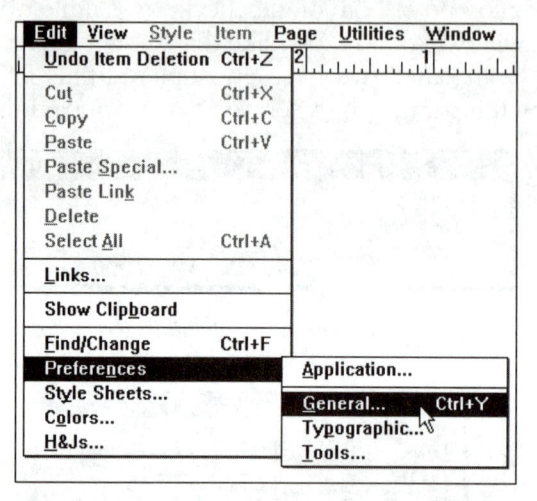

Figure 8.26 The Preferences juncture submenu.

Figure 8.27 General Preferences.

You might also notice some of the other functions here. You can change the value for greeking text. The default is 7 point. Replace this value with 2 point and you'll see a truer representation of text at reduced views—at the cost, however, of slower screen redraw. Also note that you can move the guides to a deeper level, which makes picking up objects on them easier. And the framing method for all boxes can be adjusted between framing inside (the default) to framing outside (which will not obscure box contents). More on all the preferences later.

STEPPING FORWARD

Typography offers endless possibilities for even the simplest of texts. Seeing how controls for paragraphs and stories can produce a countless range of variations, you've looked into the heart of QuarkXPress. To see more about how these features work, let's apply them to a typographically demanding medium, the newspaper.

Chapter 9

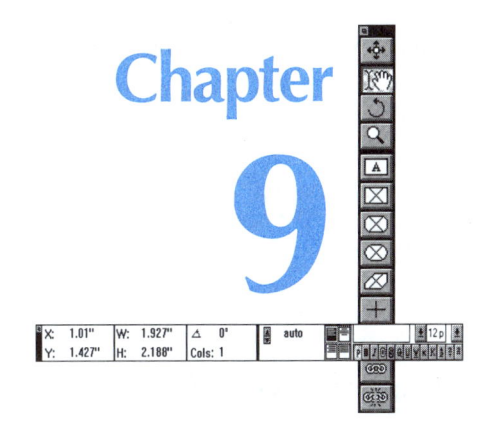

Newspapers on the Job

WHAT YOU WILL LEARN IN THIS CHAPTER

- How to set up a newspaper page layout
- How to apply hypenation and justification
- How to adjust stories on a large format page

For millions, ink-fresh newspapers start each day. On a full news day, Page One might expose readers to ten or more stories and direct them to a dozen more. Word-heavy by nature, most newspapers seek to lure a scanning, screening, discriminating audience to every story it can. Daily journalism, wrestling with the chaos of each day's events, demands typography that is lucid, provoking, and orderly.

In this chapter we'll work with a front page to put into practice those techniques introduced in Chapter 8. We'll set up hyphenation and justification, deal with indents and rules, and apply other typographical adjustments that bring order to the daily tumult of news stories.

THE FRONT PAGE

Our Page One requires a banner title, articles with headlines, and lead-ins to inside stories. We're working with a large-format document here, 23 by 13.75 inches. It folds in the middle for display in a stack or a rack, so our layout should take this into account. First we'll set up the document by creating the file, switching the measuring system, and setting margins in place.

Setting up the Newspaper Document

It's no mystery how to begin. We first turn to the File menu and choose New. In the New dialog box for width, we key in *13.75*, and for height, *23*. Setting up a strong grid is vital for a newspaper, and we opt for six columns, to keep our stories tightly in line. Conveniently, the Gutter width is already set for .167, which is 1 pica, the separation we're looking for.

We refrain from choosing "automatic text box" because the many stories on each page will each require their own variable boxes. As a result, the six columns which are laid out will serve strictly as guides. But important guides they will be, unifying the look of a variety of stories. Clicking OK, we create this newspaper-format document.

Next we change to the measurement system with which we prefer to work, then make some other document-wide display changes. Opening the Edit menu, we choose Preferences, and at the submenu that is displayed we choose General. In the General Preferences dialog box (shown in Figure 9.1) we use drop-down lists to convert the Horizontal Measure and Vertical Measure to picas.

This type-heavy newspaper will be an all-text document as far as our work is concerned. As we move along, we'll add placeholder picture boxes for photos. Being able to see text at different views is important. So, we click off the checkmark in the Greek Below checkbox. We click OK to complete our preferences adjustments.

Figure 9.1 Changing measures and display features for the document.

NOTE: Your choice of whether or not to greek text will depend on the speed with which your computer system can redraw the screen and the demands made on it by the formatting of the text. There is a trade-off here between speed of response and precision of display. The sometime sluggishness of a slower 16MHz SX machine with limited memory in the video graphics card would encourage its user to leave greeking on at the default, while the responsiveness of a 40 MHz DX machine with a megabyte or more of video memory would suggest no greeking, or greeking set at a low pixel value for greater screen-display clarity.

Next, after a change of mind, we'll use a different approach to adjust the margin guides. The margins are established in two places: the New dialog box when you create a document, and later, once the document exists, at the master pages. You reach the master pages by opening the Page menu and choosing Display. A submenu appears, as shown in Figure 9.2. Here, as in all newly created documents, there is only one master page. It's designated M1-Master1. Selecting it brings us to the facing master pages. We're here to do only one thing, readjust the margin

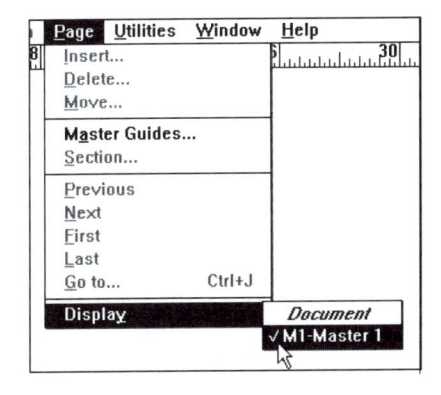

Figure 9.2 Locating the master page through submenu.

guides. For this we need only open the Page menu and choose Master Guides. When the dialog box is displayed, we key in new values in picas for the margins, in this case *3p* all around except for the inside margin, for which *2p* is typed (shown in Figure 9.3). Now the margins are set.

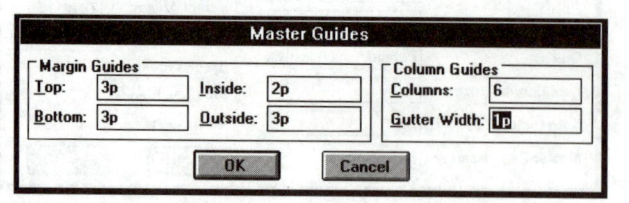

Figure 9.3 *Readjusting margin guides.*

NOTE When using the pica measuring system in QuarkXPress, it's wise to type pica values as *1p, 2p*, and so on. If the letter *p* does not follow the value, QuarkXPress assumes the value is in points (which are one-twelfth the pica value). Keying in *3* in a pica field would result in 3 points being assigned to that field, and on examining the field later you would see it appear as *p3*. The convention, then, is picas-"p"-points. A pica and a half (one pica, six points) would be displayed as *1p6*. 10 would be interpreted as p10 or 10 points, while 10p would be interpreted as 10 picas.

We return to Page 1 by opening the Page menu and choosing Display, then Document. First we pull a guide across at midheight on the page by clicking in the horizontal ruler and dragging down. Now our layout can take into account what will be displayed when the paper is folded. The page is 138 picas long, so we know that the midpoint is 69 picas from the top. We check this location by using the picture box rectangle tool to draw a box the length of the page over the page. When the box is selected, its side handles will mark the midpoint.

Finding the midpoint

Drag a box between two extremes

The item handles at the sides will fall at the midpoint

Top Matter

We're going to set up the top of this newspaper first, including the banner and accompanying information. We use the text box tool to draw a box at the top for the banner title. With the content tool selected, we choose the appropriate display font and type a size of 140 points at the Measurements palette and click on the Centering button there. At the Text Box Specifications dialog box (Item menu, Modify) we set the vertical alignment at Center. Then, back at the text box we key in the name, *Daily Times*, as shown in Figure 9.4. This begins the typesetting of Page 1. To improve banner appearance we adjust the tracking -5 by keying in that value at the Tracking field of the Measurements palette. Note that the rulers indicate picas, and the Measurements palette likewise displays values in pica units.

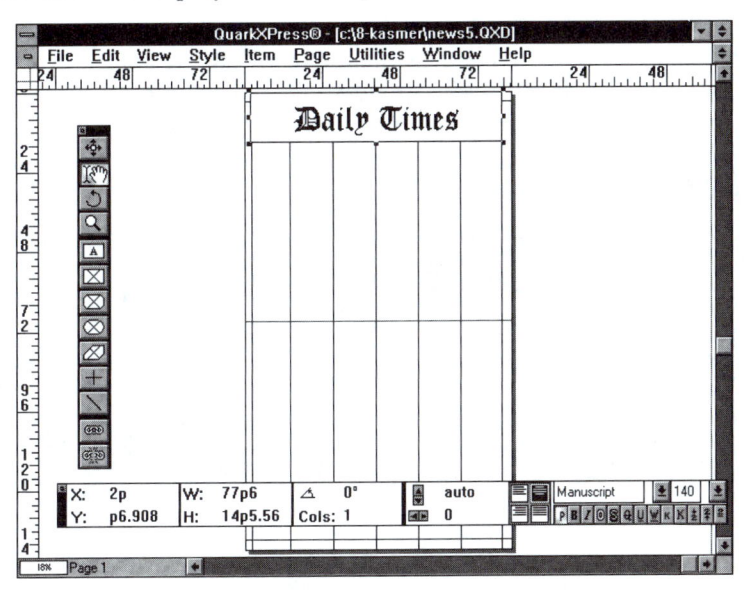

Figure 9.4 *Establishing the banner title.*

To separate the banner from the material below it, we use the rule tool and drag out a line from margin to margin. Two picas below this, we drag another line. We select the upper line, and turning to the Measurements palette, we key in *.5* in the W: field to make it half a point thick. Selecting the lower line, we key in *4* at the palette to make this line four points thick, and use the drop-down list to select the double-line attribute with a thin line over a thick one. The result is a set of enclosing lines.

Between these bounding lines we use the text box tool to drag a box across, margin to margin. In the box we type three phrases, including tabs before the last two: Final edition, the date, the price.

NOTE Many symbols and characters not apparent on the keyboard can be derived through special codes, the Windows ANSI character set. For instance, to type a cents symbol, hold the Alt key while pressing the four-digit number at the keypad, *0162*. When you release the Alt, a ¢ character will be displayed. More about ANSI characters in Chapter 18.

Selecting all (Ctrl-A) with the cursor in the text box, we use the Measurements palette to adjust type and size. Then it's time to adjust those tabs. We want to position the phrase *Final edition* flush left; the date, centered; and the price, flush right. With the cursor still in the text box, we open the Style menu and choose Tabs, thereby opening the Paragraph Tabs dialog box.

The first phrase is already in position, because the text is left-aligned. The date, however, is one default tab stop over. We want this stop to be at the center of the text box. So, we'll numerically figure the center from the width of the text box, shown in the Measurements palette as nearly 78 picas. We therefore want the date centered on 39 picas, with our wide, single-column text box. At the Paragraph Tabs dialog box, we open the Alignment drop-down list and choose Center. Using the scrolling arrows to locate 39 points in the dialog box ruler, we click there; a center tab is inserted (shown in Figure 9.5).

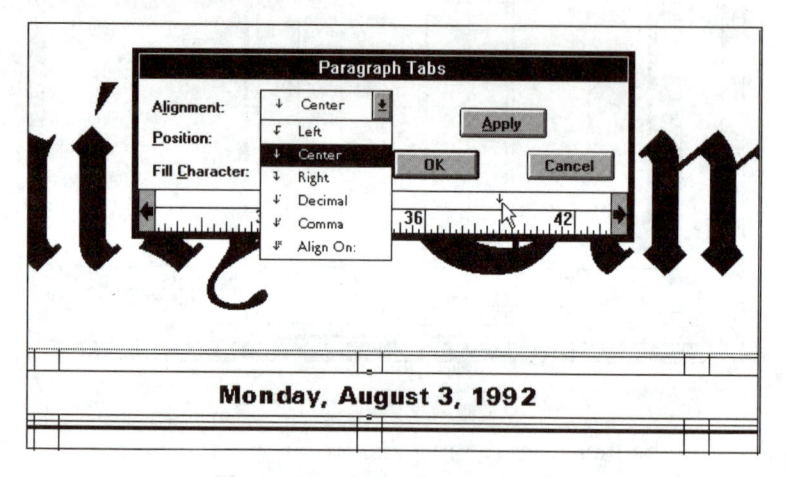

Figure 9.5 *Inserting a center tab.*

Last, there is the price. We want it aligned to the right extent of the text box. This is the second tab stop in the box. Returning to the Paragraph Tabs dialog box, we open the Alignment drop-down list and choose Right. In the position box we type in the position of the right end of the box, then click the Apply button. The price is aligned flush right, as shown in Figure 9.6.

This completes the top matter of Page 1.

The Stories

You'll notice that most newspapers follow a Page One layout format that varies only in minor points from day to day. A popular layout approach is to designate one story to run as a regular feature in a single column down the left of the page. We follow that plan here with a section labeled *Column One*. Using the text box tool at Fit in Window view, a long column box is dragged downward into the leftmost column, we rely on the Snap to Guides feature to make the box fit across the column exactly.

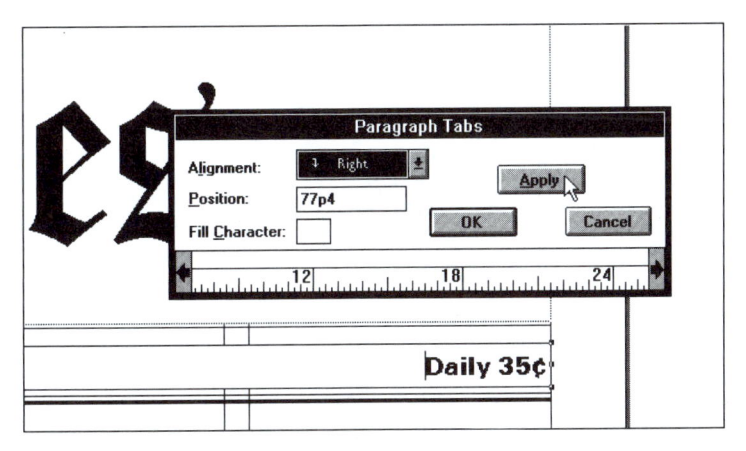

Figure 9.6 *Inserting a right tab.*

To create the column head, we type in the label, triple-click to select the line, then open the Style menu and choose Character. In the resulting dialog box we select a sans serif font, a size, All Caps, and bolding. To emphasize this label, we open the Style menu again and choose Rules. At the Paragraph Rules dialog box, we click on the checkbox marked Rule Below. After the box expands, we choose Text from the Length drop-down list. The rule will now run under our label like an offset underline. We key in a Width of 0.5 for a half point thickness. The resulting section head label is shown in Figure 9.7. Selecting OK, we turn next to the story headline.

Figure 9.7 *Character and rule formatting applied to a section head.*

In this design the body and headlines are all set in the same typeface, the ever-hardy Times Roman style. We key in a headline and a lead-in. Then, at the Measurements palette we make the following adjustments. The head is set at 30 points, the lead-in at 14. Both paragraphs are selected together and the tracking is reduced -5%.

Now the label, head, and lead-in are selected together in order to add paragraph spacing. At the Paragraph Formats dialog box (through Style menu to Formats) a value of *p6* (six points) is keyed into the Space After to separate the three paragraphs. Once we click OK, we see the three paragraphs spaced as shown in Figure 9.8.

Figure 9.8 *Uniform spacing applied to three paragraphs.*

NOTE Sometimes it's tempting to separate a paragraph from its neighbors by adding both Space Before and Space After through the Formats dialog box. Beware, this can become a trap. Because the spacing format doesn't stop with the paragraph in question, it continues to be applied as new paragraphs are successively generated. After this kind of formatting, separation of paragraphs is compounded. The space after paragraph one, for instance, will be combined with the space before paragraph two. The result can be an archipelago of paragraph islands in a sea of white space. You might want to consider using only Space After for successive paragraphs—making sure that paragraph spacing is reset following the stand-out paragraph.

In this layout we have a byline to include. Our design calls for an All Caps name set off by a thin rule from the headline and lead-in we've just completed. We begin by selecting 10 points, bold, at the Measurements palette and typing *By* and the reporter's name, *Gregory Wilson*, on a new line. Next, we drag to select just the name and open the Style menu. We choose Character and, in the Character Attributes dialog box, click All Caps. We leave the bolding setting and the other attributes as they are shown in Figure 9.9 and click OK. We're also accepting the paragraph spacing, so we leave the Formats dialog box unchanged. This byline should have a rule running above it across the column. The Style menu is opened and Rules is chosen. We click on the Rule Above checkbox and, at the expanded dialog box of Figure 9.10, choose Indents from the Length drop-down list. We also key in an offset of *20%* (to lift the rule 20 percent of the line spacing from the line) and change the Width to 0.5 points before clicking the Apply button. One look confirms this is the appearance we want, so we click the OK button.

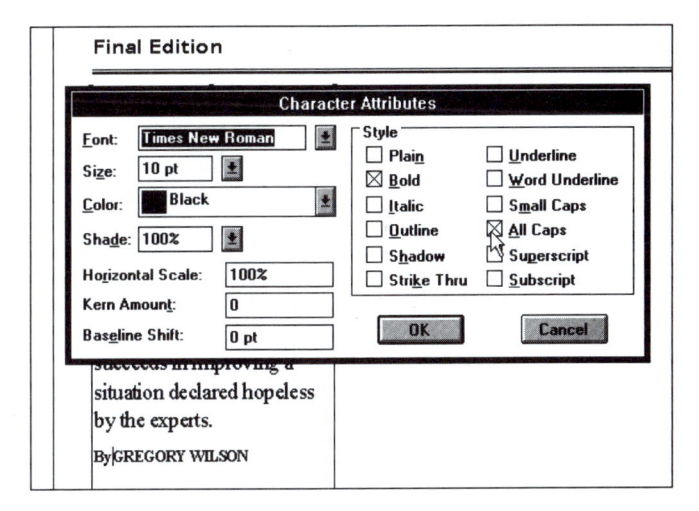

Figure 9.9 *Formatting a byline.*

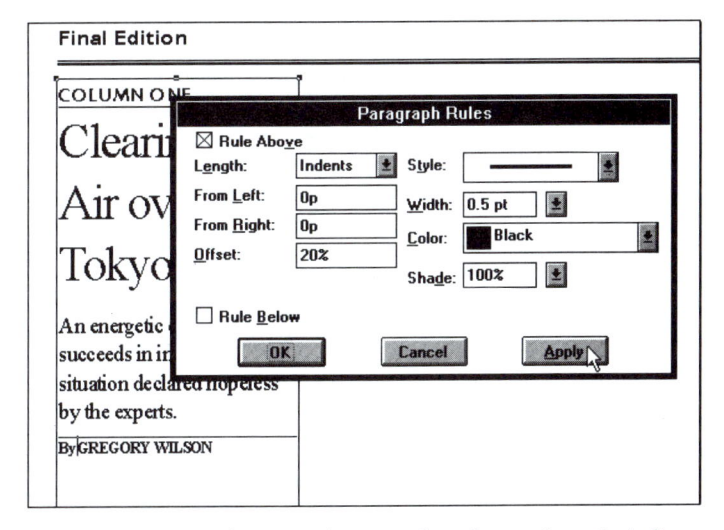

Figure 9.10 *Applying a rule across the column above the byline.*

Now it's time to add body copy into our story box. We're going to prepare for this text by adjusting the character and paragraph attributes. When the story is imported, we want its formatting to resemble the desired appearance of the final product. Here's what we do. Tapping the Enter key puts the cursor one line below the byline, where the story file will begin. Using the controls of the Measurements palette, we select plain text, Times Roman, 10 point, justified, with tracking set at zero. At the Paragraph Rules dialog box, the Rule Above checkbox is clicked to be blank, removing the rule established in the previous paragraph. Then at the Paragraph Formats dialog box (Style menu to Formats), the Space After value is set to zero since we want no interparagraph spacing in the body text. Also, the First Line indent is set to 8 points so that each paragraph will be indented about three characters. And finally the checkbox, Lock to Baseline Grid, is clicked to "x," engaging this function. The default baseline spacing of 12 points will work fine with the 10-point body type we'll be using.

With the text cursor placed where the body copy will begin, we open the File menu, choose Get Text, and double click on the file, AIRTOKYO.TXT. The story flows into the text box. Figure 9.11 shows the text with the Baseline Grid turned on.

Figure 9.11 *Body copy locked to baseline grid.*

Looking at the result, we see that a feature vital to the narrow column layout of a newspaper is not applied here. The hyphenation function is switched off. Hyphenation Off is the default for a new QuarkXPress document. We'll have to adjust the H&J specifications. Here we choose to generate a new specifications set that will be applied to body copy.

NOTE Sometimes you will want to change hyphenation or justification specifications once some text has been satisfactorily formatted in document columns. Changing an existing set of specifications, however, might also change those paragraphs already in place. All text to which another set of specifications is not applied automatically is assigned an H&J of Standard. So, in general, if you are pleased with the text already in the document, create a new set of H&J specifications.

Opening the Edit menu, we choose H&Js. At the H&Js dialog box that is displayed, we click the New button. This presents the specifications for Standard in the

Edit Hyphenation and Justification dialog box. We key in a name, *Standard2*, and then click an *x* into the Auto Hyphenation box. At this dialog box we make some other adjustments in order to avoid the looseness of the default settings. These modifications include setting the Smallest Word value to hyphenate on a five-character instead of a six-character word, changing the Minimum Before to two instead of three characters, adjusting the word spacing minimum and maximums to 90 percent and 130 percent (from 100 percent and 150 percent), and the letter spacing equivalents to -3 percent and 5 percent (from zero and 15 percent). The Single Word Justify feature is also deactivated before clicking OK.

Having made this new set of specifications, we then select the body copy and apply the new standard. This we do through the Paragraph Formats dialog box by locating Standard2 in the H&J drop-down list. Figure 9.12 shows the newly hyphenated and justified first paragraph with the specifications that adjusted it.

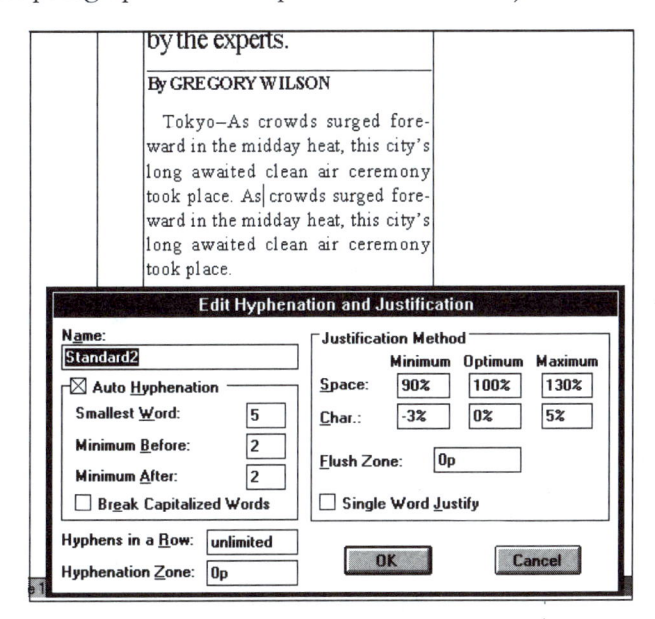

Figure 9.12   *Body copy with adjusted hyphenation and justification.*

NOTE In taking care of the body copy, we've established a Hyphenation/Justification standard, the specifications set Standard2, which can be used for any or all body copy in the paper. Developing standards for character and other formatting is performed similarly. These other standards can be saved in sets of specifications known as **style sheets**. In Chapter 10 style sheets will be explored in detail.

One small item remains to be fixed in the first paragraph. The dateline, *Tokyo*, should be capitalized. To do this we select the word by double-clicking, open the

Style menu, choose Character, then click All Caps and OK. Now the body of this story on Page 1 has been set. All that remains on this page is to signal the reader that the story has been jumped to the inside. We'll do this by adding a small continuation notice at the lower extent of the text box. Since our design calls for other stories to begin at 106 picas from the top, we produce a guide by clicking and dragging from the horizontal ruler down to that point, as indicated on the vertical ruler. Then we pull the Tokyo Air text box up above the guide.

We create another small text box for the jump notice—using the text box tool to drag one into place below the Story text box. In the Runaround Specifications dialog box (in the Item menu) we select None from the Mode drop-down list. At the text box, using the content tool we key in the jump information, choosing the same text style as the body but adding bolding at the Measurements palette. At the Formats dialog box (open Style menu), we click to *x* the Lock to Baseline Grid checkbox. The result is shown in Figure 9.13.

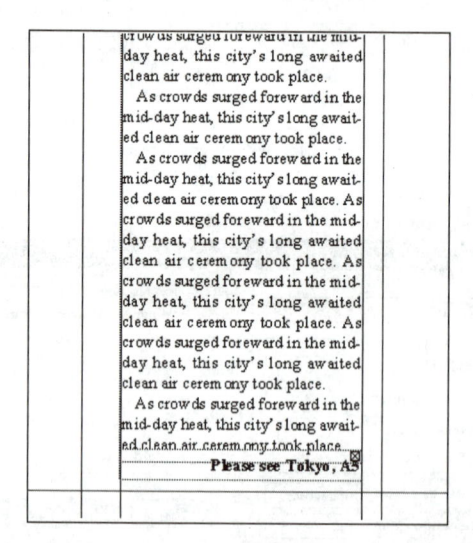

Figure 9.13   *A jump notice installed.*

Now we can fit in other stories across multiple columns at the top two-thirds of Page 1. The headline text boxes are drawn separately across the columns and left as single column boxes. The multiple column body text boxes are set through the Measurements palette to the number of columns matching their width on the grid guides. By applying the already established Standard2 hyphenation and justification specifications, using similar styles, formats, and rules, we incorporate the other stories of Page 1 into the design. A horizontal rule of 3 points is drawn to separate the two stories stacked in the rightmost columns. And because a photograph will be supplied to our specified proportions and pasted in, we use the rectangle picture box tool to drag out a picture box across three columns at the top of the layout, as shown in Figure 9.14. This serves as a placeholder for the halftone picture to be provided later.

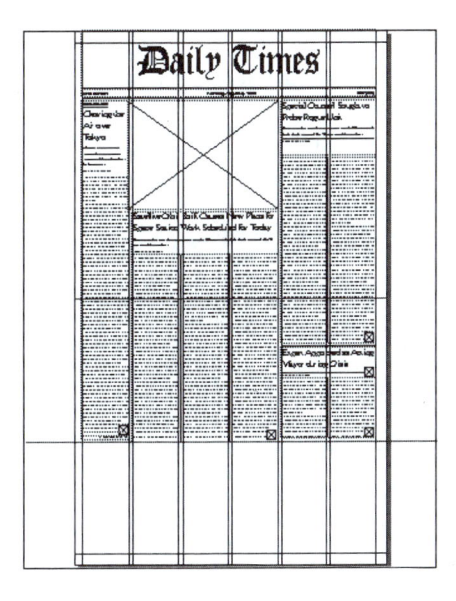

Figure 9.14 *A blank picture box as placeholder.*

The Inside Box

No Page One of a contemporary newspaper would be complete without a small table of contents built on blurbs extracted from the stories inside. In our design, that inside section is set in the two middle columns of the grid. It will be flanked by stories on either side, below a guide that we placed at 106 picas down. We'll include several short paragraphs based on articles located deeper within the paper.

We'll want a heading for the table of contents in one box, and the actual contents in another. We'll position them so they appear integrated. First we use the text box tool to draw two boxes across the two center columns, one above the other. The one on top is a short box, to hold the heading of the inside section, which fills out the space of the two columns below it. Both of these boxes will have frames. We will align them so they appear to be one box.

We draw the large box with the text box tool, from column guide to column guide, letting the Snap to Guides function pull the sides in line. Then we draw the smaller heading box the same way, placing the heading box one layer in front of the large box. We select both boxes with the item tool, open the Item menu, then choose Frames. At the dialog box we key in *1pt* and click OK. Next we open the Item menu, choosing Space/Align. At the dialog box we click the Vertical Alignment checkbox, click the Space button, leaving the value at *0p*, and at the Between drop-down list select Top Edges. Clicking OK returns us to the layout with the small box positioned over the large one and appearing like a division of that larger box.

Choosing the content tool, we click within the heading box and type *inside today's daily times*. Ctrl-A selects all the text. At the Character Attributes dialog box (Style menu to Character) shown in Figure 9.15 we format by clicking the All Caps and Bold checkboxes, make the font and size choices, and key in a 130 percent Horizontal scale for wider characters.

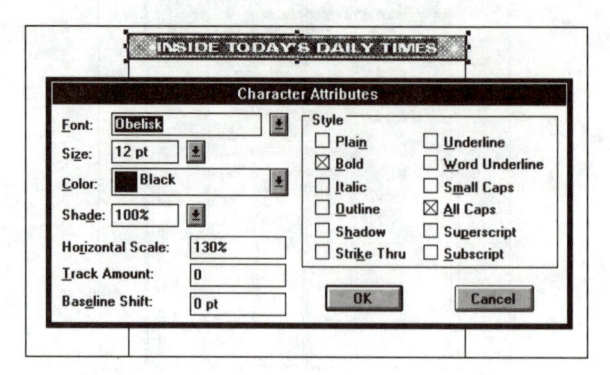

Figure 9.15 *Style formatting of the box heading.*

Next, we click below the heading in the larger box and type in the blurbs to appear there. Selecting All (Ctrl-A), we open the Character Attributes dialog box and change the font and size. Then we open the Paragraph Formats dialog box (Style menu to Formats) and adjust the left indents in two picas. The indent for the first line of each paragraph is only pulled in one pica. We also make sure to suppress the formation of widows and orphans with the Keep Lines Together checkbox. Space after each paragraph is keyed in as 8 points. Figure 9.16 shows the text and the dialog box.

Figure 9.16 *Fomatting the paragraphs.*

We also do a bit of formatting—by selecting the introductory phrase of each paragraph and bolding it through the keyboard (Ctrl-Shift-B). And we've added a tab before each page reference at the end of every paragraph. We want to adjust these tabs to be right tabs to the end of the column, so we select all (Ctrl-A). The Paragraph Tabs dialog box is opened (through the Style menu), and we make the adjustments there, as shown in Figure 9.17.

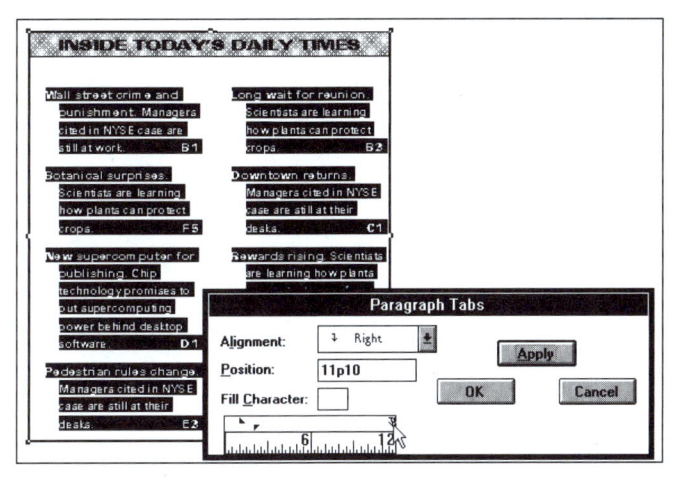

Figure 9.17 *Aligning page numbers to the right with tab adjustment.*

There is another adjustment required if the text is shifting downward within the text box. We've accomplished this by clicking on the heading box to select it and opening the Item menu, and choosing Runaround. In the specifications dialog box as shown in Figure 9.18, we've used the Mode, Item, and set its bottom offset to 24 points to push down the text in the box below a full two picas as shown.

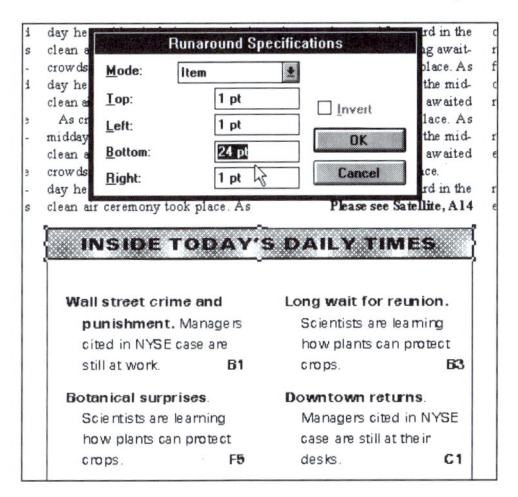

Figure 9.18 *Pushing down text through Runaround of the heading box.*

Finally, adding a story on either side of the Inside box completes the typesetting of Page One.

STEPPING FORWARD

In composing a front page you've seen how typography can make otherwise undistinguished text matter stand out from its cousins in the layout. There are still more typographical controls. Some affect text on the document-wide level, some are connected to the master pages, and others are special tricks of the program.

In the next chapter we will explore more typography, using style sheets, and document flow controls.

Chapter 10

Document Flow

WHAT YOU WILL LEARN IN THIS CHAPTER

- How to create and use master pages
- How to create and import style sheets
- How to group items
- How to anchor inline graphics and text
- How to manage multiple-page spreads
- How to set up sections
- How to number pages automatically and create jump lines

Documents grow. Pages multiply. Stories are jumped. Designs expand carrying along formatting from story to story, page to page. In this chapter we look into giving unity to QuarkXPress-generated documents. We also examine features that help integrate text, picture, and line items in versatile and visually compelling ways.

Two features of QuarkXPress are especially important for producing complex documents: master pages and style sheets. They let you carry your best formatting and layout efforts to all parts of a publication where they can be put to use. We will examine them in detail along with other page and item capabilities that make for well-integrated documents.

Master Pages

Every page is different. In some cases the difference is minor, as in novels, where the only difference in appearance may be the positions of page numbers on verso and recto pages. In other cases, the difference is so great that readers may forget which publication they are reading. Haven't you ever been momentarily waylaid by a full-page ad, and before leaving it forgotten what magazine you were holding?

Almost always, pages in a publication are graphically related to each other. It may be only by a rule positioned at the top or by page numbering. Or there may be similarity in the number and location of columns, in section headings, in graphic emblems, or in dozens of other layout items.

Using Master Pages

Much time and effort clearly can be saved by preserving and automatically transferring the repeated elements and layouts to page after page. This is the essential function of a master page. Every page in a new QuarkXPress document is automatically built on one. Called M1-Master1, it is established through the New command with certain dimensions, certain guides, margins, and perhaps a text box. It is but one of countless possible master pages.

Additional master pages can be produced and applied to either new or existing pages at any stage of document development. Also, special linking through text boxes on a master page can trigger the program to automatically generate hundreds of typeset pages. Master pages can be applied to certain pages, dissociated from others, or even removed from the document altogether.

In every single-sided document the master pages themselves are of one format, from **Blank Single Master**. In every facing-pages document the master pages can be of such single-sided format or of double-sided, from **Blank Facing Master**. These master page types provide the bases for creating new master pages or modifying existing document pages.

Master Page Designation

The Document Layout palette is a useful window onto the activity of pages and master pages. It normally appears on the screen when QuarkXPress is started. Recall that it can be called up through the View menu by choosing Show Document Layout. As shown in Figure 10.1, two menu headings, Document and Apply, appear at the top of the layout palette.

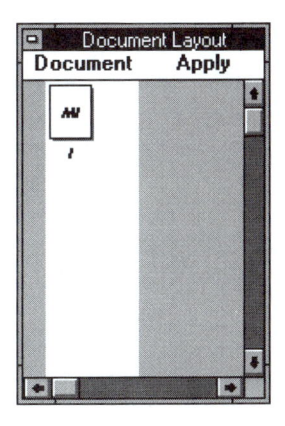

Figure 10.1 The Document Layout palette of a new document.

The Document menu refers to changes that can be made to individual pages, such as inserting pages, removing pages, or switching the layout palette to display icons for the master pages. The Apply menu is devoted to choosing one of the available master pages and applying it to an existing page.

To see what master pages are available for a newly created single-page, single-sided document, we can click on the page icon to select it, and open the Apply menu as in Figure 10.2.

Figure 10.2 A list of applicable master pages.

Here we see the simplest of master page situations. Three different master pages are represented in the drop-down list. Each of the first two, the Blank Single and Blank Facing Masters, represents a master page choice that can be applied to pages. Each provides a format that can be applied to any new or existing master pages, answering the question, Should this master page be formed as a single-sided page or part of a facing-pages spread? Note that in this case only the Blank Single Master and M1-Master 1 choices are in dark lettering and accessible. That is because this document was set up through the New dialog box as a single-sided publication with the Facing-pages checkbox unchecked.

Figure 10.3 shows the layout palette of a document with more diversity. Here you can see that the blank masters of both single and facing pages have been applied as indicated by blank page icons on pages 1, 6, and 7.

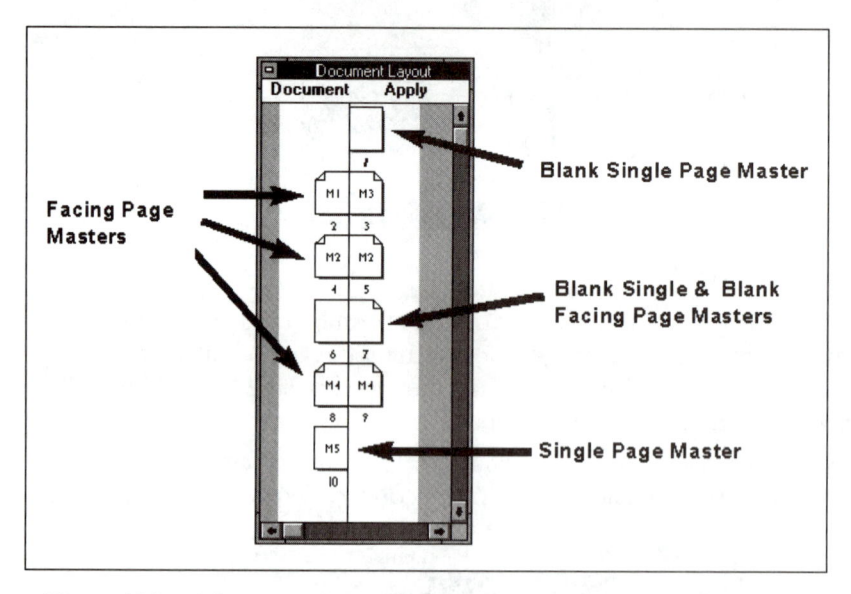

Figure 10.3 *A Document Layout showing a variety of master pages applied.*

Recall that dog-eared page icons indicate a facing-page master has been applied. Here, facing-page masters have been applied to Pages 2 through 5 and Pages 8 and 9 (indicated by M1, M3, M2, and M4 within the page icons). And notice in particular that though they are facing pages of the same spread, Pages 2 and 3 are based on different master pages, M1 and M3, respectively.

The Blank Single Master and Blank Facing Master always remain empty of all content, items, or guides (except that they reflect choices in the New dialog box regarding page dimensions and margins). The other master pages, designated M1-Master 1, M2-Master 2, and so on, can contain anything a document page is capable of holding, and more.

Access to the Master Pages

Of course, when you make a new document you create a master page with it, M1-Master 1. How can you work with this?

Let's consider a simple case. When a new document of facing pages is created with the New command, we find ourselves at a page like Page 1. If this document is expanded to a 32-page document, by adding pages through the Page menu's Insert command dialog box, the default master page, M1, will be automatically applied to the added pages as in shown Figure 10.4. Or, by using the drop-down list, you can choose to apply one of the other available masters (blank single and blank facing pages) to your pages, either through the Insert Pages dialog box or the Document Layout palette..

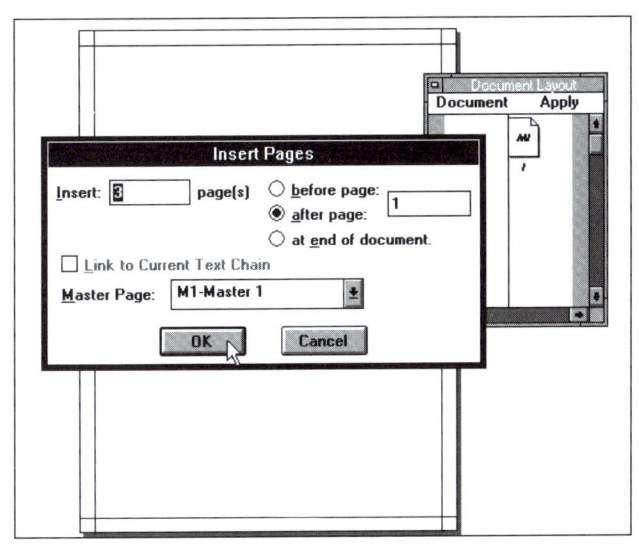

Figure 10.4   Automatic master page, M1, applied.

> **Applying a master page**
>
> At the Document Layout palette, select the page or pages
>
> Open the Apply menu and choose the master page

You can easily bring into the document window a master page (not counting the blanks, which are untouchables), by opening the Page menu and choosing Display. A submenu pops up, as shown in Figure 10.5. After sliding the mouse pointer over to the name of the master page (M1-Master 1, for example), you'll see the master page layout displayed.

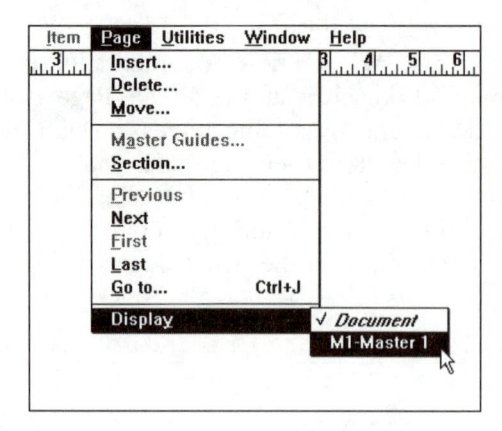

Figure 10.5   *Moving to a master page.*

> **Moving to a master page**
>
> *Open the Page menu and choose Display*
>
> *At the submenu, choose the master page*

Notice that the master page spread looks much like any document-page layout. It reflects the choices made in the New dialog box for the document. If you chose Facing Pages through the checkbox when you created the document, you'll find that M1 will be displayed as two facing pages. Margin and column guides will also be displayed, just as on a document page.

NOTE   Note that what is called a master page can be just one page, or it can be a spread of two. In cases where it is a spread, the master page can be applied to a single document page. QuarkXPress will assign the corresponding left- or right-page master page.

On the master page with guides active (View menu to Show Guides), you will also notice an icon in the upper-left corner. This is a **text chain icon** and refers to the text-linking checkbox you engaged when the document was created. If you chose to activate automatic text boxes through the checkbox in the New command, the icon will appear as a set of connected links, like the text-linking tool. Every page inserted into the document will have a text box linked to the next page's text box. This was the approach we used in creating a word processing document file. It's also the approach you might use to produce a book.

If you choose not to engage the automatic text box checkbox in the New dialog box, the master page's corner icon will appear as the unlinking tool, a set of links broken in the middle, as shown in Figure 10.6. In this case you'll see no text boxes. And automatic text box linking will be inactive.

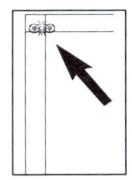

Figure 10.6   *Master page indicating automatic text box linking is inactive.*

Working in Master Pages

Working on a master page is just like doing layout or typesetting on a document page. For instance, if you want to put a rule across the top of the document page, you select the rule tool and drag out a line there. You can make all the same adjustments, such as choosing a thicker width at the Measurements palette. Of course, you'll normally lay down fewer or smaller items on a master page than you might on a document page. But remember, these items will be on every page to which the master has been applied.

Figure 10.7 shows the left page of a two-page master spread, M1, in one document. Several items, including lines, text and picture boxes, have been laid out and positioned just as they might be on a document page. A different but similar layout has been used on the right page of the same master. Together both pages represent the M1-Master 1 page spread, as shown in Figure 10.8.

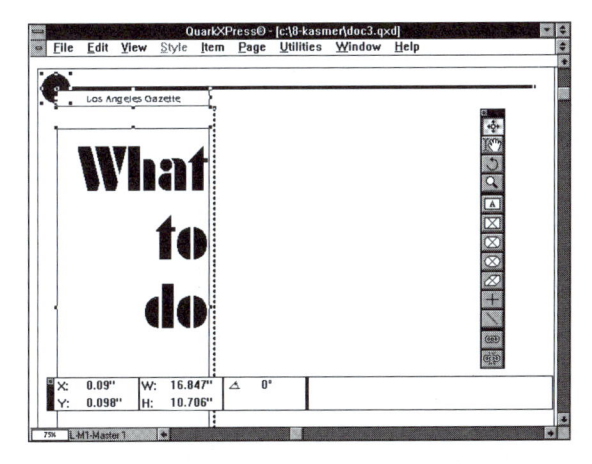

Figure 10.7   *The left member of a master page spread.*

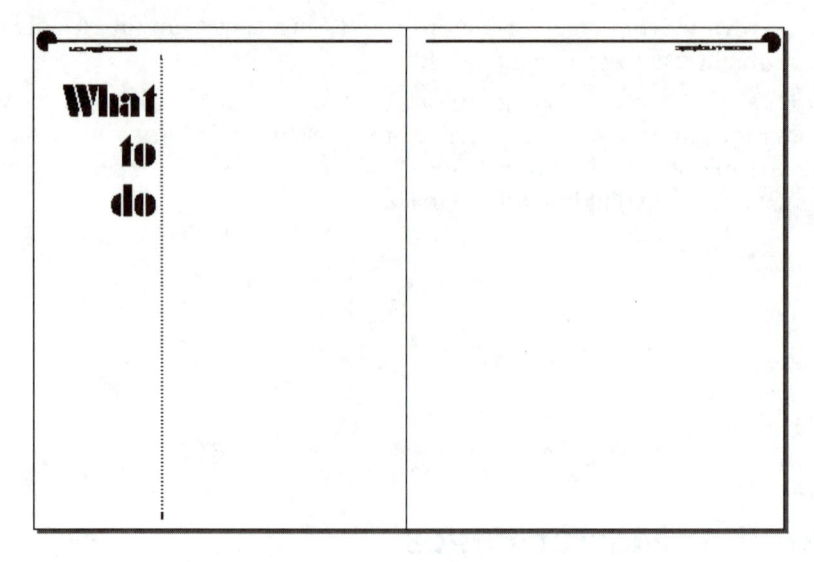

Figure 10.8 *A master page spread.*

Adjustments of Master Items on Document Pages

All document pages with master page designation will have all the items in place exactly as on the master page. But they can normally be modified, moved, and deleted just like those created on the document page.

   For instance, you can use the content tool to change the document-page text of a text box created in the master page. In Figure 10.9, an insert has been labeled by modifying the original master page item above it. You can also move items by selecting and dragging as usual.

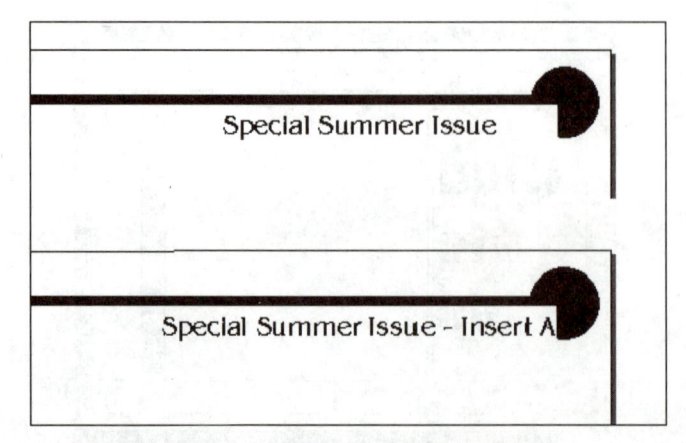

Figure 10.9 *Editing a master page item on the document page.*

However, there may be times when, because of very precise positioning requirements, you won't want master page items moved or deleted under any circumstance. For these cases, QuarkXPress provides a useful option. On the master page, you can lock items in place, just as on a document page, so that they can't be moved or resized using a tool. Just select the item or items, open the Item menu, and choose Lock. Conversely, choosing Unlock frees the items to be relocated.

Locking items

>   Select the items
>
>   Open Item menu and choose Lock

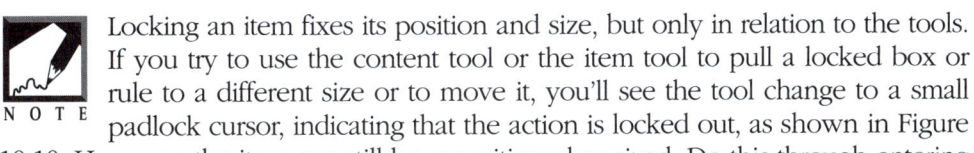

NOTE Locking an item fixes its position and size, but only in relation to the tools. If you try to use the content tool or the item tool to pull a locked box or rule to a different size or to move it, you'll see the tool change to a small padlock cursor, indicating that the action is locked out, as shown in Figure 10.10. However, the item can still be repositioned or sized. Do this through entering new values in the Measurements palette or the Specifications Box (Item menu to Modify). The contents and attributes of the locked item are subject to change as always.

Figure 10.10   *A locked item changing a Tool icon.*

Adjusting position or size of a locked item

>   Select the item
>
>   Enter new values in the Measurements palette

A text box originating on a master page may be modified in all the usual ways on a document page. Even if the box is locked, its text may be edited as usual. You can create a blank text box on the master page and fill in the blank on each document page as it comes up. This is one way to generate title pages or section-front pages that must have a unity of design while varying in content. Lines and boxes originating on a master page may also be modified on a document page.

> **NOTE** An item modification on a document page will not affect the original item on the master page. Nor will it affect similar items on other document pages.

Generating Master Pages

Aside from the automatically generated master page, M1-Master 1, and the blank master page formats that wipe off master page features when applied to a document page, numerous other master pages can be produced for any document. Master pages can be based on blank pages or on existing master pages.

The method for producing new master pages involves the Document Layout palette. It is a two-step process. First the format is chosen: single or facing-page or an existing master. Then the new master is inserted into the list of existing master pages.

To gain access to these master page controls, go to the Document Layout palette, open the Document menu, and choose Show Master Pages. The menu heading will change to Masters.

To create a new master page, open the menu, now headed Masters, and choose Insert. A submenu listing the blanks and the existing masters will open, as shown in Figure 10.11. Next, slide the pointer over and choose one of the blanks or an existing master. Move the cursor to the main palette area. It will change to the insertion tool shown in Figure 10.12. Click, and a new master page will be produced.

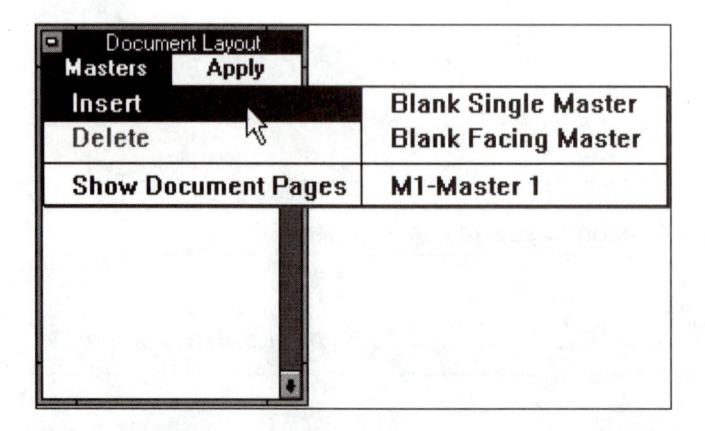

Figure 10.11 *Preparing to add a new master page.*

Figure 10.12   Inserting a new master page.

An icon will appear instantly in the list of masters, following the existing icon you've clicked below. This new master page will be labeled following the sequence of master pages that already exist in the document, M1-Master 1, M2-Master 2, and so on.

Adding a master page

>*At the Document Layout palette, open the Document menu*
>
>*Choose Show Master Pages*
>
>*Open the Masters menu*
>
>*Choose Insert and select a page format*
>
>*Move the arrow cursor into position on the list and click*

Choosing an existing master from the Insert list will create a new master page based on that existing master, with all its items.

Deleting a master page is simple and quick. So be careful and sure of your intentions. Select the icon from the palette's list by clicking. Then open the Masters menu and choose Delete. The master page will be removed without confirmation.

Removing a master page

>*At the Document Layout palette, click to select the master page icon*
>
>*Open the Masters menu and choose Delete*

Changing the basis of a master page takes just two steps. Select the master page first. Then open the Apply menu and choose the blank or the master to write over the selected master page. After a confirmation dialog box, the master page will be changed. Again, proceed with caution, because this action is not reversible through the Edit menu's Undo command.

> **Changing the format of a master page**
>
> At the Document Layout palette, click to select the master page
>
> Open the Apply menu and choose the replacement master format

To reach a master page directly from the Document palette, simply double-click on its icon. The master page will appear in the document window. You can quickly move between master pages this way. An alternative is to open the document's Page menu, choose Display, and locate the appropriate master page in the submenu.

NOTE: You can change the name of a master page, but not its prefix code (the M1, M2, and so on). For instance, M3-Master 3 can be renamed M3-Reviews Section, but not as just Reviews Section.

To rename a master page, click on its name next to the icon in the Document Layout palette. Then type in the new name. QuarkXPress will automatically reinsert the prefix that was applied to the original name. The prefix stays with the master page until it is deleted.

> **Renaming a master page**
>
> At the Document Layout palette, click on the name next to the master page
>
> Key in the new name

Automatic Page Numbers

There is one special way a master page can function interactively with the pages in the document. It can function as a vehicle for automatic page numbering. On nearly all publications this is helpful, and on long ones, especially so.

QuarkXPress handles page numbering through a placeholder inserted in a text box on the master page. The program can automatically number all the pages in a document of any length. Anywhere a placeholder is put on any master page, a corresponding page number will appear on the document page .

To set up automatic page numbering, first create a text box. Then, with the text cursor active, type Ctrl-3 within the box. This is the code for the page-number placeholder. You might note that the 3 key is home of the pound sign (#). In fact when you type in the placeholder keystroke you will see a pound sign inside angled brackets (<#>). This character code can be adjusted and formatted within the text box, just as any other text can. You can also mix text with it (for example, Page <#> or -<#>-). Figure 10.13 shows the page-number placeholder on the master page and next to it the page numbering on a corresponding document page.

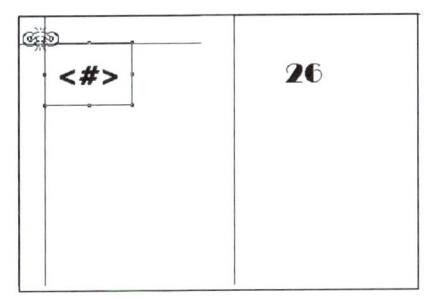

Figure 10.13   *Master page number placeholder and resulting document page number.*

Establishing automatic page numbering

At the master page, prepare a text box

Press Ctrl-3

Note that you will need to put the placeholder on both left and right master pages in a facing-pages document. One quick way to do this is to copy the text box used on one page of a facing pair and paste the duplicate on the other page of the pair. The <#> code will stand in for even or odd numbers.

STYLE SHEETS

Inevitably as you work in QuarkXPress, formatting and applying style to text, you will develop a need for greater control. You'll find you've fashioned paragraph formats and type styles that would work perfectly applied to different portions of text in the document. And so the question arises: How to reapply style and formatting specifications already laboriously set in text?

In QuarkXPress, as in other desktop publishing programs and word processors, this need is answered by a method that relies on format and style models known as style sheets. Style sheets are to text what master pages are to document pages.

The principle of style sheets is simple. You set up style and format for text paragraphs in the text itself and save the typesetting specifications in a kind of sub-document, the style sheet. Or, you can establish the style sheet and set up specifications within it directly.

Remember how H&J specifications were established? Style sheets are specifications of all the text and paragraph attributes for a paragraph. Each style sheet can be applied selectively to any of the text within a document. A style sheet can be made accessible in a variety of ways. You can create a style sheet from scratch, or format text just the way you like and then designate a style sheet based on that text. You can import style sheets from other sources, such as other QuarkXPress documents or word processors. And you can export them as well.

More than any other feature, style sheets provide for unified typography within a design document. Consider the case of subheads in an article as shown in Figure 10.14. Here you find style differences between the one-line paragraph (the subhead) and the ocean of body text that surrounds it. Each time another subhead is to be typeset, the same set of formatting and type specs will be called for. With style sheets available, the typesetting desktop publisher simply selects the paragraph and designates it a subhead through the style sheet. Without them, the typesetter must reformat each paragraph into subhead form using a list of typographical settings.

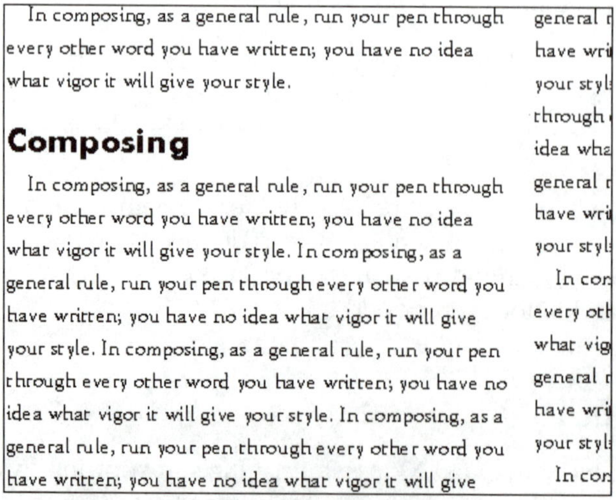

In composing, as a general rule, run your pen through every other word you have written; you have no idea what vigor it will give your style.

Composing

In composing, as a general rule, run your pen through every other word you have written; you have no idea what vigor it will give your style. In composing, as a general rule, run your pen through every other word you have written; you have no idea what vigor it will give your style. In composing, as a general rule, run your pen through every other word you have written; you have no idea what vigor it will give your style. In composing, as a general rule, run your pen through every other word you have written; you have no idea what vigor it will give

Figure 10.14 *A subheading within body text.*

Applying Style Sheets

There are two ways to associate a style with a paragraph or a selection of paragraphs. In each case, the first step is to select the paragraph or paragraphs with the content tool. Placing the cursor within it is sufficient for a single paragraph. For a range of text, select all or part of each paragraph.

One method of applying style to the selected text requires displaying a palette that lists all the style sheets available in a document. The command to do this is a Show/Hide palette command, like those we've used for the Tools, Measurements, and Document Layout palettes. To display the Style palette, open the View menu and choose Show Style Sheets. In Figure 10.15, you can see both the Show/Hide command and the palette it puts on the screen. Next, to apply a style sheet to the text, click on the name in the palette listing. All selected paragraphs will be reformatted and restyled.

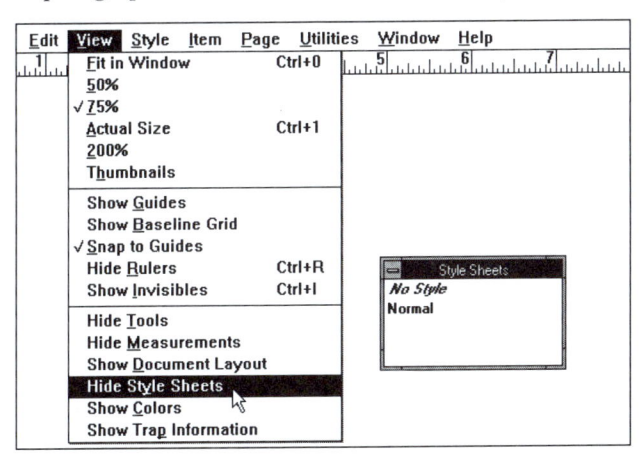

Figure 10.15 *Displaying a Style Sheets palette.*

The other method of applying style is through a submenu. Open the Style menu and choose Style Sheets. A submenu will appear, as shown in Figure 10.16. To apply the style, slide the pointer over the listing to the style sheet preferred and release the mouse button.

Applying a style sheet to text

Select the paragraph(s) with the content tool, or insert cursor

At the Style Sheets palette, click on the style sheet

or

At the Style menu, choose Style Sheets, then select the desired style sheet

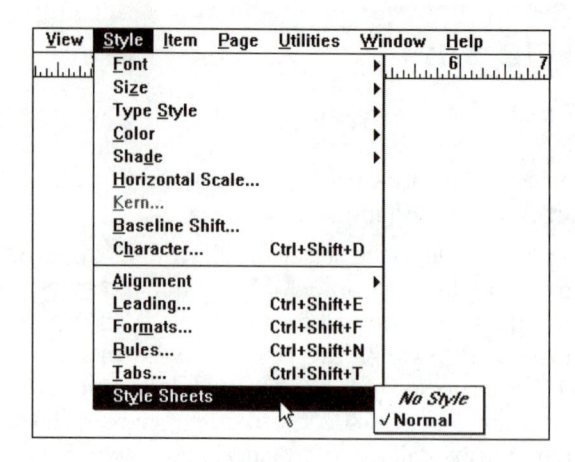

Figure 10.16 *Applying style sheets using the Style menu.*

What It Means to Have No Style

In new documents, QuarkXPress provides at least two style sheet choices, as illustrated in Figures 10.15 and 10.16. One of these, Normal, is a default style sheet automatically applied to any new text box. It specifies, as all style sheets do, the font, leading, indents, tabs, and so on in the paragraphs to which it's applied. We'll look more at this in a moment.

The other choice is No Style. No Style allows current style sheet formatting to remain on a paragraph regardless of subsequent changes to the style sheet itself. When you apply No Style to a paragraph, there is no change in its appearance. If you later reformat the style sheet that was previously applied to the paragraph, other paragraphs will take on the new formatting, but the No Style paragraph will retain the original formatting.

Figure 10.17 shows a box of text in which all the paragraphs received a Normal style sheet formatting when Normal was defined as Times Roman, Plain. Then just one paragraph, in the center, received the No Style formatting. Next the Normal style sheet specifications were changed to Arial bold. Of all the text, only the No Style paragraph in the center retained the original formatting.

Creating and Adjusting Style Sheets

How, then, to create the various style sheets that a full-length publication demands: headlines, subheads, captions, body text, pull quotes, teasers, page-jump notices, section titles, bylines, and so on? The answer lies in the style sheet controls and in a dialog box that stores specifications of paragraph formatting, paragraph rules, tabs, and character type attributes.

Document Flow ◆ **229**

> In composing, as a general rule, run your pen through every other word you have written; you have no idea what vigor it will give your style.
>
> In composing, as a general rule, run your pen through every other word you have written; you have no idea what vigor it will give your style. In composing, as a general rule, run your pen through every other word you have written; you have no idea what vigor it will give your style.
>
> In composing, as a general rule, run your pen through every other word you have written; you have no idea what vigor it will give your style.
>
> In composing, as a general rule, run your pen through every other word you have written; you have no idea what vigor it will give your style.
>
> In composing, as a general rule, run your pen through every other word you have written; you have no idea what vigor it will give your style. In composing, as a general rule, run your pen through every other word you have written; you have no idea what vigor it will give your style.
>
> In composing, as a general rule, run your pen through every other word you have written; you have no idea what vigor it will give your style.
>
> In composing, as a general rule, run your pen through every other word you have

Figure 10.17 *No Style preserves formatting for one paragraph when the style sheet is modified.*

To reach the style sheet controls, open the Edit menu and choose Style Sheets. The dialog box shown in Figure 10.18 will appear. Along the bottom, a running description is displayed of all the attributes and formats of the style sheet selected.

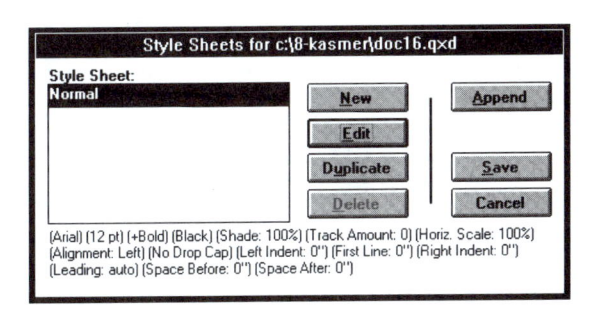

Figure 10.18 *The Style Sheets dialog box.*

If you've selected text in the document, its style and formatting will be summarized. The first four buttons in the center of the dialog box represent basic controls. At the right in the dialog box, the Append button sends QuarkXPress to the directory listings. Its function is to import into the document various style sheets that have been created elsewhere. For instance, you can locate another QuarkXPress document with dozens of style sheets or a Microsoft Word for Windows file (when the Word filter is present in the QuarkXPress directory folder), and import all the style sheets to the current document. Exceptions will be those with names the same as style sheets already existing in the document. QuarkXPress will not overwrite them.

> **Importing style sheets**
>
> > Open the Edit menu and choose Style Sheets
> >
> > At the Style Sheets dialog box, click the Append button
> >
> > In the directory windows that appear, locate the document containing desired style sheets and double-click

At the basic controls, the New button leads to the dialog box shown Figure 10.19, titled Edit Style Sheet. Specifications are set through it, and another style sheet can be created. To use selected text in the document as a basis for a new style sheet, click on New and then key in a name at the Edit Style Sheets dialog box. Click OK. Back at the Style Sheets dialog box, you'll see the name of the new style sheet displayed in the list and the specification summarized at the bottom. Click on the Save button, and the new style will be available in the document.

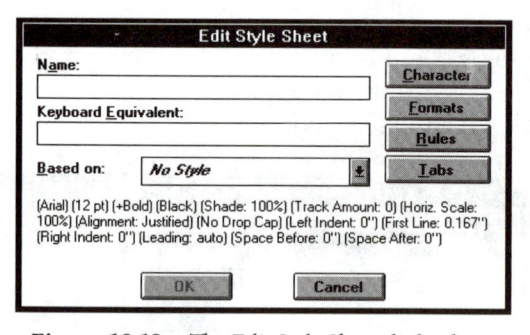

Figure 10.19 The Edit Style Sheet dialog box.

> **Creating a style from a text selection**
>
> > Select the model text
> >
> > Open the Style Sheets dialog box and choose New
> >
> > At the Edit Style Sheets dialog box, key in a name, and click the OK button
> >
> > At the Style Sheets dialog box, click Save

Each button on the right in Figure 10.19 leads to the dialog box corresponding to commands on the Style menu for text: Character Attributes, Paragraph Format, Paragraph Rules, Paragraph Tabs. Using these, adjustments can be made to all the attributes and formatting that will be applied through a style sheet, in the same way adjustments are made to text directly. Here again, you'll see the description of attributes and formats that have been specified in the dialog box.

In the first field of the dialog box, you can type in the name you wish to assign this style sheet. And you can invent and key in a keyboard shortcut that will select and apply this style sheet to text. The function keys (except for F1) are particularly well suited to serve as style sheet shortcuts.

The Edit button leads to the same dialog box and the same functionality as the New button, with one exception. The name is locked in place and can't be modified. Aside from that, you can change any existing style sheet through this command.

The Duplicate button creates a copy of the style sheet selected and leads to the Edit Style Sheet dialog box again, with the name "Copy of (whatever was selected)" in the first field. The copy will have all the text attributes and formatting from the original style sheet. You can leave this name, if you like. More likely, you'll want to key in something descriptive of the style sheet. For instance, you could design a large headline style sheet, then duplicate it, change the size of type and the tracking, and rename it as a subhead.

Removing a style sheet is simple. Select it in the list and click the Delete button. Note that the Normal style cannot be removed from a document.

When you find that the style sheets in the dialog box are suited to your uses, you can install them (new or edited) into the document all at once. Just click the Save button. This will add the changes and the new style sheets to listings in the palette and Style Sheets submenu.

> **NOTE** It's important to remember to use the Save button. Otherwise, you'll find that changes to the style sheets will not be implemented by QuarkXPress.

Basing Styles Sheets on Other Style Sheets

More often than not, much of the typography within a document is derived from other typography. For instance, subheadings frequently resemble headlines. Or second-level subheads may resemble primary subheads. Or a caption may simply be a smaller italicized version of the body text. Or headlines may be large, tightly tracked versions of the body text. Many times the difference between these elements is little more than one of size.

It's not unusual to put a lot of care into formatting a collection of interrelated headlines, subheads, or other text styles and formats, even while the design of your publication is still in development and subject to change. At some point you may find that you want to change just one or two aspects of the styles you've created—perhaps just the typeface or the horizontal width. If you had simply derived each related style sheet from another by using the Duplicate button and then renaming in the Edit dialog box, you would need to edit each style sheet separately to make changes consistent across all of them.

Fortunately, an option available within the Edit Style Sheet dialog box permits us to retain the relationships between an original style sheet and its offspring. This control works by maintaining the link to the parent style sheet, keeping track of which style sheet a later style sheet was based on. It can be engaged through the drop-down list of the Based On field. Figure 10.20 shows a style sheet named Subhead Two based on an existing style sheet named Subhead One.

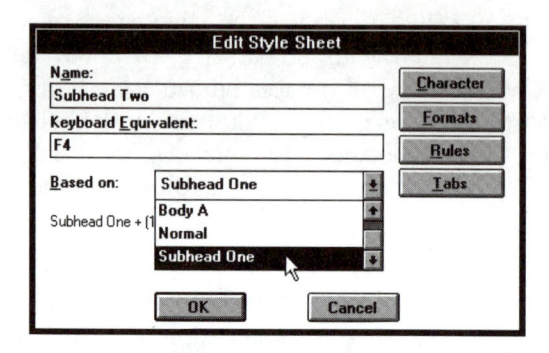

Figure 10.20 *Basing a style sheet, Subhead Two, on Subhead One.*

In this case, a change of style or format within the first style sheet will be reflected in the second. For instance, there are two levels of subheads shown in Figure 10.21. The larger, 24-point subhead, labeled Subhead One, can be seen applied to the phrases "Composing" and "Other words." The smaller, 18-point subhead is labeled Subhead Two has been applied to the phrases "Vigor" and "Run your pen." It was based on Subhead One through the Edit Style Sheet dialog box, as shown in Figure 10.20, and varies from it only in font size.

Basing one style sheet on another

Proceed as usual, creating a new style sheet or editing an existing one

In the Edit Style Sheets dialog box, open the Based On drop-down list and choose an existing style sheet

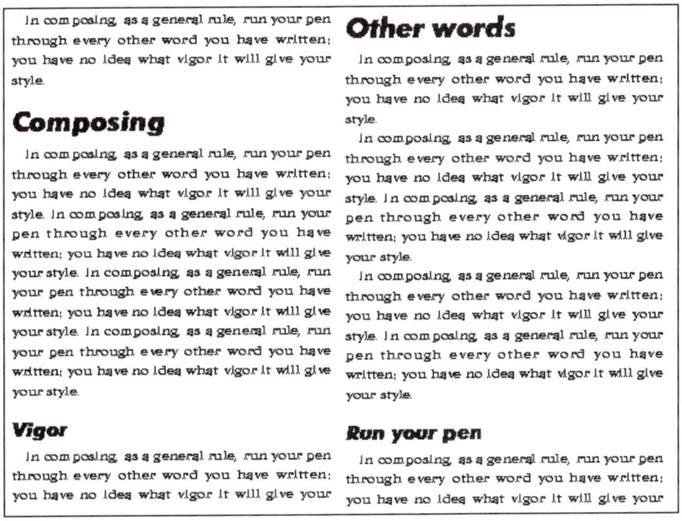

Figure 10.21   *Two levels of subheads, one based on the other.*

The font set in the specifications for Subhead One is called Futuri Black; it has been italicized. To change all the subheads, an edit was made to the Subhead One style sheet only. In the Edit Style Sheet dialog box, the font was changed to Dateline Condensed, and the italics were removed by clicking off the checkbox. Figure 10.22 shows the result. Not only have the first-level subheads (to which Subhead One style sheet was applied) changed, but the second-level subheads reflect the different typeface and font style as well, since Subhead Two is based on Subhead One.

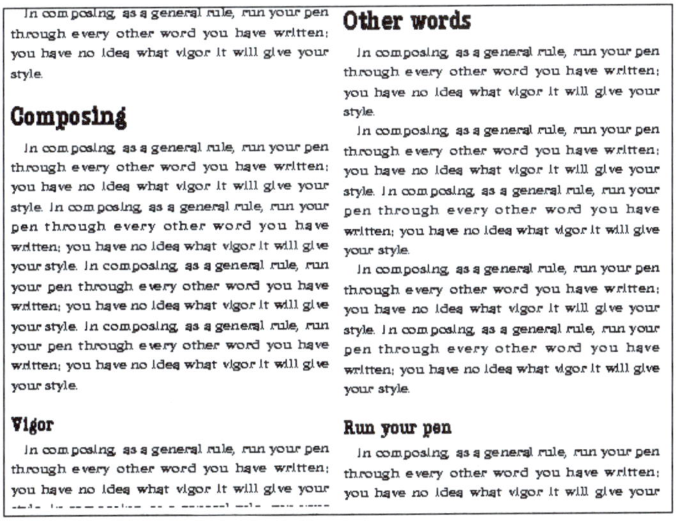

Figure 10.22   *The result of changing just the primary subhead.*

The same kinds of effects can ripple through all the pages of a QuarkXPress document of any length. Basing one style sheet on another is not limited; you could base a caption on a subhead, which was in turn based on a headline, which was based on body copy, and so on.

SPECIAL ITEM CONNECTIONS

Page elements generally appear in the document flow unrestricted by other elements. Of course, text may need to run around certain items, but it does flow on. Items can be locked in place, but they need not limit other items and their place in the scheme of the document.

But in layout work we often want to restrict items. We'd like certain picture and text boxes to appear together even if they flow on to other unseen pages. Or we see the need for certain pictures and lines to stay together. In a QuarkXPress document, there are two methods that provide ready control over such things: grouping and anchoring.

Grouping

If you've worked much with graphics software, you've no doubt already made regular use of grouping. It is a simple procedure, much like locking, except that instead of fixing an item to the page, you fix it to another item. You can group nearly any number of items—any that you can select simultaneously. This means, of course, that all the items to be grouped must be on the same page or same spread and surrounding pasteboard.

To group items, first select them all. Then open the Item menu and choose Group.

When you group items, a new, dotted bounding box forms around the group, as shown in Figure 10.23. The group will now move as a single item. If you try to drag it partly across a spread boundary, as to share the items between page spreads, the entire group will reside on either one page or the other, jumping as a group when dragged halfway across.

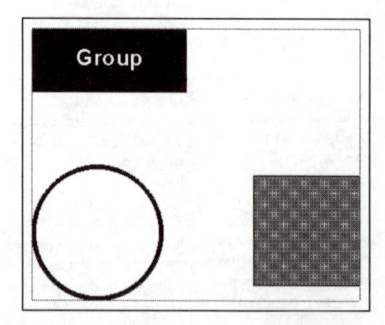

Figure 10.23   Three items grouped and their common bounding box.

To select the group, you need to click on one of the items, not simply the space that is enclosed by the bounding box. You can still modify the attributes that the group members hold in common. In fact, if you open the Item menu and choose Modify, you'll be presented with a special Group Specifications dialog box, as shown in Figure 10.24.

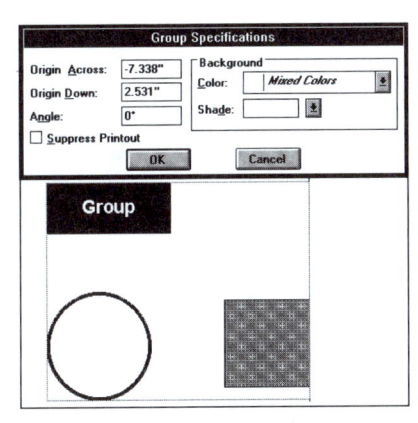

Figure 10.24 *The dialog box for modifying elements of a group.*

You can even group existing sets of grouped items. But in this case, you lose the ability to modify the resulting conglomeration.

Disassociating a group is easy. To break it up, select the group, open the Item menu and choose Ungroup.

With the Group and Ungroup controls, you can affix items to each other as needed, then remove the connection or reattach as your work requires. This is especially useful when you're doing precise positioning of multiple items.

Anchoring Inline Items

While grouping can associate text, pictures, and lines together, in doing so it treats them strictly as items. There is another method that combines text with other text or with pictures in a curious way that crosses the item/content separation usually characteristic of QuarkXPress. This method is called anchoring, and it is the principal way of inserting pictures directly into text. Often referred to as an inline graphic, the anchored picture or text box follows in the movement of text lines as though it were a single character in those lines.

The procedure goes against what we've come to expect from QuarkXPress, but it is reliable and effective.

Inserting a graphic (or text box) in line involves a peculiar twist on the usual convention of tool use. You cut with one tool and paste with another.

To place a picture (or text box) in line within text, first select the picture box with the item tool. Next, cut or copy it (Edit menu). Then select the content tool. Click a cursor insertion point within the text where the picture box will be located. Finally, paste (Edit menu). The picture box and its contents will appear within the text.

> **Anchoring a graphic or text box in line with text**
>
> *Select the item with the item tool*
>
> *Copy or cut it*
>
> *Use the content tool to click an active cursor in the text line*
>
> *Paste it*

You'll find that you can still select and modify the picture box and contents. But the item tool will be unable to select both the picture box and the text box in which it resides simultaneously. Also, if you select the picture box, only three of the usual eight handles will become active. In this way you can resize or proportion the picture box, but it remains anchored in place.

The picture box now has a dual nature. It is still a picture box. But it is also a character within the text, so it can be selected as a single character with the cursor (which may elongate to match the new character if it is large). Figure 10.25 shows a picture box of leaves anchored as the first character of text within a selected box. It could as easily have been inserted as a character in the middle of a paragraph, as shown in Figure 10.26.

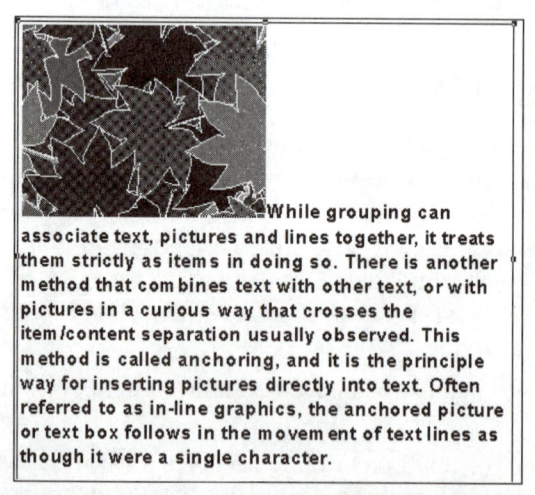

Figure 10.25 *A picture anchored to the baseline as first character.*

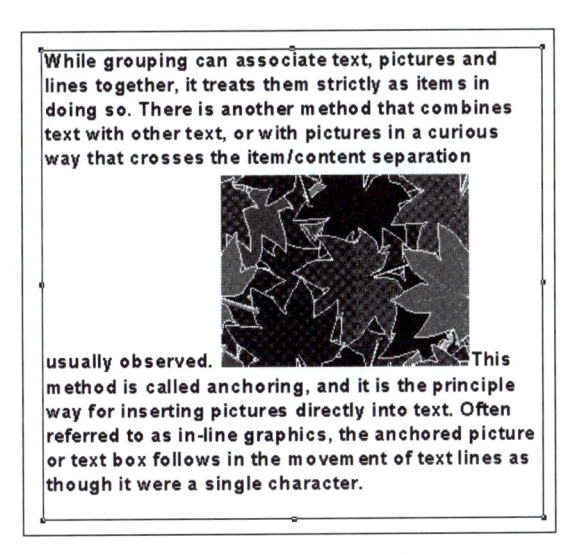

Figure 10.26 *A picture anchored to the baseline within a paragraph.*

Notice that in both cases the bottom of the character is aligned with the rest of the line. This is alignment along the baseline. And notice that because the picture is the largest character on the line, in each case it forces down the baseline for the entire line. Remember that you can still resize the inline graphic using the three handles.

There is another way to position a picture box that is anchored inline. If you select the picture box with the item tool, open the Item menu, and choose Modify, you'll be presented with an Anchored Picture Box Specifications dialog box, as shown in Figure 10.27. Notice two new controls in the upper left corner of the box, in the Align with Text section. The Baseline pushbutton was engaged by default for the boxes of figures 10.25 and 10.26. Clicking the Ascent pushbutton produces the anchoring of Figure 10.28. Here the picture box is set flush with the highest ascender of a character on that line, and then pushed down into the text, much as in runaround.

Figure 10.27 *Setting picture box inline anchor.*

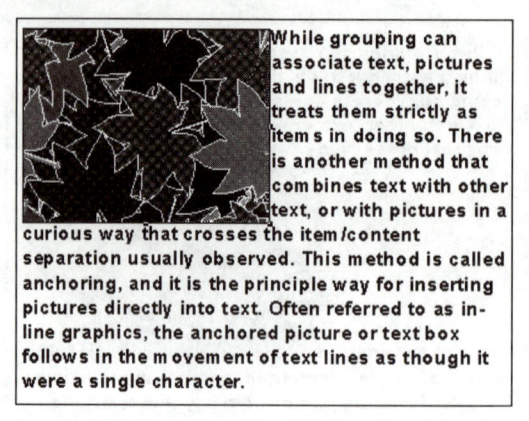

Figure 10.28 *A picture box anchored to the highest ascender.*

Creating special drop caps and graphic inserts

Anchor the item as usual and select it with the item tool

Open the Item menu and choose Modify

At Align with Text, click on Ascent

You might note that these controls could readily be used to make custom drop caps from both graphics and text boxes. All that we've seen about anchored picture boxes applies to anchored text boxes as well. Figure 10.29 illustrates a three-line text box set inline (through the same cut-and-paste method as above) with the ascender of the first line of the larger text box. In all cases, the contents of an anchored box remain accessible to modification and revision within the hosting text box. Text within an inline text box can be edited and reformatted, for instance. Similarly, picture contents can be adjusted for shading, background, and so forth.

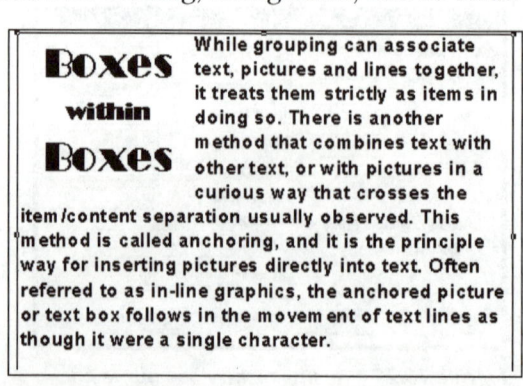

Figure 10.29 *A text box anchored to the first line of another text box.*

SPECIAL PAGE FLOWS

It is easy to become lulled into the sweet dream of predictability in any field. In publication design and layout, this dream rises out of the seeming conformity of facing-page after facing-page spread, numbered sequentially from beginning to end. Then a new project that doesn't follow this simple plan smacks into us.

Not all publications restrict their pages to simple verso-recto rhythms or running Arabic numbering. Controlling the flow of text and graphics in these exceptional circumstances is made possible by the sectioning and multiple page-spread capabilities in QuarkXPress.

One type of page flow requires such frequent readjustment as to cry to be automated, if only because the readjustments can threaten to consume inordinate amounts of our layout time in multiple-story publications. Jump lines are vital to keeping the reader's attention, but easy to overlook, even in final page proofs. Luckily, there is an easy way to let QuarkXPress keep track of them.

Multiple-Page Spreads

We need only look on the nearest magazine rack to note some significant exceptions to the two-page spread. Not every publication is limited to it, and QuarkXPress addresses this fact with the ability to expand to as many pages as will fit in the 48-inch document limit.

The place to find this is at the Document Layout palette. In laying out a publication completely with two-page spreads, you normally add a page by opening the Document menu of the palette, choosing Insert and a page master, and positioning the Insert arrow at or between pages on a spread. The new page obediently pushes pages aside to assume its position among them. The pushed pages realign themselves in new page spreads if necessary, and the effect ripples downstream through the document.

However, you can use the same approach to extend the spread out an additional page, or, as in some full-page glossy ads that fall out across your lap, to three, four, or more pages.

To add a page to expand a spread, open the Document menu. Choose Insert and the master as before, but now locate the Insert arrow to one side of the spread, and it will change into an icon of the type of master you've chosen, as shown in Figure 10.30 (single blank). Click, and the spread will automatically widen as a new page falls into place. You can use this approach to intoxicating lengths, as shown in Figure 10.31, where a five-page spread (Pages 4 through 8) has been unfurled.

240 ◆ *Teach Yourself...QuarkXPress for Windows*

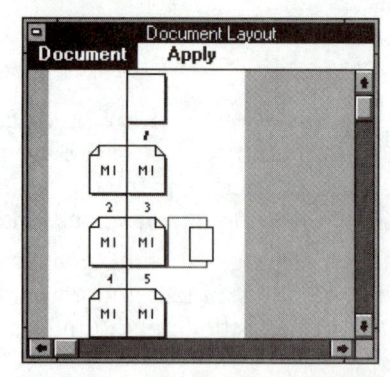

Figure 10.30 *Adding a third page to a spread.*

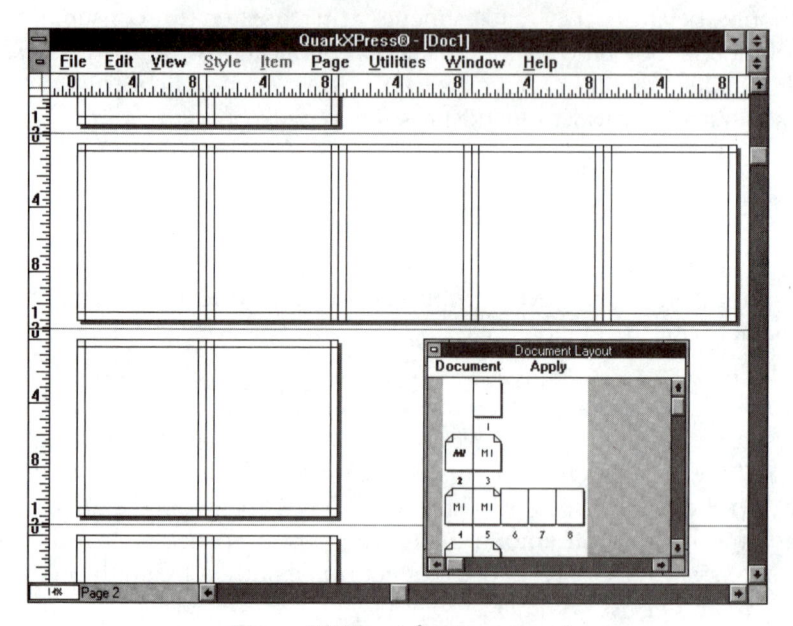

Figure 10.31 *A five-page spread.*

Expanding a page spread

> At the Document Layout palette, open the Document menu
>
> Choose Insert and the master page
>
> Pull the cursor to the outside of the spread icons and click

Sectioning

If your layout and design work involves newspapers, manuals, proposals, or various other sectioned documents, you know that the world does not always begin at Page 1 and run numerically uninterrupted to the end.

Clustering pages into sets of numbered sections is a matter of telling QuarkXPress which page will begin the section and how the numbering (or lettering) will proceed. QuarkXPress will keep track of the conventional, absolute page numbers (Arabic 1 through to the end), but will label and otherwise designate your pages according to the new scheme. You can even individualize the page labels and automatic page numbers that might appear.

To begin a section, first be sure that the page on which you want to start is prominent in the document window. Its label should appear in the Page Number field, lower-left on the horizontal scroll bar. The easiest way to get it there is to double-click to select its page icon in the Document Layout palette. Then open the Page menu and choose Section. A Section dialog box like that shown Figure 10.32 is displayed. Click an x into the Section Start checkbox.

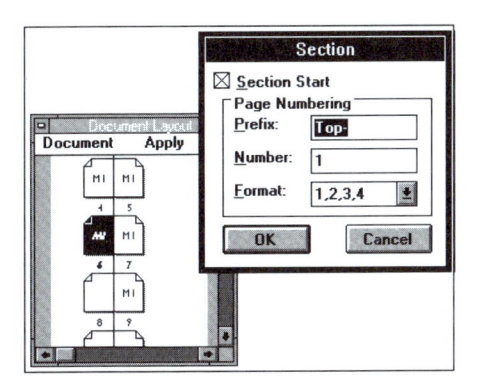

Figure 10.32 *Enabling section numbering.*

Now, under Page Numbering, you'll see a field for Prefix. You can leave this blank or type up to four characters into it. If you do type in a prefix (as "Top-" was keyed in here), the prefix will become part of the page label that appears on the document Page Number field—and that prints out if automatic page numbering has been set up on a master page.

At the next field, Number, leave the value at 1 if the section numbers/letters are to start at 1 or A. Change to another value if you want numbering to start further into the sequence. Note that for section lettering, 1 corresponds to A, 2 to B, and so on.

Finally, at the Format field, notice that a drop-down list allows for five numbering schemes, including Roman numerals, as well as lettering.

> **Sectioning pages**
>
> Select the first page of the section
>
> Open the Pages menu and choose Section
>
> Click an x into the Section Start checkbox
>
> Make other modifications in the dialog box to suit the section

Once applied, the section numbering will be in effect through all subsequent pages until another section start is applied at a downstream page. You can remove section numbering by selecting the first page of the section, opening the Section dialog box and clicking the x to clear the checkbox.

Automating Jump Lines

Have you played the "continued on...continued from" game yet? It works like this. You prepare a story that must be jumped to a later page (in QuarkXPress, create a text box and use the linking tools). You link the jumped text to the later page, continuing the story. You set up the little jump notices that say "continued on....," "continued from..." with the appropriate page numbers. Everything is in order.

Then something changes. Unexpectedly, the story is now jumped to another page. So you go back and sort out the changes in the "continued on..." and "continued from" lines. Or you forget to, and complaints of confusion stream in days or weeks later.

Because publication design and layout is a dynamic process, jump lines are easy to establish and easy to mix up. Shouldn't they be automated? Here's how.

QuarkXPress, as you've seen, can automatically number and track pages. It can also number and track jump lines. The key here, as with page numbering, is to enter the appropriate code. It is also necessary to position the jump message in a layer above the text box.

To set up a "continued on" jump line for a text box that has been linked to another page, use the text box tool to drag out a small jump-line text box. Then key in your jump message, typing in place of the page number the keystroke Ctrl-4. Next, drag the jump-line text box so that part of it is lying above the story text box.

> **NOTE**
>
> In laying jump-line boxes over stories, you should be careful of the interplay between text boxes. So, set Runaround on the jump-line box to None, and if necessary, move the box so it is just barely overlapping the text box underneath.

To set up a "continued from" jump line, proceed as above with this exception. In place of the page number, type the keystroke Ctrl-2.

> **Creating automatic jump lines**
>
> *Use the text-box tool and make a small text box after the story text box is created*
>
> *Key in the continuation notice excepting the page number*
>
> *For a "jump to" notice, key Ctrl-4; for a "jump from" notice, key Ctrl-2*
>
> *Drag the jump box until it overlaps the text box*

As Figure 10.33 shows, the jump-line page numbers, when in place, will follow the "to" and "from" relationship set up in the text chain and visible in the arrows between linked boxes.

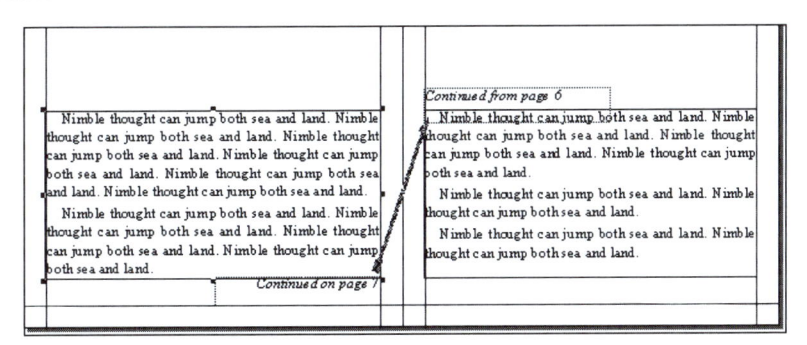

Figure 10.33   *Automatic jump-line page numbers in place.*

STEPPING FORWARD

Document flow incorporates some of the most powerful features of the program. With controls over master pages, style sheets, inline graphics anchoring, and the other methods we've covered here, you are ready to apply QuarkXPress to a wide variety of publications of great complexity.

Seeing how these techniques are used will sharpen your understanding of them. In Chapter 11, we'll explore how much a document can be assembled and refined as we go to work on catalogs and books.

Chapter 11

On the Job: Catalogs, Manuals, and Books

What You Will Learn in This Chapter

- How to apply style sheets to a catalog
- How to apply master pages to a manual
- How to use sectioning in a book
- How to apply absolute leading to inline graphics

Book-length documents present special challenges. Two kinds of publications that frequently cross into their realm are manuals and catalogs. They require as much organization and flow control as more literary tomes—and often more.

The millions of customers who rely on catalogs would turn away from them if they did not provide quick recognition and easy usage. If manuals and documentation fail in their duty to make reference information accessible, repairs would cease, installations would be stymied, and operations would falter.

Strongly organized page make-up depends on the sort of organization achievable through style sheets, master pages, and the other document flow features covered in Chapter 10.

In this chapter, we'll use our skills toward the construction of both a catalog and a manual. We'll apply the methods that make a publication into a unified piece. In doing so, we'll see just how these functions guide the elements in the document.

A Catalog

Many consumer catalogs put heavy emphasis on pictures. Others rely on the printed word to make the sale. But always, text must adhere to a consistent format established early in the catalog. Giving the armchair customer clear visual cues allows for the quick scan as well as detailed reading. For some readers the name of the product will catch the eye. Others will be engaged by the description or the price. All these things must be easily identified, usually by type style, size and format, as well as by location relative to the rest of the text. As you may have guessed, in such type-crucial situations, style sheets can play a major role.

We'll join a book catalog in progress. Our task is to set up an early page that will serve as a prototype for subsequent pages and will establish the type styles and formats to be used throughout the catalog. To do this, we plan to add heading boxes and establish style sheets for the titles and author bylines. We'll set the text to fit and include rules to further delineate each item.

Starting the Catalog Page

We set up the document by keying in pica values in the New dialog box as shown in Figure 11.1. It employs a small-format page, 40 by 50 picas, facing, with three columns established automatically and separated by a pica and a half (recall the X and Y measurements, where X is number of picas and Y is the number of points). The automatic text box is used because we're given a continuous text file that includes titles, authors, and catalog item blurbs, which will run sequentially.

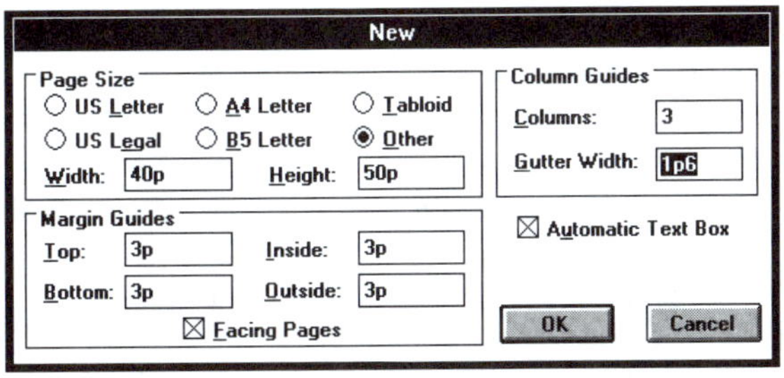

Figure 11.1   Document setup for a catalog.

Before starting to work on the first full listings page, page 4, we call up the Document Layout palette, open the Document menu and choose Show Masters. Then we double-click on the M1 master to bring it into the window. We want to fix the basic text box in place so it won't be inadvertently shifted as we add and adjust other elements on the pages. Using the item tool, we click on the text box already in place, and under the Item menu we choose Lock.

Next, returning to document Page 4, we use the text tool to drag out a long horizontal text box across the top of the page. In it we key in the page heading, selecting the Eterna font at 18 points in the Measurements palette. Then in order to reverse out the text, we select all (Ctrl-A) and set the color of type to White through the Style menu and the color of the background to Black 100 percent through the Item menu (choose Modify to Text Box Specifications).

With the text-box tool, we drag out another box to serve as a heading for listings that will appear below it. We key in the text, and at the Measurements palette, we adjust the font to Futuri black, size to 18 points, and style to Italic. Then we make horizontal scale and tracking changes for each box to achieve the preliminary layout shown in Figure 11.2, showing the upper part of the page with guides visible. Since each of the two text boxes lies on a layer above the automatic text box (always the first down on the page), we don't have to worry about any untoward text collisions. The text destined for the columns will be pushed down once it is there.

Figure 11.2   Layout of prototypical early page.

We choose the content tool and click it over the large automatic text box to insert a cursor. Using the Get Text command of the File menu, we move through the directory listing to find the word-processing file that will provide text for this page. After we double-click on the file name, the text flows into the columns below the heading *See beyond the headlines with these great books,* as shown in Figure 11.3.

Figure 11.3   Text pushed down in columns below a heading text box.

Using Style Sheets

Notice how uninviting the items seem in the listing. Our task now is to set up style sheets that will be applied to each of the book titles and author bylines to make them stand out. But first we'll set up a style sheet for the body text as a whole.

We choose the Capelli font at 10 points at the Measurements palette. Examining the appearance of the text lines, we decide after some experimentation to set them a bit tighter than normal. So we reduce tracking by setting a -5 value at the Measurements palette. The body text is acceptable now. Presumably the type attributes for it won't change, even as we adjust the other lines. But publication design, like life, is full of uncertainties. So, we want a precaution against inadvertent changes. We definitely want the means to change all the body text should the need arise.

NOTE The descriptions will soon become separated paragraphs, barricaded into relative isolation from one another by the formatting of title and byline. Later, changing even just one characteristic of each paragraph would be tedious and frustrating. By establishing a style sheet for all the descriptive text, we'll be able to do things like pull all the body text tighter or reduce leading throughout the document with just a single text change at the style sheet.

So with our cursor planted soundly within the Capelli, 10 point text, we open the Edit menu and choose Style Sheets. At the first dialog box, we click New. At the Edit Style Sheets dialog box, we approve of the features of our listing text, type in the name *List Text* as shown in Figure 11.4, and click OK, returning to the first dialog box. We click the Save button.

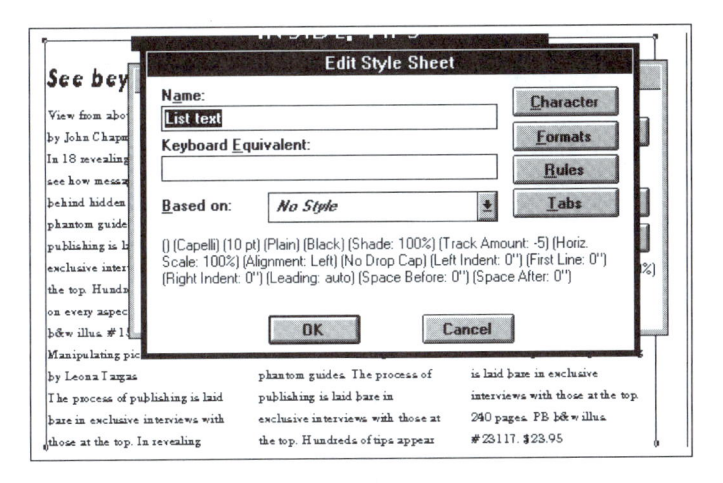

Figure 11.4 *Establishing a new style sheet based on selection.*

Now it becomes clear we'll be working with style sheets, so we open the View menu and choose Show Style Sheets. The little palette appears with *List Text* showing prominently.

We set to work on doing the whole of the first book listing. Beginning with the book title, we select by triple-clicking. For type font, we choose Futuri black; for size, 14 points. At the Measurements palette, we italicize the text, further reduce the tracking to -10. At the Style menu, we choose Horizontal Scale and key in 90 percent in the small dialog box that appears. Next, using the same approach we used to create the List Text style sheet, we go by way of the Edit menu to the dialog boxes off the Style Sheets command to create another style sheet. This one we name *Title*. We save as before.

To create a style sheet for the author's name, we do likewise, selecting the byline and italicizing it before establishing the new style sheet, *Byline* (which varies from body text at this point only in that it is italicized). Now we've set the first paragraph as shown in Figure 11.5. The resulting style sheets, represented in the adjacent palette, will serve as formatting and styling tools for all the listings to follow in the catalog.

Next we go to each title and byline in turn, clicking a cursor into the line and then clicking the Style Sheet name in the palette to apply it. When finished this way, the page looks like the one shown in Figure 11.6.

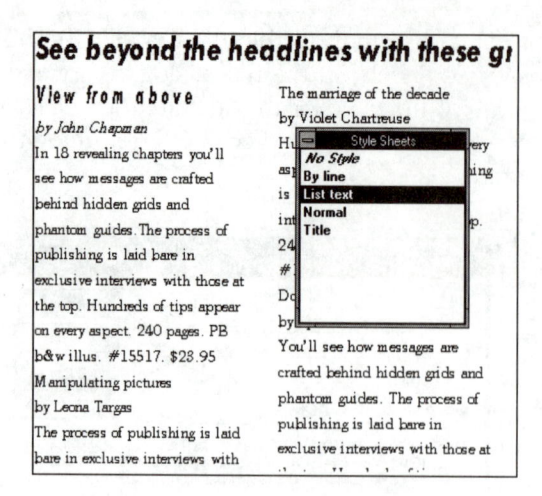

Figure 11.5 *A prototypical listing and style sheets palette.*

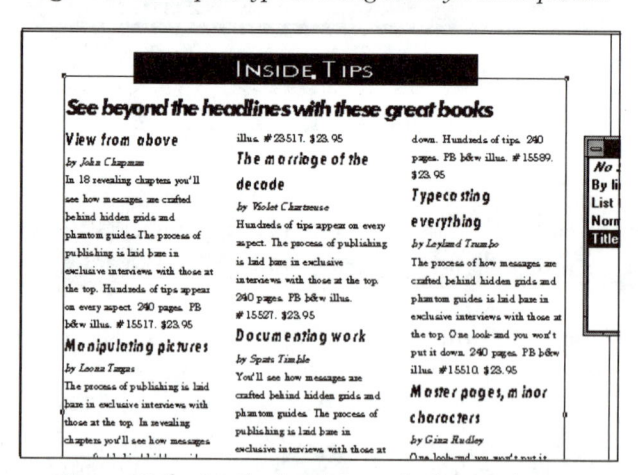

Figure 11.6 *Result of applying style sheets to listings.*

It is at this moment that we see what was overlooked. For one thing, paragraph spacing between list items is much too scant, failing to set the listings apart. We'll need to add more. Also, the leading over the title, byline, and list text, which spreads them out indiscriminately, can be reduced for a more unified appearance. And we'll need to do something to keep widows and orphans from forming. To implement these changes, we'll be going back to edit all the new style sheets, including the List Text.

> **NOTE** When creating a style sheet based on selected text, you might easily neglect to apply the style sheet to that selection. The lapse wouldn't show up immediately, of course, because the style sheet and selection would match. But should you later make changes to the style sheet, you'd notice

that the original selection hadn't changed. The correction for this is simple. Apply the style sheet to the original selection, including that text in any future changes.

To make our revisions we go first to the Byline style sheet (through the Edit menu). At the Edit Style Sheet dialog box, we click on Format (for paragraph format). At the Format dialog box, we click to engage the Keep with Next Paragraph button. This keeps the name from dragging behind the description as the latter jumps to the next column. Remember, we're setting up style sheets for all the other listings in this catalog as well. We want to anticipate what might happen even if we don't see that particular problem on this page.

Next, we go to the Title style sheet, and by the same route we click on Keep with Next Paragraph, as well as Keep Lines Together. The latter is important because we don't want a two-line headline to become widowed and decapitated. We also type over the auto value currently in the Leading field. In its place goes 12 points to match the leading of the list text.

NOTE Though the Keep with Next Paragraph feature should work all the time, you may find it helps to resize the text box to force it to finally take effect.

Final Work on the Page

Back at the page, everything looks good, except that all the listings are cramped together. The solution to this will be simple. We return to the List Text style sheet, Edit dialog box. There we go to the Space After field and key in *2p* for two picas. That should loosen up the paragraphs a bit. And, indeed, it does, as shown in Figure 11.7.

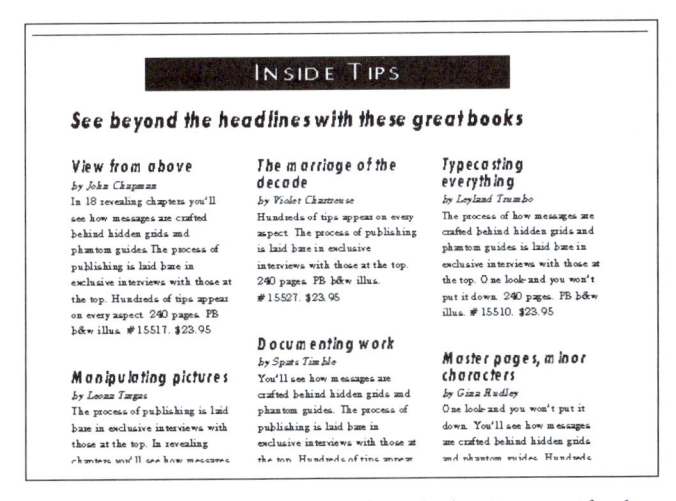

Figure 11.7 *Effect of 2 picas in the style sheet's Space After box.*

Another adjustment or two of leading and box size, and we've almost completed our layout. Still, something more is needed to set off each listing. After a bit of experimentation, we hit on an answer: Rules will be chosen to sit above each listing. To apply them, we go to the Edit Style Sheet dialog box for the Title style sheet. Clicking on the Rules button, we find ourselves at the Paragraph Rules dialog box. Here, in the dialog box settings shown in Figure 11.8, we choose a double-line rule of 2 point thickness, to be set two picas from the first baseline of the Title paragraph.

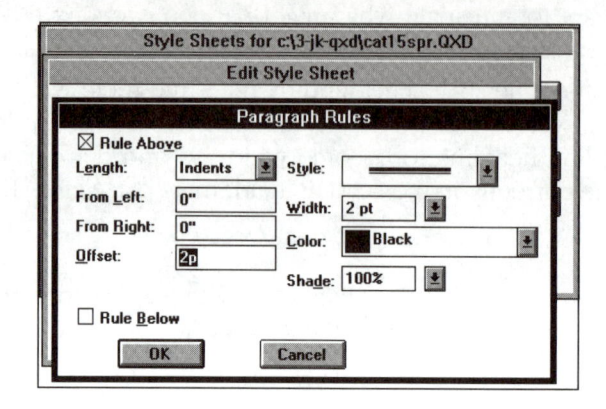

Figure 11.8   *Adding Rule Above to the style sheet.*

Saving this revised style sheet in the usual manner adjusts all the listings to the form shown in Figure 11.9. Our catalog styles are now in place and working. The rest of the catalog can be dealt with by applying these styles throughout. If the word processor supplying the text has the capability, style sheets can be transferred through the text to the word-processing program. That could also free QuarkXPress for other duties, if the work flow demanded them, while the word processor was applying styles to text to be imported to the QuarkXPress document.

A Manual

Documentation is the workhorse of the publication world. It is the ultimate in functionality and logical presentation. Some documentation breaks with tradition and is full of illustrations and white space. Manuals have changed looks significantly in recent years. But to most people, a manual has a distinctive look and feel. Effective manuals serve primarily as reference works and sometimes secondarily as training aids. They draw their strength from logical organization and clear subdivisions.

In the manual we'll be constructing, the information we're presenting must be divided into four sections, each clearly marked yet consistent with the others in format. We want readers to be able to locate each section quickly and to be well oriented when they are within a section. To clarify points within the text, small graphics will be

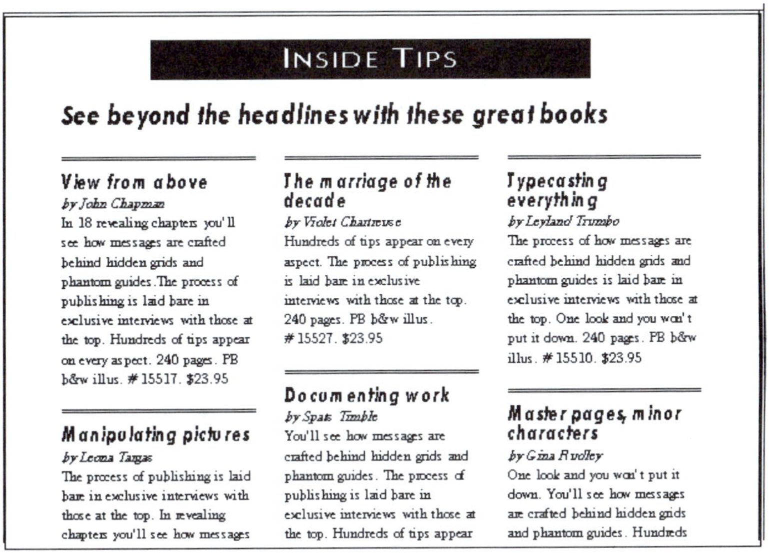

INSIDE TIPS

See beyond the headlines with these great books

View from above
by John Chapman
In 18 revealing chapters you'll see how messages are crafted behind hidden grids and phantom guides.The process of publishing is laid bare in exclusive interviews with those at the top. Hundreds of tips appear on every aspect. 240 pages. PB b&w illus. # 15517. $23.95

Manipulating pictures
by Leona Targas
The process of publishing is laid bare in exclusive interviews with those at the top. In revealing chapters you'll see how messages

The marriage of the decade
by Violet Chartreuse
Hundreds of tips appear on every aspect. The process of publishing is laid bare in exclusive interviews with those at the top. 240 pages. PB b&w illus. # 15527. $23.95

Documenting work
by Spats Timble
You'll see how messages are crafted behind hidden grids and phantom guides. The process of publishing is laid bare in exclusive interviews with those at the top. Hundreds of tips appear

Typecasting everything
by Leyland Trumbo
The process of how messages are crafted behind hidden grids and phantom guides is laid bare in exclusive interviews with those at the top. One look and you won't put it down. 240 pages. PB b&w illus. # 15510. $23.95

Master pages, minor characters
by Gina Rudley
One look and you won't put it down. You'll see how messages are crafted behind hidden grids and phantom guides. Hundreds

Figure 11.9 *All the styles in effect and finalized.*

included at certain points. To accomplish all of this, we'll be using techniques in master pages, sectioning, and anchoring in-line graphics.

Starting the Manual

The page format we've decided on is 44 picas wide by 54 picas high, with single-column facing pages, margins of 6 picas at top and bottom and 3 picas on either side. Since this will be a book-length project, we select automatic text-box generation when choosing the other features at the New dialog box. Pica is the measurement system preferred. Through the Edit menu we reach the General Preferences dialog box and set both horizontal and vertical measures, in picas.

Our plan for the layout includes text boxes 25 picas wide abutting the right margin on both verso and recto pages, a style consistent with that of many reference guides. Recall that we have Automatic Text Box engaged. To modify them in a way that will affect the entire manual, we'll need to work on the master page. So, at the Document Layout palette, we open the Document menu and choose Show Master Pages. The M1 master icon appears alone in the palette. Double-clicking on it brings the master page spread into view.

To pull each text box narrower, we grab the middle handle on its left side and drag to the right, monitoring the value Width in the Measurements palette all the while, until it indicates 25 picas as shown in Figure 11.10. Next we begin work on the basic layout of the first section, A. In setting it up we'll be setting a format to be followed for all the sections.

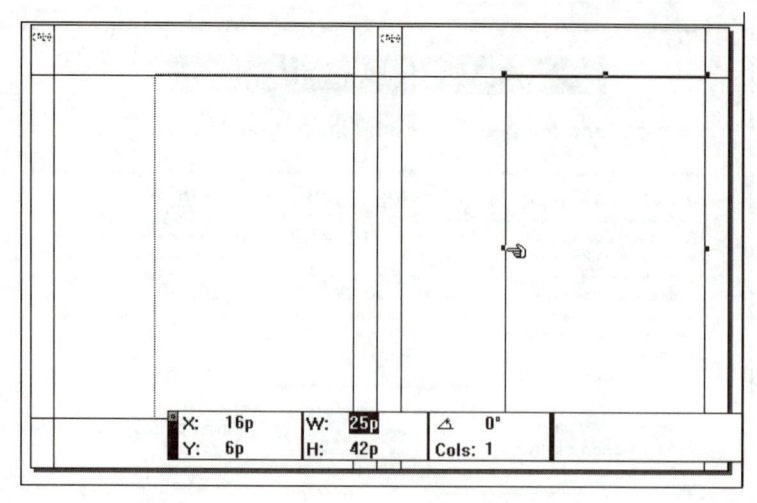

Figure 11.10 *Using the Measurements palette to monitor precise text box adjustment.*

This manual should be easy to use, so a section indicator will be located in each of the outside margins, as in a thumb index. At the verso page, using the text-box tool, we drag out a vertical box 10 picas long and 2 picas wide. Selecting the Futuri font at 48 point size in the Measurements palette, we type the letter *A* and then center it with Ctrl-Shift-C. Ctrl-A selects the text, and at the Style menu the color is set to White, and the horizontal scale to 70 percent. Using the Item menu to open the Text Box Specifications dialog box, we set the background to Black, the vertical alignment to Center, and the text offset to zero.

With the item tool, we select the text box, and then, at the Item menu, we use the Duplicate command. Then we move the cloned text box over to the mirror-image location on the recto page.

To include a section title at the top of each page, we use the text-box tool to create another text box on the verso page into which we type the section title, *INSTALLA-TION*. We reverse out the text in this box, as we did earlier, and adjust the box for size, with the aid of the Measurements palette, to line up with the text box below it. We apply tracking at the palette to spread the text across the box. Then we duplicate the box as above and position its clone above the text box of the recto page.

We create a placeholder text box for page numbers with the text-box tool, formatted and adjusted to match the others. With the cursor in the placeholder box, we type Ctrl-3 to insert the page number symbol <#>. We position the box in the lower outside corner of the verso page, duplicate it, and position the duplicate the same way on the recto page. Our master spread is now complete, as shown in Figure 11.11.

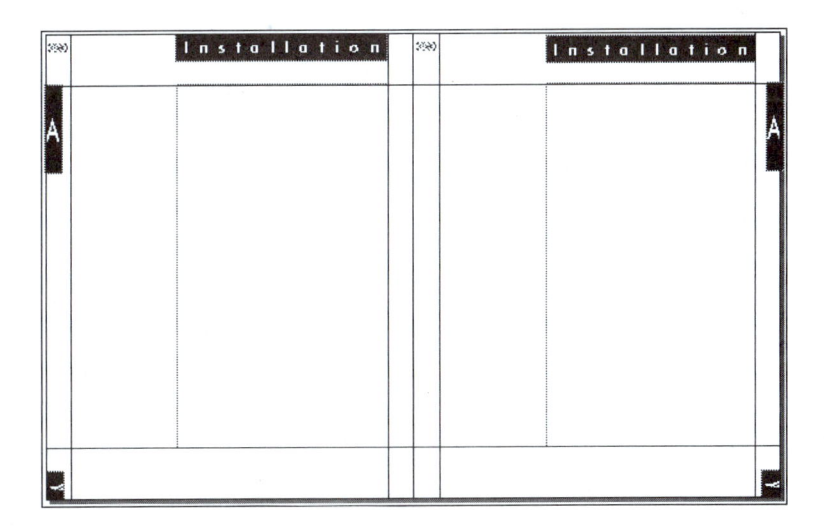

Figure 11.11   *The completed master page spread for Section A.*

Working with Sections

This is one of four sections. We want similar layouts with different labels for each section. So we will create three new masters based on this one. Here's how. First, at the Document Layout palette, we open the Masters menu and choose Insert. At the submenu that is displayed, we select M1, the master we just laid out for section A. The insert cursor is displayed and we click it below the M1 icon in the palette. A new master icon, M2, appears. Now, to work on the Section B master page, we double-click on the M2 icon. A spread identical to M1 appears on the screen.

As indicated by the name in the page number space, this is M2. To change the heading title and the section designation, we select the *A* within the section box and key in *B,* then select the box containing *Installation* and key in *Basics.* Figure 11.12 shows the program window as we work on the verso side. We follow the same pattern on the recto page of this M2 spread.

One last revision will complete the master page layout for Section B. Since we want the pages of the manual to create that thumb-index effect along the margin, we move the text boxes in the margins—the B boxes—down just the length of the box. We do this by selecting the box on each side and, at the Measurements palette, keying in a value equal to the current location of the text box (6p) plus the length of the box (10p). We put this 16p into the Y coordinate field. This shifts the box down by one box length and creates the thumb-index effect shown in Figure 11.13.

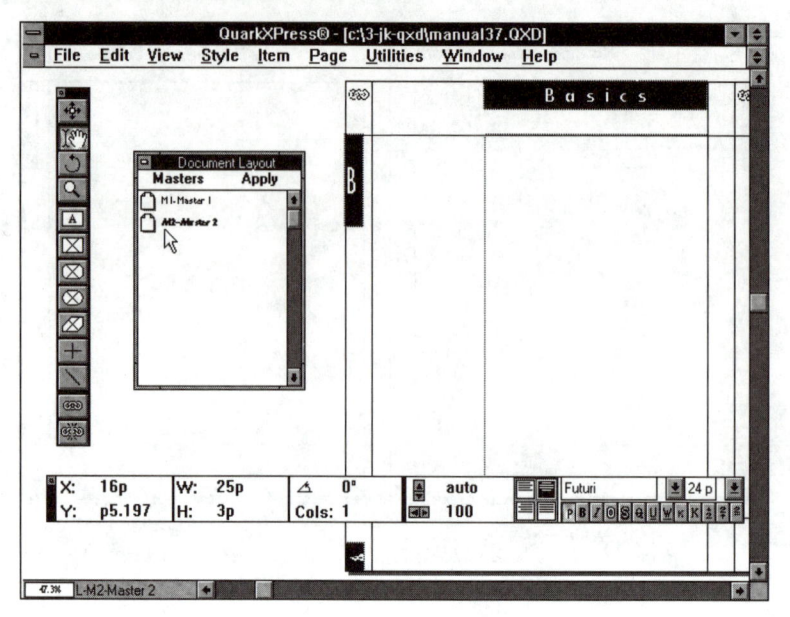

Figure 11.12   *Changing one section master to another.*

Figure 11.13   *Creating a thumb-indexed book.*

Similarly, we create and adjust master spread M3 for section C and M4 for section D, basing both on M1, keying in the corresponding section letters, and shifting the section box down by an additional 10 picas for each in turn.

As a final precaution, we return to the master M1 spread, and, with the item tool chosen, give the Select All command (Ctrl-A) and, at the Item menu, choose Lock. This prevents accidental movement or deletion of master items. For each of the other masters, M2 through M4, we do the same.

Now everything is in place for sectioning. All that remains is setting up page numbering to follow our plan. Recall that we decided numbering would begin anew with each section.

We're informed that the entire manual will run about 160 pages, and that the first six pages will be devoted to the usual front matter—table of contents, and so forth. Eight more pages will be devoted to back matter. These front and back pages will each have a layout differing completely from any of the master pages.

We'll handle these pages in order. First, we put in the front pages blank. They'll be laid out when the rest of the book is complete. This is a simple move. We open the Pages menu, choose Insert, and at the dialog box make the selections shown in Figure 11.14, typing in 6 for pages, clicking the Before Page 1 button, and choosing Blank Facing Pages from the Masters drop-down list. Next to the dialog box shown in Figure 11.14, you can see the result as displayed in the Document Layout palette.

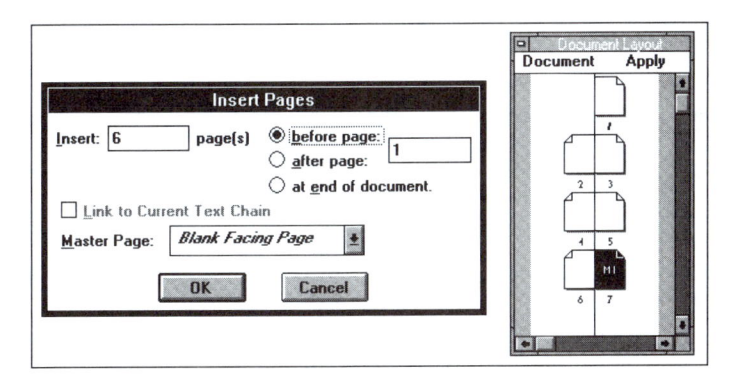

Figure 11.14 Inserting six blank pages in front of Section A.

Now, note that we're setting up pages as the text comes in. As we're given each text file, we'll import it to a single master page (M1, M2, M3, and M4 for sections A, B, C, and D, respectively) and let the Automatic Text Box function take over. The text has already been formatted in the word processor, and aside from adding a few inline graphics that have been requested, we'll accept it as is.

WARNING QuarkXPress behaves somewhat unexpectedly if you add pages from a certain master and then paste or import text into any of them. If a text overrun occurs from the box in which you paste it, and the Automatic Text Box function is engaged, the text will skip all the perfectly good pages already added to the document and form its own pages after them to handle the overrun.

For Section A, we click the content tool to put a cursor in the text box on Page 7. Then we open the File menu and choose the Get Text command. After locating the word-processed file, SectionA.doc, we double-click, and in flows the text. After twenty-three more pages are created, we find ourselves at page 30, which will be the end of Section A in our document, as shown in Figure 11.15.

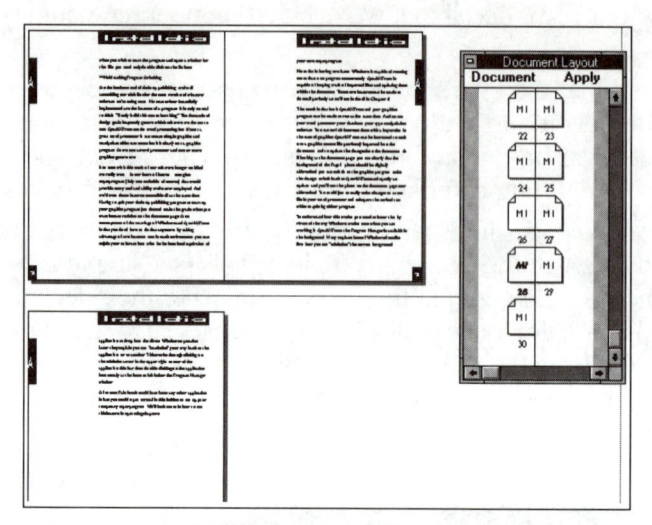

Figure 11.15   *A successful importing into the automatic text box in Section A.*

Our next step is to put the first page of Section B in place and then import the text for that section and let Automatic Text Box take over again. Since we need only insert one page, we'll turn to the Document Layout palette, where this is easily accomplished. Opening the Document menu, we choose Insert. At the submenu, we select M2, the master for Section B pages. We move the mouse tool, which changes form (finally becoming a dog-eared page tool) next to Page 30, where Page 31 would go. There we click, and the new page is inserted, as shown in Figure 11.16.

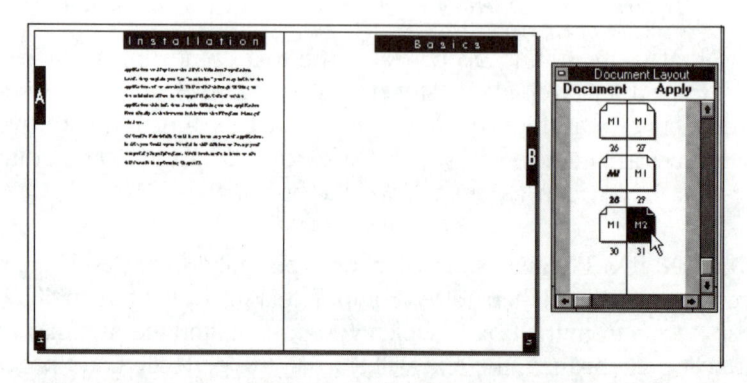

Figure 11.16   *Inserting the first Section B page from the M2 master.*

Proceeding as with Section A, we use the Get Text command to import the formatted SectionB.doc text, and let QuarkXPress automatically set it in 31 instantly-appearing pages. This puts us at Page 62. We continue, inserting the first page of Section C and importing its text, and doing the same for Section D.

We still haven't got the sections quite the way we'd like them. Remember, the pages are still numbered in a sequence running through all sections. It's our plan to number each section independently. To do this, we'll invoke the sectioning abilities of QuarkXPress. Our efforts begin at the first page of Section A, at what is now Page 7. Using the Document Layout palette, we locate the Page 7 icon and double-click on it to make the page active and selected. We confirm this by checking the page indicator field at the lower-left of the window.

Now we're in business and ready to section. This part goes simply. We open the Page menu and choose Section. At the dialog box, we click an x into the Section Start checkbox and key in a section designation of *A-* in the prefix field. We leave the numbering at Arabic (1, 2, 3) and click OK. The result is shown in Figure 11.17, with the dialog box. Notice that the page number in the corner of the layout has taken on the section designation, as has the page indicator. A small mark appears superscripted at the page number in the Document Layout palette to indicate this is the start of a section.

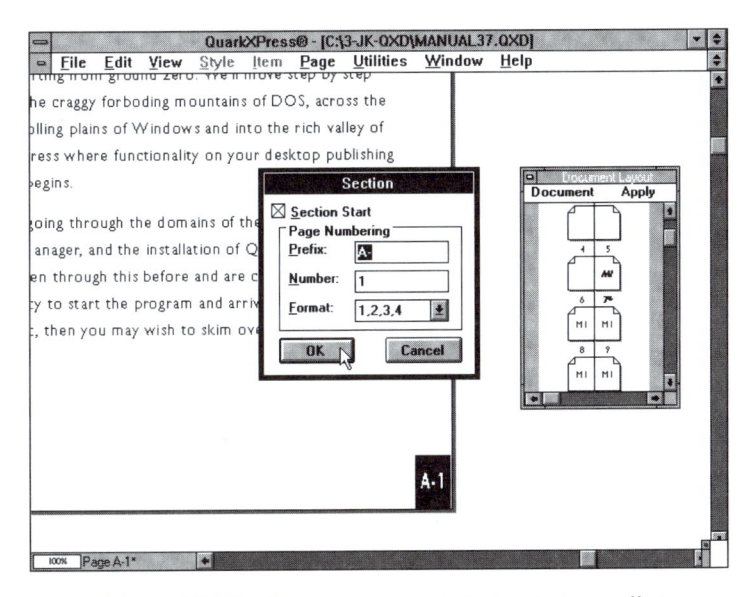

Figure 11.17 *Section A page numbering put into effect.*

> **NOTE** While the indicator will shift to reflect new section numbers, the Document palette always maintains its count in absolute terms, starting from Page 1 and running through the final page of the document.

We proceed in similar fashion to correlate page numbers with Sections B, C, and D, keying in *B-* and so on in the Section dialog box.

The final set of pages will be for back matter. We'll set these up as we did the first pages. Eight pages are allowed. We move our view to the last page (the last page of section D, known to the Document Layout as Page 152, and elsewhere as D-38). At the Page menu, we choose Insert and key in the values shown in Figure 11.18, specifying a set of Blank facing pages. Eight new empty pages fall into place, waiting for the time when the index and other back matter is ready.

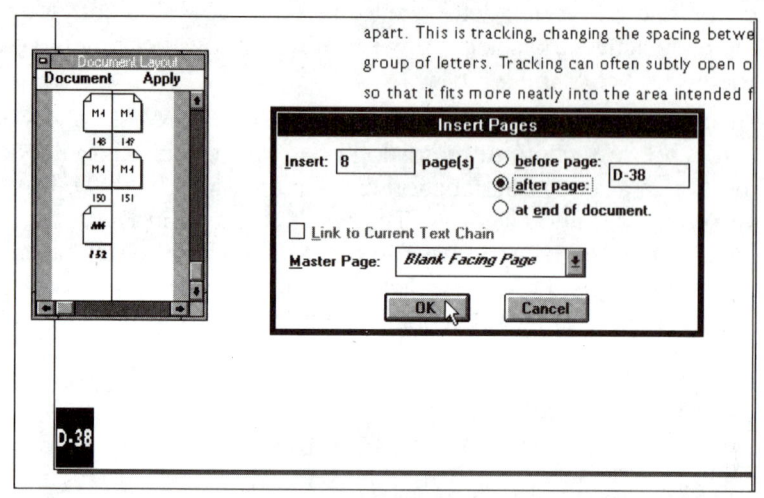

Figure 11.18 *Inserting the back pages after the last section.*

The Manual's Fine Points

Our work in page makeup for this manual is nearly complete. There are a few points to deal with on individual pages, and now we attend to them.

In addition to the text, we've been given graphics files that should be inserted into various lines of text so that readers can have instant visual confirmation of the process being described. There are to be no separate illustrations in this book. In this case, these are graphics representing tool and control interface elements described in the text.

Using the usual techniques for importing graphics, we create a picture box for each and import through the File menu's Get Picture command. Now we want to anchor each graphic in its appropriate location within the paragraph. Using the item tool, we click on the first picture box (containing the pointer-tool graphic), selecting it. Then we copy it to the clipboard with a Ctrl-C keystroke. Next, we choose the content tool, click it into position within the paragraph's text and paste with a Ctrl-V keystroke. The picture of the pointer appears. We follow the same procedure for the picture of the scroll-bar arrow. Figure 11.19 shows both picture boxes to the side of the text box and their duplicates in place within the text.

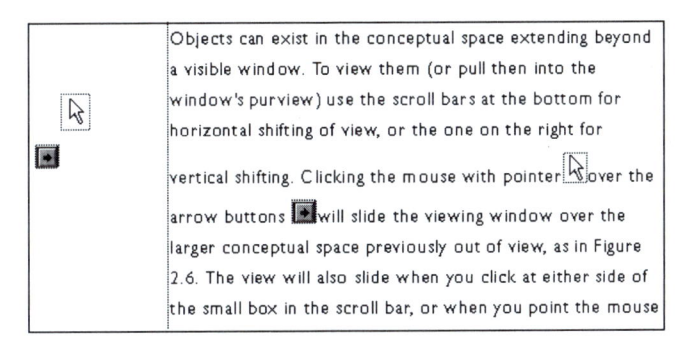

Figure 11.19 *Graphics as separate items, and anchored within text lines.*

You'll notice that the pictures are inline with the baselines in each case. But a problem has arisen. Even though the graphics are small enough to fit within the lines at regular leading, extra space has been added above them. This is because the leading was set at a relative value to the characters rather than an absolute value. This is indicated in the Measurements palette with a + sign in front of the leading value (shown in Figure 11.20). In this case the leading is not simply a positive 6 points, but rather 6 points over the type size of 12 points. Of course the graphics are recognized as having a larger point size than 12 because their height is greater than the highest ascender of type in each line. And with six points added to this greater height, the result is that extra spacing.

Figure 11.20 *Relative leading indicated in the Measurements palette.*

To fix this, we select the entire paragraph and, at the Measurements palette, select the leading field and key in an absolute 18 points. The result is the regular spacing shown in Figure 11.21. Notice we added parentheses to set off the pictures slightly from the flow of text. With several more adjustments of this kind, we finish our work on this manual, and hand the results over to await indexing, table of contents, and other front matter.

Figure 11.21 *Paragraph adjusted to absolute leading.*

STEPPING FORWARD

The skills and approaches used in assembling the catalog and manual apply to all types of books. Ironically some longer books will be simpler to lay out because they don't require sectioning or multiple master pages and style sheets. But the basics of automatic page creation apply to all.

We've already looked at graphics, their place in pictures, and how we can adjust them. But we've only seen part of the picture, so to speak. Still more modifications can greatly affect the usability and impact of images brought into the document. In Chapter 12 we investigate.

Chapter 12

Manipulating Images

WHAT YOU WILL LEARN IN THIS CHAPTER

- How to create and manipulate grayscale images
- How to adjust contrast
- How to make halftones
- How to maximize resolution
- The effects of sizing, contrast, and halftone screens on image quality

An illustration appears on the printed page after graphic techniques have been applied with judgment. Color, shading, sizing and skewing adjustments, which can be applied to all kinds of images from software-generated line drawings to scanned photographs, are just some of the variables. Certain file formats provide the opportunity for even greater and more varied manipulations of image quality. In this chapter we'll look at those manipulations and their effects on detailed graphics.

For complex graphics that range in tonal values and contrast (photographs, for instance), adjusting for optimum reproduction will determine whether clarity and subtleties of the illustration come through on the printed page. QuarkXPress offers methods of manipulation and image-editing that are often the province of graphics software.

In particular we'll be looking into the two aspects that have the greatest effect on the printability of an illustration: contrast and the handling of halftones. This discussion takes us out of the realm of line art and pictures as placeholders and simple stand-ins for illustrations in a layout. We now move into actual image fine-tuning. Here we regard the image as one which will find its way to print directly from the document. For this reason, examining and enhancing the image becomes important.

Contrast and When It Matters

To put it simply, the contrast of an image is the relation between its dark and light parts. Take your black felt marker (say Black P98, Chartpak) and draw a square on a piece of white paper, and you'll establish a vivid contrast. Draw the square with a gray marker (say Cool Gray 5 P185, Chartpak) and the contrast is reduced. Draw each square on gray paper stock, and a still lower contrast results. Switch to black paper and you'll lose all contrast.

The kinds of graphics files for which contrast is adjustable in QuarkXPress are grayscale images. That means the image consists not just of black and white areas, but also variations (grays) in shades between those extremes. Sometimes these variations are described as highlights, shadows, and middle tones.

If the graphic you're importing into QuarkXPress contains grayscales, and you plan to print it for best possible effect, then you'll have use for these controls. Grayscale images are found in many tagged image file format (TIFF) and bitmapped picture formats, identified by their respective TIFF and BMP suffixes. The TIFF is a particularly favored format that travels well from one application to the next.

What is important about these and other eligible formats is that they have the capacity for conveying grayscale information. They can describe images in black, white, or various shades of gray. Recall the shading values we've applied through the Style menu. Those were shading reductions applied uniformly over an image. Here, we're looking at shades of gray varying within an image.

OK, if contrast is already established in the imported image file, what can QuarkXPress possibly do about it? Simply, the program remembers the imported image's shades-of-gray information for each bit, and it has controls to determine how those shades will be translated into the document image. Consider that someone seeing a photographic print might say, "I like it, but it should be lighter." Making it lighter means taking every shade of gray and converting it to a lighter shade of gray. Or taking every dot or bit within the image and making that bit lighter than it was. In this case 100 percent back bits might become 80 percent bits, 10 percent bits might become 8 percent bits and so on. This is a simple translation to a less black image.

Suppose however, the critic says, "I like it, but it needs more contrast." One way to accommodate this request would be this: Take every bit that is black, or some shade of gray between 51 percent and 100 percent black, and make it black; make every bit that is white or some shade of gray between 0 percent and 50 percent, into white. The effect here would be considerably different.

In the case of simple reduced shading we suggested in the first example, the result would simply be a lighter image. In the second example, the adjusted image could be lighter or it could be darker, depending on the relative grayness of bits within the image. This second case is one example of adjusting contrast.

Figure 12.1 demonstrates the difference between the shading and contrast adjustments we have described.

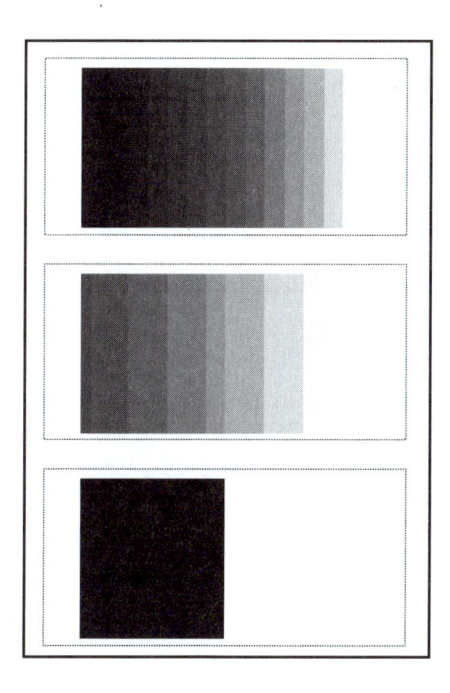

Figure 12.1   *An original grayscale image, shown at 50% shading, and with extreme contrast.*

The top box contains an image with a gradient of shading varying from left to right, 100 percent black to white. The middle box contains the same image adjusted to 50 percent of the original shading. Notice how the overall effect is a washing out of the black as all shades are reduced to half their original values.

The box at bottom contains the same image, but here the contrast has been adjusted as described earlier, using 50 percent black as the contrast cut-off criterion. Darker than 50 percent black is turned to 100 percent, while lighter than 50 percent is turned to 0 percent. Notice that the left half of the original image has turned completely black, and the right hand has turned completely white. This is extreme contrast adjustment, and just one of countless possibilities.

It's helpful to note that contrast adjustments are applied relative to the shading of the imported image. As in photographic darkroom developing, you can darken just the light shades, or lighten just the dark ones, or the reverse, or darken or lighten the middle tones, or combine various effects. Obviously, the particular contrast enhancements you choose or devise will depend on the image and the effect you desire from it. Let's see how.

Adjusting Contrast with Preset Controls

QuarkXPress provides controls that make preset adjustments of contrast in grayscale pictures. You've already seen one kind of adjustment in the form of the Negative command under the Style menu. This handles grayscale, in addition to such other factors as color complements. Recall how applying this command made white-on-black images turn into black-on-white ones. In the strictest sense, the contrast did not change, since the relative shades were simply interchanged. But the effect was inverted grayscale values.

Whenever an image is imported into a picture box, the values of its grayscales are considered normal. If fact, if you look under the Style menu when a picture is active and the content tool selected, you'll see a checkmark by the command Normal Contrast. Should you change the contrast and then later wish to reclaim the original contrast setting, you can use this command.

> ***Adjusting an image to original contrast***
>
> *Select picture with content tool active*
>
> *Open the Style menu and choose Normal Contrast*

Figure 12.2 shows the scanned image of a painting that has been imported into a picture box and is set at its original contrast—that is, the contrast at which the scanning software saved the original image.

Figure 12.2   *An image at Normal Contrast setting.*

One of the simplest and starkest contrast adjustments possible is that of the third picture box in Figure 12.1, where all is either black or white. QuarkXPress provides a similar control through a predefined command in the Style menu. The effect of this command is to change a grayscale picture into one with just two levels of shading, black and white. This effectively turns grayscale images into line art, like a figure made by a black marker drawing on white paper. In this case, the program must decide which shades are replaced with white and which with black.

Figure 12.3   *The image of 12.2 at High Contrast setting.*

The predefined command High Contrast does this by setting to white all shades lighter than 30 percent black. It likewise sets to 100 percent black all shades greater than 30 percent. Figure 12.3 shows the Figure 12.2 picture after it has been selected and had the High Contrast command applied to it. Notice that all grayscale variation has been eliminated. This is the most drastic of contrast adjustments.

> **Adjusting an image to black-and-white contrast**
>
> *Select picture with content tool active*
>
> *Open the Style menu and choose High Contrast*

Another contrast setting can change an image by forcing each of its grayscale bits to assume a gray value of one of six levels, instead of just the two (black and white) of the High Contrast command. This is a stepped contrast, listed on the Style menu as Posterized. Its effect is to take the variable grays that exist on an image and change them each to the nearest of six levels of gray, 20 percent, 40 percent, 60 percent, 80 percent, 100 percent (black), and 0 percent (white). Applying this command to the bus image produces the picture shown in Figure 12.4.

Figure 12.4   *The image of 12.2 at Posterized setting*

> **Adjusting an image to stepped contrast**
>
> *Select picture with content tool active*
>
> *Open the Style menu and choose Posterized*

At first this image may look similar to the one shown in Figure 12.2. But notice carefully the flattening out and loss of detail that results from fewer shades in many areas, particularly in the upper-most sign area above the driver. Also, you can see that the two small horizontal window decals in the lower-left of the bus window which in Figure 12.2 appeared as a darker over a lighter one, have been reduced to the same shade.

Customized Adjustments to Contrast

If your bent is toward even more picture contrast control, you may want to turn to a dialog box that provides the means to graphically set up a relationship between the contrast of the imported image and the one displayed in the document and printed through QuarkXPress. The result will be a contrast-adjusted image of your own design. Controls for this option are reached by choosing the Other Contrast command under the Style menu.

What you'll see is a dialog box titled Picture Contrast Specifications. All the controls of this dialog box are used in drawing a graph that defines a new image contrast. This new contrast is based on the original image shading. In the dialog box, the horizontal axis labeled Input and the vertical axis labeled Output plot a relation that converts from one contrast to another. If you choose Other Contrast for a picture to which a preset contrast control has been applied, you'll see that control's effect on shading values plotted in the graph.

Figure 12.5 shows the Picture Contrast dialog box for Normal Contrast. Note that the graph portrays a one-to-one relation between Input and Output. The straight diagonal line indicates an increase of Input shading matched exactly by an equal increase of Output. A 100 percent black bit will be replaced by a 100 percent black bit, a 37 percent black bit by a 37 percent black bit, and so on. That represents no change over the original image contrast—in other words, Normal Contrast.

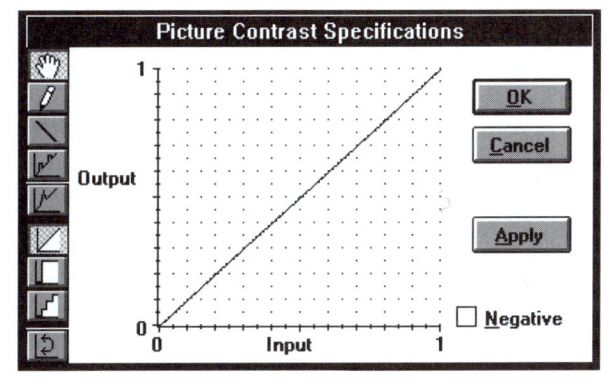

Figure 12.5 *The Picture Contrast Specifications' plot of Normal Contrast setting.*

Notice also that at the dialog box tools on the left, the fourth button from the bottom (bearing a similar diagonal line) is engaged. The Picture Contrast dialog box is an alternate way of applying the same settings as the commands we've just looked at in the Style menu. It's also a way to examine what conversion is actually performed by High Contrast and Posterized Contrast as show in Figures 12.6 and 12.7. Of course to interpret it you need some ease at reading graphs. Notice the button engaged for each of these also mimics the plotted graph of contrast Input/Output.

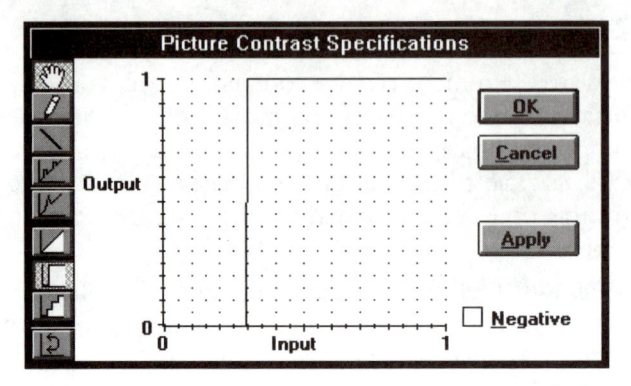

Figure 12.6 *The Picture Contrast Specifications' plot of the High Contrast setting.*

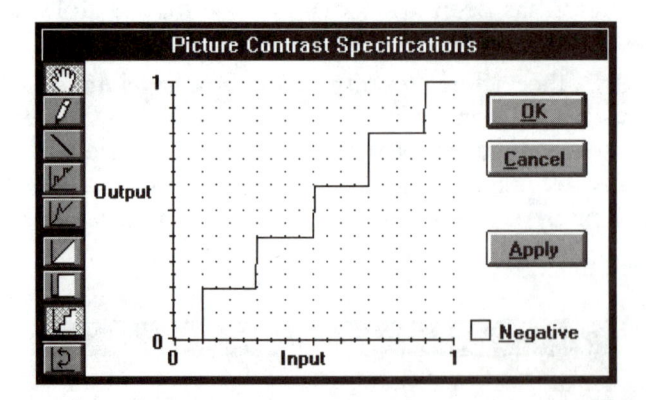

Figure 12.7 *The Picture Contrast Specifications' plot of the Posterized setting.*

The button at the bottom of the dialog box tools can be used to invert whatever Input/Output relation is established in the graph. This inversion tool flips the curve upside-down around its center. For instance, when applied where a high input shading might have resulted in a high output shading, the inversion process will plot a new relation that results in a low output shading. The combinations of effects are endless, but Figure 12.8 shows the result of applying the High Contrast button and then the inversion button.

Figure 12.8   Plot of High Contrast button, then inversion button specifications.

The hand icon button at the top of the dialog box tools allows you to shift the graph within the confines of the chart. Note that when you do so the graph will be reformed. The pencil icon button below it engages a freehand drawing tool, with which you can draw any shape graph to produce any desired relation in contrast. Using it, like using all the first five tools, gives the impression of tugging on the plot already drawn. The third tool down provides a means to draw straight lines in the graph. Figure 12.9 shows the effect of using it to draw a graph that peaks and accentuates low-percentage input shades, then drops and falls to zero of high-percentage shades.

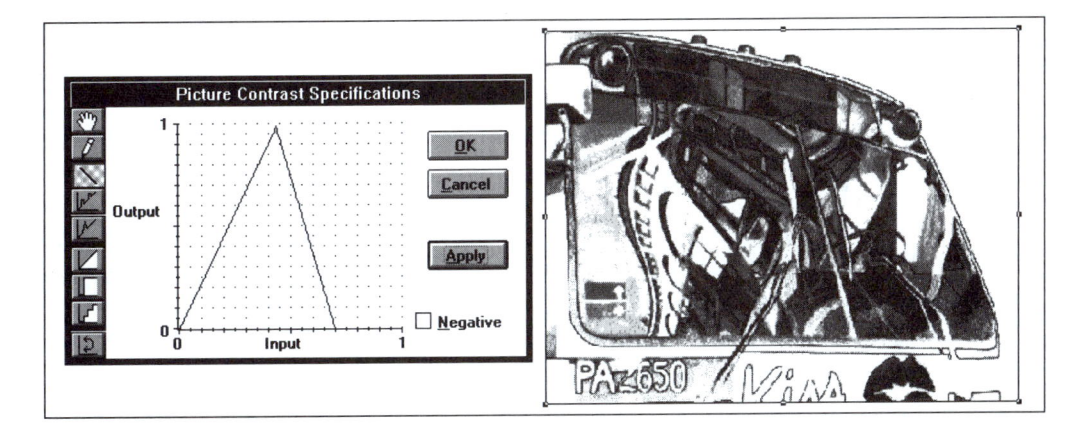

Figure 12.9   Effect of a drawn contrast graph.

The fourth and fifth buttons from the top select the plot and provide handles by which the graph can be pulled for fine-tuned adjustments. Button four provides handles between the 10 percent input marks; button Five, handles at the 10 percent marks for pulling spikes or valleys.

There is also a checkbox, in the lower-right corner, which applies the Negative command encountered earlier on the Style menu.

> **Making a custom adjustment of contrast**
>
> *Select the picture with content tool active*
>
> *Open the Style menu and choose Other Contrast*
>
> *At the dialog box, use the first five tools to draw or modify a contrast graph*
>
> *Use the last four tools and buttons to apply or invert a contrast graph*
>
> *Click the Apply button and revise as necessary*

Together, the tools of the Picture Contrast dialog box provide all the controls of QuarkXPress over relative image-shading levels. The possibilities are countless. You can accentuate normally low-percentage features and mute high-percentage ones. Add to these capabilities the shading controls, and you'll find ways you can enhance and highlight images in the document.

HALFTONES

Ink is not silver nitrate. Or, to put it another way, printing is not photography. What appears on film—or on screen—will not reproduce acceptably in print unless modification is made to convey the information inherent in the image. Continuous-tone illustrations are reproduced by translating them through a screen that results in another image known as the halftone. Through halftones, images with grays are represented in a medium that deals only with black and white (or full color and no color). And so we have photographs in newspapers, magazines, and books. A close look at any such photograph will reveal the arrangement of black dots that fools the eye into seeing gray or color tints.

The pattern of these dots is produced by photographing the continuous-tone image through a screen, which breaks the grays into dots of varying size. A collection of big dots overlaps to produce black. Smaller dots and pieces of dots simulate grays. Figure 12.10 shows an image of relatively continuous tones on the left and its screened halftone counterpart on the right. Notice how the dot formation in the halftone creates an impression of gray. Note how the dots are all smaller than a certain size. This maximum dot size is determined by the gridlike screen through which the image is captured.

Manipulating Images ◆ **273**

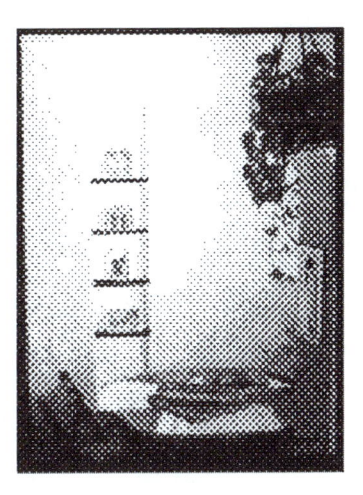

Figure 12.10 *Continuous tone image and halftone image.*

Further examination of the halftone in the figure also reveals that the dots fall into a pattern made up of lines at 45 degrees to the horizontal. This screen can be described as 45 lines per inch, dot screen, at 45 degrees. A screen can also consist of lines of varying thickness instead of dots of varying size. So the parameters for a screen are (a) lines per inch, (b) the pattern, and (c) the angle of screen rotation.

The screen is what determines and creates the halftone image from an original image. Of course, there is always some loss of image clarity when a screen is applied. But the result is an image that can be conveyed through a printing press.

QuarkXPress achieves the screening effect digitally. The result is halftone pictures that can be sent to all sorts of printers and image-setters to display a rendition of the shading in continuous-tone illustrations. The controls for halftoning are, like the contrast controls, of two types and are found in commands on the Style menu as shown in Figure 12.11.

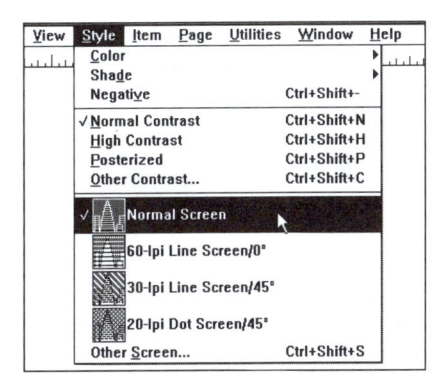

Figure 12.11 *Halftoning screen controls on the Style menu.*

Unless given other directions, the program applies a default screen to any picture image. This is represented by the Style menu command, Normal. You might find your default is set to a dot pattern of 60 lines per inch at 45 degrees. To apply a preset halftone setting to any picture image, first select the picture with the content tool. Next open the Style menu and choose any of the four screens displayed with icons there.

> **Applying preset halftone screening to an image**
>
> Select picture with content tool active
>
> Open the Style menu and choose one of the screens in the lowest box

Note that even after making these changes you probably won't notice them on your monitor. QuarkXPress doesn't display halftones unless specifically requested. Screen redraw times are considerably lengthened when halftoning is displayed. However you can specify halftone display through the final screen command in the Style menu.

You can examine an existing screen applied to a picture or specify a screen of different parameters by opening the Style menu and choosing Other Screen. A dialog box titled Picture Screening Specifications will appear, as shown in Figure 12.12. Note that both angle and screen lines per inch are adjustable here, as well as pattern type. Also presented is the checkbox control, at the lower-left of the dialog box, for displaying the halftone on your monitor.

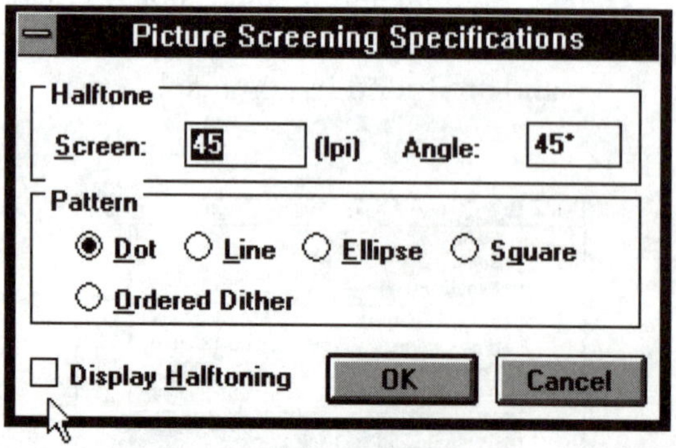

Figure 12.12 *Picture Screening Specifications dialog box from Other Screen command.*

Figure 12.13 shows the two preset dot screens of Normal (here 60 lpi/ 45 degrees, on the left) and the coarser fourth choice on the screen commands (20 lpi/45 degrees, on the right) applied to the same illustration shown earlier. Figure 12.14 shows the two preset line screens 60 lpi/zero degrees (on the left) and 30 lpi/45 degrees (on the right) applied to the illustration. Notice how the lines per inch of the screen have a drastic effect on the quality of the image, and how the choice of dot or line has a subtler, but distinctive, effect.

Figure 12.13 *Halftones of Normal Screen and 20-lpi Dot Screen/45 degrees.*

Figure 12.14 *Halftones of 60-lpi Line Screen/ zero degrees and 30-lpi Line Screen/ 45 degrees.*

Resolution

Aside from contrast and screening, a much simpler aspect of image manipulation always has a significant effect on the illustrations we include in a document file. This is enlargement and reduction, or sizing. You've already seen how to size an image. But here, let's consider what happens to image quality as a result of sizing.

To understand the effect of sizing on the types of images we're looking at in this chapter (bitmapped and grayscale) you should note that these images are like mosaics, with hundreds and thousands of little dark or light bits tiled into patterns that we recognize as images. The size of these bits is originally determined by the device and software system that puts them into a graphics file. This system may be the graphics-generating program operating in your computer, or it may be a scanner system. The bits are positioned into place in a rectilinear grid, like tiles laid into a floor.

In simple bitmaps, the bits are either black or white. In grayscale bitmaps, however, the bits can be black, white, or some shade of gray. As bitmapped images are enlarged, these pieces become apparent. At small dimensions, the clarity of a bitmapped image can appear quite sharp. In fact, reducing the size of an image is sometimes the best way to improve its apparent quality.

Enlarged several hundred percent the same image can show the underlying pattern of the bitmap grid in a way that distracts from the image itself. Figure 12.15 shows a scanned painting that has been both enlarged and reduced. In this case you can see the effect on resolution becomes clearly noticeable at 500 percent. Because each image varies, the effect of enlarging or reducing size will vary greatly from image to image. It's wise not to assume you can enlarge to any size, and to consider original size and fineness of bitmap before committing a piece of digital art to a large size.

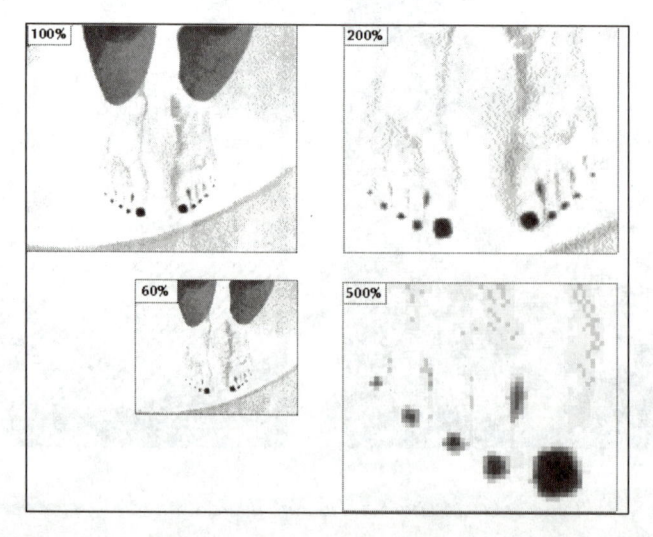

Figure 12.15 *Effect of sizing bitmapped art on image resolution.*

Stepping Forward

You've now see how images can be modified and manipulated in ways relating to resolution, contrast, halftoning, and shading. Almost all that we've said about black images applies just as well for images to which you apply color. The effects you can bring out for purposes of layout and printing will make a wider range of images available to you. The imperfectly scanned photograph, the file from a graphics program that's just a bit off—they are now within your reach.

The next step is to see when and how these techniques are applied to layout. With the wide range of magazine designs that have come into acceptance, image manipulation of the type we've just explored becomes especially useful. In Chapter 13 we'll see how using a magazine layout.

Chapter 13

On the Job: Magazine Pages

WHAT YOU WILL LEARN IN THIS CHAPTER

- How to adjust a graphic's contrast
- How to balance graphics and text flow in a pictorial article
- How to adjust halftone screens

Nowhere more than in the modern magazine are illustrations so pressed to their limits. Maximum impact demands that photographs, drawings, and paintings buoy up and carry articles along. In fact, stories without strong visuals are often shunned.

Ironically, the most visual subjects many times provide you with illustration originals never intended for reproduction in publication format. In these cases, you need to work a little magic to coax one medium to show itself favorably in another.

When illustrations are destined for output directly from a desktop-published document, image manipulation and software halftoning come into play. In this chapter we'll be laying out a strongly illustrated magazine piece. We will prepare grayscale pictures in a document for final output with the text they accompany. To do this, we'll make use of QuarkXPress's image manipulation techniques, especially those encountered in the previous chapter. We'll be interested in adjusting these digital images to optimum quality for output through an image-setter.

Assembling the Elements

The pages we're working on are 50 picas by 65 picas high and have top and bottom margins of 4 picas, inside margin of 2.5 picas, and an outside margin of 3.5 picas. The grid is made up of three columns separated by a 1-pica gutter. For our document we've engaged the Automatic Text Box feature and text chaining. Though we'll be adding other elements, they'll go on layers above the automatic box. By assuring that text runaround is engaged for these, we'll let the program help in arranging the text through the labyrinth of pictures to be laid out.

The story here is about the work of a painter. Scanned digital TIFF files of the canvases are the graphics we have to work with. Obviously, photographic prints are in many ways to be preferred to scanned files. The resolution of scanners, technological marvels that they are, lags behind that of the photographic process. But working from digital files, a great deal can be accomplished.

Since this will be a highly graphic piece, we're going to build it from the pictures out. That is, we'll establish the illustrations on three pages allotted to the story, adjust them for optimum reproduction, and then work in and typeset the body of the story and other text. We have four TIFF files and one text file. We'll also need to generate headline text and captions.

Our first move is to make a rough pictorial layout. This story is allocated the spread of Pages 32 and 33, and Page 34. And we have four pictures that, for convenience, we'll call Palm, Victorians, Porch, and Picnic. In order to work with these images, we choose to make an adjustment to the document's preset image resolution.

NOTE: Though we're making adjustments to an image in the picture, QuarkXPress is really only providing a representation of the actual graphic file. That file, which will be called on during printing output, still resides outside the document. Normally TIFF pictures are displayed at a low document-image resolution, which is what we see on screen. This is preferable if you wish to avoid lengthy redraws of the screen each time the TIFF picture is altered or when the view is changed. (Just how lengthy these redraws will be depends on your computer system.)

In order to make the adjustments we have in mind, we prefer to see the images at the fullest resolution of our monitor. So, opening the Edit menu, we choose Preferences, then Application in the submenu. At the dialog box that appears we click to remove the x in the checkbox marked "Low Resolution TIFF." Now every TIFF image we import will be displayed at highest resolution.

The Palm painting is the focus of the story, so we choose to incorporate it large on the page spread in a prominent position, starting near the upper-right and running across the fold. To bring this about, we choose the rectangular picture-box tool and draw a large picture box into which we import the Palm painting TIFF file. Using the keystroke Ctrl-Alt-Shift-F, with the picture selected and the content tool active, we proportionally enlarge the image to fit the box. Then we use the picture grabber hand (dragging with the content tool in the box) and the box handles for more adjustment to put the cropped image in place over the fold. We've deliberately done a bleed (extending the image past the end of the page) to the right to add to the sense of expanse in the image. On the left side we've pulled the picture box so far that it covers a column there, making it a four-column-plus picture box.

We're not satisfied with the contrast of the image, so we do two things. First we open the Style menu with the image selected and choose Shades, then 90 percent. Also under the Style menu, we choose Other Contrast. In the dialog box, we click the spike points button; handles appear on the straight 45-degree line of the Normal Contrast graph. We begin to distort the graph by pulling on these points, especially at the dark (to the right, the high input value) end.

After some experimenting, pulling a point then clicking the Apply button, we settle on the image setting shown in Figure 13.1. Next to it is the contrast graph that we've adjusted. You'll notice the pointer hand pulling on one of the dark end graph points at the upper-right. In order to create more distinction among the darkest shades, we've dragged points in opposite directions at the dark (or high) end of the plot. This has the effect of pulling things out of the shadows. We've also whitened out the lightest (or lowest) end of the graph.

The Victorians painting also figures into the piece early. So we position it on the spread in a picture box somewhat smaller and lower at the left on Page 32, where its portrait orientation fits well. We size and crop it to bleed off the left edge of the page, as shown in Figure 13.2.

Figure 13.1 *The adjusted contrast graph with Palm image.*

Figure 13.2 *The normal contrast Victorian image.*

This scanned image is somewhat washed out, so we again choose Other Contrast and modify the Input/Output contrast curve of the picture by using the straight-line tool. With the tool, we redraw the graph in sections, clicking the Apply button as we go to monitor the effect of the contrast distortion on the image. Reconstructing the contrast curve this way, we manage to accentuate contrast in certain tone levels and subdue it in others. Our changes bring out some of the features we value in the scanned subject. After several tries, we're able to increase the dark tones and bring out subtler features, such as curtains in the windows. We have arrived at the Picture Contrast graph shown in Figure 13.3, producing the enhanced image shown beside it.

On Page 34 of our magazine, we use the picture-box tool again to draw out two boxes into which we import the image files, Porch (at the top of the page) and Picnic (at the bottom). Again we size the images and crop them, pulling on the box handle of the Porch picture to bleed it off the page to the left. With each of these grayscale images, we encounter a need to darken the higher-percentage shades and lighten the lower ones.

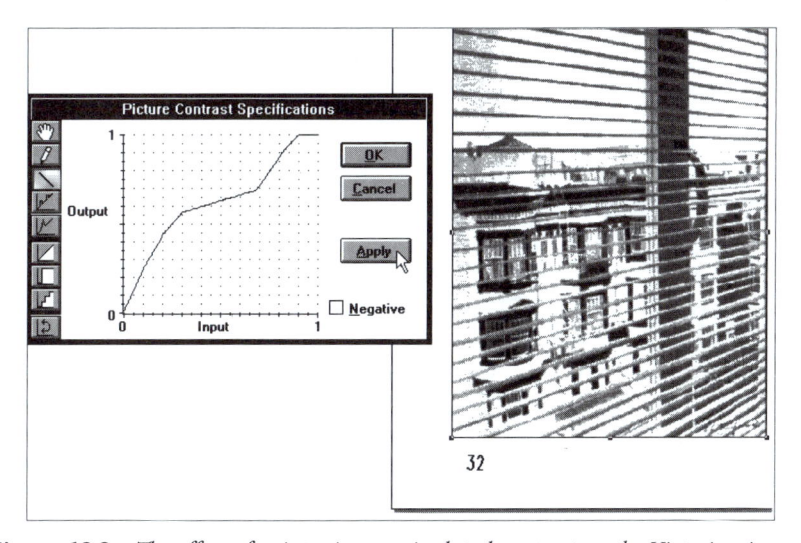

Figure 13.3   *The effect of point-wise manipulated contrast on the Victorian image.*

We do this with a method that often proves effective for us. In the dialog box presented through the Other Contrast command, using the pencil tool, we tailor each end of the Normal Contrast graph by redrawing the curve there into a taper. This bends the overall graph into an *S* shape. The gradual climb of the curve at the light end brings out the whites; the reverse curve at the dark end brings out the blacks.

In Figure 13.4 you see both images. Between them is the Picture Contrast graph we applied to each one. This kind of grayscale contrast adjustment, which exaggerates the lights and darks, often proves useful in heightening contrast without losing middle tones.

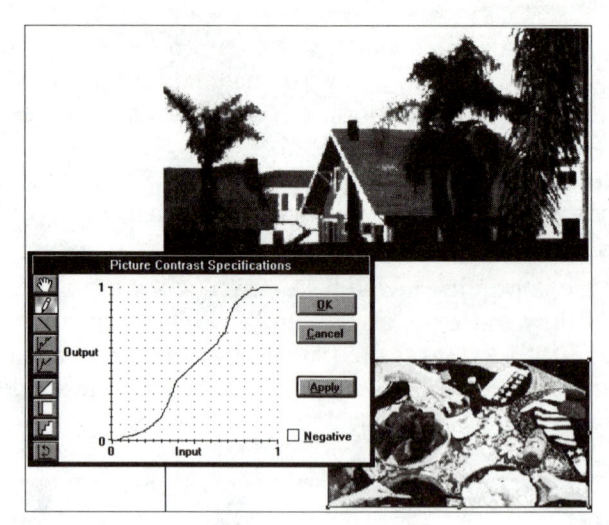

Figure 13.4 *An "S" contrast graph applied to each of two images.*

SETTING THE TEXT

Now we decide to set the text in place. Recall that this document is based on a master page spread that chains text from one page to the next in three columns. Note also that the picture boxes now in place have been created with an automatic text runaround feature active. With the content tool active, we insert a cursor in a column of the text box of Page 32 and then import through the Get Text command. The text flows, in serpentine fashion, in the column spaces around the Victorians picture, then over to Page 33 and under the Palm picture, then on to Page 34, between the Porch and Picnic pictures.

We next go to work on the typography, setting the typeface and size in the Measurements palette, establishing a new hyphenated specification with H&J's dialog box, engaging this specification and indenting the first line of each paragraph through the Paragraph Formats dialog box. We also use the text-box tool to create a new text box for the headline at the upper-left of Page 32. Into this we type the heading and then format lines both flush left and flush right to give a staggered effect. The headline text box now joins the picture boxes in pushing the body text down into available column space.

We make adjustments to the lead paragraph, formatting the first several words in all caps through the Measurements palette, and removing the first-line indent for this paragraph only through the Format dialog box.

A captions box is needed. We decide to describe both paintings in one caption, so we draw a small box to fit in at the bottom of the second column next to the Victorians picture. We key in the description, then choose a bold sans serif font and align left using the Measurements palette. We also make adjustments at the Text Box Specifications dialog box, removing the text inset and vertically aligning to the bottom of the box.

Everything on Pages 32 and 33 seems to be coming into place when we discover that the text and pictures are much too close. So, using the content tool, we select each picture box in turn and open the Item menu to choose Text Runaround where we increase the offset to 8 points all around. Now things are in order, except that the left side of our caption doesn't appear to be in line with the story text. This is because its text box was created after the Victorians picture box, and so resides on a layer above it. Since the picture box runaround will affect only those text boxes below it, we'll have to rearrange the layers. We select the picture box with the item tool and, opening the Item menu, choose Bring to Front. Now the spread, shown in Figure 13.5, is acceptable and we turn to the last page of the story.

Figure 13.5 *The spread of Pages 32 and 33, all text and pictures adjusted.*

On Page 34 we see the text already in place. Here we also increase the text runaround of the picture boxes. We create a similar caption box by copying the one from page 32, pasting it in here and then selecting the text, aligning right from the Measurements palette, and keying in the new caption.

To close the story, we insert a cursor in the last paragraph of the story itself, and at the Style menu choose Rules. We click the Rule Below checkbox and then specify a 1.5-point rule in the dialog box that is displayed. In a new line below the last paragraph, we type in a writer's credit. Then we use font and style adjustments to boldface the name and make the line stand out slightly from the rest of the story. Figure 13.6 shows a close up of this page with story and pictures complete.

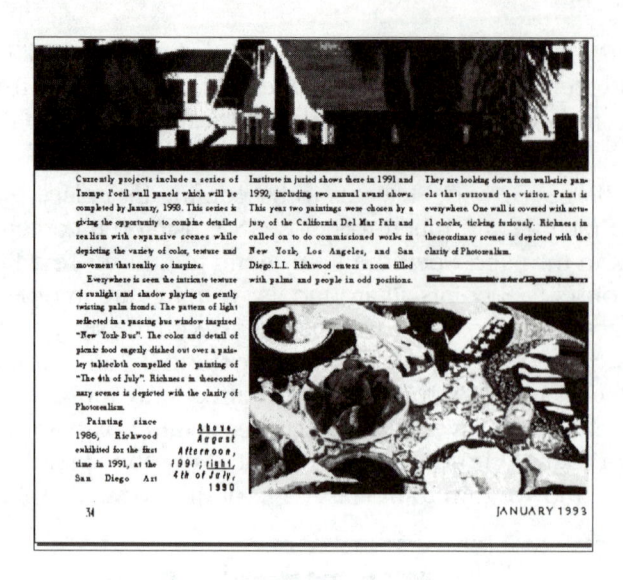

Figure 13.6 *Page 34 complete.*

HALFTONE CONSIDERATIONS

As far as layout and page make-up go, we've completed the story. But remember that this is a special case. If we had simply left space for photographs to be pasted in, or if the graphics were line drawings, which print easily, we'd be done.

But we have grayscale images to be output directly from this QuarkXPress document file. How good they look in the final film, negative, or paper output depends on the output device (image-setter, laser printer, and so on) and on the ways we prepare them within the document.

Whether we've chosen it or not, halftoning is already applied to each image. By default, a halftone setting will be in effect for each image unless we override it. The display of halftones on the monitor is normally switched off by QuarkXPress. What we've been looking at doesn't reveal the halftones that will eventually be applied to the pictures when the document is printed.

In order to see the simulated effects of halftoning, we open the Style menu and choose Other Screen. At the dialog box that appears, we click on the Display Halftone checkbox. Without making any other adjustments, we click OK. The result is a screen representation of the default halftone.

NOTE: Even very good monitor displays won't reach the clarity of an imagesetter (120 dots per inch is not quite 133 lines per inch). But for the moment, we'll hold a cautious faith that what we see is what we get.

Each picture is a special case, so we go from one to another, noting that the ultimate output device that will receive this document is capable of 133 lines per inch. At each, we try different halftone screens. Some effects show up more dramatically than others. Figure 13.7 shows the Normal Screen version (at 60 lpi) of the Victorians picture on the left, and next to it the picture at the screen setting we choose for more vividness, 133 lpi, 60 degrees, dot pattern. With the pictures set to match the output device, we have finally completed layout and prepared for printing.

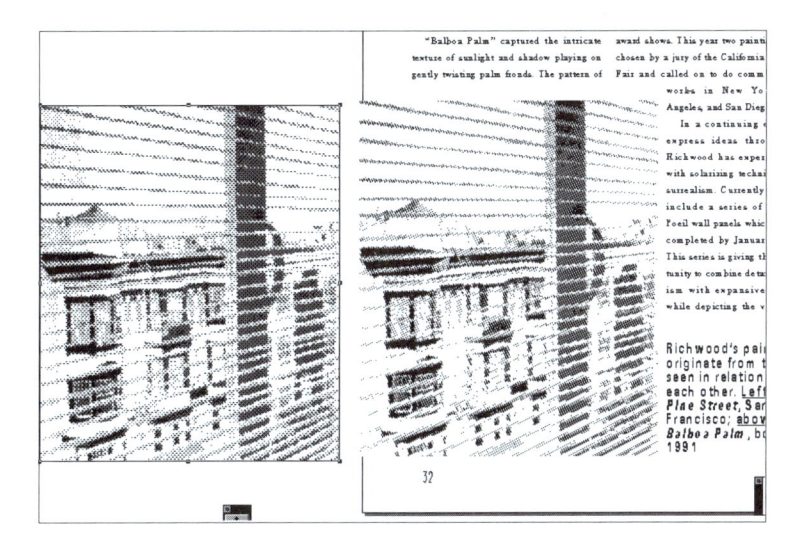

Figure 13.7   Monitor display for Normal Screen halftone and the chosen halftone.

STEPPING FORWARD

This last preparation makes use of functions often invisible in QuarkXPress—invisible, that is, until you see the printed page. Several other features affect the quality and success of final document output. Some affect whether you spend weeks or just days on a project. Others determine just what files you can gain access to. Still others affect the size and color of your page proofs and final output.

We turn to these features in the remaining chapters. For instance, we'll explore the ways to avoid the turmoil of episodic publication production. If you must prepare issues of a publication regularly, you can use QuarkXPress features to avoid duplication of effort and to speed production. In Chapter 14 we'll see how.

Chapter 14

Multiple Editions and Multiple Documents

What You Will Learn in This Chapter

- ◆ How to transfer elements between documents
- ◆ How to transfer pages between documents
- ◆ How to change formats automatically
- ◆ How to make publication templates

Once is not enough. Nowhere (well, perhaps almost nowhere) is that more true than in desktop publishing. Indeed, many one-of-a-kind books and advertisements and other unique productions are produced through desktop systems. But often, documents or pieces of them find their way into new projects. Sometimes these are direct descendants of the original document, as in subsequent magazine issues. Other times, layouts resurface to be modified into new layouts.

By working with multiple documents and multiple editions of the same document, desktop publishers expand their resource base and cut down on redundant labor. In this chapter we're going to look into ways to reapply whole pages, to update, to return to existing documents, to set up and reuse whole documents in new forms. This exploration will take us into QuarkXPress features that include thumbnails, templates, searching and replacing, and reverting.

ACROSS THE DOCUMENT BOUNDARY

QuarkXPress can present up to seven documents simultaneously open, each in its own window. Couple this with an ability to move items from one document to the other, and you have the ultimate in direct element sharing. Suppose a document exists that contains elements you'd like to use, perhaps in modified form, in a second document you're creating. Periodicals, for instance, often create special collections or booklets. Many of these are based on existing copy and designs. If your aim is to transfer elements or layout pieces from one to the other, you'll find the steps surprisingly simple, even simpler than cutting and pasting.

To copy items from one document to another, first bring both document windows into view within the program window. One way to do this is to open the Window menu and choose Tile. This command fits all open document windows into the program window space. You may need to close some other windows to use this command effectively. Or you might wish to size the windows manually to make each provide a view of the pages in question.

Next, make sure the source document's window is active by clicking on it or using the Window menu's document list. The title bar will highlight. Now select the items to be transferred. Drag them out of the source window to the destination window and release the mouse. Duplicates will be placed in the destination document.

Figure 14.1 shows such a transfer in progress. Here the *Looking Good* heading and the picture below have been selected in the window holding the Deco News tabloid, on the left. They are being dragged into the Deco Guide booklet, on the right. Notice that the items appear in the Deco Guide window at the larger view size selected for it. Once the midpoint of the selection crosses the window boundary, it jumps automatically to the adjacent window and conforms in all ways to the window parameters in effect there.

Figure 14.1   *Copying by dragging items from one document to another.*

Duplicate drags between documents

Bring both document windows into view

In the source document, select the items

Drag them across the window boundaries into the destination document and release mouse in position

Remember, these movements are not limited to just two documents. You can put three or more documents within the program window at once and drag items among them. In fact, as you drag an item it will appear momentarily in whichever window that contains the mouse tool. As you continue dragging, you'll see the item leave that document window and enter the next, and so on until you release the mouse button where the item will be deposited. Note that you can select a collection of items and drag the whole collection (in duplicate) to a different document.

NOTE Working with multiple windows like this, you would do well to exercise caution when you delete. It's easy to see items selected in one window, such as the destination window of a drag, and imagine that pressing the delete key will remove them. However, this will be the case only if these items are within the window that is active. For instance, in dragging to duplicate from source to destination windows, though the items appear selected and the mouse arrow can be seen in the destination window, the source window is the one active. So the items there would be the ones affected by a cut or delete command.

THUMBNAILS

Another method for manipulation between documents exists on the page level. This method can also be of use in reorganizing pages within a document, as an alternative to using the Document Layout palette. The access to this control is, curiously enough, through a View selection. The choice, Thumbnails, does more than change to the Lilliputian view. It engages a visual feature for moving pages.

To use this method to move pages within a document, begin by opening the View menu and choosing Thumbnails. The document will appear in an extremely small size. In this state, only the pages are accessible. If you try to select or otherwise affect the items on those pages, you'll find QuarkXPress unresponsive. To actually move a page, simply bring it into view within the window, click on it to select, drag to a new location, and release. QuarkXPress will rearrange pages as necessary to accommodate the new positioning.

When you position the mouse tool before releasing, you'll see one of several cursors appear, as they did within the Document Layout palette when moving pages there. The box cursor indicates the spread will be enlarged with the new page. The small bar-arrow cursors indicate which page will be pushed aside and downstream to make way for the new page.

The Thumbnails view offers some clever variations for page movements. To select a range of pages, click at one end of the range then hold down the Shift key and click at the other end. The entire group of pages will be highlighted and can be moved together. To select a scattered assortment of pages, click on one and then hold down the Ctrl key to click on the others. When you move one page, the others will follow and the group will be inserted where the cursor is placed.

Moving pages within a document using thumbnails

Select the pages by clicking, SHIFT-clicking, or CTRL-clicking

Drag to new location and release

To copy a page from one document to another is a similar process. It's much like copying items from document to document. With both document windows showing, make each active in turn and select the Thumbnails view for each. Next click the source document to make it active and click on the page (or pages) to be moved. Drag it across the window frames and into the destination document. Release the mouse button when the page is in position. QuarkXPress will rearrange the pages to fit.

Copying pages between documents

At the source document window, select the pages by clicking, SHIFT-clicking, or CTRL-clicking

Drag into the destination window and release

NOTE Each document created in QuarkXPress is set up in one page size. So what happens if you try to drag a page from a document of small-page format to one of large format? QuarkXPress creates a new page (or pages) of the destination document size, then puts all the elements from the source document in place, seated in the upper-left corner. But, if you try to drag from larger format to smaller, the program cancels the attempt.

Figure 14.2 shows the result of dragging Pages 1 and 3, selected with CTRL-click, from the smaller-format document (6 by 7 inches) on the right to the larger-format document (tabloid, 11 by 17 inches, after Page 4) on the left. Notice that the contents of each of the smaller duplicated pages, which are highlighted after the drag, appear tucked into the upper-left corner of the larger pages.

Bringing new pages to the document this way will also bring over any master pages, hyphenation and justification specifications, and differently named style sheets that are applied within these copied pages.

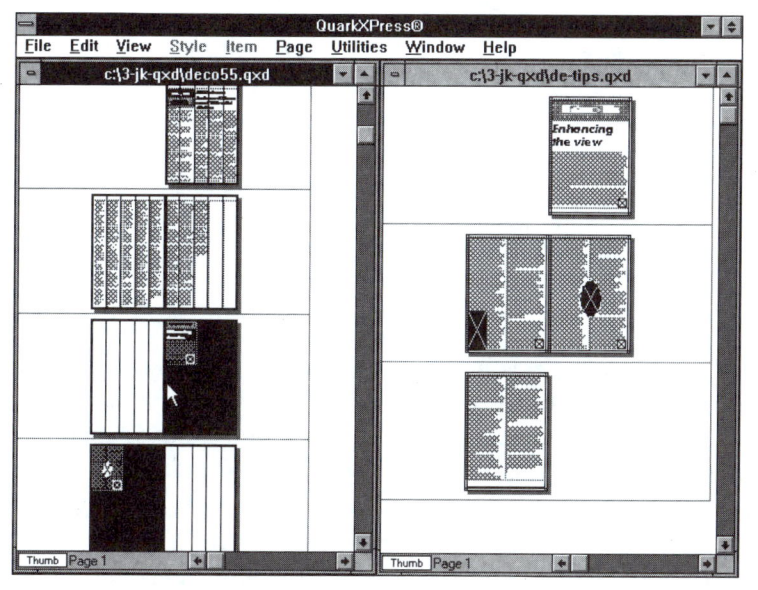

Figure 14.2 *Copying pages by dragging from a small document to a larger one.*

BLIND REPLACEMENTS AND UPDATING

Consider the manual that needs revision, or the book being prepared for a second edition, or the once-complete project that must now reflect a sheaf of last-minute changes from the editorial department. In all these cases, we're dealing with content that remains mostly the same, except for miscellaneous changes. Of course, miscellaneous changes can easily number in the hundreds on a project of any size. Still, when revision is preferable to redoing, you're looking at an updating effort.

As you've already seen, QuarkXPress provides a search and replace feature that makes quick work of changing this year's totals to last year's totals or *deliver all artwork to the art director, Hal Stinson* to *deliver all artwork to the production editor, Amelia Peters*. But by extending this feature, you can easily make global (that is, document-wide) changes in subtler and more typographic fashion.

For instance, suppose the text file you're given included the names of several books and was prepared by a person who used underlining to indicate these titles. If the standards of your publication require another type style, say bold italic, for each book title, you can easily make the change of style automatically for any title that might be already designated within the text. This would be the kind of change shown in Figure 14.3.

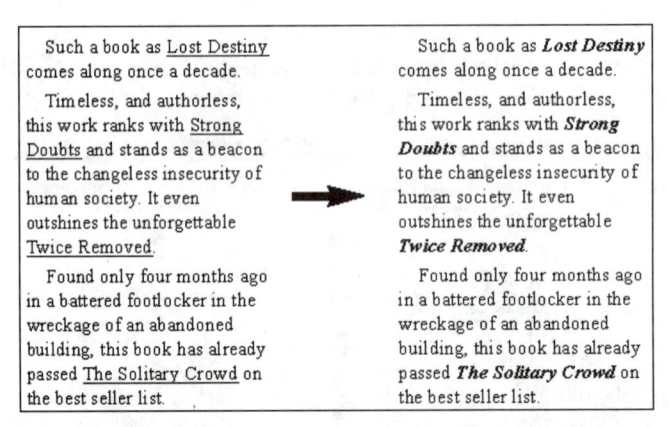

Figure 14.3 *A blind change of formatting made through the Find/Change dialog box.*

To change the type features automatically within text, open the Edit menu and choose Find/Change. At the dialog box that is displayed click to remove the x from the checkbox marked Ignore Attributes. An expanded Find/Change dialog box will be displayed that allows changes of font, size, and type style.

Under Style, you'll find that the checkboxes can be clicked blank, x-ed, or grayed. In this case, gray means not to consider that feature during the search. In this expanded search, you proceed exactly as with the simple text find/change routine, clicking Find Next, then Change or Change All, as appropriate. Figure 14.4 shows the blind search and change that automatically converted the underlines to bold italics in Figure 14.3.

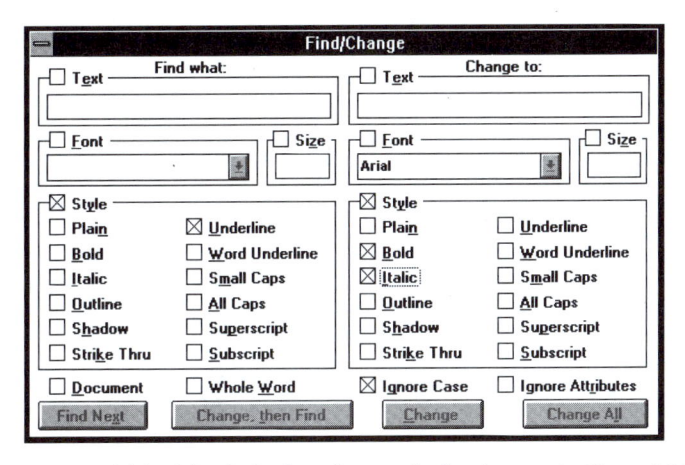

Figure 14.4   *The dialog box that made the changes in Figure 14.3.*

Note that no text is entered into either field for text. This tells QuarkXPress we're looking for a change of whatever text has the attributes indicated in the rest of the dialog box. You could also change font or font size, or use the box to search for attributes. One such search might be to locate each boldface word in a document, or each phrase in all caps.

FIXING MISTAKES AND REVERTING

A word about mistakes. We all make them; the computer makes them; the software makes them; at times the person-computer-software team makes them. Of course, it's in our interest to keep wrong turns to a minimum. But clearly, there is no progress without error at some point. The key to success is knowing when to attempt to fix the mistake, and when to just try over again.

In preparing a layout, you may encounter a situation in which you've made a number of adjustments since last saving the document. Maybe some elaborate text style and formats have been applied; perhaps a layout or series of image adjustments has been achieved. And sometimes, after doing all this, you conclude the document or page just isn't right.

Going backwards to undo every move, selection, and format application is one way to fix things. But QuarkXPress provides another method. If indeed you haven't saved the document since the beginning of these changes, then all you need do is give a single command, and the program clears the changes and returns the last saved version of the document to the window. The way to do this is simply to open the File menu and choose Revert to Saved. A dialog box will be displayed, asking for confirmation. Clicking OK brings up the earlier version.

Now, if you care to work more aggressively, you can deliberately experiment with changes to your document with an eye to this command. If you don't like the results of an experiment, then you tell QuarkXPress to revert. Realize, of course, that once done, reverting can't be undone. So you'll want to be confident that the earlier version was the preferable one. The changes you make between saves are kept in the computer's short-term memory, while the saved versions are of course kept on disk files.

Another approach to project development relies on your ability to use the Save As command under the File menu. As we saw earlier, by simply saving documents under different names, you can create a bank of possibilities to draw on for a final decision.

MULTIPLE EDITIONS AND TEMPLATES

If you plan to repeatedly access a document, to use it as a basis for developing future documents, you'll want to treat it as special. That is, you'll want to assure that it won't be inadvertently changed. This way you can return to it each time, confident that the document is the same. A file that serves as a starting point for others is known as a **template**. A template can be created and used as the basis of issue layout in a regularly reappearing publication or for a form or report that is generated more than once.

Templates serve as handy repositories for all the work that will be applied issue after issue. You can preserve ready access to layouts, page organization, special graphics, headings, logos, master pages, style sheets, hyphenation and justification specifications, custom colors (more about these in Chapter 16), and all the elements that go into the look of a publication or other document.

Making a Template

You can make a template from scratch, creating a prototype document using dummy text and pictures to get a grasp of how it will appear. Or, more practically, you can create an actual issue, being sure to save all the layouts, specifications, style sheets and preferences you might want for subsequent issues. In either case, you can then strip out the changeable text and graphics, deleting with the content tool, and leave boxes in place as appropriate.

One way to set up a template is to generate the document and save it in the usual way (as a standard document with the .QXD suffix). Then, when it's time to produce the new issue, the template can be opened and the Save As command given with a new name. For instance, you might open the template document, THEGLOBE.QXD, then make changes pertinent to the March issue, saving this new version as MARCH93.QXD, and leaving the template document unchanged. Then when the next month's production begins, you could open THEGLOBE.QXD again, make changes and save it as APRIL93.QXD.

The important point here is to be sure not to inadvertently save changes onto the original template document, except as you want to change the template. The best practice in this case is to immediately choose the Save As command after opening the template and to generate a new document by giving it a different name, even before a single change is made to the template.

Making Templates Using Save As

A second way to set up a template is to apply an obscured feature available through the Save As dialog box. To use this, key in a new file name and open the drop-down list in the lower-left of the dialog box, the one labeled Save File as Type. Here, choose the second listing, Templates.QXT. Notice that the template suffix, .QXT, identifies this as distinct from the normal .QXD document. To go back to our earlier example, with this method the file saved would be labeled THEGLOBE.QXT. Figure 14.5 shows THEGLOBE file being saved as a template.

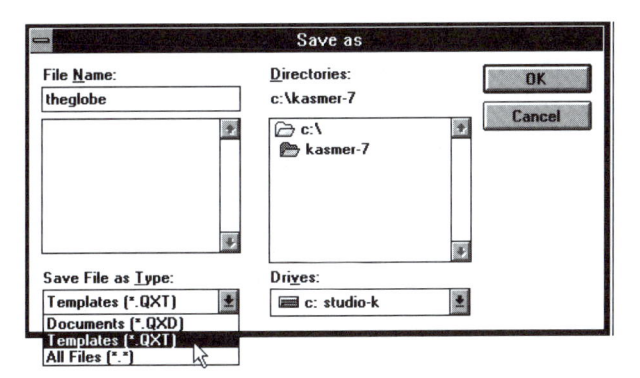

Figure 14.5 Saving a file as a template.

A template file can be opened but not altered. When you try to save it after opening, you're presented with a Save As dialog box, which prompts you to save the current document as a normal .QXD type. Note that you can also generate a new template from an existing one, saving the template in document file format and then modifying, and finally saving the modified document as a template under a different name.

STEPPING FORWARD

We've explored some of the simple, but highly effective, tools that QuarkXPress provides for updating documents, using templates, and transferring elements and pages between documents. They will prove invaluable when your document production demands efficient use of resources within QuarkXPress format.

The desktop publishing world is a bigger place than just QuarkXPress, of course. There are a number of ways of dealing with the elements that your documents need from this larger world. In Chapter 15, we'll look at what can be done to manage graphics and text within and among documents, and how to handle some special transfers.

Chapter 15

Transfers Within and Without

WHAT YOU WILL LEARN IN THIS CHAPTER

- How to collect design elements into a library
- How to export text and formatting tags
- How to deal with screen captures and EPS pages

The document provides for assembling, modifying, and creating design elements in such versatile ways that we may be tempted to use it to store and organize elements as well. While it can be acceptable for this purpose, there are other means more suited to the task.

Images, text, and even partial layouts can travel both into and out of a document. The stronger the grasp we have of these migrations, the more readily we'll be able to manage diverse elements in page makeup. In this chapter, we'll investigate some sophisticated ways we can control the flow of elements through documents. We'll look at libraries, a special type of QuarkXPress file with which you can create and manage elements. We'll also see how to export text, graphics, and layouts by command and through auxiliary software.

The Library

Library. Now there's a word that conjures up apprehension in many otherwise courageous, worldly, sophisticated adults. They picture dusty books secreted in dimly lit, tottering stacks under arcane numbering systems. A QuarkXPress library is something different; it's really just a kind of Rolodex for design elements.

You can use a library to store any item that can reside on a document page. If you put pictures in a library, all their specifications will be stored in the library with them. If you place a text box in one, formatting and style features will be stored with the text box. In effect, a library is a specialized QuarkXPress file designed only for storing items. It occupies a window, like a document. In fact, several libraries may be opened at once, and items may be interchanged between both them and documents. When taken together, the total number of open documents and libraries can reach seven, the same limit put on documents alone.

To put the library window on the screen, open the Utilities menu and choose Library. A dialog box will appear that resembles the Open dialog box of the File menu. You can use the directory windows to locate an existing library. For example, if all the QuarkXPress files are installed, you can locate a sample library within the XPRESS directory folder (inside a SAMPLES directory). Alternatively, you can make a new empty library into which you'll drag collected entries. To do this, first type a name in that first field, then click on the Create button in this dialog box. In either case, the library will be displayed onscreen, normally as a long vertical window at the right side of the program window. You can size and move this window just like any other in the Windows environment.

> **Opening or creating a library**
>
> > Open the Utilities menu and choose Library
> >
> > Locate the file through the directory windows or key in a name to create one
> >
> > Click the Open or Create button as appropriate

How do you gain access to items in a library? Use the same approach you apply to transfer items from document to document. Simply select the item and drag it to a document window or to another library window. The dragged item will be duplicated in the destination window, following the same behavior as any item dragged between document windows. And you can drag items from library to library to build different specialized sets of working collections.

You can also drag an item from a document to a library to put a duplicate of it there. Within the library every item (or selected group of items) will appear as a thumbnail, just as each of the various collections of information appears as books within a library building.

> **Using items between documents and libraries**
>
> > Position the windows of both in the program window
> >
> > Click on the window to activate it, then on the item
> >
> > Drag to the other window and release to copy the item there

All the instructions for moving a single item also apply to several items that have been selected together. In that case, however, the item selection will appear as a single thumbnail within the library. This is actually a handy way of temporarily grouping items for reuse.

How do you deal with the thumbnails within a library? In Figure 15.1 you can see a library with three items (a text box, a grayscale picture, and a recently added line with an arrowhead end cap) that have all been dragged in at different times from a document. When you drag an item or item collection to a library, two small triangles serving as markers indicate where the item will be placed. Also, the cursor becomes a pair of spectacles. By moving the mouse tool along, you can choose where in the list to drop the new item by observing the location of the triangle pair.

Figure 15.1 *Three items represented as thumbnails within a library.*

> **Positioning entries within a library**
>
> *While dragging the item(s), note the appearance of double triangles*
>
> *When the triangles mark the desired insert point, release*

The familiar Cut, Copy, Paste, and Delete functions are available within the library under its Edit menu. Using them, you can, for instance, take an entry from a library by clicking on its thumbnail and giving a Cut command. Locating the item tool elsewhere, you can give the Paste command to relocate it elsewhere within the library or to paste a copy of it within a document. Note that you can copy any thumbnail entry from a library by using the mouse to drag it out of the window, regardless of which tool has been selected from the program tool palette.

A feature particularly helpful with large library collections is the ability to name each library thumbnail. To do this, you double-click on the thumbnail, and a name dialog box is displayed. Key in the name and click OK. In Figure 15.2, the text box at the top of the library has been double-clicked to produce the dialog box next to it, where a label has been typed.

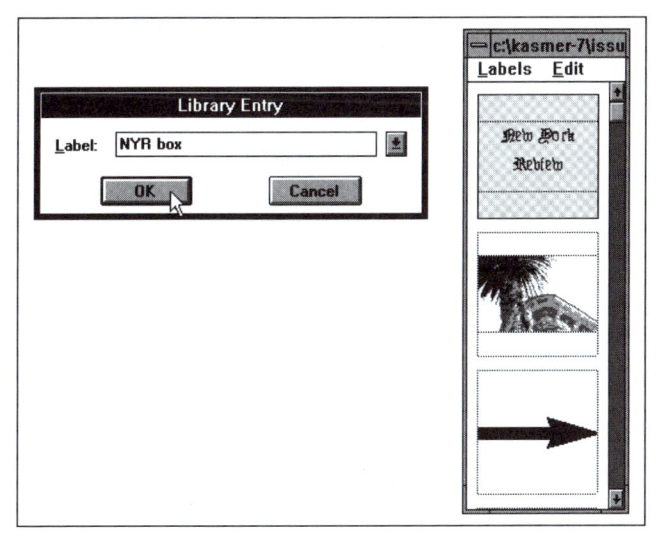

Figure 15.2 Labelling a library entry after double clicking on it.

Naming library entries

> *Double-click on the entry to call up the Library Entry dialog box*
>
> *Key in the name*
>
> *Or*
>
> *Use the drop-down list arrow to locate an existing name you'd like to apply again*
>
> *Click OK*

You can always locate a thumbnail by using the library's scroll bar. When you've named thumbnails, you can also locate them by opening the Labels menu and choosing from the alphabetical listing of names you're given, as shown in Figure 15.3. The thumbnail by itself is displayed in the library window. To return to a view of all the thumbnails, you can open the Labels menu and choose All. Or to see just those items that haven't been named, you can choose Unlabeled.

Figure 15.3 *Choosing a library entry by alphabetical name listing.*

QuarkXPress saves the library file when you close the window. However, you can instruct the program to save the library automatically each time an item is added to it. The control to engage this automatic saving is a checkbox in the Application Preferences dialog box. To locate it, open the Edit menu and choose Preferences and then the submenu, Application.

SENDING TEXT OUT OF QUARKXPRESS

Of course, when using QuarkXPress as a platform for developing designs and typesetting, we normally follow through by printing through QuarkXPress as well. But there are ways to send information established within the document out in the form of files that can be dealt with by other software.

Text is normally grist for the document layout mill in QuarkXPress. However, it may also become necessary to take text that has been processed within the document and send it out in a form that can be used in other software programs. For instance, you may wish to make the final text from your publication available so that staff members who have access only to word-processing software can work on it. To do that, you'll need to export the text in a form that allows your colleagues to gain access to it with their programs.

One control within QuarkXPress enables you to send out text in various forms—whole or partial stories. As you might guess, this is the outbound counterpart of the Get Text command. And like Get Text, the exporting command is found under the

File menu. It's labeled Save Text, and it presents a dialog box like the Get Text dialog box. The options are similar. But realize we're going the other way now. In the Get Text dialog box, you have the option of importing different file types. This allows you to draw text into the QuarkXPress document platform from a variety of sources. This variety is limited only by the available filters present in the XPress directory. In the Save Text dialog box, you can export through these same filters. But now the process leads not to a single QuarkXPress document, but to any of the word-processor types represented by available file filters.

As before, your options include the universal plain text format known as ASCII and labeled with a .TXT suffix. Recall that this is plain text at its plainest, with no style or formatting attributes included. Other export options include Microsoft Word, WordPerfect, and Rich Text (.RTF suffix) formats, as well as others. You might recall that RTF is a widely recognized file type that includes character and paragraph attributes. Figure 15.4 shows the Save Text dialog box with a file type being chosen from the drop-down list at the lower-left.

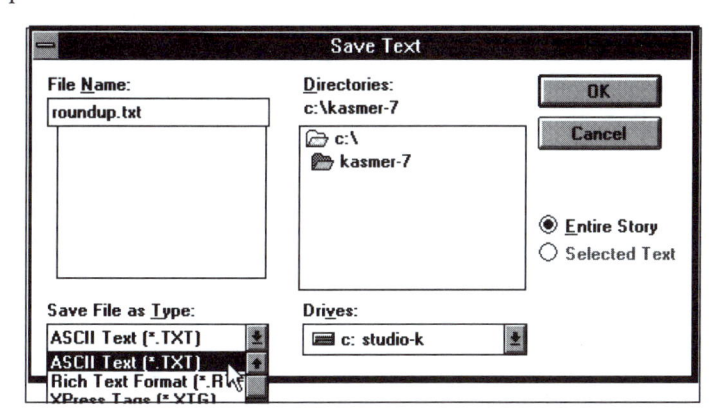

Figure 15.4 Choosing an export file type from the Save Text dialog box.

If there is any chance that you might ever need to reimport a story that has already been formatted in QuarkXPress, you'll want to consider another format that is at once universal and yet particular to QuarkXPress. This is a special text-file type in standard ASCII format. What makes it universal is the standard .TXT-file type. What makes it particular to QuarkXPress are special codes included within the text file. These are character and paragraph tags, which QuarkXPress understands, actually spelled out in the text. They signal QuarkXPress to apply formatting and styling automatically when the text is imported. This file format is found under the listing XPress Tags in the file-type drop-down list of the Save Text dialog box. Files saved in this format bear the .XTG suffix.

> **Saving formatting information in an ASCII text file**
>
> *Place the cursor within, or select, the text to be exported*
>
> *At the File menu choose Save Text*
>
> *At the dialog box, use the drop-down list to choose XPress Tags*
>
> *Click OK*

In Figure 15.5, at the left you can see a text box to which the Save Text command was applied with XPress Tags. To the right of it is the text file opened in Microsoft Word for Windows 2.0. Notice that all the text of the box is found in the text file, but it is accompanied by a number of arcane-looking notations enclosed in pairs of angle brackets. With a little attention these notations can be decoded. For instance, the first phrase, <v3.10>, indicates the version of QuarkXPress that created the document from which the text was extracted. Preceding and following each title within the text, you can see the phrase, <BI>, which indicates to switch on, then off, the boldface and italics for the words between. You could, using rather simple deductive reasoning, go through the entire comparison and derive the meanings of nearly every code.

| Such a book as ***Lost Destiny*** comes along once a decade.

Timeless, and authorless, this work ranks with ***Strong Doubts*** and stands as a beacon to the changeless insecurity of human society. It even outshines the unforgettable ***Twice Removed***.

Found only four months ago in a battered footlocker in the wreckage of an abandoned building, this book has already passed ***The Solitary Crowd*** on the best seller list. | <v3.10><e1><*L*h"Standard"*kn0*kt0*ra0*rb0*d0*p(0,14.4,0,0.0,3.6,g."U.S. English")*t(0,0,"~"):Ps100t0h100z14k0b0c"Black"f"Times New Roman">Such a book as <BI>Lost Destiny<BI> comes along once a decade.Timeless, and authorless, this work ranks with <BI>Strong Doubts<BI> and stands as a beacon to the changeless insecurity of human society. It even outshines the unforgettable <BI>Twice Removed<BI>.Found only four months ago in a battered footlocker in the wreckage of an abandoned building, this book has already passed <BI>The Solitary Crowd<BI> on the best seller list. |

Figure 15.5 *Document formatted text at left and the same text exported with XPress Tags.*

Again, the advantage of the XPress Tags file type is its ability to reimport formatting and character attributes intact. So you can work on typesetting within a document, export text in XPress Tags format for editing, and then reimport for final copyfitting without losing a bit of your typesetting effort. Of course, in this case the editor must work around these codes and regard them as unalterable. Consider also that once they are familiar, typesetting codes can be applied directly outside of QuarkXPress, in nearly any word processor. In fact, using typed codes like these has been part of traditional typesetters' jobs for decades.

Sending Layouts Out of QuarkXPress—EPS

Just as text can be sent out of QuarkXPress to be used in other programs, so can layouts, within certain limitations. In one way, the designers of QuarkXPress intended exporting to work for everything on a page at once. The approach they used was saving an entire page as a graphic image file.

The type of graphic image saved through this method is an Encapsulated Postscript, or EPS. Postscript, as you may know, is a programming language specifically designed for high-resolution printing. Several programs such as Adobe Illustrator and Aldus FreeHand work with EPS files. Because this kind of file is precise in its description, it offers a means of accurate and smooth output.

QuarkXPress can save single pages as EPS files. This means an entire page can be turned into a graphic. The command for doing this is found in the File menu, Save Page as EPS. In theory, using this EPS command to preserve elements in a document page should provide exact replicas that can be printed or manipulated from a variety of programs. You could even lay out a page in QuarkXPress, export it as EPS, paste it into PageMaker, and then print from the PageMaker document.

My own experience so far with the Save Page as EPS command in version 3.1 has produced somewhat imperfect renderings of pages. Perhaps these problems will be resolved by the time you see the program. In any event, you might want to proceed cautiously and try it out yourself before committing yourself to using this process in any of your projects.

Sending Layouts Out of QuarkXPress—Screen Capture

A method that is often overlooked for taking images outside of programs is the screen capture. This is a rather blunt way of taking an image on the screen and saving it as a bitmapped file. The reason screen capturing is often neglected is simple. In screen captures you are always limited to the resolution of the screen. For comparison, consider that a good monitor might have a resolution of 120 dots per inch while a standard laser printer will generate 300 dpi and an image-setter 1200 dpi or more. We're talking about a substantial difference in quality. Jagged letters and stair-step lines are real possibilities here.

OK, now consider the advantages. You can always capture the screen. Now, it's up to you to decide if the capability of taking an image from a QuarkXPress document offsets the lowered quality that image will present. On many occasions—perhaps most—the degraded image is unacceptable. But for those situations when some visual information on the screen must be retained or some layout or image must be transferred to another program regardless of lower resolution, the screen capture is the way to go.

What happens in a screen capture (also known ungraciously as a screen dump or a screen shot) is that the image on the screen is duplicated bit-by-bit in a file that can be used just like any other bitmapped file. The image can be brought into any software document that will read this type of file, such as a graphics, paint-style program. From there it can be edited and printed. A screen capture can be imported into a QuarkXPress document as a graphics file through the Get Picture dialog box. You can even import a screen capture of the scene in a program back into that program's document. (That's how several of the side-by-side comparison illustrations shown in this book were created.)

How do you capture the screen? One method is built into the DOS-Windows platform on which QuarkXPress works. Other methods make use of dedicated screen-capture software. If you use the DOS-Windows method, the bitmapped image will be saved to the clipboard. The other methods can save directly to newly created graphics files.

The DOS-Windows capture method works through a key on the standard 101 keyboard. It's the one labeled Print Screen. You'll probably find it on your keyboard along the top row to the right of the F12 function key. To copy and save a screen image to the clipboard, simply press the Print Screen key.

Capturing a screen image to the clipboard

Prepare the screen as desired

Press the Print Screen key

Normally the clipboard and its contents are out of view. However, you can gain viewing access to this Windows feature through QuarkXPress. Seeing the clipboard can be useful at any time when you lose track of what you most recently cut or copied, whether screen-shot or not. To take a look at the clipboard contents, open the Edit menu and choose Show Clipboard. A window labeled Clipboard Viewer is displayed. Within it, you should be able to see the screen that was displayed when you pressed the Print Screen key.

Recall that the clipboard is where text or graphics are put when the Cut or Copy commands are given. And just as in those cases, here you can bring out a copy of the clipboard contents by issuing the Paste command. To paste a captured screen in a QuarkXPress document, be sure that a picture box is selected and the content tool is active. Giving the Paste command will put the captured screen image within the picture box. In Figure 15.6, you can see the upper-left corner of a captured screen in which a QuarkXPress document is open, and within in it the Applications Preferences dialog box. For orientation, notice that the screen shot is in a picture box with a 20 percent Black background.

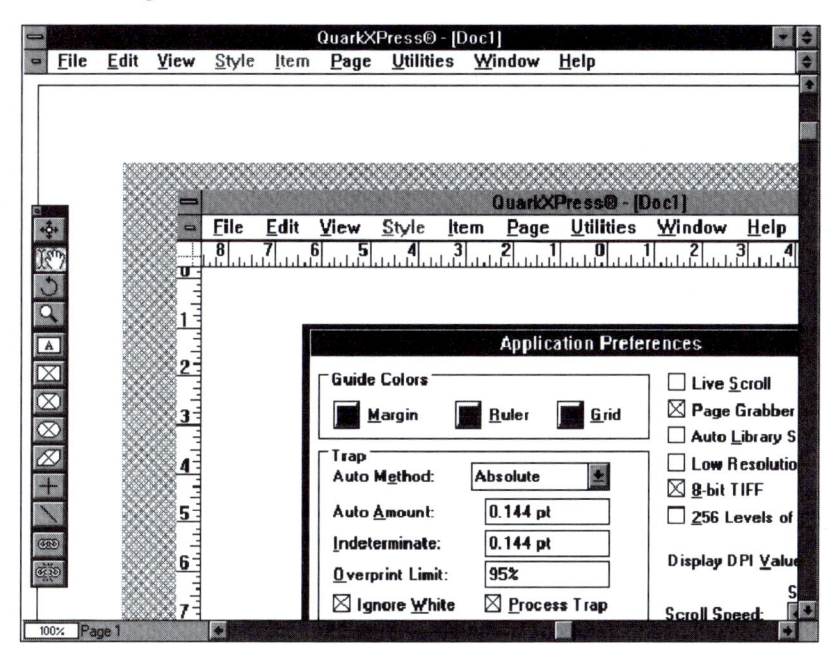

Figure 15.6 *A portion of a screen capture in a picture box.*

You can also paste the clipboard screen capture into other files through other software. For instance, you could paste the captured image into a graphics program, like Windows' Paintbrush (though this program is somewhat limited in how much of an image it can receive this way). Or the image could go into a word processor like Microsoft Word, if the program has the ability to receive graphics, as WinWord does.

Besides using this method to transfer monitor-quality images, you might find it handy to capture some settings, such as those in a dialog box, or as a quick way of providing background information when troubleshooting a document.

There are alternatives to using the Print Screen key. Various screen-capture software packages save the screen shot to an automatically generated file. These usually offer a number of file-format options. They also allow you to crop the picture before it's saved and to include the mouse tool within the captured image. (Such a program, Collage Plus, was used to tailor the illustrations in this book.)

Whichever way you go, the side-door graphics-from-screen captures are quick, reliable, and relatively easy ways to document what you see on your monitor.

Stepping Forward

These methods for handling text, images, and layouts in out-of-the-ordinary ways give you techniques for sidestepping the brick wall of file-format incompatibility. You never need be at a loss to convey to outside programs what is happening to your text or graphics at any point in their use.

Next we'll move into an area that's more an art than a science—managing color from our documents. QuarkXPress offers a feature that some competitors are now just beginning to add. That ability, to separate colors into the various plates needed for printing, is what we're going to explore in Chapter 16.

Chapter 16

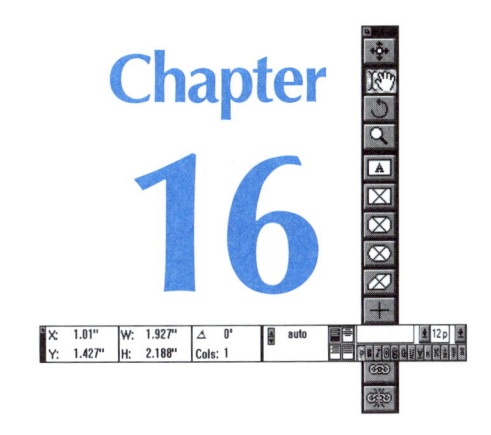

Color

WHAT YOU WILL LEARN IN THIS CHAPTER

- How to use the color wheel
- How to prepare color separations
- How to trap and blend colors

Working with color documents can be difficult. Matching colors is a subtle skill. There are schemes and models that make it easier. But predicting how a color produced using one scheme can be replicated in another is mostly a matter of judgment and experience.

This chapter is about how QuarkXPress can help you get colors from the screen to the final print run. First we'll look at various schemes QuarkXPress uses to handle colors, and how you can make use of them.

Screen Color versus Print Color

Recall the colors we applied from the Style menu back in Chapter 6. These preset colors were just a snowflake on the iceberg of colors that are available. With a good monitor and enough memory in your system's graphics card, you can see millions of colors on the screen. But here's the most amazing part: every one of these millions of colors generated on the screen is made from just three primary colors.

This may jog a memory back to elementary school. By adding red, green, and blue light together you can make virtually every other color in the spectrum. You might recall teacher talking about a rainbow, or that science class with prisms.

A variant of this is the basis of one color model, the RGB model, or red, green, and blue model. The light on your monitor—which is just a highly controlled light source, after all—is derived from an additive system such as the one you learned in grammar school. With no light added on screen, you see black. With red added, you see red. With red, green, and blue added in equal shares, you see white.

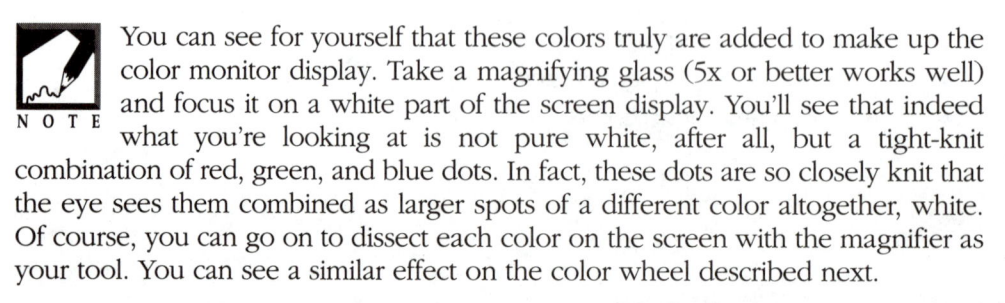

NOTE You can see for yourself that these colors truly are added to make up the color monitor display. Take a magnifying glass (5x or better works well) and focus it on a white part of the screen display. You'll see that indeed what you're looking at is not pure white, after all, but a tight-knit combination of red, green, and blue dots. In fact, these dots are so closely knit that the eye sees them combined as larger spots of a different color altogether, white. Of course, you can go on to dissect each color on the screen with the magnifier as your tool. You can see a similar effect on the color wheel described next.

If you're working on a quality color monitor, it is probably based on the RBG model. A whole class of video monitors came to be known as RGB monitors. To see the RGB model at work in your system, open the Edit menu and choose Colors. At the dialog box titled Colors for, you'll see the familiar preset colors in a listing. Now click on the New button, and a dialog titled Edit Color will be displayed. Be sure that the model RGB is selected from the drop-down list.

As shown in Figure 16.1, this is where you can design your own color or modify one already in place. To see how the RGB model works, note the wheel at the right of the box. This is the color wheel. It represents, in its fashion, all the colors of the spectrum. At this point you'll within it see a small black box in the center. The three fields below the wheel show 100 percent each of red, green, and blue. This, as we have just seen, creates the color white.

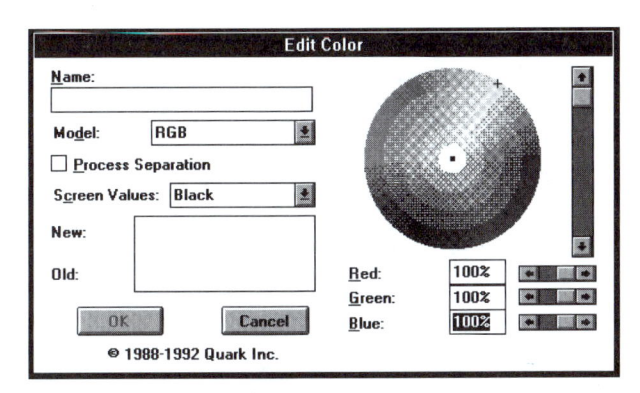

Figure 16.1 *The Colors dialog box with color wheel indicating white.*

Each position on the wheel represents a different color. You can verify this by dragging the tool (a pair of crosshairs seen in the figure in the upper right of the wheel) with the mouse button down. The values of the additive colors will be shown in the percentage fields below the wheel as you move. Note that the tool in Figure 16.1 is in the position representing yellow (100 percent green and 100 percent red), but because the mouse has not been clicked, the original value, white, is still the one represented in those values. To the lower left of the dialog above the Cancel button is a box that displays the color currently selected on the wheel, (opposite New) as well as the original color which is being edited (opposite Old). These solid color bars provide a large contiguous area for you to see more clearly how the colors (on the monitor) appear.

As you drag along the edge of the wheel with the mouse button down, you select colors which are composed of varying percentages of two colors and zero percent of the third. The center of the wheel is, as mentioned, white. Positions between the center and the circumference represent assorted non-zero combinations of red, green and blue. Note that you can also adjust colors by moving the sliders adjacent to each primary color-percentage field, or by typing in percentage values in those fields. In all cases, the new color will appear in the New/Old color box at the left.

> **Producing a color**
>
> At the edit menu, choose Colors
>
> At the dialog, click New
>
> Use the mouse tool to click at a color on the color wheel
>
> Or
>
> Type in values of percentage of each color in the field boxes
>
> Or
>
> Use the sliders to combine colors
>
> Monitor the resulting color at the color bar
>
> Click OK at the Edit Color dialog and then Save at the Color dialog

You can also add varying amounts of black to any color you're editing. This is done with a vertical slider bar to the right of the color wheel. At its uppermost position, the slider adds no black; at its lowermost, 100 percent black.

NOTE You can make use of the color wheel and colors even if you use a black-and-white monitor. Of course you'll lose your visual feedback. However, if you know the percentage combinations of the colors you want, you can prepare them in the Edit Color dialog, like a colorblind painter systematically mixing from labeled tubes of paint.

You can experiment with the RGB system, and use it to provide custom colors for your layout document. Later, QuarkXPress can separate the colors for the individual runs they'll need to make through your printer's presses. But here's the rub: While the monitor uses an additive system to make colors, ink by its very nature uses a subtractive system. This means that as light—white light which contains the whole of the visible color spectrum—falls on a color of ink, we see that particular color because all the other colors are subtracted out of the light and only the visible one is reflected to our eye.

There is enough translation difficulty between one ink-based color model and another. But translating between a subtractive model and an additive model requires a mental leap, and, when all is said and done, a good eye and experience.

The prevailing color model used by printers is one in which the colors cyan, magenta, yellow, and black are blended to produce a desired color. This model, CMYK, is clearly based on different foundation than the RGB model. However, both ultimately perform the same function. That is, they both represent colors that are not present by a combination of colors that are. You can choose a color in any model and then switch to a different model. Figure 16.2 shows the dialog for the color red, which was chosen in the RGB model (by setting the slider controls to 100 percent red, 0 percent green, and 0 percent blue), but that now appears in the CMYK model. Note the values that produce red are a combination of two colors in this model. Yet we're still looking at the same color. Just its representation has changed. You can select any available model through the drop-down list of the Model field.

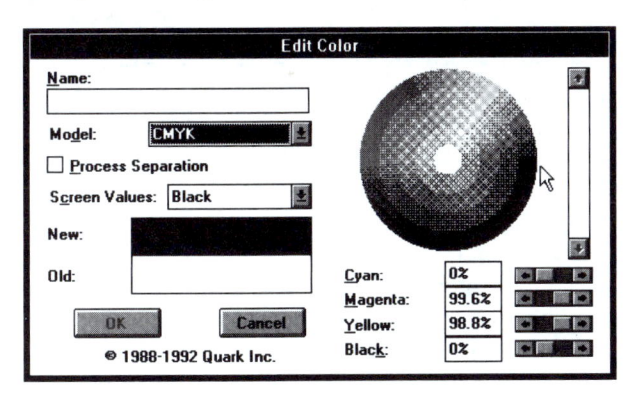

Figure 16.2 *The color, Red, as viewed in the CMYK color model of the Edit Color dialog.*

Keep in mind that we can use the Edit Color dialog box to create or change colors. These new colors will then be available to be applied through the Style menu to the items in our document.

OTHER MODELS AND PRINTERS

Another color-mixing scheme provided in the Edit Color dialog is one that allows you to choose a pigment (hue), its proportion (saturation), and its brightness (black or lack of it). This is the HSB model, an approach which brings us back to tubes of paint pigments. You also choose this scheme from the drop-down list for Model. Note, as in Figure 16.3, that you'll find similar sliders under the color wheel as in the RGB and CMYK models. But now the top slider/field will be the determiner of color; the second slider will determine tint; and the last will serve the same function as the vertical black-adding slider to the right of the wheel. As you move the Hue slider, the small color marker will move around in a circle. As you move the tint slider, the marker will move radially toward or away from the center of the wheel.

As you may know, other widely accepted color models exist that are somewhat less scientific in their approach but are more generally understood. These are the commercial color-matching systems. QuarkXPress offers use of three such systems through the Model drop-down list. They work on the premise that a large number of color swatches can provide for many, if not most, of the choices needed in color layouts.

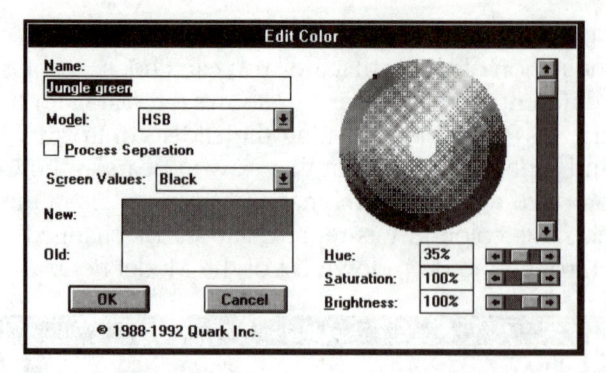

Figure 16.3 *The Hue-Saturation-Brightness color model presented in the Edit Color dialog.*

The three systems here—Pantone, Trumatch, and Focoltone—are each different commercial products. But they're all represented in the same way. Figure 16.4 shows the Pantone matching system as presented in the Edit Color dialog. In this scheme, you scroll through the swatches in the box, which has replaced the color wheel. When you find a color that matches what you'd like to include in the document, you click on it and then OK. Most of the colors are designated by number, but some are indicated by name. (That's an indication of an evolved, rather than strictly designed, approach.) These matching models can be viewed and edited through the color-wheel models and vice versa.

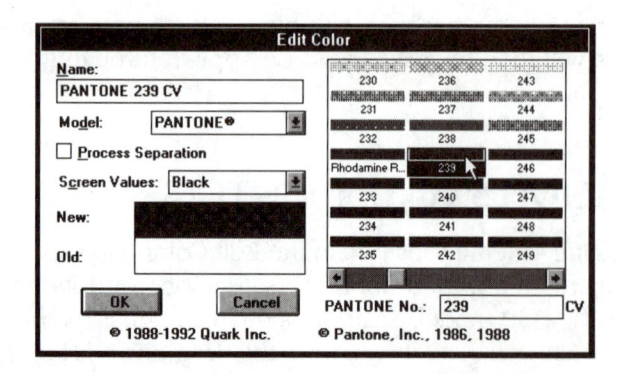

Figure 16.4 *The Pantone matching system presented in the Edit Color dialog.*

COLOR SEPARATIONS

If we had a tube of paint for every color we wanted to produce, there would be no need for blending. If a magic color printer worked directly from the QuarkXPress document, we could simply assign colors, click the Print button and watch our thousands of copies stream from the presses. While this is currently almost possible on a small scale through color proofing output printers, the reality of large-scale printing is that we need to reduce our color demands to simple instructions in which a limited number of colors are used to create the full range in our documents.

Printers work with two types of colors. One is spot color, consisting of the designated colors that the premixed ink can be found to match. This is often used with color-matching systems like the Pantone system. The other type is process color, a means of separating nearly any color into its component colors within the CMYK model. Most colors can be so separated into a four-color equivalent.

The way QuarkXPress handles these separations is to print a separate version of each page to correspond to the separate printing plates that will apply each of the CMYK colors in the presses. In the print run, each page may be printed on four times to produce the range of colors needed. But you need to designate which colors will be treated as process color. To do so, click to engage an "X" in the Process Separation checkbox in the Edit Color dialog box. Then, whenever you print separations, QuarkXPress will know to organize this color into its cyan, magenta, yellow and black components before separate printing of each. Putting into effect the separation of a color, as well as including new or edited colors in the Style menu, is finally assured by clicking the Save button in the Colors for dialog box.

Preparing colors for separation

In the Edit Color dialog, display the color to be separated

Click an "X" into the Process Separation checkbox

Prior to printing in the Print dialog box, click an "X" into the Make Separations checkbox

A document can be output as separations of spot color as well as process colors. And both spot and process colors can be output from the same document concurrently. The final step to this color separation process from QuarkXPress comes during printing. You can take care of this when you give the Print command at the File menu. Click to put an "X" in the checkbox labeled "Make Separations, near the bottom of the dialog. When the pages are printed to a PostScript printer, each separated color will come out on its own page, ready for the printing department to prepare for the presses.

TRAPPING COLORS

When multiple colors are eventually printed on the same page in the printing press, they come together. The way they come together is determined by the way the inks from the separate plates align when they meet the paper. Things are imperfect in printing presses, as they are in most of life. So QuarkXPress provides for the way inks will meet in a common approach known as trapping. If your document includes a red square over a blue background, for instance, QuarkXPress will remove the blue behind the square, so the colors don't mix in intended ways. This way, the red prints over white and appears as red as you intended.

However, when the high-speed presses are finally turning your document into ink-and-paper reality, the red square might not line up exactly over the cutout. The white could peek through, creating wholly unplanned visual effects. The most obvious proof of the inaccuracy of multicolor printing can be found in many of the Sunday newspaper comic strips, where a character's eyes can be found mysteriously migrated toward one temple, like a flounder's.

To compensate for this kind of effect, QuarkXPress automatically overprints slightly, to overlap the adjacent colors. This trapping method is adjustable, if you prefer, through two dialog boxes. One is document-wide, and in fact applies to all documents that are actively being printed. It's found in the Application Preferences, reached through the Edit menu by choosing Preferences, then the submenu. Figure 16.5 shows the Trap section within this dialog box. The other way to adjust trapping is color-by-color through the Color dialog box under the Edit menu. Here, by clicking Edit Trap button, you'll reach the Trap Specifications dialog box for the color you've selected. In the example of Figure 16.6, the color green, is being given a 0.2 point trapping value through the field box next to the Trap button.

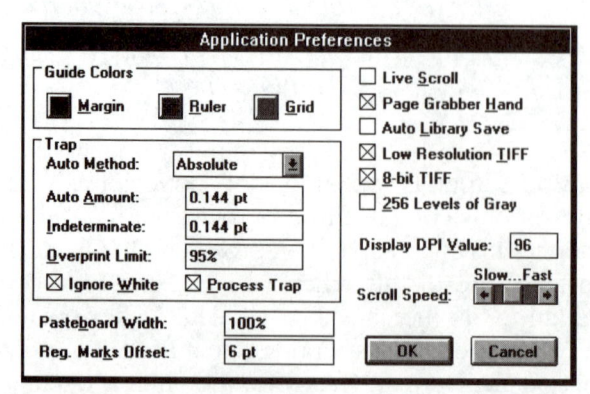

Figure 16.5 *The Application Preferences dialog box containing Trap specifications.*

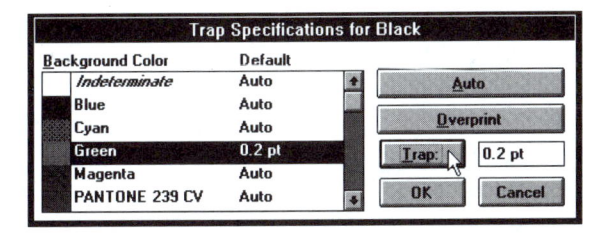

Figure 16.6 *Applying a trapping value to the color Green.*

THE COLOR PALETTE AND BLENDING COLORS

As you've seen, the lively and subliminal effects of adding color to a publication result in no small way from the designer's scrutiny and attention to detail. Color work can be made a little easier by using a tool through which you can apply colors to items and backgrounds, as you might apply styles to text. In the spirit of the Measurements palette, the Style palette and the Document Layout palette, QuarkXPress provides the Colors palette, as shown in Figure 16.7. You can choose colors and shadings for items, frames, pictures, text and backgrounds.

Figure 16.7 *The Colors palette.*

   Most of the controls work in a straightforward fashion. The first button on the left at the top applies to the frame of the item selected, the next to the text or picture content within the selected box, and the last to the background of the box in question. Tint or shading of color can be selected through the drop-down list and field value to the right of the buttons. Occupying most of the Colors palette is the scrolling list of colors. As you create new colors, they're added here as well. To apply a color, select the object, click one of the three top buttons to indicate which aspect to color, click on a color in the list, and apply a tint, if desired, through the drop-down list or value field.

There is also a control for blending background shades and colors. For instance, you could blend the background of a text box from a 50 percent black to a 10 percent black horizontally and produce a box that lightened from left to right. Similarly, you can blend from one color or one color tint to another. First select the item. Then choose Linear Blend from the drop-down list below the first row of buttons in the palette. Next, click the round button labeled #1, choose a color and tint. Then click the round button labeled #2, and choose a second color and tint. If the angular value next to these buttons is zero degrees, you'll see a blend of color and shade from left to right when the item tool is chosen.

Creating a color blend in background

Select the picture or text box with the item tool

From the drop-down list in the Colors Palette, chose Linear Blend

Click the #1 button; click a color and a shading

Click the #2 button; click a color and a shading

Zero degrees represents the horizontal. You can change this value to 45 degrees for the oblique, or 90 degrees for the vertical, or any other angle within the circle of 360 degrees, and the blend will run in the direction chosen. The blend feature is a handy one that can add some variation to text or picture backgrounds.

STEPPING FORWARD

Color can be an elusive goal. No other aspect of publication production demands so much subjective judgment. Fortunately, with the techniques introduced here you have a start on producing the colors you want for your documents. Experience and familiarity will be the best guides in the long run.

Bringing your documents to print involves much more than color replication. There are factors of font and image usage that become crucial in the actual printing process, whether you're proofing with a laser printer or sending final output to an image-setter. This is also where the large formats meet the reality of small paper sizes. And printing long documents can steal away precious eleventh-hour computer time if you let it. In the next chapter, we'll explore the ways to make your printing flow as smoothly as possible. We'll look at surprise problems that can be avoided. And we'll see how to get the best results regardless of the output device available to your project.

Chapter 17

Printing

WHAT YOU WILL LEARN IN THIS CHAPTER

- How to update images
- How to track font usage
- How to replace font choices
- How to output documents to printers
- How to use the Print Manager
- How to install printer drivers

In printing, the what-you-see turns into the what-you-get. Printing must successfully translate digital computer files into a film, paper, print, or negative visual master, or all the work of design, layout, typesetting, image adjustment, and so forth, is for nothing.

It sounds so simple. And, indeed, printing often requires no more than opening a menu and giving a command. However, it's a little like sailing a ship. When conditions are calm and the course unobstructed, it's a simple matter. But as the complexity of the document grows, as it becomes out of the ordinary in any way, as font and picture decisions are made for effective design rather than convenience, the waters may not be so smooth.

In this chapter we're going to look at how you can manage your document files through the sometimes turbulent printing process. We'll see what can be done in advance and how to facilitate the output session. We'll look at font management, picture management, printers, drivers, and dealing with over- and undersized pages.

CHECKS AND CONNECTIONS

One thing is easily overlooked while a document is being produced: The QuarkXPress program does not act alone. As we're guiding it to lay out and typeset pages, the software calls on other software and files behind the scenes. Several of these lie always within easy reach of the program, within the same directory folder.

Others are brought in from outside as needed. We introduce some ourselves when we call up a file or insert a disk into the floppy drive. Some of the files used by QuarkXPress that are not part of the QuarkXPress software package must be present during printing for our labors to come to fruition. Principal among these are many fonts and graphics files imported into a document.

Image Sources

Consider first the large image files we might be using in a document. Scans and elaborate grayscale renderings can occupy large amounts of storage space. When QuarkXPress imports these images, you may remember, it is really importing a screen representation while establishing a link outside the document to the original file. Through this link the program is able to use the graphics file to direct printing of the image at the highest possible resolution.

Now just imagine for a moment all the things that could happen to complicate this arrangement. When all the information required for printing is contained securely within a single document file, that's one thing. But when QuarkXPress must seek out a graphics file in order to print, well, what if it's been moved? What if an image has been altered in the file, but not on the document? What if the floppy disk from which you imported the image is in a briefcase at 30,000 feet headed for Rome?

To make your printing flawless, you'll want to assure that the sources for all images in the document are available to QuarkXPress when the final print command is given. Note that if you are simply generating laser proofs, and picture quality is the least of your concerns, then having the sources at hand for the program is not important. In this case QuarkXPress will use the rendering it uses for screen display. Of course, this is of coarser quality, but you may find it acceptable if positioning and cropping are your current concerns.

However, when the time comes to print to the image-setter, or even to print the best possible laser copy, then you'll need to provide the source file to QuarkXPress. The program tries to keep track of the status of each source for every picture within a document. If a source is moved, QuarkXPress will know. If a source image is modified in some way by outside software, the program knows that, too. You can check on the status for each source. And you can take action to reestablish or update linkages between your document and the source file.

You do both through a single dialog box. To see the status of the document's picture-source files, open the Utilities menu and choose Picture Usage. A dialog box similar to the one shown in Figure 17.1 will appear listing the drive and file path of the source files, the document page on which each is used, file type suffix, and status of the source file.

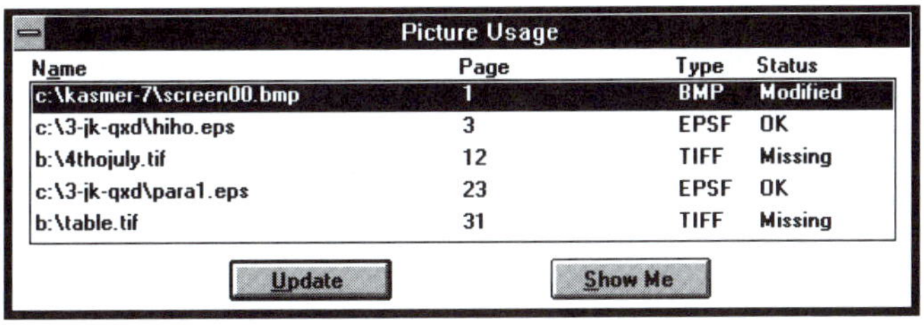

Name	Page	Type	Status
c:\kasmer-7\screen00.bmp	1	BMP	Modified
c:\3-jk-qxd\hiho.eps	3	EPSF	OK
b:\4thojuly.tif	12	TIFF	Missing
c:\3-jk-qxd\para1.eps	23	EPSF	OK
b:\table.tif	31	TIFF	Missing

Figure 17.1   *A document's Picture Usage dialog box indicating status of source files.*

In Figure 17.1, notice the status for the Page 1 picture file is *Modified*. This file was originally imported to the document and later altered in a graphics program. The pictures on Pages 3 and 23 are listed as *OK*; QuarkXPress can use the sources without problem.

The pictures on Pages 12 and 31 are listed as *Missing*; QuarkXPress couldn't locate either of them. In this case you might notice that the file path indicates these source files were imported from a different disk drive, b, the floppy drive. What has happened is that the source floppy disk has been removed from the system. This is a particularly easy mistake to make.

Updating

To make sure all the sources are in order and up to date, you'll need to use the Update button. Select the file you want to update by clicking on it. Or select several files by the Shift-click or Ctrl-click methods. Then click on Update. All questionable files will be addressed individually in the dialog boxes that appear in turn. In the case of a Modified file, a confirmation dialog box will appear. Click OK, and the new source file is linked to the document. In the case of a Missing file, a dialog box asks you to locate the file. You use it just as you would an Open dialog box.

> *Updating picture sources*
>
> *At the Utilities menu, choose Picture Usage*
>
> *At the dialog box, select the missing or modified file and click the Update button*
>
> *Follow directions as they are displayed*

To examine a picture on location at the page where it appears, select the file and then click the Show Me button. QuarkXPress will scroll through the document to the page where the picture is. This can help you to clarify just which picture is in need of updating or what was the subject of that missing source file.

FONTS IN A DOCUMENT

If there is any one support on which all of desktop publishing rests, it is the availability of fonts. Electronic typefaces are a high form of graphic unequaled in their ability to change the look, effectiveness, mood, and subliminal message of a layout. They are a constantly shifting foundation, however, as new fonts are added and new formats of fonts evolve.

In this commercial arena, a variety of contenders vie for market position. For instance, a current standard has developed around fonts in the Adobe format. That one type of font should be standard is more an indication of history and marketing placement than of any inherent superiority. Other fine fonts are available from other vendors. Among them are the TrueType fonts, some of which were introduced with Windows 3.1.

How the Program Deals with Fonts

In some ways, QuarkXPress treats fonts as it does graphics files. Let's consider Adobe fonts for the moment. Generally, they can be displayed on screen only if the font file is present. The file must also be present for printing. It used to be that you needed a font file for each size you wanted to be able to see on your monitor. However, Adobe developed a program that could work in conjunction with desktop publishing, word processing, and other software to produce screen representations of fonts at any size from files of just one font size. This is Adobe Type Manager or ATM.

If you're using Adobe fonts for serious desktop publishing, you are almost certainly using ATM. This program works in the background to assist with printing, as well. To add or remove Adobe fonts, you can start the ATM control panel program, which would reside on your hard drive. Operation is quite simple. You select from a list of fonts in either adding or removing. Having the font files present during printing is essential. Otherwise often ugly substitutions of other fonts are likely.

TrueType fonts can also be added or removed. In fact, starting with Windows 3.1, a similar font installer/remover can be found by opening the Control Panel within the Main program group. Some TrueType fonts can also be imbedded within a document file, so that during printing the document itself provides the font information. This is sure to simplify font and document management as it becomes more common.

Keeping Track of Fonts

Currently, the odds are very good that you'll need to assure the proper fonts are available when printing occurs. Of course, if printing means outputting the document to a laser printer directly from the same computer system you used to create and lay it out, there should be no problem with fonts.

However, if you're sending your file out to a pre-press shop or service bureau for output from their system, watch out! The number and variety of fonts each carries can vary. And you'd be surprised how an otherwise thorough shop can be missing that one font you were sure they would have on hand. Even within your own office, you may find that when you move your file to another computer, a different set of fonts may reside on it. These differences, by the way, are not usually obvious. Often just one or two fonts are different or missing.

One wise approach to take in dealing with fonts and your documents is this: Make a list of the fonts used in the document. This sounds simple until you start to go through, page by page, trying to note every special heading or, harder still, all the special fonts within the main body text. However, QuarkXPress can do all this automatically. Remember the expanded Find/Change dialog box for dealing with text style revisions? QuarkXPress presents a similar dialog box whose main purpose is to identify or change fonts already applied in the document.

To use this feature, open the Utilities menu and choose Font Usage. A dialog box will appear. To see a list of every font used within the document, click on the arrow for the drop-down list next to font name field. You'll see a list of fonts, as shown in Figure 17.2. Preceding each font name, in angle brackets, you'll notice an indication of the style of font present in the document, if the font appears in bold, italic, or plain text. Should one appear in more than one of these styles, then the list will show each style with font name. You can make a note of these. Or you can use the methods for screen capture to provide an instant visual file of the dialog box.

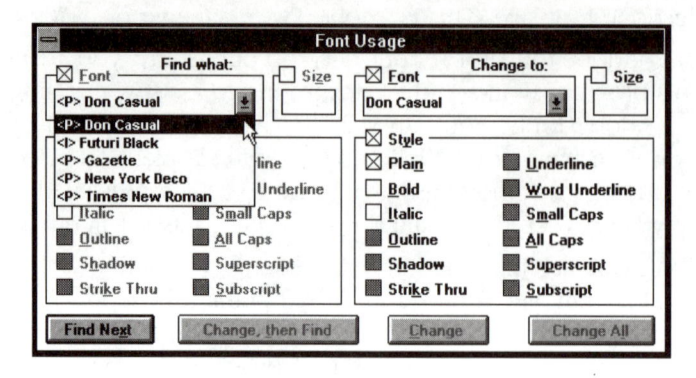

Figure 17.2 *Using a document's Font Usage dialog box to get a list of active fonts.*

> **Collecting a list of fonts in a document**
>
> *At the Utilities menu, choose Font Usage*
>
> *At the dialog box, open the drop-down list at the font field*

You can use this dialog box to make changes throughout the document. Say you just gained access to the Futuri black font and you want to replace recurring Helvetica in your completed document with it. Following the same procedure as with the expanded Find/Change dialog box, you can make that change in one operation.

> **Replacing fonts document-wide**
>
> *At the Utilities menu, choose Font Usage*
>
> *At the dialog box, select font and style to be replaced under Find What*
>
> *Select new font and style under Change To*

NOTE: This dialog box may be a bit unresponsive to displaying the changes you make in it. To see a current list of fonts after making a change, you may need to close the dialog box, by clicking on the close button in the upper-left of the box, and then reopen it. But the newly opened dialog box should accurately reflect the font status of your document.

READYING A PRINT

Of course, you're going to need to send the QuarkXPress file somewhere in order to get a physical print of the document. Use the Printer Setup dialog box to select the printer and specify how you want the print session to proceed. You can bring up this dialog box by opening the File menu and choosing Printer Setup, or (on your way to print) by choosing Print and then pressing the Setup button in that dialog box. The dialog box, shown in Figure 17.3, provides in the uppermost box a means for selecting the printer to receive QuarkXPress's output. At the second button, labeled Specific Printer, you can choose from among those connected printers for which printer drivers have been installed. This is good for switching among your draft printer, page proofing laser printer, and final output image-setter, for instance. The Options button will provide you with access to adjustments made available by the specific driver for the printer selected.

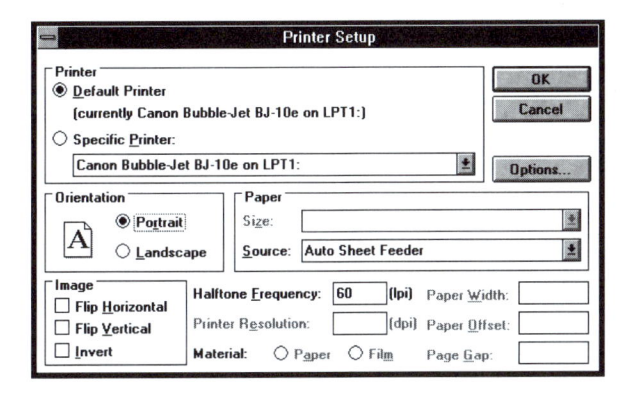

Figure 17.3 *The Printer Setup dialog box.*

The Orientation and Paper boxes simply relate to printer logistics. The Image box allows for mirror images, Flip Horizontal and Flip Vertical, and for a negative image, Invert. The choices in the unboxed lower-right section of the dialog box refer to PostScript control and image placement on roll-fed image-setters. Note that if you're working with the same printer repeatedly, you need only check the printer setup initially, and thereafter you can leave it alone until the occasion calls for some variation.

This is a good time to check that all systems are go at the printer itself: paper, film, trays in place. Cables connected. Power on.

TO PRINT

Another gauntlet seems to present itself the first time you open the Print dialog box from the File menu. Will this never end? In fact, the choices before you seldom need all be considered together. As with the Printer Setup dialog box, often when you're doing simple proofing you can find a set of specifications that works and then use it until there is reason to change. This may mean simply choosing the Print command and clicking OK immediately at the dialog box.

At times you'll want more control than is already established in the Print specifications. For instance, you can print multiple copies of a document. To do so, simply type in the number in the Copies field of the Print dialog box, as shown in Figure 17.4. If your work is focusing on a portion of the document, you can print a range of pages rather than the entire document. Click the Pages button to the left of From, and key in the starting and concluding pages you want.

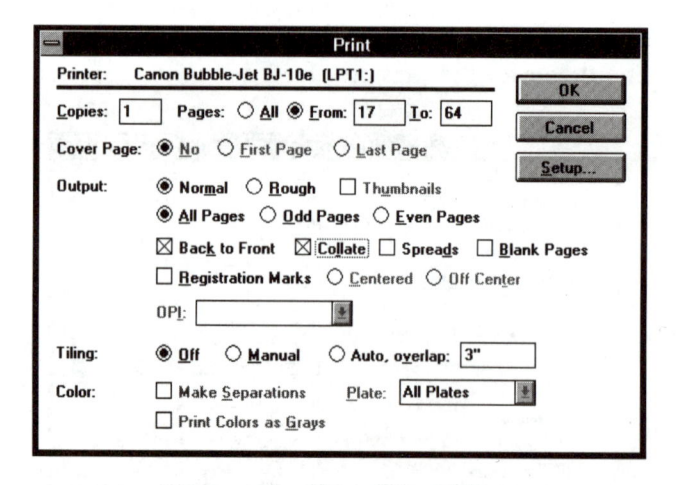

Figure 17.4   *The Print dialog box.*

Another useful option allows printing of just the odd or even pages. If you're doing a mock-up of a double-sided publication on your proofing printer, you can click first on the Odd Pages button (about halfway down the dialog box), gather the printed pages, turn them over, reinsert in your paper feeder, and then issue the Print command with the Even Pages button clicked. You'll have a double-sided printed document.

Printing a double-sided document

At the Print dialog box, engage the Odd Pages button

Print as usual

Turn the pages over and reinsert in the paper feeder

At the Print dialog box, engage the Even Pages button

Print as usual

If you want your computer system to do the paper shuffling instead of doing it yourself, you may want to click an x in the Back to Front checkbox. Similarly, if you're doing multiple copies and you want each set grouped together into a document, then be sure to click an x into Collate.

Note that in running color separations, the printer staff needs to know how to align each of the color plates. Clicking an x into Registration Marks provides a guide in the form of small crosses within circles in the margins of each separation. From these marks, alignment can be controlled for each color printing. Engaging this checkbox also provides crop marks for trimming excess paper from a page format smaller than the paper format. Clicking the Off Center button is useful if you're concerned that the printers might inadvertently rotate your separation plates upside down.

How do you get a 48-inch square document page out of a letter-size capacity laser printer? The answer is that it comes in pieces. By clicking the Auto button at the Tiling line in the dialog box, you turn on QuarkXPress's ability to section a large on-screen image into a tiled mosaic with a specified overlap.

You can also manually tile pages one at a time. First, at the document window, drag the zero-point crosshairs from the upper-left corner of where the rulers meet, to the point you want to serve as upper-left in that tile. Then, at the dialog box, click on Manual. The page will print. Repeat this process until the entire page is printed in pieces.

The last section on Color is where the Make Separations feature is engaged for printing. You can also specify that colors be printed as the corresponding shade of gray. Back at the Output section is another route to printing simulated proofs. Here, click on the Rough button to have pictures print as boxed x's. Of course, the actual print command for these specifications is initiated by clicking the OK button.

> **Tiling a page**
>
> On the document page point, assure that the rulers are showing
>
> Click at the crosshairs where the rulers meet, and drag to upper-left of desired tile
>
> At the Print dialog box, click to engage the Manual button at Tiling
>
> Proceed as usual for printing a single page, clicking the OK button
>
> Repeat the process for each section of the page

Using the Print Manager

Whatever settings and specifications you prepare for your document, QuarkXPress doesn't actually pass them on to the printer. This is the job of the Print Manager program of Windows. The Print Manager is the perfect assistant. It normally works behind the scenes, but it can be called forward when you need to change the normal flow of work.

When you give the print command from QuarkXPress or any other Windows-based software, you'll notice that the program screen returns to you ready for further developments while the printer is still receiving instructions from your computer. The Print Manager has taken over the task of seeing the print job through. This is one of the reasons you can issue print commands for several different files, and be back at the program screen before the first of those pages has come out of the printer. Print orders sent to the Print Manager are actually put in a line to be printed in order behind the scenes.

You can see the print queue listed within the Print Manager window, as shown in Figure 17.5. Call this window up on screen through the Program Manager by opening the Main program group and double-clicking on the Print Manager icon. The file first on the list is preceded by a small printer icon, indicating that it is actively being sent to the printer. Other files will be numbered in their order in the queue.

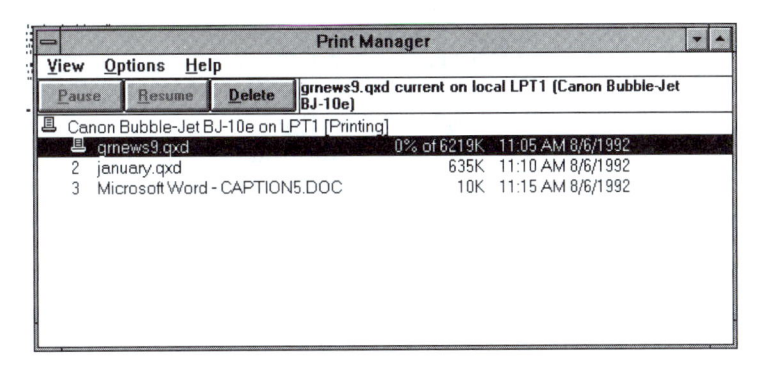

Figure 17.5 *The Print Manager window.*

NOTE Note that every time you give the print command from within a program such as QuarkXPress or a word processor, a small message dialog box appears stating that the active file is printing. Actually, the file is being sent to the Print Manager. That's why sometimes the program returns to active status even before your laser printer begins moving paper into position.

You can stop the sending of the file to the printer at the Print Manager with the Pause button and start it again with the Resume button. You can reorder files in the print queue by highlighting one and, when the upward-pointing arrow appears, dragging it to a new position in line. (Note that you can't bump the one currently printing.) You can remove files from the print line-up altogether with the Delete button.

Controlling print flow

In the Program Manager, open the Main group and double-click on the Print Manager icon

Select and drag to reorder the queue of files

Click on the Pause, Resume, and Delete buttons as appropriate

---

By controlling the Print Manager, you can expedite the print flow, and correct printer-based, as well as program-based, mistakes.

INSTALLING PRINTER DRIVERS

Another feature of the Windows programs may prove useful if you need to change or upgrade your printer connections. Note that the Print Manager works through software installed specifically for each output, or print, device. These are known as printer drivers. If you add a different type or model of printer to your system, chances are you'll need to install specific printer driver software. If it's one of the many already planned for in the Windows system, this is easy. You'll need your windows installation disks, or the install disk for your printer.

At the Program Manager, open the Main program group, and then double-click on the Control Panel. As this window opens, you'll see an icon labeled Printers. Double-click on it and click the Add button. A list of printers will appear, as shown in figure 17.6. Select the one that matches yours and double click. If you don't see it listed, then click the first choice for unlisted or generic. Next click the Install button, and a dialog box instruction will be displayed asking you to insert the disk in one of the floppy drives. Do so and continue with the instructions that follow. Within a few minutes, your new printer will be installed.

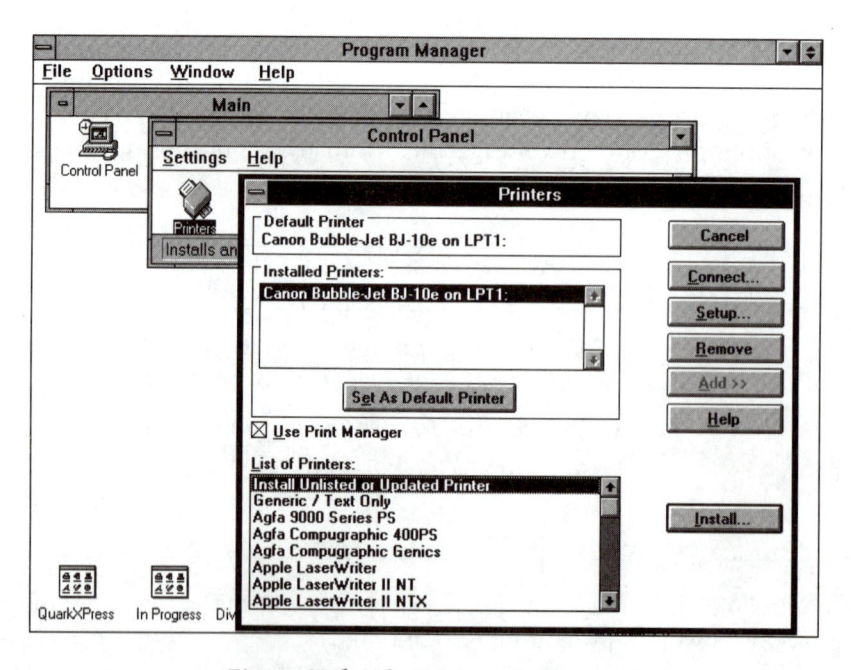

Figure 17.6   *The Printers window.*

> **Installing a printer driver**
>
> *At the Program Manager, open the Main window*
>
> *Double-click on the Control Panel icon and double-click on the Printers Icon*
>
> *At the Printers dialog box, click on the Add button*
>
> *Click to select a printer driver and then click the Install button*
>
> *Follow the disk directions*

You can also use this dialog box to software-select the port at the back of the computer where the printer is physically connected. Gain access to this control by clicking the Connect button. You can control those features of the printer itself made accessible by the printer driver; do this through the Setup button. And you can eliminate an installed printer driver through the Remove button.

STEPPING FORWARD

Printing, the last step in the desktop publishing process, is crucial whether the job is an eleventh-hour final film output or a page proof of your layout in development. Fonts, pictures, and document requirements still need attention at this point. Using the update techniques shown in this chapter makes achieving successful printing a relatively straightforward matter. Of course there will always be surprises. But adaptation is the key to improvement.

You've come nearly full-circle now, from the original idea or sketch to finished pages. Your journeys through the processes of QuarkXPress have shown you what is possible and how. What you do with these skills will speak volumes.

Chapter 18

Beyond the Usual Methods

WHAT YOU WILL LEARN IN THIS CHAPTER

- ◆ Keyboard shortcuts
- ◆ How to access instant views
- ◆ How to select through layers
- ◆ How to make one-stroke hanging indents
- ◆ The Windows-ANSI character set
- ◆ Special symbols

Once you begin to acquire skills in QuarkXPress, there is no end to the possibilities. The many methods and techniques you've encountered and come to call your own are just a springboard to the next level of skill. If you've used the preceding chapters to teach yourself QuarkXPress, this is the point where you'll benefit from a few well-chosen refinements.

The aim of this book has been dual: to make you proficient with QuarkXPress, and to help you progress with desktop publishing. This has meant showing you how things work in the Windows-QuarkXPress environment, as well as showing you how to accomplish essential tasks. All the methods and examples have been devoted to showing you how to design and produce practical projects quickly. Along the way there have been chapters showing you alternatives.

This chapter presents shortcuts, tips, and suggestions for working with QuarkXPress, going beyond the methods presented in previous chapters. Some people call them power techniques. We'll uncover ways to save time and improve the product—from producing graphics with your keyboard to presetting program defaults.

KEYBOARD SHORTCUTS

When you use a method frequently, it's natural to want to engage it more quickly. Throughout most of this book we've seen the straightforward ways to do things in QuarkXPress. But by this point you can identify which techniques you'd like to streamline.

Shortcuts seem like a great idea. But they impose a price of their own. Exchanging established routine for speed of operation, you often have to remember some offbeat sequence or keystroke. This is not a problem when your method comes up frequently. But take just two weeks off and you can find yourself fumbling to recall those arcane key combinations. So the key is to learn and use shortcuts only as needed.

CTRL KEY SHORTCUTS

The most obvious shortcuts are the keyboard Ctrl equivalents of the menu commands. You can find them opposite each command when you open a menu and their form is easily understood. Each command that has a keystroke equivalent will operate when the Ctrl key is held down while some other key (or keys) is pressed. For instance, you can give the Cut command by using the keystroke, Ctrl-X—the keystroke abbreviated to the right of the command. These keystrokes exist for somewhat less than half of the menu commands.

ALT KEY SHORTCUTS

Another easy shortcut is provided by the Windows interface through the Alt key. In case you're not familiar with it, you might like to know that this approach will work in any Windows-based program. If you're fast with the keyboard, you probably experience some slowdown each time you shift your hand to the mouse. But you can give almost any command through the keyboard, whether or not it has been assigned a Ctrl keystroke equivalent.

By pressing the Alt key you can engage the menu bar through the keyboard just as readily as through the mouse. When the keyboard/menu link is established, the document-close button at the extreme left of the menu bar is highlighted.

Then to open a menu, just press the key corresponding to the underlined letter. In the case of QuarkXPress this is always the first letter of the menu title: F to open the File menu, E to open the Edit menu, and so on. With the menu open, you can extend this approach by looking for the underlined letter at each command. Press this key and the command is activated. The Alt keystroke method provides two advantages over the Ctrl key method: 1) you can address any menu command through it; and 2) it is entirely visual, presenting clues so that you don't have to memorize keystrokes.

To display the clipboard, for instance, you press the Alt key (and release), then the E key (to open the Edit menu), then the B key (to give the Show Clipboard command).

MOMENTARY ITEM TOOL

When you're using the content tool, you may often find yourself needing to use the item tool for just a moment. For instance, you might want to drag a text box to a new location before continuing to edit the contents.

You can momentarily invoke the item tool when the content tool is selected by holding down the Ctrl key. You'll see the mouse cursor change to a four-arrow tool. Then you can press the mouse button and drag the box to a new location. When you release the Ctrl key, the content tool is once again in force.

Quick switching from content to item tool

Hold down the Ctrl key, and proceed as with item tool

Release to reactivate Content tool

TEXT SIZING

As you know, the Measurements palette provides a convenient alternative to opening the Style menu to change the size of selected text. However, an even quicker method is available through the keyboard. This method is limited to the size increments available in the drop-down size listing of either the Measurements palette or Style menu. But it's fast.

To increase the font size from the keyboard to the next higher increment, hold down the Ctrl and Shift keys and press the right angle bracket key, >. To reduce the size hold down Ctrl and Shift and press the left angle bracket key, <.

Sizing text by keystrokes

Select text and hold down Ctrl and Shift keys

Press > key to enlarge, < to reduce

CLICK ZOOMING

Without a doubt, two of the most useful views are Actual Size and Fit in Window. Adjusting items life-size, then pulling back to look at the whole page (spread) is frequently called for during page layout. Using the menu, you can switch between these views by choosing commands. But if the mouse you're using has two buttons, you can switch views instantly. Simply click the right side button and the view will toggle between these two sizes.

If the view has been set to something other than Fit in Window or Actual Size, clicking this button will return it to 100 percent first. A second click will then display at Fit in Window.

The particular usefulness of this feature however, goes beyond changing viewing magnifications. By using the tool as a centering pointer, you can position any part of the Fit in Window view in the center of the Actual view. So, rather than move across a spread with the grabber hand, it's often faster to simply click that right button and put the whole spread into Fit in Window view, locate the part of interest with the mouse tool, and click back to 100 percent view.

> **Toggling views and centering views with the mouse**
>
> *To view at Fit in Window when seeing Actual Size, click right side mouse button*
>
> *To view at Actual Size at a particular location when seeing Fit in Window, position tool cursor and click*

SELECTING THROUGH LAYERS

If your layout calls for items of about the same size to be layered, or for many items to be layered all in a pile, you will probably encounter the inconvenience and frustration of being unable to reach a particular item to make some modification. The tedious solution is to move items out of the way, sending them to the back in a revised stacking order. Then after making the modifications, you restack the items in their original layering order.

But there is a better way. With either item or content tool selected, hold down Alt-Ctrl-Shift at the keyboard. Point at the stack and click once for each layer you want to descend. Items within the stack will become selected singly, one after the other, from the top down. They will not move out of stacking order, but will simply become accessible. After you've selected the appropriate item, you can proceed as usual, while you modify it.

> **Selecting through the layered items in a stack**
>
> *Hold Alt-Ctrl-Shift and point into the stack*
>
> *Click once to select the topmost item, click again for each backward layer*

SIMPLE, DIRECT WORD COUNTING

There is a simple way to get a word count from QuarkXPress. It's easy to use, but obscure. To determine the number of words in a story, use the Spelling feature.

Here's how it works: Put the text cursor in the story. Open the Utilities menu and choose Spelling. Then at the submenu, choose Story. Before actually checking spelling, the program will present an informational dialog box indicating the total number of words, the number that appear only once, and the number that the spell checker cannot match with its list. Click OK and the Check Story dialog box will appear. If you don't care to run the spelling check, simply click Cancel.

> **Running a word count**
>
> *Insert the text cursor*
>
> *Open the Utilities menu, choose Spelling, then Story*

QUICK PAGE MOVES

The Page Up and Page Down keys in QuarkXPress don't actually do what their names imply. To move one page through the window using the keyboard, hold the Shift key while pressing either one. The screen will respond accordingly. But notice that with each key-press the page that appears will be positioned with its upper left margin seated in the upper left corner of the window, regardless of where on the previous page the display was fixed.

In similar fashion, you can move to the first page or last page by holding the Ctrl key as you press the Page Up (for Page 1) or Page Down (for last page) keys.

> **Moving through pages by keyboard**
>
> *Shift-Page Up and Shift-Page Down*
>
> *Or Ctrl-Page Up for first page and Ctrl-Page Down for last*

ONE-STEP HANGING INDENTS

We've discussed ways to adjust paragraphs from the Paragraph Formats and Tabs dialog boxes, including establishing hanging indents. There is a direct, character-based method for hanging indents. It requires that you place a hidden character to serve as a marker under which the remainder of a paragraph will indent. You can put this marker in the first, second, or a later line, then the following lines in the paragraph will indent under it.

To create an instant hanging indent this way, insert the text cursor within the line above those you wish to indent, at the point where they ought to indent. Hold down the Ctrl key and press the backslash key, \. The lines starting below this will indent immediately.

Inserting a hang-below character

Position cursor in line above desired indent line

Key in Ctrl-

This creates an invisible character whose effect will be applied until the character is removed. To remove it, select the space at which you've inserted it and press Backspace. Note also that if you move the characters on that line so that the invisible "indent here" character moves too, then all the lines below in the paragraph will move to the new indent position, following the marker.

Adding Typographers' Quotes, Common Marks, and Symbols

If you are typing in QuarkXPress and choose to type in quotes, they will appear in nonspecific typewriter fashion (") as you type from the keyboard. For typographically standard open and closed quotes, hold the Alt and Shift keys while typing the angle brackets (< and >).

Following the same approach, you can produce registered marks (Alt-Shift-R), copyright marks (Alt-Shift-C), and bullets (Alt-Shift-8).

Windows offers a similar scheme with a full character set that can be typed through the Alt key and the numerical keypad. For instance, to type a bullet you hold the Alt key down, while typing at the keypad, 0149. To produce a $\frac{1}{4}$ mark, do the same, typing at the keypad, 0188. The set of characters for TrueType fonts runs from 32 to 127 (the standard keyboard characters), and from 0128 to 0255 (the special characters). These are known as the ANSI character set.

Producing the ANSI character set

Hold down the Alt key and press the four digit code (0128 to 0255) at the numeric keypad

---

SETTING DEFAULTS AND PREFERENCES

Throughout the chapters we've encountered the effects of defaults and preference settings. You've seen how changing the settings in preferences will change defaults for the document that's open at the time. But as you work you'll want to begin from a set of preferences that match your approach to projects. The Application Preferences dialog box resets certain defaults for the program. These apply whenever it is running subsequently. The other three Preferences dialog boxes—General, Typographic, and Tools—apply only to documents open at the time of resetting.

But you can establish defaults in these specifications to be in effect whenever the program is subsequently started. To do so, simply clear the program window of any document windows by closing all open documents. Then set up the default specifications in each Preference dialog box and exit the program immediately without opening a document. When you start QuarkXPress the next time the newly set preferences will be in effect for all new documents.

Setting startup defaults for any preference

With QuarkXPress running, assure that all documents are closed

Set up specifications under the Edit menu, Preferences

Exit the program

WHERE TO?

You had some goal when you first picked up this book—perhaps to just use an exceptional program for completing your current project; perhaps to gain a solid grounding of skills in software that will become your constant work companion; perhaps even to gain a footing with desktop publishing for the first time. But having arrived here, in control of a tool with wide reach, you can now execute many more design and layout decisions.

This book has attempted to hand the controls of QuarkXPress over to you and to demonstrate practical methods. Readers and viewers of your handiwork appreciate your attention and energy. The extra effort makes a difference. The judicious use of QuarkXPress can only improve your results in the long run.

Your proficiency with the program need not end here. The one certainty in desktop publishing is that no one knows it all. No one source can tell it all. If your game is to seek out other sources, by all means proceed. You'll find some recommendations in Appendix B.

Comparing your work with others, putting the software through its paces, generating your own wish list of things your system should do—these are all useful ways of improving. Going back to the program to see how it can do something you've never tried before will increase layout, design, and typesetting skills as well as improve your skills at handling the software. Experimentation is the best way to find what works best for you. You are the final judge of that.

Now you have all you need to make design and production work based on QuarkXPress second nature. Now is the time to let your own spirit show through each project you undertake. It has been the sincere pleasure of this author to help you teach yourself this program.

If you have thoughts about QuarkXPress, the book, or desktop publishing, you're welcome to share them with the author. Write to Studio K, Box 3562, San Diego, California 92163.

Appendix A

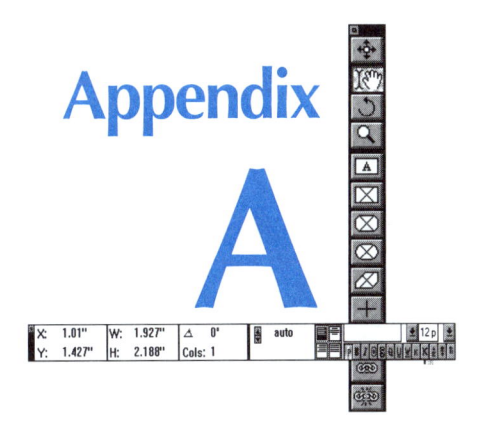

QuarkXPress Methods At-a-Glance

The main text of the chapters offers the full explanations of methods and techniques in the program. Here you'll find the At-a-Glance summaries of more than a hundred of those methods. All are listed according to the chapters in which they appear. This provides a ready reference to the context in which each summary emerged.

In a few cases these At-a-Glances appeared in two chapter:, a methods chapter and an on-the-job chapter. Where that has occurred, the summaries have been listed in each chapter.

Chapter 2: The Windows/QuarkXPress Marriage

Starting Windows in DOS

>*win (for 386-enhanced mode)*
>*or*
>*win/2 (for standard mode)*

Moving an object in Windows

>*Select with click*
>*Drag to new location*
>*Release*

Scrolling window views

>*Click scroll bar arrow*
>*or*
>*Drag scroll bar box*
>*or*
>*Click in scroll bar outside box*

Sizing objects

>*Position pointer (on side or corner handle) until it becomes double arrow (or other sizing tool)*
>*Drag to new shape and size*

Starting a program

>*Locate icon in Program Manager (or File Manager directory listing)*
>*Double-click on it*

Switching from Program Manager to File Manager

>*Open Main window*
>*Locate and double-click on File Manager*

Making file backups

>*Drag file icon/name to another drive*

Linking a file to a program

>*In File Manager select the file*
>*Open File menu, choose Associate*
>*Click Browse, locate and select program*

Appendix A ◆ 347

Instant switching between programs

Hold Alt key, press Tab repeatedly until program name appears
Release Alt

Chapter 3: Working with Documents

Opening a file by pathname

At the File menu choose Open
Type path to document in this form: drive:\directory\directory...\file.qxd

Viewing pasteboard with pages

Ctrl + At View menu choose Fit in window

Precision percentage views

Double-click value in percentage view display
Key in new percentage
Enter

Selecting tools from the keyboard

Ctrl-Tab to move downward through buttons, or to show palette
Ctrl-Shift-Tab to move upward

Modifying through Measurements palette

Select item and locate attribute in palette
Highlight attribute value and type in new value
or
Select new value from drop-down list
Press Enter

Magnifying view with zoom tool

Position tool over point to anchor
Click repeatedly until magnification is achieved

Reducing view with zoom tool

Position tool over point to anchor
Hold Ctrl key and click repeatedly until reduction is achieved

Precision magnification with zoom tool

Choose rectangular area to magnify
Position zoom tool at one corner
Hold Alt key and drag diagonally to create enclosing box
Release

Using the grabber hand

With any tool but the zoom selected, hold the Alt key
Press mouse button and drag page through window view

Using the selecting box

With item tool drag a box to enclose any part of item(s)

Positioning with the Measurements palette

Select item
Key in new location as X and Y values

Selecting scattered items

Hold Shift key and click on each item
(Deselect with second click)

Selecting a range of pages in Document Layout

Click on page at one end of range
Scroll to other end in Document Layout
Hold Shift key and click on page at other end

Selecting scattered pages in Document Layout

Hold Ctrl key and click on each page
(Deselect with second click)

Moving to adjacent pages by grabber hand

Hold Alt key and drag pages through window view
    up to higher numbers
    down to lower
    sideways on spreads

Moving to a page by Document Layout

In the palette scroll to locate page icon
Double-click to bring page into window

Appendix A ◆ **349**

Moving items to distant pages in the document

Select item(s) and at Edit menu choose Cut
Locate destination page
At Edit menu choose Paste

Chapter 4: Type and Text Formatting

Making a text box

Choose text box tool
Choose rectangular area in which to place box
Position text box tool at one corner of chosen area
Drag diagonally until box fits area chosen

Clipboard text transfers

Select the text with content tool and at the Edit menu choose Cut or Copy
Select the recipient text box with content tool
(Set insertion cursor or selection if necessary)
At the Edit menu choose Paste

Importing text

Assure that text box is selected with content tool active
At File menu choose Get Text
Select file in dialog box listings or by pathname

Selecting text by powerstrokes

Use the content tool to do the following
    One word—double-click
    One line—triple-click
    One paragraph—quadruple-click

Kerning at the text palette

Position I-beam text cursor between letters
Use palette arrows for incremental changes (10 units each)
or
Key in kern value and press Enter

Adjusting columns at the palette

> Select text box with either item or content tool
> Select value in Cols field at palette
> Key in new value and press Enter

Chapter 5: Newsletters on the Job

Starting a program

> Locate icon in Program Manager (or File Manager directory listing)
> Double-click on it

Using the grabber hand

> With any tool but the zoom selected, hold the Alt key
> Press mouse button and drag page through window view

Basic QuarkXPress character codes

> New line   \n
> New paragraph   \p
> Tab   \t

Word counting

> In Find/Change dialog box Find What field type in one space, and in the Change To field type in one space
> Proceed to Change all
> The number of changes cited equals virtually the number of words

Chapter 6: Pictures, Boxes, and Interaction

Importing a graphic

> Activate a picture box tool and draw a box
> Assure the content tool is selected
> At the File menu choose Get Picture
> Locate the graphic file in the dialog box and double-click

Reshaping, resizing the picture image

> Ctrl-drag the picture box handles

Making a polygon picture box

Using the polygon tool, click at each angle in turn
Return to the first click point and double-click
Using the picture grabber, position the Content tool over the picture box
Drag the image through the window

Instant fitting of image within picture box

Ctrl-Shift-F

Instant fitting of image proportionally within picture box

Ctrl-Shift-Alt-F

Reversing type

Select text
Open Specifications dialog box, set background to Black, 100%
Open Style menu, choosing Color as White

Using the rotation tool

Select the box
Click a fulcrum point
Drag out a rotation lever
Pull the lever around the point

Creating a guideline

Assure that the rulers are displayed
Point in the rule oriented as the guideline will be and drag out a line

Establishing text runaround

Assure the runaround item is selected and above the text
At the Item menu choose Runaround, select the Mode and set the offset spacing

Adjusting a manual image

Drag the side or handle into place
Add or remove handles using Ctrl-click

Establishing a text chain

Using the Linking tool click on the first box in the chain
Click on every other box in order

Linking a text box in an existing text chain

Using the linking tool click on the box before the insertion point
Click on the new text box

Breaking a text chain

Select the Unlinking tool
Click on an arrowhead or tailfeather

Removing one box from a text chain

Select the Unlinking tool
Shift-click on the unwanted box

Chapter 7: Guides on the Job

Pulling a guide that extends across a spread

Point the cursor in the horizontal ruler above the pasteboard
Pull directly down

Momentarily switching to the item tool

With any but the zoom tool engaged, hold down the Ctrl key

Scaling a box proportionally by sight

Draw a line through and beyond the opposite corners of the box
Resize the box by dragging one corner along the line

Locating nonprinting character codes in text

Open the View menu and choose Show Invisibles

Creating hanging indents

In the Paragraph Formats dialog box drag the left indent over
Drag the first line indent back leftward of the left indent

Adjusting indents

Select the paragraph(s)
In the Paragraph Formats dialog box locate the ruler
Slide the triangular markers into place as follows: first line indent, small to marker; left indent, small bottom marker; right indent, large marker
Or key values into corresponding fields

Chapter 9: Newspapers on the Job

Finding the midpoint

Drag a box between two extremes
The item handles at the sides will fall at the midpoint

Chapter 10: Document Flow

Applying a master page

At the Document Layout palette, select the page or pages
Open the Apply menu and choose the master page

Moving to a master page

Open the Page menu, and choose Display
At the submenu choose the master page

Locking items

Select the items
Open Item menu, choose Lock

Adjusting position or size of a locked item

Select the item
Enter new values in the Measurements palette

Adding a master pages

At the Document Layout palette, open the Document menu
Choose Show Master Pages
Open the Masters menu
Choose Insert and select a page format
Move the arrow cursor into position on the list and click

Removing a master page

At the Document Layout palette click to select the page master icon
Open the Masters menu and choose Delete

Changing the format of a master page

At the Document Layout palette click to select the master page
Open the Apply menu and choose the replacement master format

Renaming a master page

At the Document Layout palette click on the name next to the master page
Key in the new name

Establishing automatic page numbering

At the master page, prepare a text box
Press the Ctrl-3 keystroke

Applying a style sheet to text

Select the paragraph(s) with the content tool, or insert cursor
At the Style Sheets palette, click on the style sheet
or
At the Style menu, choose Style Sheets, then the style sheet

Importing style sheets

Open the Edit menu and choose Style Sheets
At the Style Sheets dialog box, click the Append button
In the directory windows that appear, locate the document containing desired style sheets and double-click

Creating a style from a text selection

Select the model text
Open the Style Sheets dialog box and choose New
At the Edit Style Sheets dialog box key in a name and click OK
At the Style Sheets dialog box click Save

Expanding a page spread

At the Document Layout palette open the Document menu
Choose Insert and the master page
Pull the cursor to the outside of the spread icons and click

Basing a style sheet on another

Proceed as usual, creating a new style sheet or editing an existing one

In the Edit Style Sheets dialog box open the Based On drop-down list and choose an existing style sheet

Anchoring a graphic or text box in-line with text

Select the item with the item tool
Copy or cut it
Use the content tool to click an active cursor in the test line
Paste it

Creating special drop caps and graphic inserts

Anchor the item as usual and select it with the item tool
Open the Item menu and choose Modify
At Align with Text, click on Ascent

Sectioning pages

Select the first page of the section
Open the Pages menu and choose Section
Click an x into the Section Start checkbox
Make other modifications in the dialog box to suit the section

Creating automatic jump lines

Use the text box tool and make a small text box after the story text box is created
Key in the continuation notice excepting the page number
For a jump-to notice, key Ctrl-4; for a jump-from notice, key Ctrl-2
Drag the jump box until it overlaps the text box

Chapter 12: Manipulating Images

Adjusting an image to original contrast

Select picture with content tool active
Open the Style menu and choose Normal Contrast

Adjusting an image to black and white contrast

Select picture with content tool active
Open the Style menu and choose High Contrast

Adjusting an image to stepped contrast

Select picture with content tool active
Open the Style menu and choose Posterized

Making a custom adjustment of contrast

Select the picture with content tool active
Open the Style menu and choose Other Contrast
At the dialog box use the first five tools to draw or modify a contrast graph
Use the last four tools and buttons to apply or invert a contrast graph
Click the Apply button and revise as necessary

Applying preset halftone screening to an image

Select picture with content tool active
Open the Style menu and choose one of the screens in the lowest box

Chapter 14: Multiple Editions and Multiple Documents

Duplicate drags between documents

Bring both document windows into view
In the source document select the items
Drag them across the window boundaries into the destination document and release mouse in position

Moving pages within a document using thumbnails

Select the pages by clicking, Shift-clicking, or Ctrl-clicking
Drag to new location and release

Copying pages between documents

At the source document window select the pages by clicking, Shift-clicking, or Ctrl-clicking
Drag into the destination window and release

Chapter 15: Transfers Within and Without

Opening or creating a library
Open the Utilities menu, choose Library
Proceed to locate the file through the directory windows, or key in an name to create one
Click the Open or Create button as appropriate

Using items between documents and libraries

Position the windows of both in the program window
Click on the window to activate it, then on the item(s)
Drag to the other window and release to copy the item there

Positioning entries within a library

While dragging the item(s) note the appearance of double triangles
When the triangles mark the desired insert point release

Naming library entries

Double-click on the entry to call up the Library Entry dialog box
Key in the name
Or
Use the drop-down list arrow to locate an existing name you'd like to apply again
Click OK

Saving formatting information in an ASCII text file

Place the cursor within, or select, the text to be exported
At the File menu choose Save Text
At the dialog box use the drop-down list to choose XPress Tags
Click OK

Capturing a screen image to the clipboard

Prepare the screen as desired
Press the Print Screen key

Chapter 16: Color

Producing a color

At the edit menu, choose Colors
At the dialog box, click New
Use the mouse tool to click at a color on the color wheel
Or
Type in values of percentage of each color in the field boxes
Or
Use the sliders to combine colors
Monitor the resulting color at the color bar
Click OK at the Edit Color dialog box, then Save at the Color dialog box

Preparing colors for separation

In the Edit Color dialog box, display the color to be separated
Click an x into the Process Separation checkbox
Prior to printing in the Print dialog box, click an x into the Make Separations checkbox

Creating a color blend in background

Select the picture or text box with the item tool
From the drop-down list in the Colors Palette, chose Linear Blend
Click the #1 button, click a color and a shading
Click the #2 button, click a color and a shading

Chapter 17: Printing

Updating picture sources

At the Utilities menu, choose Picture Usage
At the dialog box select the missing or modified file and click Update button
Follow directions as they appear

Collecting a list of fonts in a document

At the Utilities menu, choose Font Usage
At the dialog box open the drop-down list at the font field

Appendix A ◆ **359**

Replacing fonts document-wide

> At the Utilities menu, choose Font Usage
> At the dialog box select font and style to be replaced under Find
> Select new font and style under Change

Printing a double-sided document

> At the Print dialog box, engage the Odd Pages button
> Print as usual
> Turn the pages over and reinsert in the paper feeder
> At the Print dialog box, engage the Even Pages button
> Print as usual

Tiling a page

> On the document page point assure that the rulers are showing
> Click at the crosshairs where the rulers meet and drag to upper left of desired tile
> At the Print dialog box, click to engage the Manual button at Tiling
> Proceed as usual for printing a single page, clicking the OK button
> Repeat the process for each section of the page

Controlling print flow

> In the Program Manager, open the Main group and double-click on the Print Manager icon
> Select and drag to reorder the queue of files
> Click on the Pause, Resume, and Delete buttons as appropriate

Installing a printer driver

> At the Program Manager, open the Main window
> Double-click on the Control Panel icon, then double-click on the Printers Icon
> At the Printers dialog box, click on the Add button
> Click to select a printer driver, then click the Install button
> Follow the disk directions

Chapter 18: Beyond the Usual Methods

Quick switching from content to item tool

> Hold down the Ctrl key, and proceed as with item tool
> Release to reactive content tool

Sizing text by keystrokes

Select text and hold down Ctrl and Shift keys
Press > key to enlarge, < to reduce

Toggling views and centering views with the mouse

To view at Fit in Window when seeing Actual Size, click right side mouse button
To view at Actual Size at a particular location when seeing Fit in Window, position tool cursor and click

Selecting through the layered items in a stack

Hold Alt-Ctrl-Shift and point into the stack
Click once to select the topmost item, click again for each backward layer

Running a word count

Insert the text cursor
Open the Utilities menu, choose Spelling, then Story

Moving through pages by keyboard

Shift-Page Up
and Shift-Page Down
Or Ctrl-Page Up for first page and Ctrl-page Down for last

Inserting a hang-below character

Position cursor in line above desired indent line
Key in Ctrl-

Producing the ANSI character set

Hold down the Alt key and press the four digit code (0128 to 0255) at the numeric keypad

Setting startup defaults for any preference

With QuarkXPress running assure that all documents are closed
Set up specifications under the Edit menu, Preferences
Exit the program

Appendix B

The Desktop Publisher's Short List Resource Guide

This listing is by no means exhaustive. It includes a selected group of books and publications found to be useful to my clients and—it is hoped—to the readers of this book.

Books

***Great Pages* by Jan V. White.** Detailed but off-the-cuff remarks on publication design, typography, and approaches to page design, useful to both desktop and traditional designers. White is particularly adept at putting into words what other designers point, sketch, and murmur about.

***Editing by Design* by Jan V. White.** A wry energy drives this book, which very successfully bridges the gap between the graphic design and editorial sides of the publishing. The book offers methods of editorial planning, layout, and printing, with emphasis on practical details of publication design.

Designing for Magazines **by Jan V. White.** A counterpart to White's *Editing by Design*, but with emphasis on examples, this book seeks to show what designs succeed and why.

Newsletters from the Desktop **by Roger C. Parker.** Good at breaking down the newsletter (and some of desktop publishing process) into component parts. Parker's titles have gained wide popularity, perhaps for their directness and easy reading.

Basic Desktop Design and Layout **by David Collier and Bob Cotton.** This very visual book is full of examples in progress. Though not a step-by-step reference, it does provide insight into the design and development process by giving snapshots of various effects.

Graphic Design Cookbook **by Leonard Koren and R. Wippo Meckler.** The temptation in this 100 percent layout book is to believe that you can perhaps just copy the ideas directly to your project. In reality, it serves best as a page-through wake-up call to your creativity, getting you thinking rather than giving you direct answers.

Windows 3.1 Secrets **by Brian Livingston.** If you start from the index, you'll find this thousand-page reference useful for sorting out many of the peculiarities and abilities of the Windows world. The author is a columnist, and the book reflects this, offering lots of explanations and problem-solving in easily managed, but isolated, chunks.

Publishing Newsletters **by Howard Penn Hudson.** Though slanted toward manual layout and traditional typesetting, Hudson's book provides the lowdown on all aspects of bringing out a newsletter from basic planning and production through marketing.

How to Do Leaflets, Newsletters and Newspapers **by Nancy Brigham, et al.** This down-home, grass-roots, large-format book carries lots of line drawings that convey the start-to-finish process of newsletters and newspapers. The advice is solid, with a kitchen-table, tight-budget slant.

PUBLICATIONS

Publish. Though its focus seem to have wandered, this magazine has followed desktop publishing since the early days and continues to do so. It alternates between generic desktop wisdom and product-specific information.

Windows Magazine. A hefty source of what's going on in the Windows world, this publication offers lots of reviews and tips on compatible hardware and software.

PC Computing. An ad-heavy magazine with articles relating to the latest PC machines. Emphasis leans toward hardware, though software is covered, too.

Magazine Design and Production. No-nonsense production technology coverage that views desktop publishing as a peripheral part of the larger process.

The Newsletter on Newsletters. Comments and updates on the newsletter business by the author of *Publishing Newsletters*.

Index

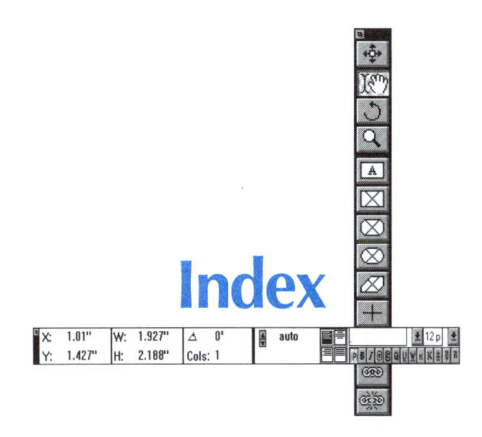

A

Actual Size view, 48-49, 338
Adobe fonts, 324-325
Adobe Type Manager (ATM), 25, 324-325
alignment
 of multiple items, 148-149
 paragraph, 87-88
 vertical, 184
Alt key shortcuts, 337
anchoring, 235-238, 260-261
ANSI characters, 201, 341
Apply button, in Paragraph Formats dialog box, 177
Apply menu, in Document Layout palette, 215

Arrow buttons, in scroll bars, 21
ASCII text files, 78
 exporting text to, 305-306
Associate command, in File Manager, 33-34
Auto Image runaround mode, 153
Automatic Text Box feature, 43

B

backgrounds, box, 138-139
backing up document files, 33
Back to Front checkbox, 329
banner, newspaper, 200-201
baseline grids, 185-187
bitmapped images, 141
Blank Facing Master, 214-216

Blank Single Master, 214-216
blending colors, 320
body text
    in contemporary newsletter, 107
    in letterhead newsletter, 99-104
    newspaper stories, 205-207
bold typefaces, 98
bounding box around multiple items, 147-148
boxes. *See also* picture boxes; text boxes
    backgrounds of, 138-139
    characteristics of, 135-136
    reshaping, 168-169
    rotating, 143-144
    scaling proportionately by sight, 162
bullets, 341
byline, 204
    in a catalog, 249

C

Cancel button, 25
captions box, 284-285
Cascading document windows, 46-47
catalog, 246-152
    final work on, 251-152
    style sheets for, 248-151
    setting up the document for, 246-147
chaining text, 154-156
Change All button, 82
Change button, 82
Change then Find button, 82
character codes, nonprinting, 174-175
click-drag procedure, 32
Clipboard, 76-77
    capturing a screen image to, 308-309
Close All command, 47
CMYK model, 314-315, 317
codes, paragraph and character, 102-103
Collate checkbox, 329
color-matching systems, 315-316
colors
    blending, 320
    of box backgrounds, 138-139
    of frames, 137
    picture content, 141-142
    screen versus print, 312-315
    trapping, 318
color separations, 316-317, 329
Colors palette, 319
color wheel, 313
Column Guides section, in New dialog box, 43
columns, 90-92
compatibility, text-file, 77
content tool, 74-76
"continued on..." notices. *See* jump lines
contrast, 264-272, 281-284
    adjusting
        customized adjustments, 269-272
        with preset controls, 266-269
conventions used in this book, 2-3
copy-fitting, 104-106
copying
    files, with a mouse, 33-34
    items
        between documents and libraries, 301
        from one document to another, 290-291

pages from one document to another, 292-293
copyright marks, 341
creating documents, 41-43
crop marks, 329
Ctrl key shortcuts, 336
cut-and-paste method, 69

D

dateline, 207-208
defaults, 342
Delete command, in Pages menu, 67
deleting. *See also* removing
    master pages, 223
    a paragraph, 101
dialog boxes, 24-25
directories, QuarkXPress, 28
Document checkbox, in Find/Change dialog box, 82
document files, 9-10
Document Layout palette, 11, 52, 67-68
    master pages and, 215-216
Document menu, in Document Layout palette, 215
documents. *See also* files
    creating, 41-43
    currently open, 47
    opening existing, 43-45
    saving, 47-48
document windows, 44. *See also* windows
    adjusting, 46-47
dog-eared page icons, 216
DOS (Disk Operating System), 16-19
DOS command prompt, 17
double-sided documents, printing, 328
dragging files and directories, 32-33
dragging method for moving a selected item, 62-63
drive windows, in File Manager, 30-32
drop caps, 190, 238
drop-down list, 54

E

Edit Color dialog box, 312-315
Edit Style Sheet dialog box, 230-232
environment, QuarkXPress as an, 8
EPS files, 307
exporting
    layouts outside QuarkXPress
        EPS files, 307
        by screen capture, 307-310
    text, 77-78, 304-307

F

facing-page master pages, 216, 218-220
Facing Pages checkbox, in New dialog box, 42
feedback loop, 55
File Manager, 28-29
    Associate command in, 33-34
    switching to, 30
files. *See also* documents
    dragging, 32-33
    importing and exporting, 77-78
    linking to programs, 33-34
filters, 77
Find button, 82

Find/Change command, 102
  for fonts, 326
Find/Change dialog box, 81-82, 102
  blind change of formatting made through, 294-295
First Line field, in Paragraph Formats dialog box, 176
First Numerical field, in Paragraph Formats dialog box, 176
Fit in Window view, 49, 338
fitting copy, 104-106
flashing cursor, 74-76
Flush Zone, 183
fonts (typefaces), 85, 324-327
  changing size of
    keyboard method, 338
  keeping track of, 325-26
  replacing, 326
Font Usage dialog box, 326
formatting
  blind change of, 294
  reapplication of, 117
frames, 136-37

G

General Preferences dialog box, measurement system in, 194
Get Picture dialog box, 126-27
Get Text dialog box, 78-79
grabber hand, 60-61
  moving to another page with, 68
  for pictures, 132-33
  using, 97
graphics. *See* pictures

graphic user interfaces (GUI), 19
grayscale images. *See* contrast; halftones
greeking text, 198-199
grids, baseline, 185-187
grouping, 234-235
Group Specifications dialog box, 235
guide brochure, 158-166
guides (guidelines), 146-147
  that extend across a spread, 159
Gutter Width field, in New dialog box, 43

H

halftones, 272-275, 286-287
hand, pointing. *See* pointing hand
H&J dialog box, 179-181, 206-207
handles (handle boxes), 23
  reshaping a polygon and, 169
hanging indents, 177-179
  one-step, 340-341
headlines, 203, 208
horizontal scaling, 188-189
HSB model, 315-316
hyphenation, 179-181, 206-207
Hyphenation Zone, 181

I

icon, QuarkXPress, 28
Ignore Attributes checkbox, in Find/Change dialog box, 82
Ignore Case checkbox, in Find/Change dialog box, 82
illustrations. *See* pictures
images. *See* pictures

importing
	pictures, 130
	style sheets, 229-230
	text, 77-78, 100
indents
	hanging, 177-179
		one-step, 340-341
	in Paragraph Formats dialog box, 176-179
in-line items, anchoring, 235-238
Insert Pages command, 65-66
inside box, for newspapers, 209-211
installing QuarkXPress, 25-27
interface, 10
invisibles, showing/hiding, 174
items, 13. *See also* objects
item tool, 74
	momentarily switching to, 160, 337

J

jump lines, 239
	automatic, 242-243
jump notice, 208
justification, 179-180, 182-184, 206-207
	methods of, 182-183
	vertical, 184-185

K

Keep Lines Together feature, 187, 251
Keep with Next Paragraph feature, 251
kerning, 88-90
keyboard shortcuts, 336-337
	for selecting tools, 53
	for switching between programs, 36

L

layering, 149-151
layers, selecting items through, 339
layouts, exporting
	EPS files, 307
	by screen capture, 307-310
leading (line spacing), 88
	baseline grids, 185-187
	increasing, 105
	relative versus absolute, 261
Left Indent field, in Paragraph Formats dialog box, 176
letterhead, for letterhead newsletter, 94-99
letterhead newsletter, 94-106
	fitting copy, 104-106
	letterhead for, 94-99
	typesetting body text for, 99-104
libraries, 300-304
Line palette, 55
line spacing. *See* leading
linking text boxes, 154-156, 218-219
linking tool, 154
locking items, 221

M

magazine article, 280-287
	assembling the elements of, 280-283
	contrast of images in, 281-284
	halftones in, 286-287
	setting the text for, 284-286
magnifying view with zoom tool, 57-59
	by area, 58
mailer space, in newsletter, 110-111

manual, 252-261
Manual Image runaround mode, 153
margin guides, 42, 199-200
master pages, 214-225
    access to, 217-219
    adjustments on document pages and, 220-222
    applying, 217
    changing format of, 224
    designation of, 215-216
    facing-page, 216, 218-220
    generating, 222-224
    linking text boxes and, 218-219
    locking items in, 221
    for a manual using sections, 255-259
    moving to, 218
    removing, 223
    renaming, 224
    working on, 219-220
Measurements palette, 11, 41, 52, 54-56
    creating a text box and, 74-75
    moving items with, 63-64
    for text. *See* Text palette
measurementy system, pica, 193-194, 200
Menu bar, 41
menus, 10
Microsoft Word, 305
midpoint, finding the, 200
Minimize arrow, 35
minimizing a program, 35-36
mistakes, fixing, 295-296
mouse, 32-33
    toggling views and centering views with, 339

mouse-based tools, 11
mouse pointer. *See* pointer
moving. *See also* positioning
    around the page, 60-61
    items (objects), 19-21
        between documents and libraries, 301
        drag method, 62-63
        with Measurements palette, 63-64
        multiple, 65
        between pages, 69-70
    to pages, 68-69
    through pages by keyboard, 340
    pages within a document using thumbnails, 292
    palettes, 52
multiple copies of a document, printing, 328
multiple documents, 290-296
    copying items between, 290
multiple editions, 296
museum guidebook, 167-172

N

nameplate, newsletter, 108-110
Negative command, 142, 163
New dialog box, 41-42
    for letterhead newsletter, 95
newsletter
    contemporary, 106-122
        mailer section of, 110-111
        nameplate for, 108-110
        preparing body text for, 107

table of contents, 118-119
    text layout on page 1 of, 116-118
    text layout on page 2 of, 112-114
    text layout on page 3 of, 114-116
    text layout on page 4 of, 120-222
letterhead, 94-106
    fitting copy, 104-106
    letterhead for, 94-99
    typesetting body text for, 99-104
newspapers, 198-211
    stories in, 202-209
        body copy, 205-207
        byline, 204
        column head, 203
        column one box, 202
        dateline, 207-208
        headlines, 203, 208
        inside box of, 209-211
        jump notice, 208
        paragraph spacing, 203-204
    setting up the document for, 198-200
    top matter for, 200-202
nonprinting character codes, 174-175
Normal style sheet, 228
No Style option, 228

O

objects. *See also* pictures
    resizing, 22-24
    selecting, 19
odd or even pages, printing, 328
OK button, 25
Open dialog box, 44-45
opening documents, 43-45

orientation, 143
orphans, 187-188, 250-251
orthogonal line tool. *See* rule tool
oval picture box tool, 125
overview of QuarkXPress, 8-14

P

page icons, dog-eared, 216
page numbers, 105
    adding pages and, 66
    automatic, 224-225
    for sections, 241, 257, 259-260
pages
    adding, 65-66
    in Document Layout palette, 67-68
    moving around, 60-61
    moving through, by keyboard, 340
    moving to, 68-69
    removing, 66-67
    sectioning, 241-242
page size, 48
Page Size section, in New dialog box, 42
page spreads, 42
    adding pages and, 66
    multiple-page, 239-240
Page Up and Page Down keys, 340
page views. *See* views
palettes, 11, 52
Pantone matching system, 316-317
paragraph alignment, 87-88
paragraph codes, 102
Paragraph Formats dialog box, 174-179
    spacing in, 203-204
paragraph rules, 193

Paragraph Rules dialog box, 252
paragraphs
    formatting, 86, 102-103, 174-179
    spacing, 203-204
pasteboard, 49-50
path, 44
Percent view, 50-51
percent views, with zoom tool, 57-59
picas, 85, 193-194
picture boxes
    anchoring, 235-238
    backgrounds of, 138-139
    characteristics of, 135-136
    frames of, 136-137
    importing into, 126-130
    instant fitting of pictures within, 135
    rotating, 143-144
    shaping and sizing, 130-132
picture grabber hand, 132-133
pictures (graphics), 12-13, 124
    anchoring, 235-238, 260-261
    content colors, 141-142
    contrast of, 264-272, 281-284
    cropping, 130-132, 162
    file formats for, 126
    grabber hand for, 132-133
    halftones, 272-275, 286-287
    importing, 125-130
    in magazine article, 280-287
    resolution of, 276
    shaping and sizing, 134-135
    skewing, 145-146
    source files for, 322-323
        updating, 324

Picture Usage dialog box, 323
pointer (tool; cursor)
    flashing, 74-76
    moving an object with, 19-21
pointing hand, 74-75
points, 85, 200
polygon picture box tool, 125, 129-130
positioning, 61, *See also* moving
    items in relation to one another, 148
    with the Measurements palette, 63-64
    picture boxes, 163-165
preferences, 342
Preferences command, 194
Print dialog box, 328-330
printer drivers, 332-333
Printer Setup dialog box, 327
printing
    image source files and, 322-323
    options for, 328-330
    setting up printers for, 327-328
    updating picture sources for, 324
Print Manager, 330-331
print queue, 330-331
process color, 317
program group, 29
program icons, QuarkXPress, 28-29
Program Manager, 17, 21
    getting to, 25-26
programs
    linking to files, 33-34
    starting (running)
        from File Manager, 32
        by linking files to programs, 33-34

switching between, 35-36

Q

QuarkXPress
    defaults and preferences, 342
    installing, 25-27
    overview of, 8-14
    program icon for, 28-29
    screen displayed after starting, 40-41
    as start-up application, 29
    system requirements, 25
    User Registration disk, 27
quotes, 78
    open and closed, 341
.QXD suffix, 45, 47, 296-297

R

rectangle picture box tool, 124
reducing view with zoom tool, 58
registered marks, 341
registering QuarkXPress, 27
Registration marks checkbox, 329
removing. *See also* deleting
    a box from a text chain, 156
    pages, 66-67
renaming a master page, 224
replacing fonts, 326
Reshape Polygon command, 169-170
resizing objects, 22-24, 134-135
resolution, 276
reverse text, 143, 170
reverting to last saved version, 295-296
RGB model, 312-315

Rich Text Format (RTF), 78
Right Indent field, in Paragraph Formats dialog box, 176
rotating
    boxes, 143-144
    pictures within boxes, 145
    text boxes, 166
rounded-corner rectangle picture box tool, 125
RTF format, 305
RTF (Rich Text Format), 78
rulers, 146
rules
    paragraph, 193
    in style sheets, 252
rule tool, 52
runaround. *See* text runaround
Runaround Specifications dialog box, 152-153

S

Save As command, 296
    making templates using, 297
Save Text command, 305
saving documents, 47-48, 96
scaling, horizontal, 188-189
scroll bars, 21
searching and replacing text, 81-82
section indicator, 254-256
sectioning, 241-242
sections in a manual, 252-260
section title, 254
selecting
    items, 62

through layers, 339
multiple items, 147-148
scattered items, 65
text
all the text, 105
within text boxes, 84
tools, 53
universal method for, 19
selecting box, 62
shading. *See also* contrast
of picture elements, 142
shortcuts
keyboard, 336-37
momentary item tool, 337
sizing text by keystrokes, 338
zooming with the mouse, 338-339
Show Baseline Grid command, 185
Show Guides/Hide Guides toggle command, 147
Show Invisibles/Hide Invisibles toggle command, 174
Show Rulers/Hide Rulers toggle command, 146
sizing. *See also* resizing objects
resolution and, 276
skewing, 145-146
Snap to Guides feature, 147, 163
Space/Align command, 149, 161, 163-164
spacing. *See* kerning; leading; tracking
justification and, 182
multiple items, 148-149
paragraphs, 203-204
Specifications dialog boxes, 139-141
spot color, 317

starting (running) programs
from File Manager, 32
by linking files to programs, 33-34
start-up application, making QuarkXPress a, 29
Startup window (or folder), 29-30
Style menu, 139-140
style sheet palette, 227
style sheets, 207, 225-234
applying, 227-228
based on other style sheets, 231-234
based on selected text, 229-231, 250-251
for a catalog, 248-251
creating and adjusting, 228-231
definition and principle of, 226
importing, 229-230
No Style option and, 228
removing, 231
Style Sheets dialog box, 229-230
system requirements, 25

T

table of contents
of a newsletter, 118-119
for a newspaper, 209-211
tab markers, 192
tabs, 190-192
templates, 296-297
text, 12-13
body
in contemporary newsletter, 107
in letterhead newsletter, 99-104
newspaper stories, 205-207

content tool and, 75-76
importing and exporting, 77-78, 100
reversing, 170
selecting
    all the text, 105
    within text boxes, 84
in word processing documents, 80-81
text boxes
    anchoring, 238
    backgrounds of, 138-139
    characteristics of, 135-136
    clipboard used to put text in, 76-77
    effects of creating, 74-75
    frames of, 136-137
    keying text directly in, 76
    linking, 154-156, 218-219
    making, 72-75
    rotating, 143-144, 166
    selecting text within, 84
    text overruns in, 79-80
    unlinking, 155-156
text chain icon, 218
text chaining, 154-156
Text Format (ASCII Format), 78
Text palette, 84-86
text runaround, 99, 151-153
    custom, 167-168
thumb-index effect, 255-256
thumbnails, 292
    in libraries, 301
Thumbnails view, 49-50
TIFF files, 264, 280-281
Tile command, 44

Tiling options, in Print dialog box, 329-330
tools. *See also* specific tools
    applying, 53-54
    selecting, 53
Tools palette, 41, 52-54. *See also* specific tools
    picture tools, 124-125
tracking, 88-90
trapping colors, 318
TrueType fonts, 324-325
.TXT files, 78, 305
type, 83
type control, 83
type font. *See* fonts
type size, 85
type style, 86
    blind changes of, 294-295
    reapplication of, 117

U

underlining, 103-104
unlinking text boxes, 155-156
User Registration disk, 27

V

vertical alignment, 184-185
View menu, 48-49
View Percent field, 50-51
views, 48-49

W

Whole Word checkbox, in Find/Change dialog box, 82

widows, 187-188, 250-251
Windows, Microsoft, 37
    dialog boxes in, 24-25
    enhanced mode, 17
    File Manager, 28-29
        Associate command in, 33-34
        switching to, 30
    mouse in, 32-33
    moving an object in, 19-21
    Program Manager, 17, 21
        getting to, 25-26
    reasons for using, 18-19
    resizing objects in, 22-24
    standard mode, 17
    starting, 17-18
windows
    displaying two concurrently, 108-109
    document, 44
        adjusting, 46-47

    moving, 19-21
    multiple, 290-291
    scroll bars in, 21-22
word counts, 112-113, 339-340
WordPerfect, 305
word processing, 80-81
word processing documents, setting up, 80

X

X and Y coordinates, 54, 135
xpress.exe, 29
XPress Tags, 305-306
.XTG suffix, 305

Z

zooming, mouse method of, 338-339
zoom tool, 57-59